The Psychological and Social Impact
of Physical Disability

Robert P. Marinelli *draws on an extensive background in rehabilitation and rehabilitation counseling, on and off the campus. Currently an Associate Professor in the Department of Counseling and Rehabilitation, College of Human Resources and Education, at West Virginia University, he has held faculty appointments at Boston University and at Pennsylvania State University, where he received his doctorate in 1971. A former consultant to both the Veterans Administration and rehabilitation facilities, and past-president of the Massachusetts Rehabilitation Counseling Association, Professor Marinelli was an incorporator and member of the Board of Directors of the Boston Center for Independent Living, a community facility for severely disabled adults. He is currently a consultant for Eastern Rehabilitation Associates, a rehabilitation training and consulting firm, and the Social Security Administration. He has, in addition, published widely in areas related to psychological and vocational issues in rehabilitation.*

Arthur E. Dell Orto *is Chairman of the Department of Rehabilitation Counseling, Sargent College of Allied Health Professions, Boston University. Since obtaining his Ph.D. from Michigan State University in 1970, he has engaged in a wide range of rehabilitation activities: as President of the Massachusetts Rehabilitation Association, as psychological consultant to the Veterans Administration, as rehabilitation psychologist in private practice, and as President of Eastern Rehabilitation Associates. He has also been a program consultant to various rehabilitation programs in Colombia, South America, in conjunction with the Massachusetts Partners of the Americas Rehabilitation and Education Program, of which he has been co-chairman. His publications and research interests include the application of structured experiential group therapy approaches to various populations and the role and resources of the family during the rehabilitation process.*

The Psychological and Social Impact of Physical Disability

ROBERT P. MARINELLI
and
ARTHUR E. DELL ORTO
Editors

SPRINGER PUBLISHING COMPANY, New York

We dedicate this book to Bernard Kutner, Ph.D., who died unexpectedly on December 9, 1975. Bernie was our Dean, colleague, and friend. He will long be remembered for his academic contributions and leadership in the field of physical disability and rehabilitation as well as for his humanity and concern for others. He was a man who had a dream, lived it, and gave it life so that it lives today. The dream was that rehabilitation be more than a word, a practice, or a process—that it be a way of life.

Springer Publishing Company, Inc.

200 Park Avenue South
New York, N.Y. 10003

77 78 79 80 81 / 10 9 8 7 6 5 4 3 2 1

Library of Congress Cataloging in Publication Data

Main entry under title:

The Psychological and social impact of physical disability.
   Bibliography: p.
   Includes index.
   1. Physically handicapped—Psychology—Addresses, essays, lectures. 2. Rehabilitation—United States—Addresses, essays, lectures. I. Marinelli, Robert P. II. Orto, Arthur E. Dell.
HV1553.P75   155.9'16   76-58556
ISBN 0-8261-2210-8

Printed in the United States of America

CONTENTS

FOREWORD

At its Eleventh World Congress in Dublin, Rehabilitation International, the nongovernmental federation of national and international organizations providing rehabilitation services for the disabled in 61 countries, unanimously adopted a resolution declaring the period 1970–1980 to be The Decade of Rehabilitation. The high expectations expressed in this resolution were fulfilled at least in part when in 1975 the United Nations General Assembly adopted the Declaration on the Rights of Disabled Persons. This volume is an appropriate American contribution to the Decade of Rehabilitation since its many excellent articles, together with the editors' introductions to the eight parts of the book, document the conceptual and methodological advances that have been made in this country. The sense of this United Nations Declaration is reflected throughout the text.

I am particularly glad to find in many of the chapters an emphasis on programming for children, substantiating a developmental approach to rehabilitation which, of necessity, leads to an increasing recognition of the importance of early intervention. Also, even though the book is geared mainly to physical disability, the editors have selected many articles which make clear that the fields of mental retardation and mental illness have similar needs and must be included in comprehensive planning and programming.

This volume is addressed to a broad audience encompassing many disciplines as well as the dynamic forces of the rehabilitation volunteer, the interested citizen, and above all the ever more alert consumers. Moreover, I hope it will become a primary text in the training of the rehabilitation counselor to whose professional identity, awareness, and training both Dr. Marinelli and Dr. Dell Orto have devoted so much of their own careers.

Nowhere in the pages of this volume, including the hundreds of references, does there appear the name of Mary E. Switzer. This is not surprising, considering that Mary Switzer was a leader and doer more so than a writer. It was under her inspired and inspiring leadership over two decades, first as Director of the U.S. Office of Vocational Rehabilitation and later as Administrator of the Social and Rehabilitation Services in the U.S. Department of Health, Education and Welfare, that rehabilitation became a major concern of national and state government. Her strong interest in research, experimentation, and demonstration resulted in the funding for much of the work on which this book is based. But the momentum generated in years past is in danger of running out, and all of us in the field of rehabilitation, whether as counselors, administrators, researchers, academicians, consumers, or interested citizens, need to be concerned with regeneration of forceful, dynamic rehabilitation leadership in the national government so that we can continue to build soundly toward the future and maintain the progress so amply documented in this volume.

Gunnar Dybwad, J.D.
Florence Heller Graduate School
for Advanced Studies in Social Welfare,
Brandeis University

PREFACE

The rehabilitation process is a journey, not a destination. It is limited only by the ability of our society to provide the necessary means to continue this journey, to extend its range, and to provide quality rehabilitation services to persons in need. While there have been significant gains in the rehabilitation of physically disabled persons, much work remains to be done. However, we are hampered by the existence of ignorance, negativism, and prejudice related both to disability and to those affected by it.

The purpose of this book is to explore physical disability in light of its psychological and social implications in order to obtain a clearer understanding of the important issues noted above. The hope is that, with this understanding, we can better meet the challenges facing rehabilitation today. We must do more than we have done, go places where we have not been, and be less fearful of failure if we are not to sacrifice potential success.

While the focus of this book is on physical disability, we recognize that persons with physical disabilities share many of the same life experiences of those who are not disabled, as well as those who have mental and/or social disabilities. We further acknowledge that persons with physical handicaps sometimes have accompanying mental and social handicaps. So, although the *major* focus of this book is upon physically handicapped persons, readers whose main interests rest with the socially or mentally handicapped persons will find useful information and resources herein. Also, because of the general issues that transcend specific types of disabilities—physical, mental, or social—the reader will find frequent reference to the problems of mental retardation, emotional disorders, and other disabilities.

The orientation of this text is different from that of most other edited volumes in this field, which concentrate on the psychological and/or social problems of specific physical disabilities. Our organization begins with the assumption that physical disability affects different facets of a person's existence. Therefore, we present readings that discuss the impact of disability on a variety of areas of human life. The topics covered include the impact of disability on the child and the family, the personal meaning of disability, the interpersonal impact of disability, attitudes toward disabled persons, sexuality and disability, and disabled consumers.

The emphasis throughout the book is on providing the reader with an understanding of the impact of disability and the practical problems of disabled persons. Considerable stress on helping the person with a disability is reflected in the readings, particularly in Part VIII. Articles were selected on the basis of their significance in relation to this book's topics of interest. They were also chosen for their appeal and importance to a wide variety of helpers in the rehabilitation field.

This book is largely a compilation of the works of others. We thank those authors and publishers who have given us permission to reprint their publications. We would like especially to acknowledge our colleagues in the Department of Rehabilitation Counseling at Boston University, particularly Bob Lasky and Bill Anthony, who contributed major articles to this book. Paul Power and LeRoy Spaniol provided encouragement and support. Our wives, Irene and Barbara, typed, proofread, and gave valuable counsel. We would also like to thank our staff, Hannah Kwartler, Denise Roberge, and Rosemary Hess, for their clerical help, and our former students, Steve Valle and Jeanne Cioffi Pressman, who assisted us in the library review.

Robert P. Marinelli
Arthur E. Dell Orto

CONTRIBUTORS

Dan L. Adler, Ph.D.
American Association of University Professors
Washington, D.C.

Thomas P. Anderson, M.D.
University of Minnesota Medical School
Minneapolis, Minnesota

William A. Anthony, Ph.D.
Boston University
Boston, Massachusetts

Aaron Aucrbach, Ph.D.
The Hebrew University of Jerusalem
Jerusalem, Israel

Constance U. Battle, M.D.
The George Washington School of Medicine
Washington, D.C.

Jean L. Bloom, Ph.D.
Edinboro State College
Edinboro, Pennsylvania

Betty E. Cogswell, Ph.D.
University of North Carolina
Chapel Hill, North Carolina

Theodore M. Cole, M.D.
University of Minnesota Medical School
Minneapolis, Minnesota

Victor Cummings, M.D.
Albert Einstein College of Medicine
Bronx, New York

Arthur E. Dell Orto, Ph.D.
Boston University
Boston, Massachusetts

Tamara Dembo, Ph.D.
Clark University
Worcester, Massachusetts

Milton Diamond, Ph.D.
University of Hawaii School of Medicine
Honolulu, Hawaii

R. William English, Ph.D.
University of Oregon
Eugene, Oregon

David J. French, Ph.D.
Claremont Graduate School
Claremont, California

H. H. Garner, M.D.
The Chicago Medical School
Chicago, Illinois

H. Jon Geis, Ph.D.
Clinical Psychologist in private practice
New York, New York

William Gellman, Ph.D.
Jewish Vocational Service of Chicago
Chicago, Illinois

Ernest R. Griffith, M.D.
University of Cincinnati School of Medicine
Cincinnati, Ohio

William A. Hawke, M.D.
The Hospital for Crippled Children
Toronto, Ontario

George W. Hohmann, Ph.D.
University of Arizona College of Medicine
Tucson, Arizona

Marceline E. Jaques, Ph.D.
State University of New York at Buffalo
Buffalo, New York

Robert Allen Keith, Ph.D.
California State University at Los Angeles
Los Angeles, California

Nancy Kerr, Ph.D.
Arizona State University
Tempe, Arizona

William Kir-Stimon, Ph.D.
William Kir-Stimon, Ph.D., and Associates
Flossmoor, Illinois

Bernard Kutner, Ph.D. (Deceased)
Boston University
Boston, Massachusetts

Gloria Ladieu-Leviton, Ph.D. (Deceased)
Schwab Rehabilitation Hospital
Chicago, Illinois

Robert G. Lasky, Ph.D.
Boston University
Boston, Massachusetts

Robert E. McDowell, Ph.D.
Claremont Graduate School
Claremont, California

Tom Magner
Teacher of mentally retarded children
Dubuque, Iowa

Robert P. Marinelli, D.Ed.
West Virginia University
Morgantown, West Virginia

Kathryn P. Meadow, Ph.D.
University of California at San Francisco
San Francisco, California

Lloyd Meadow, Ph.D.
San Francisco State University
San Francisco, California

Leslie D. Park
United Cerebral Palsy of New York City, Inc.
New York, New York

Kathleen M. Patterson
Erie Community College
Buffalo, New York

Franklin C. Shontz, Ph.D.
University of Kansas
Lawrence, Kansas

Silas P. Singh, Ph.D.
Southern Illinois University
Carbondale, Illinois

Jerome S. Tobis, M.D.
University of California School of Medicine
Irvine, California

Roberta B. Trieschmann, Ph.D.
University of Cincinnati School of Medicine
Cincinnati, Ohio

Jean Vanier
l'Arche Movement
Oise, France

Frederick A. Whitehouse, Ed.D.
Hofstra University
Hempstead, New York

Beatrice A. Wright, Ph.D.
University of Kansas
Lawrence, Kansas

Part I

Perspective on Disability

The impact of disability is felt both by the person with the disability and by those with whom that person comes in contact. The individual's own response to his or her disability and the way others respond to the disabled person have significant implications for the rehabilitation worker as well as for the rehabilitation process. The purpose of Part I is to sensitize the reader to these general issues.

In "Somatopsychic Concepts" Garner makes the important differentiation between psychosomatic manifestations—a concept generally familiar to health professionals—and somatopsychic ones—a concept less familiar but with implications as significant. Garner's emphasis is on a holistic approach to disability. His discussion of psychological factors and their effect on the individual's response to illness and disability provides the reader with a clarification of the complexity of the human organism and the processes that affect it.

Historically, the "medical model" has had significant impact upon the practice of rehabilitation. Anderson compares this model with the model used in the helping process and discusses the implications of each for rehabilitation. The importance of rehabilitation workers' recognizing their frame of reference in working with clients is emphasized, as well as the importance of exposure to alternative models.

The value system of contemporary America is questioned by Park, particularly as it relates to the normalization of handicapped people. He provides suggestions for overcoming the numerous barriers to normality for disabled persons in our culture.

In the final article in Part I, Gellman, a foremost rehabilitation philosopher and practitioner, presents projections for the future in the field of physical disability. His projections, which are based largely on socioeconomic trends, take the reader from the current status and practice of rehabilitation to its status and practice through the 1980s. His differentiation of rehabilitation goals into (1) enablement, (2) normalization, and (3) integration provides a unique model for understanding rehabilitation services and practitioners.

1

Somatopsychic Concepts

H. H. Garner

It is necessary to effectively encompass the problems involved in evaluating the sick patient as a total person and do justice to the needs of the practicing physician in establishing working diagnostic, prognostic, and treatment concepts of the patient. The utilization of a classification of the person seeking medical help as having either a psychosomatic or somatopsychic disturbance has been found useful. The psychosomatic disorders are those in which psychic elements are more significant for initiating the changes expressed in chemical, physiological, or structural alterations that create the symptoms responsible for the patient's complaints. There are those individuals who have some disturbance in the biochemistry, physiology, or structure of the body as the more significant initial factor in the development of illness with the psychic element in the symptom syndrome overlying the somatic factor.

A number of patients seem to fall into a classification in which the initiating element has not been determined. Some evidence to date suggests that psychic factors in the nature of a specific psychic conflict are the initiating stimulus. Hypertension, some asthmatic attacks, ulcerative colitis, migraine, and possibly rheumatoid arthritis have been considered such syndromes. In the following discussions, these disorders will be considered among the psychosomatic disturbances.

The shock therapies (Kalinowsky), the concept of stress as described by Selye, the use of ACTH and other hormones, and the newer psychopharmacology renewed the consideration of the somatopsychic aspects of a "holistic" view of man. There is no doubt that the change in a patient's mentation and behavior associated with brain tumors and with the psychosurgical procedures (Freeman and Watts) requires both

From *Psychosomatics,* 7 (1966), 329–337. Copyright © 1966 by the Academy of Psychosomatic Medicine. Reprinted by permission of the Managing Editor.

physiological and psychological explanations. Certainly, no explanation is possible in terms of either one of these disciplines alone. Adrian suggests that the sciences are converging and that Berger's discovery that the human brain is in a state of continual electrical oscillation was an important step in understanding the physical origins of nervous activity and, therefore, the physical origins of behavior. The work on reverberating circuits and feedback phenomena (Wiener) is contributing to bringing the information from the clinical psychiatrists on perception, thought, feeling, and behavior into closer juxtaposition to information coming from the basic scientists.

The term *somatopsychic* was used by Meyerson who pointed out the frequent emphasis on psychosomatic manifestations and the relatively less frequent discussion of the role played by bodily ills in the total disturbance of the person. A quote from Steiglitz is quite appropriate:

> Man, the individual, lives in two concomitant environments. Both are complex. The tissues and chemical reactions and the equilibrium of the organism constitute the realm of the biological sciences; the social, external environment is the realm of social medicine; clinical medicine, between these two, is concerned with the indivisible individual. Psyche and soma, internal homeostasis, growth and atrophy, and adaptation to external environmental forces are all part of the domain of clinical medicine.

Any such arbitrary delineation as is expressed in the term "somatopsychic" is made for convenience of discussion. Integrating approaches to disease requires concurrent studies, from organic, psychological, psychodynamic, and psychosocial viewpoints (Kruse).

Somatopsychic influences fall into two broad categories. (1) Some somatopsychic influences are an expression of the involvement of the tissues of the highest integrating organ of the body, the brain. Significant alteration in the tissues of the brain may change perceptual, integrative, conceptual, and executive functions in response to internal and external stimuli, which will have far-reaching implications. (2) The disturbances of somatic structures other than the brain. All tissue damage of structures other than the brain will influence the perceptual, integrating, conceptual, and executive functions of the brain. Dysfunction in biochemical and physiological function has feedback influences which directly affect the brain function or do so through psychological effects. The disturbances in perceptual, integrative, and behavioral responses related to brain changes will require separate elaboration.

SOMATIC DISTURBANCES AFFECT THE PSYCHE

Hereditary and constitutional factors help determine intelligence, temperament, and personality development. Intelligence will have an important influence. A mental defective might, for instance, be unable to intellectually understand a symptom such as pain in the abdomen as being related to a bowel obstruction as well as a patient whose intelligence enables him to appreciate the significance of obstruction to passage of contents in a hollow organ. The intelligent person would be operated on for bowel obstruction. The mentally defective person might require surgery for peritonitis and gangrene of the bowel.

Glandular alterations produce changes in the internal environment of a more subtle nature than that produced by major cellular or physiological change. Adolescence and the climacteric, for instance, are periods in life when changes in the sex hormones create a different internal environment. The previously balanced psychological and physiological state is thrown out of gear. New adaptations become necessary. The therapeutic use of potent steroids creates hormonal imbalance of a less subtle intensity and with greater speed and therefore calls for adaptive and defensive reaction on the part of the individual. The psychologic responses will depend upon factors other than the total dose of hormone used and will include the character structure of the person and the status of the illness before receiving the treatment (chronicity, etc.), pain and other symptoms, family attitude, physician attitude, etc.

The alteration in body function induced by the steroids is felt as ego dystonic (the person does not feel he is responding to body and environmental stimuli in the manner characteristic for him). Anxiety, guilt, shame, a sense of helplessness or hopelessness, lack of contentment, joy, and other affect changes may occur in response to regression to a psychologically less mature level. Patients whose character makeup predisposes them to further need for defenses may develop phobic, obsessional, ritualistic, and paranoid reactions. Failure of these defenses may lead to partial or total disintegration and disorganization of mental function.

Rome and Braceland have described the changes noted in patients when they have had cortisone therapy over a long period of time as follows: psychosexual conflicts previously latent become of clinical intensity; heterosexual interest wanes; aggressiveness and bitterness may replace libidinal interests; a hypochrondriacal concern with the physical self may create emotional lability and a disturbance in sleep pattern. When the steroid therapy produces a Cushing-like syndrome, integrated goal-directed functions of the individual may fail.

The total personality prior to the development of the disturbed structural and physiological functioning crucially affects the response to illness. All the previous experiences of the individual help determine how he is affected by the changes. Some of these factors are :

a. Developmental experiences (physical and psychological)
b. Family, social, and cultural influences (psychosocial effects)
c. Special symbolic meaning of the experiences (psychodynamic factors)
d. Motivation, level of aspiration, tolerance for frustration

Everyone may use all the reactions of regression and defense simultaneously. The degree to which any particular reaction is utilized helps determine the nature of the psychological pattern. When frustrated in goal-directed behavior, the individual reacts by functioning with behavior based on previously employed adaptations. It must be remembered, however, that a regressive type of adaptation to a need for love and security might well be concurrent with rather mature types of reactions in many other spheres of the person's life. How the previous personality may determine the special meaning of a somatic disturbance is illustrated by reactions to a simple dermatological lesion such as sebaceous adenoma. The obsessive-compulsive person might interpret it as a beginning cancer; the patient with repressed sexual masturbatory tendencies might finger it as if it were a phallus; and the person with a need to prove his strength, his perfection and effectiveness might completely ignore its existence as if it were not present.

The symbolic meaning of the disturbance has far-reaching implications. In general, the greater the tissue injury, disfigurement, and loss of effective function, the more likely it is that somatopsychic influences will be felt. However, the loss of a toe, for instance, may have special symbolic significance which might lead to disability disproportionate to the functional loss. Body image concepts are intimately tied to symbolic significance of any change in body structure (Kubie). The body image is determined largely by stimuli from the periphery, particularly the kinesthetic senses, touch, and pain, and to a lesser extent the special senses, and has important implications in mind-body relationships. The special senses, i.e., sight, hearing, etc., on the other hand, are particularly involved in distinguishing the "I" from the "non-I." Whenever the body image is disturbed by disease, amputation, or disfigurement, one may expect the needs of the individual for recognition, prestige, and denial of loss of parts which are invested with considerable emotional feeling, to become evident. Feelings of being irretrievably lost and unloved because one felt loved and accepted when beautiful, uninjured, or "perfect," and rejected when not perfect, are especially evident where the value system to which the patient was exposed stressed the importance of beauty and physical wholeness. The phantom limb is a case in point. It may be characterized by the illusion that the extremity is present. Neurologically, the phantom represents the organized impression of the patient's image of the body before the loss of the limb and should disappear when the stimuli which produced the organized sensory impressions of the limb in the parietotemporal center of the brain no longer appear. The phantom shrinks with time. A wish-fulfilling hallucination, however, may retain the limb indefinitely and illustrates how one type of somatic disturbance can alter mental functioning. The painful phantom, through intractable pain, may be found to serve a need to expiate feelings of guilt. The patient may feel that the organ which offended was the organ punished according to the talion principle of an eye for an eye and a tooth for a tooth (Kolb).

It is necessary to realize that the experience of any physical loss goes beyond the painful distortion of the body image, beyond one's image of oneself as a physical being. It involves the image of one's self as a social being whose family, social relationships, occupation, hobbies may become altered from a cherished ideal. One's independence, self-sufficiency, and autonomy may have to be surrendered.

The time, circumstances, extent, type, and speed of the immediate somatic disturbance affecting the individual are also important. How time and circumstances contribute significantly to somatopsychic disability is readily seen in the behavior of a soldier with an injury to an extremity who shows continuous improvement in physical well-being as he moves further from the battlefield, but who has an exacerbation of symptoms if confronted with the need to return to the battlefield. A civilian with a similar injury may show progressive disability as he moves from home to industrial surgeon's office and, finally, to the hospital. A civilian with an injury to the index finger of the right hand might have a variety of symptoms of a disabling nature, but a similar injury to a rifleman might be associated with the absence of any symptoms. In children with chronic illnesses which do not seriously impede locomotion, the psychic conflict between the desire to be active, assertive, and aggressive and the wish to be passive to satisfy the overprotective mother, especially where such overprotection has been very excessively determined by the mother's guilt, is crucial (Browne et al).

Anxiety Accompanies Any Illness
in Which Physical Integrity Is Threatened

Anxiety has been considered as a response secondary to or accompanying biochemical and physiologic changes. The relationship of stress to adrenocortical function was emphasized in Selye's concepts. Persky described the effects of stress interviews in raising the plasma hydrocortisone levels and urinary hydroxycorticoid excretion as further evidence of the neurohormonal relationship to anxiety. Anxiety has been described as arising from various levels of personality organization and development. Essentially these are the threats of : (1) complete helplessness, which derives from the earliest infancy, and separation from those to whom there is a necessary relationship, e.g., separation from mother; (2) physical injury when the value placed on mastery of environment and self-assertive powers is significant; and finally (3) social disapproval or loss of self-esteem from taboos and restrictions against egoistic strivings. The internalization of such taboos and restrictions is responsible for the development of the superego or conscience. When they have become internalized, the individual feels a threat of disapproval without external evidences of being rejected (Freud). Reaction of the individual to brain defect has been described as the catastrophic reaction. Goldstein finds that the smallest failures may be followed by considerable anxiety; any objective failure or inadequate response creates a situation to which the patient acts as if endangered. To avoid the anxiety, a series of defensive responses is developed which modifies the symptomatology of the brain-injured person. For instance, withdrawal and modification of behavior (increased orderliness, punctuality, and concentration on limited activities) prevent exposure to tasks which might lead to catastrophic reaction. Denial has also been mentioned as a significant symptom in somatic defects other than brain damage. Yielding to the defect and performing the new preferred behavior which automatically ensues or developing overcompensated, consciously contrived, preferred behavior constitute attempts to manage the anxiety produced by somatic changes whether in the brain or other organs.

The pathophysiology of psychosomatic disorders, among others, includes the fact that emotional stress finds expression in the vascular structures by ischemic effects on the arterial wall, resulting in local edema, atrophy and necrosis, hemorrhage, thrombosis, and possibly aneurysmal formation and rupture. Capillary changes include increased permeability, the passage of proteins and, finally, red blood cells. The structures being supplied by the vessels in spasm may develop edema, hemorrhage, degeneration of tissue fibres, and finally necrosis. In the brain, necrosis is followed by cyst formation and gliosis. In the stomach and other mucous-membrane-lined structures, ulceration and scarring will follow. Thus the anxiety can act to further somatic change.

Symptoms seen as defensive reactions to anxiety over somatic disability have been described by Wittkower as follows:

1. Increased absorption with the self, self-love (narcissistic withdrawal of object libido).
    a. Withdrawal from important persons in one's milieu.
    b. Withdrawal of a more general nature into a circumscribed world, e.g., patients in institutions may isolate themselves completely.
2. Hypochondriacal symptoms tend to overlay those due to the disability caused in the organ. (This has been expressed as investment of the injured part with libido withdrawn from objects.)
3. Increased phantasy life, expressive reactions (crying, etc.), and loquacity are means of expressing the activity being blocked from external expression.
4. Increased dependency desires and need for affection (primarily of infantile needs) are mobilized. There is recognition of the illness' value in permitting capitalization on the problems and conflicts of a psychosocial nature—secondary gain.
5. Overevaluation of authority, the doctor, nurses, etc. results from dependent and infantile cravings.
6. Aggressiveness, irritability, and bitterness may be expressions of a realistic distrust of the motives of others in helping the patient, but more frequently are reactions to finding that the dependent, infantile strivings for protection and affection are not fulfilled in keeping with the patient's wishes and expectations.
7. Feelings of shame, masochistic acceptance of pain, and passive resignation to illness may all serve the adaptive needs of the individual in dealing with unacceptable impulses of a sexual or aggressive nature.
8. Denial of illness and sacrifice of one part for another are also seen as methods of maintaining self-esteem and dealing with threats of loss of mastery of environment. Weinstein and Kahn stress the significance of the premorbid personality in determining this defense.
9. Confabulation is another means of establishing a relatedness to environment. Denial and confabulation may, especially in the brain-injured person, be accompanied by disorientation for time and place.
10. Faith in one's invulnerability is a prime factor in determining reaction to the shattering blows of illness (Masserman).

Pain frequently illuminates the somatic-psychic relatedness. In our society and in Judaeo-Christian cultures the acceptance and even the aggrandizement of suffering, pain, and illness is a social attitude which markedly influences medical practice. To be ill or to have pain may warrant: removal from dangerous situations (during war, etc.), enable the maintenance of self-esteem (to be kept from playing in a football game), and may lead to being compensated financially for a loss (dizziness and similar symptoms after a head injury are readily compensable if attributed to a concussion but are not as readily accepted if attributed to conflicts over a sense of lack of security and balance). The emphasis on pursuing the complaint of pain in medical examinations requires consideration. Szasz describes some of the problems in defining pain and the methods used for determining the presence of pain. If physical examination and reasonably adequate exploration of the physiochemical alterations which would help substantiate the presence of a physical alteration fail to explain the pain, the continued search or watchful, intensive concern with finding early signs of an undiscovered disease is seldom warranted. Although we may all have such undiscovered ailments, there is much reason to doubt that excessive vigilance is to the benefit of the patient. Such vigilance serves primarily the needs of the physician. Sometimes it coincides with certain psychological needs of the patient, as, for example, in cases of hypochondriasis.

It is evident that the local stimulus explanation of pain does not do full justice to the facts. Many patients have minor local irritants and react as if major changes are occurring. A severe wound which by all standards could be expected to be very painful may go unrecognized in the heat of battle or the excitement of a game. The associations that may accompany the experience of the local stimulus may affect the evaluation of pain. Patients with local chest conditions ordinarily causing mild pain might very well have severe chest pain if they associate their condition with a coronary occlusion. Pain is usually more severe at night, to which anyone with a toothache can attest. The elements of isolation, loneliness, and the withdrawal of stimuli from the outer world change the evaluation of pain. The expectation of relief and its effect on the evaluation of pain is known to most physicians. Relief will occur before the pain-relieving agent could have possibly had time to act, or a placebo given by a person in whom the patient has faith will change the evaluation of pain.

In the interpersonal (one person to another context of mother, father, sibling) the sensation of pain and reporting of pain to another person may be followed by sympathy, interest, or affection so that experiencing of pain is rewarded. The satisfaction from the reward may outweigh the discomfort of pain. Loss or separation of objects (parents, friends, etc.) may evoke the affect of pain which brings the rewarding experience of sympathetic affection.

Engel summarizes the circumstances which predispose to psychic pain as follows :

1. Pain may serve as a warning signal of possible damage or loss of a body.
2. Pain becomes associated with a pleasurable experience, and pain becomes the price for reestablishing that experience. (Pain in the child → crying response → comforting from loved person → relief of pain).
3. Pain is inflicted for being "bad." Accordingly, pain can be the evidence that one has been bad. It also serves the purpose of indicating that no further punishment is necessary. The linkage of pain and punishment is related to the seeking of pain and punishment for expiation of guilt.
4. Pain may serve as a defense against aggression. Aggression is associated with the possibility of inflicting pain but also with the possibility of suffering pain inflicted by others. Pain may serve as a warning against aggression.
5. Sexual excitement may become associated with painful conflicts or actual pain. Pain as a psychological warning signal may appear when provoking situations arouse sexual impulses.

BRAIN CHANGES AND SOMATOPSYCHIC EFFECTS

Alteration in brain structure or chemistry must be considered in a separate category from that of other organs when discussing somatopsychic influences. Brain changes are associated with psychological disturbances : changes in perception, concept formation, mood, and behavior. These disturbances can be specifically related to brain alteration in the same manner that pathology in any organ produces modification of function, irritative phenomena, or loss of function. Furthermore, somatopsychic influences of a secondary nature may be engrafted upon the primary dysfunction of the brain in a complex manner. Psychological reactions to brain injury are dependent on the nature, extent, and location of the lesion and when during life the lesion occurred. *The type of pathology,* whether tumor, trauma, infection, metabolic disorder, toxic agent, thermal, electrical, vascular, or degenerative, may not be, in some instances, as significant with regard to specific effects as the speed with which the etiological agent affects the nervous system. For instance, fast-growing tumors in a location may create disturbances which are quite different from slow-growing tumors in the same area. Infections superimpose symptoms which result from the invasion by a unique organism and the specific response of the brain to that particular organism, i.e., cell body degeneration in poliomyelitis, perivascular infiltration with syphilis. Further complicating the clinical picture may be the body response to fever. Traumatic effects, if severe, are very apt to have generalized influences which interfere with consciousness. Toxic agents, post-traumatic states, fever, and certain metabolic disturbances may be associated with general hyperirritability of the brain, tension states with gross hypersensitivity and hyperirritability to stimuli from within and without and varying states of delirium or irrational behavior. Decreased responsiveness to stimuli may be seen in tumors, post-traumatic recovery, and in later stages of recovery from toxic or infectious pathology. Cloudiness, drowsiness, slowing of thought, and perplexity, difficulty in grasping problems, indecision, slowing of speech and motor functions, tardy responses to sensory stimuli, apathy, and mood changes in keeping with generalized cerebral dysfunction, somnolence, and coma may all be present. Dementing effects produced by generalized injury to the brain are more likely to follow severe trauma or severe toxic effects as in chronic alcoholism, generalized vascular effects (cerebral arteriosclerosis), cerebral degenerative disease (senility, Pick's Disease). Loss of recent memory, poor recall, disorientation as to time, place, and person, defective general knowledge, and poor judgment are the usual symptoms. States of decreased responsiveness to stimuli merge into states of dementia. Repeated brain trauma, concussion, or contusion as seen in boxers may produce such a clinical picture.

Symptoms due to overall effects when brain damage is severe are unique. Kurt Goldstein has made major contributions to the understanding of the severely brain-damaged person through his studies of war injuries. He emphasizes that the whole behavior of the person in a given moment must be studied, the condition of the total psychophysical personality. Most of the symptomatology is an expression of disturbed function in vision, sensation, mobility, and speech concurrently, which in turn relates to damage to a specific capacity, the abstract attitude. *Damage to the abstract attitude* results in stereotyped and reserved behavior, poor spontaneity, initiative, and the capacity for making choices. Severe brain damage results in the higher level brain functions being primarily affected. *Brain function is reduced from the voluntary to the automatic-emotional level of functioning.* However, the automatic and emotional responses show a modification of their function with a loss or impairment of the higher level function of the abstract attitude. Goldstein sees as an explanation that *the emotional attitude is less subject to the effects of severe trauma than the abstract attitude.* He discloses that under circumstances which create the atmosphere for the emotional attitude, a patient may show the appropriate affect but will be unable to respond to a request to behave in a manner intended to demonstrate that affect. For instance, a patient, if asked to behave like an angry person, would find it impossible to do so, but in a situation provoking anger all the behavior characteristics of an angry response are produced.

The significance of when pathology occurs is illustrated by the difference in effects created by similar pathology in a child's brain as compared to that of an adult.

Symptoms further represent the direct sequelae of damage to a definite region, whether singly or in groups. They include : headache, dizziness, convulsions, sensory defects in the periphery, weakness or paralysis of motor function or disorganization of motor control (tremors, tics, choreiform or dystonic movements, clonus, nystagmus, etc.), speech and language defects, sense organ defects (smell, sight, taste, hearing). The area affected shows a rise in the threshold for response to stimuli, retardation of excitement, and a tendency to perseveration and repetition. In addition, one finds release phenomena or isolation of the undamaged area from the damaged so that inadequate stimuli produce a response; responses are of greater duration and are influenced abnormally by inadequate stimuli. Confusion in understanding the nature of the dysfunction which results from disordered thought processes and behavioral patterns is created by the fact that they are commonly not associated with any ready evidence of structural pathology. The following are descriptions of areas of pathology often associated with mental changes.

1. Frontal lobe loss of function produced by tumor, trauma, removal, and other causes has been remarkable for the insignificant changes noted by many. Bilateral frontal lobe pathology when extensive is associated with : impairment of attention, ready distractability, poor retention and learning (the ability to associate and synthesize), poor restraint of emotions (anger and hostility are easily displayed), euphoria and boasting, impairment of abstraction and judgment, slowness, stereotyping, and impulsiveness (Bruckner).

2. Temporal lobe pathology, especially when associated with a discharging type of lesion, may create clinical pictures confused at times with schizophrenic reactions. Attacks may begin with uncinate fits characterized by chewing, smacking of lips, tasting movements carried on automatically. Motor activity performed as an automatism, dressing and undressing, aggressive reactions, and more complex motor activity are part of the picture of so-called psychomotor epilepsy. Disturbances of mental content are a constant feature : sensory hallucinations of smell and taste, vivid imagery of a visual scene or musical tune, distortions in perceiving the size and

distance of objects and body parts, déjà-vu phenomena (I have experienced this before), unpleasant affects of fear and depression.

3. Parietal lobe tumors and destructive lesions of the parietal lobe primarily affect positional and tactile discriminations. Mental phenomena apt to be confused with nonorganic psychiatric syndromes are more related to affections of the left posterior parietal lobe which may produce difficulty in speech reception, dyslexia, dysphasia, finger dysgnosia, dyscalculia. Sensory and visual inattention have been described as caused by parietal lobe lesions.

4. Corpus callosum tumors create a distinctive picture in which mental symptoms are prominent. Apathy, drowsiness, depression, and memory defect are among the commonest symptoms.

SPECIAL PROBLEMS

Somatopsychic factors in the chronically disabled person are very pertinent to present-day medical and social problems. Chronic invalidism creates somatopsychic problems which are more or less uniform for the group as a whole. Similar problems occur from the effects of chronic diseases of the neuromuscular osseous system or the internal organs and are independent of the specific problems that might occur due to differences of disability created by infection, trauma, toxins, thermal agents, metabolic and nutritional disease, heredity and congenital malformations, degenerative changes of undetermined origin. Attempts to remaster control of the environment are more important to patients suffering from neuromuscular osseous diseases and those affecting the brain. The degree of incapacity, the nature of previous skills and occupation, the weight placed on them, and the loss of important senses will be among the major factors in determining capacity to deal with problems and events requiring such skills. A baseball player, for instance, may react to the loss of a hand with a much greater degree of apathy than a lawyer.

The somatopsychic disorders of the aging are associated with the awareness of loss of prestige, lovability, and sexual potency as well as attempts to deny loss of integrity of body and mind and fear of rejection. The need to develop defenses such as regression to dependency, depression, and demanding irritable aggressivity are attempts to restore a sense of value. Further complications are brought about by the disturbances in memory, recall, and retention and a more profound breakdown in the integrative functioning of the brain (Palmer).

Somatic influences on mental illness may be dramatic. It is not at all uncommon to see a severely psychotic patient experience complete remission for overt psychotic manifestations when some acute illness or surgical intervention or severe trauma intrudes on the patient's disordered psyche. Possibly, the shock therapies have no greater specificity for improving a psychotic patient than is inherent in the response to any overwhelming somatic change. The particular symbolic meaning to the patient of illnesses, structural alterations, and physical treatment leading to recovery from mental dysfunction require individual investigation. It may be said that any process affecting the psyche so as to create a new state of balance, or necessitating reactivation of psychic functioning on a more mature level may be followed by improvement in the mental state. A threat to vital processes of life may mobilize all the latent constructive forces to deal with the new problem; the conflict which maintained the psychotic state no longer is a major problem.

The use of physical handicaps as a means of problem-solving for the person is probably culturally determined. In a culture in which disability is not associated with sympathetic understanding and emphasis on medical care, it is questionable if it would have the same protective value. It is interesting to note that the presence of physical evidence of handicap or continued realistic trauma and fear may be factors in protection from psychoses. Schecter finds a preponderance of neurotic rather than psychotic defenses in orthopedically handicapped children. The defenses of denial, regression, undoing reaction formation, and displacement are particularly mentioned. A defense against painful perceptions through apathy, blandness, and lack of affect was noted. The deformity may become an accepted part of the body image because of its secondary gain value and may serve the person as a fetishistic object.

THERAPY

It is only proper that all the therapeutic efforts possible be utilized to help the patient toward restoration of health (Solomon.) Analysis, suggestion, persuasion, reorganization of habits, insight, insofar as it can be given, and many chemical and physical means are helpful. The patient showing structural alterations and physiological and chemical dysfunction should be the recipient of such psychotherapeutic measures as are for his benefit and can be offered to him by his physician in addition to physiochemical therapeutics. This must be done in keeping with the capabilities of the physician, the realistic potentialities of the situation, and the patient's ability to utilize them.

REFERENCES

1. Adrian, E. D. The Mental and the Physical Origins of Behavior. *Int. J. Psychoan.* 28 :1–6, 1946.
2. Browne, W. J., Mally, M. A., and Kane, R. P. Psychosocial Aspects of Hemophilia. *Amer. J. Orthopsychiat.* 30 :730–740, 1960.
3. Bruckner, R. M. *Intellectual Functions of the Frontal Lobes.* New York : Macmillan, 1936.
4. Ecker, A. Emotional Stress Before Strokes : Preliminary Report of 20 Cases. *Ann. Int. Med.,* 40 :49–56, 1954.
5. Engel, G. *Psychological Development in Health and Disease.* Philadelphia : W. B. Saunders, 1962.
6. Freeman, W. and Watts, J. W. *Psychosurgery.* Springfield, Ill. : C. C. Thomas, 1942.
7. Freud, Anna. *The Ego and Mechanisms of Defense.* New York : International Universities Press, 1946.
8. Goldstein, Kurt. *The Organism, A Holistic Approach to Biology Derived from Pathological Data in Man.* New York : American Book, 1939.
9. Hardy, J. D., Wolff, H. G., and Goodell, H. *Pain Sensations and Reactions.* Baltimore : Williams & Wilkins, 1952.
10. Harrower, Molly (Ed.). *Medical and Psychological Teamwork in the Care of the Chronically Ill.* Springfield, Ill. : C. C. Thomas, 1955.
11. Jackson, J. H. *Selected Writings.* (Ed.), Taylor, J., New York : Basic Books, 1958.
12. Kalinowsky, L. B. and Hoch, P. H. *Shock Treatment. Psychosurgery and Other Somatic Treatment in Psychiatry.* New York : Grune & Stratton, 1952.
13. Kolb, L. C. The Painful Phantom. *Psychology, Physiology and Treatment.* Springfield, Ill. : C. C. Thomas, 1954.
14. Kruse, H. D. (Ed.). *Integrating the Approaches to Mental Disease.* New York : P. B. Hoeber, 1957.
15. Kubie, L. S. The Basis of a Classification of Disorders from the Psychosomatic Standpoint. *Bull. New York Acad. Med.* 20 :46–65, 1944.
16. Masserman, J. Faith and Delusion in Psychotherapy : The UR Defenses of Man. *Amer. J. Psychiat.* 110 :324–333, 1964.
17. Meyerson, Abraham. Psychosomatic and Somatopsychics. *Psychiat. Quart.* 14 :665–675, 1940.
18. Nemiah, John C. *Foundations of Psychopathology.* New York : Oxford University Press, 1961.
19. Palmer, H., Braceland, F. A., and Hastings, D. Somatopsychic Disorders of Old Age. *Amer. J. Psychiat.* 91 :856–863, 1943.

20. Persky, H., Grinker, R. R., Sbashin, M. A., Korchin, S. J., Basowitz, H., and Chevalier, J. A. Adrenal Cortical Function in Anxious Human Subjects : Plasma Level and Urinary Excretion of Hydrocortisone. *Arch. Neurol. & Psychiat.* 76 :549–558, 1956.

21. Prange, Arthur J. The Psychophysiologic Aspects of Pain. *The New Physician* 14 :247–250 (Sept.) 1965.

22. Rome, H. and Braceland, F. The Role of ACTH, Cortisone, and Hydrocortisone in the Provocation of Certain Psychological Responses, in S. Bernard Wortis, *Publ. Assoc. Res. Nerv. Ment. Dis.* (273–279). Baltimore : Williams & Wilkins, 1953.

23. Schechter, M. D. The Orthopedically Handicapped Child. *Arch. Gen. Psychiat.* 4 :247–253, 1961.

24. Selye, Hans. The General Adaptation Syndrome and the Diseases of Adaptation. *J. Clin. Endocrin.* 6 :117–230, 1946.

25. Solomon, A. P. Rehabilitation of Patients with Psychologically Protracted Convalescence. *Arch. Phys. Ther.* 24 :270–276, 1943.

26. Steiglitz, E. The Integration of Social and Clinical Medicine. Address to Acad. of Med., New York, March 19, 1947.

27. Szasz, T. The Nature of Pain. *Arch. Neurol. and Psychiat.* 74 :174–181, 1955.

28. Weinstein, E. A. and Kahn, R. L. *Denial of Illness.* Springfield, Ill. : C. C. Thomas, 1955.

29. Wiener, Norbert. *Cybernetics.* New York : Wiley & Sons, Inc., 1948.

30. Wittkower, Eric D. and Cleghorn, R. A. (Eds.). *Recent Developments in Psychosomatic Medicine.* Philadelphia : Lippincott, 1954.

2

An Alternative Frame of Reference for Rehabilitation: The Helping Process versus the Medical Model

Thomas P. Anderson

A difference in the reaction to the patient who is having difficulty with his emotional reactions to his illness or disability is sometimes observed between those rehabilitation professionals trained under the medical model (physicians, nurses, and various therapists) and those trained in the behavioral sciences (such as psychologists and social workers).[1,2] Could it be that these two types of professionals approach the patient from different frames of reference?[3] Because rehabilitation services often have patients of this type, it is meaningful to take a further look at the approach to the patient, contrasting these two frames of reference.

To begin, one may ask, "How does the rehabilitation professional attain satisfactions from his relationship with the patient?" Several answers can be put forth: (1) he eradicates disease, (2) he cures the patient, (3) he solves the patient's problems, and (4) he, along with the rehabilitation team, helps the patient to solve problems. Which of these achievements is the most important to the rehabilitation profession? Is it also the one in which he has the most teaching and training? The significant point here is that many rehabilitation professionals, not trained in the behavioral sciences, have had the least training in the accomplishment which they consider to be the most important. If these four behaviors or accomplishments are viewed from the standpoint of frames of reference used in rehabilitation, it becomes apparent that the first three probably all could come under the frame of reference called the medical model of which surgery is the most pronounced example. The fourth one could be said to represent the frame of reference of the help-

From *Archives of Physical Medicine and Rehabilitation*, 56 (1975), 101–104. Copyright © 1975 by the American Congress of Rehabilitation Medicine and the American Academy of Physical Medicine and Rehabilitation. Reprinted by permission of the Managing Editor.

ing professions, such as psychology, social work, and counseling. There are probably many other frames of reference, operating either consciously or unconsciously, that are also involved in our day-to-day dealings with rehabilitation patients and their problems. However, only these two frames of reference will be considered. Their similarities are probably greater than their differences,[4] but it will serve the purposes of this presentation to look mainly at the differences and contrast them from a variety of aspects. This look will be a simple speculative one not based on scientific studies or fact but merely on the opinions of the author. It will be directed at the doctor-patient relationship under the medical model and the professional-client relationship under the helping professions. The aspects which will be considered are :

1. Activity of both the professional and the client.
2. The basis for trust.
3. Problem solving (including both successes and failures).
4. The client's ability to handle future problems as a result of the pro-fessional-client relationship.

Under the medical model the professional is usually active while the client is often passive; whereas in the helping professions the professional is listening and counseling, but it is the client who eventually takes the action. To many, a scene typical of a physician's office is one in which the patient is lying horizontally and passively while the professional actively does something to him, either in examining or treating. In con-trast, conceptions of a typical scene in the office of the helping profes-sional is one in which the client is actively talking, gaining insight, and planning what future action he will take. Which of these scenes is more appropriate for rehabilitation?

What is the basis for the client's trust of the professional? In the medical model the basis is more often on the expertise and authority of the professional or on the client's response to the stereotype of the profes-sional, for example, "faith in your doctor"; whereas in the helping profes-sions' model, trust does not appear so automatically but grows slowly based on a personal relationship, on mutuality, and on the joint develop-ment of this trust. How does the patient in rehabilitation develop trust in the professional? Does it develop slowly or automatically?

When the client brings a problem to the professional, one of the first steps in solution is the identification of the problem. Under the helping professions' model, the professional assists the client in a joint exploration of the problem, while in the medical model the professional directs questions to the patient, examines him, analyzes the information gained, employs deductive reasoning, and finally arrives at a proper diagnosis. This latter method, of course, is proper, practical, and expedient in acute crisis medicine.

The client's participation in this problem identification also differs greatly. Under the helping professions' model the client is given the responsibility for drawing conclusions and making decisions; whereas under the medical model he usually simply answers the professional's questions. For the problems facing the rehabilitation patient, how much responsibility do we give the patient in drawing conclusions and identifying his problems?

After the problem has been properly identified, how do the two types of professionals start working on its solution? In the helping professions' model, the professional and the client make a joint exploration of alternative solutions; whereas in the medical model the professional tends more often to give directions to the patient and assume that the patient understands and is willing to go along with the plan for solution. Furthermore, in the helping professions' model, the client is encouraged to select which alternative he is going to follow, while in the medical model the client supposedly follows the professional's directions. However, sometimes he does not follow them. There has accumulated in recent years in the medical literature more than 60 articles about patients' compliance with physicians' orders.[5-9] A good many conclusions are drawn from these studies. Two that are pertinent for this consideration are : (1) the more authoritarian or authoristic the professional, the less compliant is the client; and (2) the more severe the illness or disability, the less compliant is the client with the professional's recommendations. These two findings would seem to have particular importance in rehabilitation. In chronic illness and disability, is it the professional who treats the illness or is it the patient (or patient and his family) who actually carries out the routine treatment day after day? Hence, it behooves us in rehabilitation not only to instruct well the patient and his family in the daily home treatment program but also to see that the patient is involved in identifying his problems. It is of great importance that the patient understands his illness or disability and the reasons for and importance of the treatment regimen so that he and his family will be well motivated to carry out the professional's recommendations.

Continuing this process of contrasting these two frames of reference, consider the problem solution. What happens when the problem has been solved successfully? In the medical model, the professional can feel warm and good with the patient but often this satisfaction has developed at the expense of the patient's dependency relationship on him. The professional also can get a sense of satisfaction from having solved a problem. In contrast, in the helping professions, the professional gives the client credit for the success, praises him, and reinforces the client's self-confidence as manager of his own problems. The professional gets his satisfaction in helping the client to grow.

How does the client react to this success in problem solving? In the medical model he often is grateful to the professional for solving his problem and hence puts the professional above himself. In the helping professions the client is usually grateful for help (not for the solution), for the warm equality of the relationship, and for the opportunity for personal growth.

When the solution to the problem fails, feelings of fault and blame naturally arise, either expressed or unexpressed. Under which frame of reference in such cases is it easier for both the professional and the client to feel less guilty and defensive? In the actual carrying-out of the plans for the common problems of rehabilitation patients, on whom is the responsibility for action more dependent, the professional(s) or the client? As professionals, do we transfer that responsibility to the client clearly and directly? If not, could it be our medical frame of reference that interferes?

Having gone through this experience of problem solving, what happens to the client when he is faced with a similar problem in the future? The person who has had experience involving the helping professions' frame of reference can attempt exploring this new problem alone by using the previously learned model. If this attempt alone is not successful, then he returns to the professional for help, not for solution. Whereas in the medical model it may not occur to the client to explore his new problem alone. He just goes directly to the professional and seeks his solution.

A final way in which these two frames of reference might be contrasted is looking at them from the standpoint of transactional analysis. In this concept of personality functioning, developed by Berne and his followers,[10] it is proposed that within each individual there are three forces operating, one at a time or simultaneously: the child, the parent, and the adult. The child says, "I want"; the parent says, "I should" or "I should not"; and the adult says, "Here are my alternatives." In the medical model the professional all too often uses his "parent" to speak down to the client's "child." Whereas in the helping professions' model, the professional uses his "adult" to communicate with the client's "adult," which makes it much easier for the client to reciprocate. It might help for every rehabilitation professional to play the role of a client experiencing another professional using his "parent" to talk down to his client's "child." Then the one role-playing the client could attempt to respond with his "adult." He would find that responding as an adult to a parent-child challenge from the professional is difficult; yet we with a background in the medical frame of reference often expect this behavior of our patients.

What are the labels that are placed on the protocol or procedure of these two frames of reference? In the medical model we usually call it diagnosis and management; in the helping professions it is called "the helping process."

At this point an orientation to the helping process is indicated. A full review of the literature would be inappropriate for this admittedly loose, speculative, philosophical discussion. Fortunately, a description of some pertinent aspects of the helping process has already been prepared by Nylen, Mitchell, and Stout[11] and is summarized below. The following aspects will be covered: definition, relationship between helper and helpee, requirements, dynamics, and barriers both to receiving help and giving help.

Definition. The helping process is a helper trying to influence or affect the helpee's thinking and/or actions; the helper does not take action himself but instead assists the helpee to take the action. The desire to be helpful is natural, but in rehabilitation it often leads to doing the task for the helpee instead of assisting him in doing it, which is more difficult. We in rehabilitation often encounter this problem in the patient's well-intentioned relative who finds it quicker and easier to dress the disabled person than to allow him to do it for himself, albeit more slowly.

Relationship between helper and helpee. Important factors which influence this relationship are: the needs, the values, and the feelings (of not only the helpee but also the helper), of which each may or may not be aware. Forces influencing this relationship are not only verbal communication but some of the nonverbal behaviors (that is, posture, gestures, facial expressions, and eye movements), which are often revealing of attitudes, unaware as well as aware.

Requirements. Listening is required on both sides, but more by the helper. A joint exploration of the problem is made by both the helpee and the helper, instead of just by the team as often is the case in rehabilitation. The helper's compulsion to rush to solution, an American cultural tradition, results in the solution becoming the helper's, and hence the attitude of the helpee may be ambivalent. The helpee can be positive and active if he feels he decided on the plan of solution. Trust, which should be mutual, is important but takes time to develop, each giving verbal recognition to it when it exists and when it does not.

Dynamics. The needs, values, and feelings, both aware and unaware, of both the helper and helpee are affecting each other in this relationship for the purpose of attacking the problem. After agreeing to a contract,

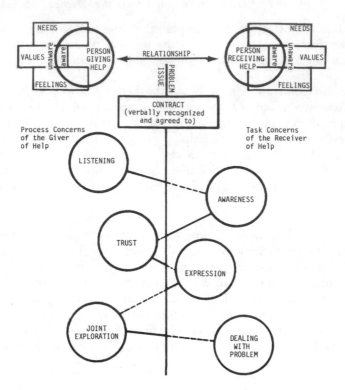

Dynamics of the helping process. (Reproduced with permission of Marilyn Harris, Ph.D.)

the helper does a lot of listening to the helpee who by talking and explaining increases his awareness. In this process the helper consciously and openly works on the development of trust. As expression of this trust is given by the helpee also, progress is made toward the joint exploration of the problem, which finally leads to the helpee's decisions on how he is going to be dealing with the problem.

Barriers to the helping process.   Difficulties and misperceptions, which serve as barriers to the helpee's receiving help, are : refusing to admit that he has a problem, not trusting the helper, being reluctant to achieve self-growth and self-understanding, and feeling his problem is unique and hence insoluble or impossible or that his acceptance of help increases his dependency on the helper. Pitfalls for the helper are : overpraising the helpee, not waiting for the helpee to discover the identity of the problem for himself with assistance only, or forcing on the helpee his own diagnosis and plan of solution of the problem (as rehabilitation teams are prone to do).

There is much more which could and should be said about the helping process. However, perhaps enough has been covered to consider the following two questions: Is it important for the rehabilitation professional to consider his frame of reference to the patient and the patient's problems? Secondly, should those rehabilitation professionals trained under the medical model frame of reference have an opportunity to become aware of the helping process as practiced in the helping professions?

REFERENCES

1. Rogers, C. R. Client-Centered Therapy : its current practice, implications, and theory. Boston, Houghton Mifflin Co., Publishers, 1951.
2. Rogers, C. R. On Becoming A Person : a therapist's view of psychotherapy. Chapter 17, Boston, Houghton Mifflin Co., Publishers, 1961.
3. Ullman, I. P., Krasner, I. (Eds). Case Studies in Behavior Modification. New York, Holt, 1965.
4. Leviton, G. Professional and client viewpoints on rehabilitation issues. Rehabil Psychol *20* :1–80, 1973.
5. Davis, M. S. Physiologic, psychological and demographic factors in patient compliance with doctor's orders. Med Care *6* :115–122, 1968.
6. Davis, M. S. Variations in patients' compliance with doctors' advice : empirical analysis of patterns of communication. Am J Public Health *58* :274–288, 1968.
7. Francis, V., Korsch, B. M., Morris, M. J. Gaps in doctor-patient communication : patients' response to medical advice. N Engl J Med *280* :535–540, 1969.
8. Gordis, I., Markowitz, M. Factors related to patient's failure to follow long-term medical recommendations. VIII Annual Meeting Association Ambulatory Pediatric Services, Atlantic City, April 30, 1968.
9. Korsch, B. M., Gozzi, E. K., Francis, V. Gaps in doctor-patient communication : I. doctor-patient interaction and patient satisfaction. Pediatrics *42* :855–871, 1968.
10. Harris, T. A. I'm OK—You're OK : practical guide to transactional analysis. New York, Harper and Row, Publishers, 1969.

11. Nylen, D., Mitchell, J. R., Stout, A. Handbook of Staff Development and Human Relations Training: Materials Developed for Use in Africa. Washington, D.C., National Training Laboratories Institute for Applied Behavioral Science, and Copenhagen, Denmark, the European Institute for Trans-National Studies in Group and Organization Development.

3

Barriers to Normality for the Handicapped Adult in the United States

Leslie D. Park

In a brilliant paper presented to an international conference in the fall of 1973, Gunnar Dybwad, professor of human development at Brandeis University in Massachusetts, gave us some perceptive definitions of what we commonly call "normalization." Dr. Dybwad says, "Normal on our earth is trouble and strife, trial and tribulation, and the handicapped person has a right to be exposed to it. Normalization thus includes the dignity of risk." He further states, "The origin of the effort to introduce the concept of normalization was the realization that a specific strategy had to be developed to counteract the process of denormalization which over the past 75 years has made such deep inroads into society's dealing with handicapped individuals."

In other words, normalization is a rational attempt to deal with the very conditions that have tended to deepen and reinforce prejudice and tended to set the severely handicapped apart from the rest of society.

From these remarks we can see that the elements of normalization involve:

1. Righting the wrongs of the past.
2. Bringing the handicapped back into the mainstream of society.
3. Developing the "normal" as a risk process that involves the elimination of the "sanitized life" and substituting for it the possibility of failure as well as the possibility of greater rewards.

All that I believe about life, man, and man's relationship to God tells me that life is or ought to be, "an adventure and a novelty." It is

From *Rehabilitation Literature, 36* (1975), 108–111. Copyright © 1975 by the National Easter Seal Society for Crippled Children and Adults. Reprinted by permission of the Editor.

this aspect of life that speaks of vigor, vitality, and the satisfactions we all seek. This is "normal" in the brightest sense.

BARRIERS TO NORMALITY

I would like to set forth what I believe are the barriers in the United States that prevent the normalization process for handicapped adults. I mention adults because I believe that the adolescent is really at the beginning stages of adult life and the same problems and barriers persist throughout life.

Barrier No. 1:
A Confused Value System by a Confused Government Makes Normalization for the Handicapped Virtually Impossible

It is a fact that the United States is a country built around the philosophy of "rugged individualism." We have had physical frontiers in the United States for many years, and they are only now beginning to disappear. One who travels in the American West knows that there are literally thousands and thousands of square miles of unsettled land that still beckon to the adventurous homesteader. Nevertheless, this is no longer the challenge it was 100 years ago, and people increasingly live in cities and urban settlements, and the idea of "rugged individualism" has long since succumbed to more popular and realistic concepts. In spite of this, we have a social system in the United States that has still not caught up with the change from the principle of rugged individualism to *social interdependence*. This may be best illustrated by the fact that the United States is perhaps the only technically advanced country in the world that does not have a health system for its citizens, lags seriously in penal reform, and has only in the past few years developed a "right to education law" for the handicapped. At the present time we offer to our handicapped citizens social security and pension payments that are below the subsistence level.

To a very large degree, riches and ability to make money are still the standards of success in the United States. When we speak of making handicapped people "contributing members of society," we almost mean *financially* contributing members. Our country still finds it much easier for the "rich" handicapped person to "make it" than the "poor" one. Although this is true of most industrialized countries, it is *more true* in the United States. This may be illustrated by the following facts :

1. *Achievement* by the handicapped is almost always totally related to having a job or working.
2. The United States has the most widely advertised "Hire the Handi-

capped population effectively. We are only now attempting to do this, paying attention to "hiring."

A young handicapped girl I know, an accomplished painter, recently had an art show. Although the show was highly successful, and her artistic talent won wide acclaim, most people did not feel that the girl was really much of an artist until she had evidence of having sold some of her paintings. The value of her work became suddenly more acceptable when the product of her hands became a salable item. This attitude is widespread in the United States at this time. It makes it virtually impossible for handicapped people to achieve any measure of satisfaction or success in activities that do not produce financial rewards.

In a recent presentation made to one of our legislative bodies, we had occasion to illustrate that, if one were to draw a line down the middle of the page and label one side of that line "no work" and the other side "work," he would find that on the "no work" side vast expenditures were being made by the government for the care of handicapped people in institutions and in all types of community services. The great economic investment government has in the handicapped lies on the "no work" side. Bringing people out of institutions for the retarded and into more effective community-based programs reduces by thousands of dollars the expenditures of government for the care of such persons. (In 1974, the annual cost of caring for one retarded child in a New York institution was $20,000.)

On the "work side" of the line, the person who holds a job is almost always holding a limited job. The taxes he pays are quite small (less than $1,200) in relationship to the saving that can be realized by the government on the "no work" side of the line. Only in recent years has this concept become evident to the Congress of the United States, and only now are we beginning to develop legislation for programs that will assist handicapped people to live in the community and carry on effective adult activities without "work for pay."

Probably no event in the social history of our country is as revealing as the recently completed "War on Poverty." You will recall that this was a national program announced by former President Lyndon Johnson. It had all of the trappings of a Normandy Beach Invasion, including massive expenditures, "crash" programs looking for quick results, and the use of the poor themselves to oversee their own programs of progress. The wreckage of this disastrous war is all over the landscape! Not only was the program highly *unsuccessful,* it also was extremely wasteful and created a bitterness on the part of the taxpayers that will make it very difficult to bring about other needed social reforms. In many ways there is a built-in American impatience with chronic "here and now" problems and with slow procedures. We are generous givers to acute international calamity. Let there be an earthquake in Nicaragua, a famine in North Africa, floods in China, and there will be an outpouring of American dollars. But the problems of the handicapped are constantly with us and so escape our notice!

In a further confusion about value systems I must mention the changing role of the family. When you speak of "the family," one pictures a mother and a father (usually a white mother and a white father) and two or three healthy children. This is becoming the atypical family in many communities of America today. We have the common portrait of interracial marriages, mothers of illegitimate children choosing to raise children without a father, changes in the law that are now under consideration to have lesbian women and homosexual men raise adopted children, and a variety of patterns that change altogether the usual pattern of what constitutes the family.

In the very successful family conferences conducted by United Cerebral Palsy of New York City, we bring together family units with handicapped children for week-long counseling and recreation programs. Only very rarely do we see "intact" families appearing at these conferences. It is quite usual for us to see a mother with two or three children, an older retarded daughter, a grandmother, or a nearby neighbor coming to the conference as a "family" unit. This confusion about the social order and national value systems is perhaps the greatest barrier to providing answers to the complex problems of the handicapped in the United States.

Barrier No. 2:
The Mobility Dilemma

Much has been written concerning the development of normal patterns for the adolescent child and how these relate to the handicapped child. One of the themes heard over and over again is the natural desire and healthy tendency for the adolescent to break away from usual family ties and to develop a sense of independence. Almost always this means an ability to get away from the family physically. In the United States, now made up of hundreds of suburbs, this inevitably means the ability to drive a car and get away from the home via the automobile.

One of the first cerebral palsied people I ever knew was a boy who lived in Chicago. He would get around the neighborhood by using a coaster wagon such as children use. He was able to push with one leg and steer the wagon with one hand. He almost always had a box of pencils, shoelaces, and chewing gum that he sold to people in the neighborhood. His sole system of mobility was his wagon.

I have had experience in conducting community studies in 32 different communities, both large and small. In each of these communities we discovered that transportation was a primary problem for the handicapped. In most instances, if an effective transportation system could have been developed, the number of people served by community resources would have doubled.

We must say, then, that the problem of transportation and mobility is a barrier to normality in the United States, as it is in many other countries of the world.

Barrier No. 3:
The Lack of Entry System for Adolescents in the World of Work

From the time an adolescent completes his school years until the time he is old enough to establish a home and represent himself as a reasonably stable member of the community, there is a period of great confusion. This applies to handicapped as well as nonhandicapped young people. There is *no* system of preparation and entry into the world of work except by the most haphazard and discriminatory practices. This is evident by the fact that many trade unions discriminate openly against the training and employment of black workers and minority groups. It can be seen in the high cost of education in the United States, which still makes college a possibility only for the well-to-do, the intellectually gifted, or the exceptional athlete. It is further compounded by the fact that there is an increasing disenchantment with college education as a proper vehicle into the world of useful and satisfying work.

This problem manifests itself by the confusion that presently exists concerning what to do in the training of *older* handicapped children, such as the mentally retarded and the cerebral palsied. Inevitably, in the school systems in the United States, you will find a very early effort to get older handicapped children, such as the mentally retarded and the cerebral palsied, into "vocational programs." The assumption is, of course, that because these children are handicapped they should know what they want to do in the world of work at a much earlier age.

I have a very serious concern about the limitations of the sheltered workshop concept. It has never made much sense to me. I do not see the logic of gathering a group of handicapped people and putting them *all* into *a* place where they sit down at benches and do *handwork*, when at the very outset we know these people have a serious limitation in their hand function! Sheltered workshop work around the world is surprisingly similar. We may also see that the subcontract, industrial type of work carried on in the average sheltered workshop goes contrary to work trends in the world.

At the present time, areas of work that are growing at an unprecedented rate are sales and service. Little or nothing is being done to develop sales and service occupations for seriously handicapped people.

We still try to make the workshop the main avenue of vocational service. Wide experimentation is needed in the next decade to develop alternatives to this pattern of work for seriously handicapped people.

Alternatives in the work system are likewise needed with such things as apprenticeships and a restoration of apprenticeship training. New patterns are needed, such as the Australian plan of mixing handicapped and nonhandicapped people in an entire industry (so successfully carried on in Centre-Industries in Sydney). White collar and service occupations geared to handicapped people and sales programs providing meaningful income to disabled people are needed. I have rarely been in a major city in the world and not seen a cerebral palsied person working at a newsstand, cigar counter, or candy store in the metropolitan area.

A further item related to this barrier has to do with training that still exists for many nonexistent jobs. We still see handicapped people trained in chaircaning and the making of potholders! I don't mean to demean these activities, but they are illustrative of the fact that there simply is not a realistic vocational objective for much of the work training carried on for the handicapped in the world.

Barrier No. 4:
Lack of Implemented Technology, Bioengineering

Let me make a bold statement at the very beginning of this discussion, "I have never met a handicapped person who could have not been functionally improved by applied technology."

The rehabilitation movement has *not* embraced bioengineering as a part of the team activity in the same way it has embraced physiotherapy, speech therapy, and medical services. Today, there exists "off-the-shelf technology" with many useful devices for feeding, transporting, and assisting the handicapped to live more effective lives. We are very remiss as a rehabilitation community in not building these technological advances into our day-to-day rehabilitation programs. It is a serious flaw in our activities.

In the United States, technology has "spun off" many useful technological advances that we must capture if we are to serve the handicapped population effectively. We are only now attempting to do this, but I fear we have not mobilized to do it effectively.

SOME ANSWERS TO THE BARRIERS

Let me now move to what I think are some promising ways to remove the barriers I have discussed.

The Value System

It would certainly be presumptuous to suggest that one single organization could tell its government how to get its values in order. Nevertheless, I think this is a time in history when voluntary agencies need to play a very specific role. I see our role in this decade as one of "model-building." Nothing affects government as much as seeing real, living, working models of programs that can change situations. *Now* is the time for us to be building programs that work, programs that are cost-effective, programs that call us into accountability, programs that are effectively housed in appropriate buildings. *We must take to ourselves the establishment of clear rehabilitation goals (this is very rarely done), develop the strategies to meet these goals, and develop the tools to evaluate our results.*

If we develop one or two working models of what can be done with handicapped people by the effective use of all that we know, we will demonstrate to our government *how* it can be done best. The day is rapidly coming when governments will awaken to the fact that rehabilitation is not only the humanitarian thing to do, but the *economical* thing to do. Models are needed to do the job effectively. Before government spends millions, we as nongovernmental groups must spend hundreds to learn how it can best be done.

Religion as a Value in Rehabilitation

One of the astonishing things about the times in which we live is how confused our value system really is. Today it is no longer taboo to talk about or show films of the most explicit sexual acts between adults. (They do not even have to be man and woman!) Nevertheless, it is absolutely taboo to talk about religion or man's relationship to God as essential to successful living (and certainly not as an objective of rehabilitation)! I completely reject the idea of eliminating religion from what must be suggested to the handicapped as an important contribution to their lives. I do not suggest that a formal program of religious training be added to rehabilitation services; however, I do not think we should ignore religion as a primary motivating factor in the lives of many people in this world. I am not necessarily talking about organized religion through traditional church groups, but what I am talking about is a basic relationship of *man* to *God* (as opposed to man's relationship to man).

Philosophical Clarity

To a very large degree we are confused in the rehabilitation movement about what we really are. There are those who suggest that we are practicing a science and therefore must adhere to rather strict scientific rules. If you pull arm A, you can expect reaction B. Others say that rehabilitation is simply an art, and the real skill is in the knowledge and techniques of the artist. I submit to you that what we are doing is both an art *and* a science. We must not be confused about what is scientific and what is artistic in our efforts.

I do not anticipate that machines will ever be able to do the work in which we are all engaged, in special education, psychological counseling, vocational training, medical management, and so on. At the same time I am not prepared to say that the most effective type of human rehabilitation can be carried on *without* the application of scientific principles in what we know about learning, medicine, and human behavior. *In short, what I am saying is that we must know much more about our craft.*

At the present time in our work in New York we have accepted the philosophy of "simulating the norm" as a pattern for effective work with the cerebral palsied. If it is normal for a child to go to school until the age of 18, we try to simulate that norm. If it is normal for an adult to marry and establish a home and have a family, we help people simulate this norm. This is a very reasonable objective, and yet it is an extremely difficult one.

Handicapped Hold Key to Attitudes in the Next Generation

I would like to suggest to the handicapped themselves that they have a tremendous role to play. It is perhaps a role that is not fully realized by the organized disabled groups around the world. I believe *this* generation of handicapped people is making it possible for the next generation to live better or worse by how they conduct themselves. The embittered, cranky, poorly kept, and untidy handicapped person is unquestionably making it more difficult for the next generation of disabled people to be accepted.

Growth in Those Who Help

Perhaps one of the great achievements of rehabilitation in our time will *not* be in what we actually do with and for disabled people but rather *what we are doing for ourselves and for the nonhandicapped world.*

Edwin Markham put the whole issue in the most effective language when he gave us these words:

> We are all fools until we see that in the human plan,
> Nothing is worth the making, unless it makes the man.
> Why build these cities glorious if man unbuilded goes?
> In vain we build the world unless the builder also grows.

As builders of the rehabilitation world of the future we have a responsibility to grow ourselves if we are ever to remove the barriers to normality that we presently face.

4

Projections in the Field
of Physical Disability

William Gellman

INTRODUCTION

The subject of developmental disabilities is a relatively new and increasingly significant rehabilitation area. Throughout the country, efforts are under way to unify the field of developmental disability and to chart its future course.

Magazines such as *Futurist,* books such as *Future Shock* by Alvin Toffler, learned papers by Bell,[1] Kahn[8] and Dubos[5] project differing visions of possible futures and forecast new vistas for tomorrow's programing. We in rehabilitation and our comrades-at-arms in special education and social welfare anticipate 1980 programs for the physically disabled that will resemble today's activities on their behalf. However, each morning's newspaper tells of changes in the programmatic landscape and of the need to map the terra incognita of the immediate present if we are to plan for a possible unknown future. We know what will appear.

Manpower projects for the field of physical disability are signals or guidelines for determining the number and type of personnel necessary to meet the rehabilitation demands of the physically handicapped in 1980. Manpower projections in physical disability should be seen in the perspective of and as part of a more comprehensive set of forecasts charting the future course of developmental disabilities. Estimates of manpower in rehabilitation necessarily involve consideration of: (1) socioeconomic factors that influence the demands of physically handicapped persons and their advocates for service, (2) society's acceptance of physically handicapped persons, and (3) trends in rehabilitation methodology.[7]

From *Rehabilitation Literature,* 35 (1974), 2–9. Copyright © 1974 by the National Easter Seal Society for Crippled Children and Adults. Reprinted by permission of the Editor.

This paper will discuss the current rehabilitation status of the physically disabled, socioeconomic conditions in 1980, rehabilitation trends, and the manpower projections based upon analyses of these trends.

REHABILITATION AND THE PHYSICALLY DISABLED

Disabled people constitute a significant proportion of the population of the United States. Although there are various estimates of the extent of disability, the precise dimensions of the problem are unknown. Senator Dole[4] estimates that some 42 million persons are handicapped in some way, although not all of them may have disabling conditions that restrict activities. The National Center for Health Statistics[22] states that during 1970 approximately 23.6 million persons, representing 11.8 percent of the civilian, noninstitutional population, had some degree of limitation of activity as the result of one or more chronic conditions. This estimate includes 8.9 percent who were limited in their major activity. Limitation of activity is a measure of long-term reduction in activity resulting from chronic disease or impairment and is defined as inability to carry on the usual activity for one's age-sex group, such as working, keeping house, or going to school, restriction in the amount or kind of usual activity, or restriction in relation to other activities (civic, church, or recreation).

The National Center[21] estimates that from July, 1965, to June, 1967, 6,300,000 persons experienced some degree of mobility limitation and that 5 of the 18 million disabled adults between the ages of 18 and 64 years could benefit from vocational rehabilitation. Wilder's analyses[21] of the 6.3 million persons with mobility limitations indicates that 38.4 percent were unable to carry on major activity and that 43.6 percent were limited in the major activity. These figures, which indicate that some 5 million persons may be able to use rehabilitation services, are in accord with the Rehabilitation Services Administration[15] estimate of 4.6 million persons aged 16 to 64 years as the potential vocational rehabilitation population.

According to estimates of the Bureau of Education for the Handicapped,[20] of a population of 7,083,500 children in the United States between the ages of 0 and 19 years, 750,000, or 9.4 percent, are handicapped. The crippled are 348,000, or 4.9 percent, of the handicapped group. Special education services are provided for 182,000 crippled children, or 52.2 percent, by 11,000 special education teachers. An estimated 12,200 teachers are needed for additional service to the crippled group.

The Rehabilitation Services Administration estimates that in 1973 state rehabilitation agencies will rehabilitate 326,000 handicapped persons. If the distribution of disabling conditions is similar to that of 1970, the percentage of the physically handicapped who are rehabilitated will be 21.5 percent. The difference between the number of physically handicapped requiring rehabilitation and the number of those rehabilitated is a measure of the current need for rehabilitation services, which parallels that reported for special education. There is no question of the need for additional rehabilitation and special education services at this time.

Prevalence of physical disability is increasing as the population grows and as medical, biological, and technical advances lengthen the life span. The change in life expectancy from 63 years in 1943 to 70.3 years in 1968 has increased the number of persons in our society prone to illness or injury. The National Health Education Committee[10] estimates that improved medical knowledge saved 8 million lives between 1944 and 1967 and that of the $7\frac{1}{2}$ million still alive, about 63 percent are not working.

The statistical information deals with physical disabilities and limitation of activities. Rehabilitation practice distinguishes a handicap from a disability and the resulting physical incapacity. The handicap refers to the decrement in functioning resulting from the impact of a negative self-image or negative social attitudes toward the disabled. Not all disabilities result in handicaps. The transmutation of a disability into a handicap appears to be a function of the severity of the disability and the process of social handicapping. The prevention of handicapping is a continuing rehabilitation task.

A related problem in rehabilitation is that of increasing the capacity of the disabled to cope with negative social attitudes.[11,12] The person with a physical disability may be barred from work or from normal interaction because of differences in appearance, mannerisms, behavior, or performance that may lead others to regard him as atypical or deviant and cause him to see himself as unproductive and to perceive himself as different or stigmatized. The restrictions imposed by these personal and social handicaps diminish the physically handicapped's capacity for effective performance in major cultural roles. The disabled person must be able to withstand the presence of societal bias, which shapes the self-image of the physically disabled and leads him to see himself as unable to achieve.[6] He must be able to avoid seeing himself in the mirror of social prejudice and to escape the self-depreciation that transforms a physically disabled person into a socially handicapped person.

These rehabilitation problems (self-handicapping and inability to cope with social prejudices and physical disability) shape the goals of rehabilitation as a healing and a helping discipline as: (1) enablement— eliminating or reducing disabling conditions that restrict activities or cause handicaps; (2) normalization—developing competencies necessary for adequate role performance in major social areas, and (3) integration —participating in the life of the general community, a process that includes altering the social and physical environment to enable the physically disabled to participate.[14]

Rehabilitation manpower can be categorized in terms of the rehabilitation goals. (See Table 1.) There are approximately 28,500 nonmedical professionals concerned with activation of physically disabled persons. The professions involved are occupational therapists, physical

Table 1. Rehabilitation Personnel—1972

		Serving Physically Disabled	Total
Enablement			
1. Occupational therapists and aides		6,000	13,500
2. Physical therapists and assistants		20,000	25,000
3. Prosthetists		1,300*	1,300
4. Medical social workers		1,200	6,000
	Subtotal	28,500	45,800
Normalization			
5. Special education teachers		11,000	124,000
6. Speech pathologists and audiologists		4,400*	22,000
7. Psychologists		2,000*	10,000
8. Rehabilitation counselors		2,600*	13,000
9. Recreation workers		2,000*	10,000
10. Psychiatric social workers		100	500
	Subtotal	22,100	179,500
Integration			
11. Vocational placement counselors		200*	1,000
12. Social psychologists		0*	0
13. Community organization workers		200*	1,000
	Subtotal	400	2,000
	Total	51,000	227,300

Items 1, 2, 3, 4, 6, 7, 8, and 9 are from the *Occupational Outlook Handbook*.[18]
Items 5, 10, 11, 12, and 13 are estimates.
Column 1 uses 20 percent as the percentage of rehabilitation personnel serving the physically disabled for all items asterisked. The figure for special education teachers is an estimate of the Bureau of Education of the Handicapped. The figures for occupational therapists and physical therapists are the author's estimates.

therapists, prosthetists, and medical social workers. Normalization of activities for the disabled involves about 22,100 professionals, among whom are special education teachers, speech pathologists and audiologists, psychologists, rehabilitation counselors, recreation workers, and psychiatric social workers. Approximately 400 professionals are involved in integrating the disabled into the community, consisting primarily of placement workers, social psychologists, and community workers. The total of the preceding figures, 51,000, is our estimate of the number serving the physically disabled. Our estimate for all rehabilitation personnel is 227,300.

Current Status of Rehabilitation

At present, rehabilitation programs and manpower are insufficient to meet service needs. There is an uneven rate of progress within the field. Through the discovery and use of psychological knowledge on the impact of stress upon personality structure, we are better able to prevent the transformation of a disabled person into a handicapped person. Social handicapping is still a major block to rehabilitation because of the resistance of social attitudes to change.

Biomedical advances and the early initiation of rehabilitation have speeded the process of enablement or activation. An example is the patient's use of a prosthesis shortly after amputation of a leg with the result that the patient is mobile within a relatively short period of time. The pace of normalization is somewhat slower because of the continuing tendency to segregate or insulate the incapacitated, so that societal role functioning is retarded or arrested. Integration of the physically disabled into the full range of community and social activities is proceeding slowly. The fight for the elimination of environmental barriers in housing, transportation, and recreation is still in its infancy.

The level of unemployment, an important factor in rehabilitation, is still high. With the percentage of unemployed at 5 percent, the incapacitated find it difficult to secure employment.

SOCIOECONOMIC TRENDS

Size of the total labor force in 1980 is projected at 90.8 million, an average increase of 1.5 million a year.[19] The percentage of workers in the various age groups is expected to be: 23 percent in the 16 to 24 bracket; 44.7 percent in the 25 to 44 age group, 29.1 percent in the 45 to 64 age group, and 3.2 percent in the over 65 years of age. The 25 to 44 group will constitute an increasing segment of the labor force, while the other 3 age groups will be reduced. The demographic characteristics of the 1980 employment market suggest that the physically disabled may encounter greater competition in securing employment because of greater numbers in the prime working age group of 25 to 44.

It is difficult to predict the unemployment level in 1980. Factors to be considered are government efforts to promote full employment, the extent of public service employment, the balance of trade, the rapidity of technological change, the relation of full employment to inflation, and the general economic level. We would suggest a 4 percent level of unemployment in 1980 as compared with the current 5 percent. The decrease in unemployment should improve opportunities for the physically handicapped.

The emergence of the United States as a postindustrial nation accentuates existing occupational trends that are repatterning the economy. Probably the major change is the transformation from a producing to a service economy with a redistribution of jobs involving an increase in the service sector and a decrease in manufacturing. The U.S. Department of Labor[17] sees a decline in the number of unskilled and agricultural jobs, a higher skill level for semiskilled jobs and an increase in the number of service, professional, and managerial positions. Blue-collar jobs will constitute a smaller proportion of the job market although the total number of blue-collar jobs will increase by 2 million as compared with 1970.

Kahn and Wiener[8] see the increasing importance of service, "occupations [which] are heavily concentrated in the government, the professions, the nonprofit groups, and the like, this implies . . . a shift from the private business enterprise as the major source of innovation, attention, and prominence in society." Government, service, and non-profit institutions will assume greater importance as employers. Job requirements will have higher educational levels as the computer and use of data banks become more prominent in these institutions.

Occupational displacement and obsolescence because of technology will occur with greater rapidity. It is estimated that at present an individual will change his occupation six times during his working life. Changes in social demands and technological improvements will create a greater need for occupational shifts during an individual's career. A large percentage of the work force will require reschooling at various times to acquire new skills. Retraining the occupationally displaced and reorganizing their intellectual and experiential skills will become an ongoing function of educational and rehabilitation agencies.

According to Bell[1] the transformation of our society into the post-industrial era is accompanied by rapid technological advancement. The social changes consequent to the technological and economic developments influence the process of rehabilitation. Among these changes are :

Megalopolitization

The continued movement of population to major metropolitan areas is transforming the metropolis into a megalopolis and accentuating difficult urban and suburban problems. Demographers forecast the mergence of three megalopolitan complexes in the United States, centering on New York, Chicago, and Los Angeles, inhabited by a more heterogeneous population. Such megalopolises will be characterized by psychological overcrowding, insufficient social, health, and welfare services, and inadequate public transportation. The pressures and strains of everyday living will result in interpersonal frustrations and intensified psychological problems for persons under stress, such as the physically disabled, who will face also the barrier of lessened mobility unless mass transportation systems improve.

Increased Wealth

The wealth of the country will continue to grow. The gross national product will increase. The 1971 median income of $10,285 for a family of four will increase substantially. There will be a greater diffusion of goods, services, and privileges. The proportion of persons who are considered poverty-stricken will decrease from the present $12\frac{1}{2}$ percent.

Population Changes

In 1980 the population will have a greater proportion of older persons. While the percentage of young people aged 14 to 19 years will decrease, the proportion will still be significant, some 25 percent. Together, the youth and aged will comprise a sizable segment of the total population. Physically handicapped persons in these groups will require extensive, specialized rehabilitation services.

Lifetime Learning

The school system will be incorporated into a lifetime pattern of alternating school and work, extending schooling and retraining beyond the first three decades of life. The school-work cycle will begin near the close of the high school period and continue through the postsecondary school period into the preretirement phase of the work career. Lifetime schooling will become a prerequisite for job advancement. The ability to learn and to achieve through learning will be more necessary, as occupations become more skilled and more abstract.

Social Problems

Problems of alienation and identity will become more pronounced in 1980. Social and individual problems will be intensified by earlier separation from the family and continued competitive pressures. The life-span school-work, school-work pattern will limit the energy available for nonwork life areas and render people more susceptible to the diffusion of a problem originating in one life sector into all aspects of life—home, school, work, and social relationships.

Implications

The implications of these trends will affect all aspects of rehabilitation. Enablement—the activation of clients through improving residual capacities—will continue to improve with advances in medicine and psychology. Normalization—functioning at a level that permits the disabled to participate in various social roles—will become more feasible through improved rehabilitation technics and a more open society that will encourage training for major societal roles.

Integration into the community will pose problems. On the negative side, social stresses will accentuate psychological stress. The number of physically disabled will increase. Prejudices may become more overt, rendering it more difficult for the physically disabled to participate fully in community activities. Richardson[11] states that prejudice against the physically handicapped appears by the age of six. If bias toward those with atypical physical appearance or mannerisms appears to be almost endemic, there is little possibility of basic changes in social attitudes by 1980. The occupational field will be more open and receptive to the disabled. However, the physically disabled will face the same problems in other fields that they do now, though at a slightly reduced scale. Living in a home adapted for the disabled, traveling by public conveyances, participating in social groups, and being accepted in work or community activities will pose difficulties.

If our gross national product increases to the $1.4 trillion estimated for 1980, there is the possibility that more funds and efforts will be transferred to rehabilitation. Wickenden[23] speaks of the necessity for more goods and services if we are to meet the needs of our country and of underdeveloped countries. Keyserling[9] points out that, under full employment, funds will be available to meet social service needs. It is possible, as Keyserling believes, that with additional funds available in 1980 the processes of normalizing and integrating the disabled into the community may become an accepted part of the social service system.

Rehabilitation Trends

A major trend in rehabilitation is the emerging perception of the physically disabled person as a social being rather than as a solitary person facing the problem of physical incapacity. The changed viewpoint stems from the perception that the various aspects of man—biological, psychological, social, and cultural—are interrelated. The early history of rehabilitation illustrates the movement toward a holistic approach. When rehabilitation began as a helping discipline, the emphasis was upon physical restoration as a distinct function separated from the patient. With the realization that physical restoration was insufficient to enable the severely disabled to cope with the demands of daily living, rehabilitation became concerned with the disabled person in the home. As the disabled learned to function in the home and to move about in the community, the difficulties of finding employment became more apparent. Job placement became a primary task for rehabilitation. With increasing awareness of the importance of psychological and sociocultural factors, rehabilitation restated its core problem as enabling the rehabilitant to function adequately in a productive role in the family and society. This reformulation emphasizes the social problems faced by the rehabilitant as a member of a family, work, or social group.

As rehabilitation moves toward greater use of the social environment as a therapeutic tool, there is a tendency to de-emphasize psychotherapeutic counseling as a rehabilitation technic and to emphasize the use of more situational tools such as rehabilitation workshops for evaluative and adjustive purposes. For example, the rehabilitation workshop uses work as a situational tool to assess and modify working behavior and attitudes, and the psychosocial aspects of the work environment as a controlled stimulus setting in which to influence a client's work adjustment. The work done in such workshops is real work for which the rehabilitants are paid.

Another trend is active intervention to secure work and other opportunities for the physically handicapped. Many personnel men and businessmen misunderstand and fear disability in themselves and in others. Uncertainty, fear, and prejudice create unwillingness to hire a disabled person. The decision not to employ may reflect an unwitting bias rather than an analysis of the rehabilitant's capabilities. Similar barriers and hurdles exist for the disabled and disadvantaged in familial, social, or communal life sectors. The family may not be able to accept the rehabilitant as a nondisabled person. Public gatherings may not provide for inclusion of handicapped persons in wheelchairs. Schools are often unwilling to provide services to older handicapped youths or to accept severely disabled children.

Also significant is the trend expressed by the physically handicapped's view of rehabilitation as a right rather than a privilege. Consumerism is reflected in U.S. Sen. Jacob Javit's Bill of Rights for the Mentally Retarded and in class action suits based upon the rights of handicapped for education and treatment. The handicapped and their advocates are asking for participation in decisions affecting allocation of funds. Irving Bluestone[2] sees "the right of each person to participate meaningfully in the decisionmaking process affecting his welfare as part of the democratization of welfare."

Deinstitutionalization of the physically disabled is a rehabilitation goal that will increase in importance as we near 1980. The movement of the institutionalized disabled clients into the community is proceeding at a steady pace. The trend reflects the union of therapeutic belief in the efficacy of a community approach and of the cost benefits of emptying institutions. Under these conditions, we can anticipate that a greater number of the physically disabled will live in the community with partial or full supporting services.

To summarize, the newer trends in rehabilitation are changing the structure and functioning of the rehabilitation process. Rehabilitation professionals are becoming more involved with the family and the community. They are beginning to use situational technics and to serve in a variety of nontraditional settings. Fully trained staff are being supplemented by paraprofessionals and volunteers. Physically disabled persons are playing a more active role in determining their treatment and are beginning to participate in setting goals for their own rehabilitation and in evaluating the results.

PROJECTIONS FOR 1980

Need for Rehabilitation Services

The review of socioeconomic and rehabilitation trends indicates that the number of physically disabled persons will increase because of the growth in population, the lengthened life-span, and medical advances in the treatment of the injured and ill. A greater proportion will live in the community. The need for rehabilitation and rehabilitation personnel will increase. With a gross national product estimated at 1.4 trillion in 1980, the increase in the national wealth will make it possible to provide more rehabilitation and educational services for this group if the political climate is favorable. Recent events suggest a possible change.

Rehabilitation Goal

Integrating the physically disabled into the community will emerge as the primary rehabilitation goal and as a more significant criterion of rehabilitation success.

Manpower Projections

The Rehabilitation Services Administration estimates that there will be an increase in the number of rehabilitants to 612,000 in 1978, as compared with approximately 300,000 in 1973. The agency states alternatively that, in order to continue to rehabilitate the same proportion of the eligible population, the program will have to increase by 17 percent in fiscal year 1978 over fiscal year 1973 levels.

We would estimate a 33 percent growth in rehabilitation personnel between 1970 and 1980, this rate paralleling the increase in government employment as estimated by the Bureau of Labor Statistics.[18] Since government is a source of employment for a substantial proportion of

Table 2.   Estimated Rehabilitation Personnel—1980

	Serving Physically Disabled[1]	Total[2]
Enablement		
1. Occupational therapists and aides	7,980	17,955
2. Physical therapists and assistants	26,600	33,250
3. Prosthetists	1,729	1,729
4. Medical social workers	1,596	7,980
Subtotal	37,905	60,914
Normalization		
5. Special education teachers	14,630	164,920
6. Speech pathologists and audiologists	5,852	29,260
7. Psychologists	2,660	13,300
8. Rehabilitation counselors	3,458	17,290
9. Recreation workers	2,660	13,300
10. Psychiatric social workers	133	665
Subtotal	29,393	238,735
Integration		
11. Vocational placement counselors	266	1,330
12. Social psychologists	200	1,000
13. Community organization workers	266	1,330
Subtotal	732	3,660
Total	68,030	303,309

[1] For basis of estimates see Table 1.
[2] Based upon an estimated 33 percent increase.

rehabilitation personnel and of direct or indirect finding of the costs of rehabilitation in voluntary health and welfare agencies, we can assume that government policies will determine the level of rehabilitation and of rehabilitation personnel. On that assumption, rehabilitation personnel engaged in assisting the physically disabled will approximate 68,030 out of a total of 303,309 rehabilitation personnel. Table 2 indicates the anticipated distribution by specialties of rehabilitation personnel serving the physically disabled. The table includes paraprofessional personnel but excludes volunteers. It can be assumed that the use of volunteers will increase, as will the proportion of paraprofessionals.

Training

The training of rehabilitation personnel will be modified to include a greater number of work-school programs that will provide on-the-job experience throughout the educational period. Rehabilitation training will be treated as an apprenticeship program similar to the training of artists in the Middle Ages. The quality of performance will be more important than level of academic learning.

Involved in training will be the use of situational technics and the ability to sense the psychosocial potentials of various settings for changing role performance. The training will emphasize technics and methods of changing public attitudes and behavior toward the physically disabled on the part of the public and of significant figures in the employment and social fields.

Training will be multiprofessional. The rehabilitator will be expected to learn two distinct specialties so that he can bridge the gap between specialties and function as a team member who can understand and use the approaches of other disciplines. For example, the occupational therapist may receive training as a workshop evaluator. The rehabilitation counselor may be trained as a social psychologist. This suggests the possibility of the partial consolidation or merging of professions such as those in which dual training is received.

Nature of Work

The changing view of the physically disabled person will add community services as a third level to rehabilitation to complement and extend individual and family service. Community services can effectuate the rehabilitation goal of integrating the incapacitated client into community life. Community services will focus upon smoothing the rehabilitant's entry or re-entry into the community, facilitating his performances and adaptation in community roles, and changing community attitudes toward the disabled. Rehabilitation will use community workers, vocational counselors, and social psychologists to ease the transition of the handicapped client from the sheltering agency to the general community.

The nature of the work of most rehabilitation personnel will change with the addition of the sociopsychological component, which will serve as a common bond between specialties and as a basis for community action. Rehabilitation personnel will spend additional time in the community changing the social environment and facilitating client adaptation. The focus on situational technic will lead rehabilitation personnel into working in new settings to enable the physically disabled to learn to enact productive roles in society.

Place of Work

Although most rehabilitation work will be done for public and private agencies, a small but substantial proportion will be engaged in industry and in private practice.

CONCLUSION

The outlook for rehabilitation personnel in the field of physical disability reflects value judgments and trend analysis. This paper assumes that the values of society in 1980 will favor a moderate expansion in funding rehabilitation services for the physically disabled and be somewhat more accepting of crippled persons' living and functioning in the community. The trend analysis suggests methodological changes in rehabilitation to conform to the goal of integrating the physically disabled into the rehabilitation process and the community. Training of rehabilitation personnel will move toward the use of apprenticeship programs providing extended work experience in two rehabilitation specialties.

Perhaps the most important feature in the rehabilitation landscape will be the re-emergence of social action and advocacy on the part of rehabilitation personnel and clients. The events of the last few years have demonstrated that manpower projections are illusory in the absence of effective political power. The validity of optimistic manpower projections in the broad field of human service depends ultimately upon our willingness to turn forecasts into self-fulfilling prophecies.

REFERENCES

1. Bell, Daniel. The Year 2000—The Trajectory of an Idea. *Daedalus* (J. of Am. Acad. of Arts and Sciences). Summer, 1967. 96 :3 :639–655.

2. Bluestone, Irving. *Toward Economic Democracy at the Workplace.* National Conference on Social Welfare, Atlantic City, N.J., May 29, 1973.

3. Brody, Ralph and Rosenberg, Marvin. *New Directions in Public Social Service: Threat or Challenge.* National Conference on Social Welfare, Atlantic City, N.J., May, 1973.

4. Dole, Robert. Handicapped Americans : Speech of Hon. Robert Dole of Kansas in the Senate of the United States, Monday, April 14, 1969. *Congressional Record.* 91st Congress, First Session. 7 p.

5. Dubos, Rene Jules. *The Dreams of Reason: Science and Utopias.* New York, Columbia Univ. Pr., 1961.

6. Gellman, William. Roots of Prejudice Against the Handicapped. *J. Rehab.* Jan.–Feb., 1959. 25 :1 :4–6, 25.

7. Gellman, William. Social Trends and the Jewish Vocational Service of 1980. *J. Jewish Communal Service.* Summer, 1970. 46 :4 :297–304.

8. Kahn, Herman and Wiener, Anthony J. The Next Thirty-Three Years : A Framework for Speculation. *Daedalus* (J. of Am. Acad. of Arts and Sciences). Summer, 1967. 96 :3 :705–732.

9. Keyserling, Mary. *The Economics of Full Employment.* National Conference on Social Welfare, Atlantic City, N.J., May 28, 1973.

10. National Health Education Committee. *Facts on the Major Killing and Crippling Diseases in the U.S.* New York : The Committee, 1971.

11. Richardson, Stephen A. Cultural Uniformity in Reaction to Physical Disabilities. *Am. Sociological Rev.* Apr., 1961. 26 :2 :241–247.

12. Safilios-Rothschild, Constantina. *The Sociology and Social Psychology of Disability and Rehabilitation.* New York : Random House, 1970.

13. Schon, Donald A. *Technology and Change: The New Heraclitus.* New York : Delacorte Pr., 1967.

14. Sterner, Richard. *Services for the Handicapped in Sweden.* Bromma, Sweden : Swedish Central Committee for Rehabilitation, 1972.

15. U.S. Department of Health, Education, and Welfare. Social and Rehabilitation Service. Rehabilitation Services Administration. *Statistical Notes.* No. 30, June, 1972.

16. U.S. Department of Health, Education, and Welfare. Social and Rehabilitation Service. Rehabilitation Services Administration. *RSA Long Range Plan, FY 1974–1978.* (Draft) May 15, 1972.

17. U.S. Department of Labor. *U.S. Manpower in the 1970's: Opportunity and Challenge.* Washington, D.C. : The Dept., 1970.

18. U.S. Department of Labor. Bureau of Labor Statistics. *Occupational Outlook Handbook, 1972–73 Edition. Statistics Bulletin 1700.*

19. U.S. Department of Labor. Bureau of Labor Statistics. *The U.S. Labor Force: Projections to 1985. Special Labor Force Report 119,* 1970.

20. U.S. Office of Education. Bureau of Education of the Handicapped.

Handicapped Children in the United States and Special Education Personnel Required, 1968–1969. Washington, D.C. : The Bureau.

21. U.S. Public Health Service. National Center for Health Statistics. *Chronic Conditions and Limitations of Activity and Mobility, July 1965–June 1967. Series 10, No. 61.* Washington, D.C. : Govt. Print. Off., 1971.

22. U.S. Public Health Service. National Center for Health Statistics. *Current Estimates from the Health Interview Survey, United States— 1970. DHEW Pubn. No. (HSM) 72–1054.* Washington, D.C. : U.S. Govt. Print. Off., May, 1972.

23. Wickenden, Elizabeth. *Sharing Prosperity: Income Policy Options in an Affluent Society.* Madison, Wis. : Industrial Relations Research Association, 1968.

Part II

Disability:
The Child and the Family

Disability may be present congenitally, or it may be acquired at any time during the life span of a person. Part II focuses on the impact of a disabled child upon the family. In addition, suggestions are presented for therapeutic intervention.

In an article focusing upon socialization, Battle examines the dynamic relationship between the child with a handicap and significant others. Emphasis is upon the relationship of the child with the mother and on the important developmental tasks to be acquired by children with handicaps. Alternatives to overcoming the social barriers for children with handicaps are suggested.

The Meadows, in their article, discuss the difficulties in adjusting to the role of being a parent of a child who is handicapped. Technical and emotional aspects of this role as they relate to the parents' acceptance of the child are presented. An understanding of these factors can assist those working in rehabilitation to help parents make an effective adjustment to their child, which, in turn, will help the child's emotional and social development.

Hawke and Auerbach present a dynamic multidisciplinary model to aid children with handicaps. They discuss the beneficial and harmful aspects of team approaches and provide suggestions for improving the rehabilitation process as it applies to children who have disabilities.

The stage of development at which disability occurs has important implications for the process of rehabilitation. The child of today is the adult of tomorrow. Early, meaningful intervention is therefore a necessity if problems of disability are to be overcome.

5

Disruptions in the Socialization
of a Young, Severely Handicapped Child

Constance U. Battle

In addition to the usual developmental tasks, a handicapped child must make unique, complex adjustments to himself, to his handicapping condition, and to his immediate world. It is likely that a few of the additional burdens he faces include the adjustment to numerous medical examinations, hospitalizations, and an exposure to a larger-than-usual group at an early age for evaluation of his condition. Other adjustments must be made to parents and to a world disturbed about his condition, people who may be curious or ridicule him. Finally, part of coping involves acceptance of his functional limitations, his state of dependency, constant frustration in attempting tasks and in communicating, and occasionally physical discomforts from procedures, treatments, immobility, and changes as a result of physical growth and development. The effects of a physical handicap influence all aspects of the child's growth and development, all areas of his life.

Richardson[24] alludes to the commonly held but erroneous concept of a neat, single effect of disability. A physical disability may in fact impair not only motor functioning but also one or several of other functional capacities—sensory, intellectual, behavioral, and social. Although the most obvious handicap of a child with cerebral palsy might be in the area of gross motor disability (for example, his inability to walk), he may also have equally significant or worse problems resulting from sensory impairment, so that he does not appreciate where his leg is, or he may have poor depth perception, difficulty chewing, or speaking, or attending to someone. What often happens, unfortunately, is that all efforts to restore or maximize function of the child are focused on the system most involved or the most easily assessed system.

From *Rehabilitation Literature*, 35 (1974), 130–140. Copyright © 1974 by the National Easter Seal Society for Crippled Children and Adults. Reprinted by permission of the Editor.

The handicapped child, it is clear, is prevented from taking part in the normal course of human interaction that comprises the process of socialization of any child because of two barriers or obstacles. The first barrier results from the *physiologic limitations* inherent in the condition, e.g., the child can't walk or can't talk. The second barrier is a consequence of the *psychological and social limitations* on the part of the child himself as a result of the blunting effects of a handicap mentioned by Richardson,[26] and a consequence as well of the spontaneous illogical, negative reactions on the part of others (normal) to the child with a handicap, his different appearance and behavior. Some like Shaffer[34] believe that evidence suggests that it is unlikely that social attitudes toward the handicaps and deformities of cerebral palsied children contribute to the frequency of psychiatric disturbances shown by them. More plausible to him is the likelihood that brain injury in some children may result in a deficiency of social perception, which may in turn distort the child's pattern of social interactions. Richardson's viewpoint[26] represents, perhaps, the middle ground since he does consider the intrinsic and extrinsic blunting effects of a handicapping condition of a child and has studied with others in considerable detail the attitudes of normal boys and girls to handicapped children, and to handicapping conditions in abstract considerations.[13,25,27,29] The findings of M. O. Shere's study[37] of 30 twin pairs (one twin had cerebral palsy, the other did not) suggest that the condition of cerebral palsy does not necessarily cause social and emotional maladjustment. The parental behavior toward the child was found instead to be instrumental in setting the pattern of the child's behavior.

The purpose of this paper will be to review certain aspects of both categories of barriers that interfere with normal socialization from the moment of birth through the beginning of the school years, the time period to be discussed here. A child with profound neuromuscular impairment, such as seen in cerebral palsy, will be considered as an example since his impairment presents one of the most global handicapping conditions seen in childhood. From this point on, the term *handicap* will be used with the distinctions set forth by Susser and Watson.[39]*

The Socialization Process in the Infant

A brief review of some fundamental aspects of the process of socialization in the normal child will be presented along with indications of points

---

*Susser and Watson distinguish three components of *handicap*: organic, functional, and social. *Impairment* is the organic component, a static condition of the process of disease. *Disability* is the functional component, or the limitation of function imposed by the impairment and the individual's psychologic reaction to it. *Handicap* is the social component, the manner and degree in which the primary impairment and functional disability limit the performance of social roles and relations with others. It is this third component that most closely suits the purposes of this paper.

where disruptions in that process in the life of a child with a handicap might occur. A definition of *socialization* cited by McNeil[20] from a psychological dictionary by English and English will suit the purposes of this paper well :

> socialization : the process whereby a person (esp., a child) acquires sensitivity to social stimuli (esp., the pressures and obligations of group life) and learns to get along with, and to behave like, others in his group or culture; the process of becoming a social being . . .[8]

Kagan[15] presents a similar, fuller definition indicating in detail which behaviors and values are socialized. It will become clear that both the mandatory relationships (parental) in the first years of life and the voluntary social relationships from age three through the school years are influenced significantly by the existence of a physical disability.

Harriet Rheingold[22] has put forth several assertions about the normal newborn infant contrary to those generally held, in maintaining that the human infant begins life as a social organism, that he socializes others more than he is socialized, and that he behaves in a social fashion while very young. These assertions would also seem to hold true for the handicapped newborn. The infant is a social being by biologic origin since he is in contact with other organisms from the moment of birth. He is at the very least a member of a dyad composed of himself and his mother and is probably a member of a much larger group. Assuming that the handicapped child is not ill as a newborn, i.e., is normal and well except for the handicapping condition, then at least one member of the dyad, the mother, is in disequilibrium during the perinatal time. The mother is experiencing shock, deep sadness, depression, guilt, anger, embarrassment, revulsion, personal responsibility, uncertainty about personal worth and about managerial ability because her creative products are defective.[9,14,16,19,21,31,38] The ritual surrounding the child's birth may be upset. The family cancels religious or family celebrations because of their distress or their sense of embarrassment. The larger group may stay away because of their own sense of embarrassment or uneasiness about seeing the baby, about "what to say," "how to act." The larger social group around the handicapped child as a newborn then may be "restricted" by the wishes of the larger group itself or the wishes of the family. Richardson[24] points out that there are no generally known alternative patterns of behavior for use by the family of the newborn handicapped child during the weeks immediately after birth.

The assertions of H. Rheingold alluded to above are qualified to apply to infants during the first year of life or so, until that time when effortless locomotion is achieved. Since the handicapped child under consideration will never achieve locomotion, one may perhaps translate these observations to the handicapped child. The newborn infant and the young handicapped child are much alike in several ways. They are both totally dependent on others since they cannot locomote, cannot grasp an object, and thus can do little if anything for themselves. Such infants must be fed, cleaned, moved, stimulated not to fret, protected from danger. During that first year of life, society does not expect the infant to acquire any social skills. He is not expected to cooperate, to be altruistic, or to demonstrate behavior appropriate to his sex. There is another similarity since society most likely does not expect acquisition of social skills of the handicapped child either, and he perhaps senses this attitude. Not only is he slow in acquiring social skills in managing relationships with normal persons, but their treatment of him also can retard the socialization process.

It must be noted, even when one is trying to stress that the infant is a socializer, that the infant's behavior is modified by what social encounters he has. The infant is socialized and is responsive to people because they have become associated with satisfactions resulting from certain caretaking operations. His social behavior, in turn, has been reinforced by the responses of people to his responses to them. One can compare this aspect of socialization in the handicapped child. If the handicapped child is easily cared for, then even the most profoundly physically impaired child can be socialized to this degree. If, on the other hand, it is difficult in the first few months for the mother, particularly if the handicapped child is a first baby, to feed the infant, to cuddle him, to get him to sleep, to position him, to keep him entertained, to learn to respond to his cues successfully, there is the likelihood that the handicapped child and his mother will be socializing one another on this elementary or basic level but not in a desirable fashion.

Commenting on the lack of studies of mother-child interaction in the earliest days of life, Campbell[3] suggested that sucking might be a suitable measure of the mother-child relationship since it has been studied extensively and is recognized as varying with external stimuli. Food intake is known to be influenced by maternal handling. Each infant and mother must acquire feeding and sucking skills, respectively, and can influence or modify the behavior of the other significantly. The handicapped child with severe cerebral palsy has poor sucking, swallowing, and feeding mechanisms, never allowing the mother to acquire skill in feeding him. Feeding her infant successfully is one skill that a mother views as central to her "mothering" process. The mother may be puzzled or even frightened by her infant's behavior patterns, which she recognizes are not normal. Adding to her uneasiness is the expectation of society that this time should be a rewarding one for mother and child. At this time another reason for the uneasiness of the mother of a handicapped child occasionally seen may be the mother's observation that there is some other person (a grandmother, friend, or baby-sitter) who is essentially not emotionally involved and who is the only person who can make her difficult child feel totally satisfied or who has some success in feeding him.

Freeman[11] noted that the rhythmicity of certain functions may not be so readily established in the handicapped child and may further interfere with smooth mother-child interaction. Certain characteristics manifested as personality traits, but which may be a direct consequence of the handicapping condition, such as excessive passivity or placidity, or restlessness and demanding behavior, may bother some mothers in a child's first year of life. When she is bothered, the mother's response to her infant's responses may be negative.[36] The handicapped infant will sense his world as chaotic, uncomfortable, unsatisfying, inconsistent as a consequence, at that time in life when the normal child is developing a sense of basic trust that his needs will be met. Other external disruptions to the socialization process in the first year occur when the handicapped child has to be hospitalized for any acute illness, or diagnostic or therapeutic procedures necessitated by the handicapping condition. The hospitalization results in two traumatic experiences for the infant : separation from the mother and exposure to various frightening and painful experiences.

Many of the disruptions to the socialization process have been alluded to above. Each one of these disruptions interferes in itself with the infant's ability to socialize and be socialized. Not only do such factors as the mother's not being able to cuddle the baby interfere with his socialization process, but her fatigue from the stress and the additional attention and care needed by the child as a result of the physical impairment prevent her from devoting time and energy to the child's intellectual and social development. A study conducted in Israel revealed that characteristically both *distant* and *involved* mothers of severely handicapped children with cerebral palsy overlooked the role they should play in providing their child with sufficient opportunities for object-contact in their child's cognitive development.[35] These mothers of children who had outgrown the infancy phase, but yet were as helpless as very young infants, did not provide toys or other objects for play, or did not place toys where they could be reached easily.

A dramatic example of how a multihandicapping condition in an infant can disturb the mother-child relationship has been presented by Freedman and others,[10] who reviewed the first 18 months of life of a baby multihandicapped due to maternal rubella. Since the mother of this infant had three earlier successful experiences in rearing her first three sons, it was reasonable to assume that she was able to operate effectively in the "average" expectable mother-child relationship. She was not, however, prepared for the complications of the task of mothering a rubella baby. Since the infant's condition was considered contagious for a while, his care fell exclusively on her. The infant showed a tendency for particular postures. As a result, it was difficult to carry, not to mention cuddle, a baby who persisted in keeping his head retracted and his back arched. As is the usual case when multiple systems are affected, he experienced a decrease in environmental stimulation, which did, in fact, result in sensory deprivation. In addition to having an absolute reduction and qualitative alteration of sensory input due to defective end organs, he was also ill much of the time and was difficult to feed as well as to handle.

Not only was the neonatal period frustrating for his mother, but as he grew older his problems required a proportion of the mother's time considerably greater than what she had spent on the other children at his age. Because of poor feeding, she had to feed him round the clock every three hours for the first three months of his life. It was necessary for her to hold him to nurse until he was 14 months of age. At 18 months of age, he still had to be held in his mother's lap to be fed solids. At the time of the report, the mother was taking him twice a week to various medical clinics, which were part of the rubella program where they lived.

Although, as is readily seen, the mother spent a great deal of time with the child, it was clear to the observers that the care of this child was carried out in a perfunctory manner. She was described as willing to attempt what the professional team asked of her. When the child failed to respond to her ministrations or opposed them with irritation, she was quickly discouraged. Much was done *for him*, but little *with him*, according to Freedman. The child's response to his mother's attention provided the mother with no incentive to act otherwise. Well in advance of his first birthday, the mother characterized the child as one of those children who don't like to be bothered. This fact was verified by the observers.

Such a single example is dramatic. It is likely that a similar situation of parent-child interaction when the child is severely handicapped is not at all so unique or uncommon. In this instance the child had a significant degree of mental retardation superimposed upon his many complicated system malformations and dysfunctions. It is quite possible for the identical picture to exist in a child with a severe handicapping condition in whom there is no mental retardation or only slight mental retardation, and consequently the potential exists for some degree of normal socialization.

A normal infant, especially if he is the first child, socializes his parents in two obvious ways: he causes definite rearrangement of the parents' psychological world, as well as a rearrangement of the family's living quarters. Becoming a parent emotionally causes marked psychologic shifts. Acquisition of baby furniture and finding an undisturbed spot for baby to sleep cause shifts of equal magnitude in the physical world of the family. The baby profoundly affects the parts of the mental lives of the parents that hold their wishes, dreams, and fears about his future appearance, health, intellect, and personality, and about the extent to which he will fulfill their expectations. This process is intensified when the child is handicapped, and the parents' psychologic extension in the child is thwarted.

In addition, Richardson[24] points out that when a physical abnormality is identified at birth there is some evidence that the parents' initial attention to the baby's bodily appearance and functions will be enormously intensified as well by constantly looking at the baby, talking about the problems, and attempting to cover up the problem. It is suggested that this preoccupation may provide a reason for avoiding a more human relationship with the child or it may result from feelings of guilt for having produced a handicapped child.

The normal infant's powerful socializers are his smile, his cry, and to a lesser extent his vocalizations. Noting that one frequently observes "answering" social and, in particular, vocal play between mother and child, Rheingold and others[23] investigated whether the adults' responses may therefore play an important part in maintaining and developing social responsiveness in the child. The results of this study of 21 infants with a median age of 3 months suggest that the social vocalizing of infants and, more generally, their social responsiveness may be modified by the responses adults make to them. The smile is a delight to the parents. The cry has been called a social signal by which the infant insures his own survival. Since the cry is so aversive, originated by the infant, it cannot be ignored. If the handicapped child or child with a birth injury cries excessively or with a disturbing, high-pitched cry or cannot be comforted, the mother-child relationship is further distorted. Vocalizations also have importance as the beginnings of speech, an additional tool in the service of socialization. The infant up to a year, until he begins to walk, is somewhat helpless physically, not socially, as has been demonstrated.

Socially the handicapped infant as well as the normal infant is responsive to and initiates social response from others. He also has three powerful tools : the smile, the cry, and the contented babbling, to insure that his needs are met. Unlike the normal child, the handicapped child may remain at this stage much longer, for several or all his years. Current social-psychological theory of behavioral exchange suggests that the single most powerful reinforcer in social interaction is social approval. The assumption has been made here that the parents truly love their handicapped child but have difficulty in relating to him for the various reasons mentioned. Of course, the problem becomes severe if the parents withhold their love or withdraw their love, acknowledged as the most powerful socializing agent there is during early childhood.

It is not clear whether impoverishment of social relationships or opportunities for socialization have more important consequences at one age level or another. Is there a critical period for the formation of basic social relationships? The question has been reviewed recently by Connolly.[5] There is good evidence of the existence of sensitive periods for the establishment of primary social bonds in many species. Studies in humans in which the mother-child relationship did not develop or was disrupted provide evidence in support of the basic contention for sensitive periods during which the human infant is maximally sensitive to social contacts with its mother, contacts that will lead to the cementing of an affectional bond. Do the parents of a handicapped child need guidance and assistance to modify any abnormal responses very early? Do they on the other hand have to originate alternative ways or opportunities for socialization if these cannot be experienced in the usual way? Is it alright to allow the child to progress in socialization at his own pace? Is there, in fact, anything that can be done? These are some of the questions raised by a consideration of the disruptions in the interpersonal relationships of the child during his first year of life which result from a handicapping condition.

Socialization Processes in the Young Child

The very early aspects of socialization, involving mainly aspects of the mother-child relationship, have been reviewed above. Similarities and dissimilarities were noted between the socialization process in the normal and handicapped child. The next portion of this paper will be concerned with the socialization process in the young child. The following topics will be covered: mechanisms of socialization, aspects of human behavior in the normal young child that must be socialized; biologic needs and socializations; general modes of interacting with the environment; dependency and independence; emergence of a clear body-image, of self-concept, or self-esteem; role-learning, particularly the sex role; imitation; relationships with the siblings and with the peer group; and opportunities for play and for participation in interpersonal relationships. Each of these aspects of early childhood socialization is markedly altered in the child who is handicapped.

Kagan[15] has reviewed the four major mechanisms of socialization, which, he notes, are similar for all cultures, although the content of what is socialized differs across cultures. Each of the four mechanisms—desire for reward, fear of punishment, identification, and imitation—is strongest at different periods of development and facilitates different aspects of the socialization process. Kagan asserts that acquisition and suppression of values and beliefs are less likely to be facilitated by watching others behave and more likely to be the product of identification with a desirable model. The process of *identification* is seen in the desire of the child to be similar to particular persons he has grown to respect, love, and admire.

After the first year of life, there are five aspects of human behavior in the normal young child that must be socialized : feeding and weaning, toileting and elimination, sex needs and practices, aggression needs and practices, and, finally, dependency needs and behavior.[17] Most of these aspects, if not all, cannot be socialized in the usual way in the handicapped child because his body structure and its functions are not normal. He cannot suck, swallow, or chew well. He cannot sit up steadily or walk, or defend himself or his toys. He is unable to learn about sex differences by exploration or learn about his sex role through play and imitation. He may not be able to handle his own bathroom needs. He must remain dependent on others for help in all areas of his life.

Many lists have been compiled of biologic and universal needs such as thirst, hunger, comfort-seeking, freedom from pain, aggression, and probably activity, curiosity, or the need for exploration.[17]

This last need system, the need for exploration, mentioned by McCandless, is the one need that can never be satisfied by the child with severe cerebral palsy, which limits markedly his exploration, so important for certain pleasures in life, for the acquisition of knowledge, and for achieving independence. Some needs are satisfied without social dependency, or, indeed, interaction, such as air-hunger, while other needs must be satisfied within a social setting, such as hunger, elimination, and aggression. McCandless points out that it is these socially conspicuous needs in all likelihood that are important in personality and social development.

In reviewing Bruner's three general modes of interaction with the environment, McCandless[17] infers that the socialized individual must have mastered all three systems. The first mode of interaction with the environment involves the near-receptors—the how-to-do-it mechanisms—the hands. Next, the child must consolidate his vision and other distance receptors; he must learn how to perceive, coordinate, and anticipate. Finally, the fabric of language or symbolic mastery of the environment must be mastered. Each of these three modes is characteristic, respectively, of the years in preschool, elementary school, and the onset of adolescent years. The implications for the handicapped child become clear. He cannot interact with the environment with his hands. The hands of the child with cerebral palsy will not go where he wants them to, will not grasp a toy effectively, or will not hold on to a toy he has succeeded in grasping. By contrast, he may grasp effectively through his eyes, he may interact through his eyes. Sometimes, eye contact is his only path for communication. Some children with cerebral palsy, though, lack depth perception, have strabismus, or perceive the world visually in strange ways. Often these children are fearful in this incorrectly perceived world.

> One five-year-old boy, crying in his wheelchair, was asked why he was crying. He responded that he was afraid of the floor. Another child performed well in his special education classroom but broke out into a panic when he had to accompany the class into a large auditorium for gymnastics. He screamed and walked close to the walls until he could be allowed to leave. When back in the small classroom with windows, which he could use to align himself, he again performed well.

Often the child with cerebral palsy cannot speak at all or speaks in a highly unintelligible manner, even though he may have a normal or even high intelligence quotient. All three of these modes of interaction with the environment may be distorted or unattainable for the handicapped child.

Another area that is to be mastered by all children was alluded to earlier—the complete dependence of the infant. Complete dependence must be established early by giving the infant immediate, generous and consistent rewards for all his demands so that in this loving atmosphere he can establish trust. In turn, the bliss of complete dependence must be dissipated later through the child's fear of the loss of parental love and support and by reinforcing independent behavior. If the infant's needs are not gratified at once, he learns that he is not the center of the universe, but is subject to forces outside himself. This realization is the child's first awareness that other persons are important. The child must achieve independence in order to live a satisfying adult life. The parents through highly selective reinforcement can encourage the child toward independent behavior and help him to seek influence of others besides themselves, in particular the influence of the child's peers. Parents of normal children can unfortunately also reinforce dependency behavior such as crying, whining, lap-sitting, and attention-seeking. It is not uncommon to see parents of handicapped children reinforcing dependency behavior. E. Shere and Kastenbaum[36] suggest that the ambivalent retaliation/dependency-fostering behaviors seem a poor substitute for normal pleasure in mother-child interactions.

What are the implications for the handicapped child who must gain independence? Is it possible for the child to become emotionally independent when he is in fact totally physically dependent on the parents? Scott[32] argues that institutions for the handicapped blind adult, for instance, coerce the individual to be dependent in return for financial and other help. The person, in point of fact, may not be dependent emotionally but is taught to be dependent. A similar phenomenon may occur early within the family of a handicapped child.

Important in the social development of the child, in fact, the most salient of the child's many social roles, is the individual's sex role. The child comes to learn his sex role through psychologic identification with the parent of the same sex and by imitation of that parent through play. The child also models himself in many ways (socializes) after the parent of the opposite sex. This cross-identification, or cross-modeling, is also probably socially useful so long as it goes along with established social patterns. It would seem that the handicapped child can never achieve an awareness of himself as a boy (or as a girl) since his impairment may prevent him from role-playing and imitation opportunities.

There is an extensive literature in social psychology, however, which deals with social learning that occurs independent of any active imitation opportunities. Bandura[1] has reviewed extensively the conceptualizations of vicarious or observational learning. Certain theories would suggest that a handicapped child may learn despite the inability to role-play much in the same way as the normal child described by Bandura does. Most persons, for example, exhibiting snake phobias have never had any direct aversive experiences with reptiles; similarly, children may acquire, on the basis of exposure to modeled stimulus correlations, intense emotional attitudes toward members of unpopular minority groups or nationalities with whom they have little or no personal contact.

Such evidence of no-trial learning is encouraging when translated to the learning processes of the handicapped child. The inability to role-play or to imitate because of the physical limitations of the handicapping conditions may not preclude his learning on a vicarious basis. The physical limitations may not be so major an obstacle as has been thought in the past.

One of the better-studied areas of family structure in the socialization of the normal child is birth order. This topic will not be treated here, since much literature is available on this area, indicating that birth order is probably not a very important factor. The relationship to siblings has additional importance in the socialization of the handicapped child. Intense sibling rivalry may arise because parents often do not apply the same standards to their normal children and their handicapped child. Parents, too, face the dilemma of how to praise their normal children without at the same time increasing the feelings of inadequacy and "differentness" on the part of the handicapped child. Freeman[11] points out the marked reaction of handicapped children between the ages of three and six to being surpassed by their normal younger siblings. At this time the handicapped child also begins to realize that he is different from others.

Second only to the parents (including the siblings) in the socialization of the child is the influence of the peer group. McCandless[17] has listed concisely many generalizations from a review of the literature. The peer group is indispensable in role rehearsal, dimensions of cooperative and competitive behavior, expression of aggression, and dependency. The peer group also supplies important confirmation-disconfirmation of self-judgments of competence and self-esteem, as well as a reference point for self-evaluation of elementary sexuality. If the child does not have a peer group or cannot communicate with his peer group, he is deprived of this aspect of the socialization process.

The opportunity and the ability or skills to *play* become increasingly important in the preschool years. In the normal instance, play enables the child to master anxiety, fears, and passivity and to learn imitative patterns. In a discussion about the socialization of blind children, Scott[33] notes that the primary mechanism by which a child learns to internalize the behavior of others is play. Like the blind child who cannot see the other roles, the handicapped child also has a major limitation in his role playing, since he cannot walk or make his limbs accomplish some task or talk.

Entering school is a major event in childhood. It has become more common for handicapped children, even those with severe or multiple-handicapping conditions, to attend school, because of recently enacted legislation, e.g., Illinois provides for placement of all handicapped children from ages 3 to 21 years. McCandless[17] asserts that in American society competence seems to lead more than anything else to self-esteem, which is the core of adequate personal social adjustment (cf., Edgerton[7]). School is one of the major testing grounds of competence for the child. The handicapped child does not have an opportunity to socialize with the peer neighborhood children because of limitations in ambulation, his mother's overprotectiveness, or rejection by other children on account of his being different. At least, he has the opportunity to socialize and be be socialized in the classroom. In general, to the present, the development of social skills in the classroom for the handicapped child has not received major emphasis. The major thrust has been in developing other skills such as speech and language, learning the three R's.

As Richardson[24] points out, parallels have been drawn between the stigma attached to persons who are handicapped and the stigma of minority groups and are important in school placement of the handicapped child. Differences between the two groups are significant. Persons born into a minority group learn in their socialization from their minority culture how to deal with the majority culture. In addition, because they develop social skills primarily with adults and peers within their minority group, the behavior inhibitions common to minority/majority social interactions are operating only a small part of the time. In contrast, it is most unlikely that the handicapped child will have parents, neighbors, sibs, or peers with the same handicapping conditions from whom he can gain experience in dealing with others. In general, he will be surrounded by nonhandicapped persons and will share the general negative values toward the handicapped. Furthermore, it is unlikely that he will have an opportunity to develop social skills freely with persons who share his handicap, as Richardson further notes.

In summary, it appears that a child with a physical handicap will encounter more difficulty than a child from a minority group in gaining experience in behavioral skills in general, and specifically in the skills for social relationships with the majority group. Such considerations have implications for school placement: Should a handicapped child be placed in a class with normal children insofar as he is able? Should he be placed with peer handicapped children as much as possible? Or should he have opportunity for socialization with both groups? From the above discussion, it seems reasonable to conclude that the last alternative will provide the most satisfactory socialization process.

Since there are good reasons both for placement in the "normal" classroom and for placement in the "handicapped" classroom, a combination would seem to serve the needs of the handicapped child best. He should have the opportunity to be in a classroom with normal children if he can compete academically, for he will have normal models, can interact with normal persons, and can develop certain specialized skills in managing his social relationships with the nonhandicapped; he will be dealing mainly with this group throughout his life. The value of placement with handicapped children, on the other hand, lies in three areas: opportunity for models of persons who have made good adjustments despite the same obstacles, the comfort of being with similar persons, and the opportunity to compete successfully at least occasionally.

Increasing recognition of the value of interaction between nonhandicapped and handicapped children is seen in the trend to include handicapped children in national children's television shows. Fred Rogers, of "Mister Rogers' Neighborhood," is including a youngster with short-leg braces in several filming sequences.[30] "Sesame Street" has selected 10 handicapped youngsters to participate with other nonhandicapped youngsters in the show's street scene.[40]

Occasionally children with handicaps are unfortunately treated as if they are *sick*, with all the social role connotations that are associated with sickness, as Richardson indicates.[24] The parents give the handicapped child less responsibility, place fewer limits on his behavior, have increased tolerance for deviant behavior, and indulge his personal whims, often at the expense of the other children in the family. The effects of each of these alterations in the socialization of the child would seem to have a profound impact.

A study was referred to earlier concerning the inability of mothers of severely handicapped infants to provide play-learning experiences for their infants.[35] In contrast some parents are able to facilitate the development of their handicapped child. A group of 60 mothers of cerebral palsied children and 60 carefully matched mothers of normal children from the New York area were compared.[2] One of many important findings was that Jewish mothers provide significantly more social opportunities for their cerebral palsied children than either Catholic or Protestant mothers. This study in 1959 also showed that mothers of cerebral palsied children were significantly more overprotective and maritally conflicted than mothers of nonhandicapped children. Mothers of younger handicapped children were found to be socially withdrawn as well. In general, mothers of the handicapped children had some of the following characteristics: guilt, rejection, and unrealistic attitudes. In a later study, Collins[4] administered a set of personality tests to mothers of children with cerebral palsy who had participated in an education program for the parents of a child with cerebral palsy. He concluded that such programs have demonstrated definite evidence of helping mothers of afflicted children to maintain normal personality patterns, since these mothers did not show personality changes leading to feelings of inferiority, introversion, and depression.

It is obvious that a child with a handicap will have less experience in social relationships than a nonhandicapped child. With the passage of time, the child becomes deeply concerned about his physical disability. As isolated as he is, the handicapped child will not be sufficiently isolated or sheltered to prevent his learning about the negative values associated with his physical disability or the depreciation of value of the handicapped person in society. As a result he will tend to depreciate himself. It has been demonstrated that handicapped children are very realistic in their self-descriptions.

Richardson and others[28] have obtained self-descriptions from 107 children with handicaps and 128 nonhandicapped children ages 9 to 11 years at a summer camp. The differences between these two groups appeared to reflect the functional restriction on physical activity, deprivation of social experience, and the psychological impact of the handicap. Although the handicapped children share in peer values, for example, they are aware that they cannot live up to the expectations that stem from the high value placed on physical activities. Gardner,[12] at the 1970 American Academy for Cerebral Palsy annual meeting, described how the child with cerebral palsy is frustrated in his attempts both physically and psychologically. His frustration begins at birth because the condition interferes with satisfactory interaction between parent and child. The result is that the child lacks self-esteem and behaves as if he were alone in the social world and of no personal consequence to it. The reactions of a child with cerebral palsy, according to Gardner, of extreme rage at disappointment or extreme, inappropriate joy over reward stem from this self-esteemless state. The child with cerebral palsy does comprehend that he is abnormal. He may, in fact, perceive his damaged state as a massive rejection of him as a person.

Several studies, reviewed by Richardson,[24] suggest that the non-handicapped child who is likely to initiate contact with a handicapped child is more likely isolated, has less general social experience, and has learned the values of his peers less. These findings, especially true for boys, suggest that, even when the handicapped child does participate in a social relationship with a peer, there is a chance that the relationship will not be so beneficial as it might be, since children who do initiate contact with him will be those who are less successful in social relationships, those who hold atypical values, those for whom physical disability cues have low perceptual salience, or those who like others to be dependent on them.

Another flaw in the relationship between the handicapped child and the normal child surmised by Richardson from a review of other studies is the fact that the handicapped person does not receive accurate or spontaneous feedback from others, who feel that they must be especially considerate or careful of the feelings of someone who is handicapped. Absence of accurate feedback makes it difficult if not impossible for the handicapped child to learn what others think of him, to learn appropriate behavior, and to develop social skills ultimately. Not only does the handicapped child have more difficulty in establishing social relationships, but those he does establish are apt to be imperfect. Awareness of these facts makes it clear that the handicapped does not encounter barriers to establishing social relationships only initially. Barriers exist for him at every turn in a relationship.

As Richardson[24] has stated from the evidence that a physical handicap impoverishes the experiences needed for a child's socialization, it appears that there is a cumulative loss in the types of social relationships established (both mandatory and voluntary) in the socialization process of the handicapped child, which results from the obstacles imposed by the physical disability. Thus far, a handicapped child's limitations in establishing a voluntary social relationship with his peers have been considered. In some instances a handicapped child may succeed in establishing a rewarding social relationship with an adult, a teacher, a neighbor, or relative who is able to view the child as a child with a handicap and not as a handicapped child. From these encounters he may acquire some rewarding experiences and have the opportunity to learn and practice social skills, if his parents are able to facilitate such relationships.

DISCUSSION

It is important that persons dealing with the handicapped child and his family, such as physicians, nurses, teachers, social workers, psychologists, and playground counselors, all persons dealing with children in any way, develop awareness or sensitivity regarding social barriers for the child with a handicap. This review raises more questions than it answers. Some areas are seen to be critical for intervention by the pediatrician and paramedical personnel dealing with the family of a handicapped child. More investigation is needed to attempt to understand the importance of the birth of a handicapped child, the nature of the parental response to learning about the child's condition, and, finally, the resolution or adaptation to many varied, uncomfortable initial feelings.

Some questions must be answered: Are there critical periods for acquiring socialization skills? If so, once past, can intervention reverse the effects of early deprivation in the socialization experience? How can the parents help to enable their handicapped child to play, to establish social relationships and the usual early friendships? Must the parent make special efforts to encourage neighborhood children to visit her house or yard so her child will have opportunities; should the mother resort to bribing children to play with her child at first, with such enticements as her active participation or novelties?

> On moving to a new neighborhood, one mother invited all the mothers on her block to her house for coffee and cake in order to meet them, to introduce her handicapped child, and to invite them to allow or even to send their children over to play.

Parents should be aided in every possible way, in areas not directly concerned with the handicapping condition, to allow them to be sufficiently free of undue stresses and uncomfortable feelings, so that they do have energies to invest in the socialization of their handicapped child. The implications of Collins' study[4] are important: An education program for parents of a child with cerebral palsy helped mothers to maintain normal personality patterns. If the mother can be assisted in general management problems, if someone will listen to her worries, attend to her fears, help her to anticipate or meet future problem areas, she will be more at ease, comfortable in the mothering process of a handicapped child.

Often advice for a piece of equipment for moving the child about can make a sufficient difference in the mother's energy level. Guidance for recreational and educational programs on television, or outside the home such as swimming or summer camp for the handicapped child, must be provided as well for the handicapped child and his family.

Denhoff[6] notes that children with severe cerebral palsy are prevented from participating in after-school activities mainly because of lack of transportation or due to architectural barriers in the playground. According to Denhoff, the Professional Services Program Committee of the United Cerebral Palsy Association has assumed the responsibility to see that transportation and recreational facilities are modified to assist the handicapped child to be with his normal peers more often. Research is under way to modify the concept of the spaceship module to school, playground, and other facilities for opportunity for socialization. Another committee, the Architecture and Engineering Sciences Committee, is exploring behavior-shaping environments, such as outdoor-indoor playgrounds. Similar innovations would help to facilitate the socialization process for the handicapped youngster simply by enabling him to be where other children are.

What about the implications for school placement? Should the child be placed with other handicapped children where competition will be appropriate? Should he have exposure to normal classroom experiences as well as for normal models for behavior? One school initiates its handicapped children slowly into the regular school program, by sending the handicapped child to one-classperiod-a-day music with the normal children.

The finding of Collins[4] that the parents of handicapped children may function in a better-adjusted manner if they receive support from some outside group also suggests that facilities dealing with the handicapped child must not isolate him in their thinking from his family. Helping the entire family may be the best or only way to help him. The finding that Jewish mothers provide more social opportunities for their children[2] also merits further study to determine why and how these mothers are able to encourage more socialization in their handicapped children.

A consideration of the three general modes of interaction with the environment alluded to by McCandless[17] has implications in assisting the parents and the teachers of a handicapped child to facilitate the child's ability to interact with his environment. To facilitate *hand mechanisms*, programs of physical and occupational therapy are necessary, as well as simple measures such as providing toys that can be grasped easily or are simple to operate, or building a two-inch railing around the table in front of the child, which will keep the toys within his hand and arm range. Sensory experiences, such as feeling water or sand, smelling a flower, petting a kitten, must be provided for the child who cannot obtain these experiences on his own. It is equally important to develop *eye skills*. The child can be taught to communicate many feelings with his eyes and to communicate even more fully through the use of communication boards.[18] The highest level of interaction with the environment is the *linguistic or symbolic* mastery of the environment. In addition to communication board systems, the child can be helped to verbalize a definite "yes" or "no," a simpler yet significant step forward for communication with others.

Perhaps this review will have accomplished enough if it has made us merely consider the magnitude of the social disruptions and barriers for the young handicapped child. Unfortunately, these social barriers increase; as the child grows older, he drops farther and farther behind his normal peers. The basic issue remaining to be determined is: What are the long-term effects of the above-mentioned disruptions in the socialization process of the young handicapped child? It is hoped that this review will move us medical scientists to join with social scientists in answering Richardson's[25] exhortation to study the social conditions that influence children.

REFERENCES

1. Bandura, A. Vicarious Processes : A Case of No-Trial Learning. In : Berkowitz, Leonard, *ed. Advances in Experimental Social Psychology.* New York : Academic Press, 1965.

2. Boles, Glen. Personality Factors in Mothers of Cerebral Palsied Children. *Genetic Psychol. Monographs.* 1959. 59 : 159–218.

3. Campbell, D. Sucking as an Index of Mother-Child Interactions. Paper presented at the *Fourth Symposium on Oral Sensation and Perception: Development in the Fetus and Infant.* National Institutes of Health, Bethesda, Md., 1972.

4. Collins, Hardin A. Introversion and Depression in Mothers of Cerebral Palsied Children. *Missouri Med.* Oct., 1965. 62 : 10 : 847–850.

5. Connolly, Kevin. Learning and the Concept of Critical Periods in Infancy. *Developmental Med. and Child Neurol.* Dec., 1972. 14 : 6 : 705–714.

6. Denhoff, Eric. Cerebral Palsy, chap. 43A, p. 997–1025, in : Wallace, Helen M., and others. *Maternal and Child Health Practice: Problems, Resources and Methods of Delivery.* Springfield, Ill. : Charles C Thomas, 1973.

7. Edgerton, Robert B. *The Cloak of Competence: Stigma in the Lives of the Mentally Retarded.* Berkeley, Calif. : University of California Press, 1967.

8. English, Horace B. and English, Ava Champney. *A Comprehensive Dictionary of Psychological and Psychoanalytical Terms: A Guide to Usage.* New York : Longmans, Green and Co., 1958. p. 508.

9. Faigel, Harris C. Small Expectation: The Vulnerable Child Syndrome. *GP.* Sept., 1966. 34:3:78–84.

10. Freedman, David A., Fox-Kalenda, Betty J., and Brown, Stuart L. A Multihandicapped Rubella Baby: The First 18 Months. *J. Am. Acad. of Child Psychiatry.* 1970. 9:2:298–317.

11. Freeman, Roger D. Emotional Reactions of Handicapped Children. *Rehab. Lit.* Sept., 1967. 28:9:274–282.

12. Gardner, Riley W. Evolution and Brain Injury: The Impact of Deprivation on Cognitive-Affective Structures, chap. 14, p. 241–251, in: Sapir, Selma G., and Nitzburg, Ann C. *Children with Learning Problems: Readings in a Developmental-Interaction Approach.* New York: Bruner/Mazel, Publishers, 1973. Reprinted from: *Bull. Menninger Clinic.* Mar., 1971. 35:2:113–124.

13. Goodman, Norman, and others. Variant Reactions to Physical Disabilities. *Am. Sociological Rev.* June, 1963. 28:3:429–435.

14. Howell, Sarah Esselstyn. Psychiatric Aspects of Habilitation. *Pediatric Clin. of North America.* Feb., 1973. 20:1:203–219.

15. Kagan, Jerome. Personality Development, chap. 7, p. 282–349, in: Talbot, Nathan B., Kagan, Jerome, and Eisenberg, Leon. *Behavioral Science in Pediatric Med.* Philadelphia: W. B. Saunders, 1971.

16. Kennedy, James F. Maternal Reactions to the Birth of a Defective Baby. *Social Casework.* July, 1970. 51:7:410–416.

17. McCandless, Boyd R. Childhood Socialization, p. 791–819, in: Goslin, David A., ed. *Handbook of Socialization Theory and Research.* Chicago: Rand McNally, 1969.

18. McDonald, Eugene T. and Schultz, Adeline R. Communication Boards for Cerebral-Palsied Children. *J. Speech and Hearing Disorders.* Feb., 1973. 38:1:73–88.

19. MacKeith, R. Physician's Aid for Parents of the Handicapped. *Medical Tribune.* Sept. 22, 1971. p. 18.

20. McNeil, Elton B. The Nature of Socialization, in: McNeil, Elton B. *Human Socialization.* Belmont, Calif.: Brooks/Cole Publishing Co., [1969].

21. Menolascino, Frank J. Parents of the Mentally Retarded: An Operational Approach to Diagnosis and Treatment. *J. Am. Acad. of Child Psychiatry.* Oct., 1968. 7:4:589–602.

22. Rheingold, Harriet L. The Social and Socializing Infant, p. 779–790, in: Goslin, David A., ed. *Handbook of Socialization Theory and Research.* Chicago: Rand McNally, 1969.

23. Rheingold, Harriet L., Gewirtz, Jacob L., and Ross, Helen W. Social Conditioning of Vocalizations in the Infant. *J. Comparative and Physiological Psychology.* Feb., 1959. 52:1:68–73.

24. Richardson, Stephen A. The Effect of Physical Disability on the Socialization of a Child, p. 1047–1063, in: Goslin, David A., ed.

Handbook of Socialization Theory and Research. Chicago : Rand McNally, 1969.

25. Richardson, Stephen A. Patterns of Medical and Social Research in Pediatrics. *Acta Paediat. Scand.* 1970. 59 :265–272.

26. Richardson, Stephen A. Some Social Psychological Consequences of Handicapping. *Pediatrics.* Aug., 1963. 32 :2 :291–297.

27. Richardson, Stephen A., and others. Cultural Uniformity in Reaction to Physical Disabilities. *Am. Sociological Rev.* Apr., 1961. 26 :2 :241–247.

28. Richardson, Stephen A., Hastorf, Albert H., and Dornbusch, Sanford M. Effects of Physical Disability on a Child's Description of Himself. *Child Development.* Sept., 1964. 35 :3 :893–907.

29. Richardson, Stephen A. and Royce, Jacqueline. Race and Physical Handicap in Children's Preference for Other Children. *Child Development.* June, 1968. 39 :2 :467–480.

30. Rogers, Fred. Personal communication, 1973.

31. Roos, Philip. Psychological Counseling with Parents of Retarded Children. *Mental Retardation.* Dec., 1963. 1 :6 :345–350.

32. Scott, Robert A. *The Making of Blind Men, A Study of Adult Socialization.* New York : Russell Sage Foundation, 1969.

33. Scott, Robert A. The Socialization of Blind Children, p. 1025–1045, in : Goslin, David A., ed. *Handbook of Socialization Theory and Research.* Chicago : Rand McNally, 1969.

34. Shaffer, David. Psychiatric Aspects of Brain Injury in Childhood : A Review. *Developmental Med. and Child Neurol.* Apr., 1973. 15 :2 :211–220.

35. Shere, Eugenia S. Patterns of Child Rearing in Cerebral Palsy : Effects upon the Child's Cognitive Development. *Pediatrics Digest.* May, 1971. p. 28.

36. Shere, Eugenia and Kastenbaum, Robert. Mother-Child Interaction in Cerebral Palsy : Environmental and Psychosocial Obstacles to Cognitive Development. *Genetic Psychol. Monographs.* May, 1966. 73 :2 :255–335.

37. Shere, Marie Orr. The Socio-Emotional Development of the Twin Who Has Cerebral Palsy. *Cerebral Palsy Rev.* Jan.–Feb., 1957. 18 :1 :16–18.

38. Solnit, Albert J. and Stark, Mary H. Mourning and the Birth of a Defective Child, p. 523–537, in : *Psychoanalytic Study of the Child, vol. 16.* New York : International Universities Press, 1961.

39. Susser, Mervyn W. and Watson, W. *Sociology in Medicine, ed. 2.* London : Oxford University Press, 1971.

40. There's More Than Counting on "Sesame Street" Now. *UCP Crusader.* (news item) 1973. No. 2, p. 5.

6

Changing Role Perceptions for Parents of Handicapped Children

Kathryn P. Meadow

Lloyd Meadow

Transition to any new role requires socialization—learning new ways of behaving and seeing oneself. Parenthood itself involves a set of behaviors and attitudes which must be learned. Parenthood, however,

> . . . typically offers an adult a series of opportunities for enriching his own identity—opportunities for concrete affirmation of his generativity, for increased self-knowledge, for vicarious approximation of his ego ideals and for experiencing his effectiveness in bringing a productive situation to fulfillment [Cummings, Bayley, & Rie, 1966, p. 595].

Persons who have been socialized to this conception of parenthood through their previous children and those who are parents for the first time face a different socialization process when they meet the task as parents of a handicapped child. It has been said that "no parent is ever prepared to be the parent of a handicapped child. The identification of a mother and father in that role always comes as a painful surprise [Barsch, 1968, p. 9]." Some modification will be suggested to this broad statement later; however, it is certainly true that the socialization to the role of parent of a handicapped child is a transition to an unwanted and distasteful status for most if not all who find themselves in this position.

Two broad categories can be utilized to characterize the role of "parent of handicapped child." These include the instrumental or technical aspects of the role to be learned and the expressive or emotional aspects of the role to be assimilated (Parsons and Bales, 1955). Examples

Reprinted from *Exceptional Children*, 38 (1971), 21–27. Reprinted with permission of the Council for Exceptional Children and the authors. Copyright © 1971 by the Council for Exceptional Children.

of instrumental aspects of the role include learning ways to help a cerebral palsied child to use his muscles (Schiller, 1961) or learning how to help a deaf child use and regulate a hearing aid. The expressive aspects of this role include learning to cope with feelings of guilt, shame, and sorrow; learning to cope with responses of pity, rejection, and avoidance from neighbors (Begab, 1956; Roos, 1963); learning to cope with responses of grief and denial from relatives; learning to cope with the temptation either to overprotect or to underprotect the child; and learning to cope with the emotional problems which develop in relation to the disability.

Although it is useful to differentiate these instrumental and expressive aspects of the role of parent of handicapped child, they are interwoven. There are expressive aspects of every instrumental task, and the parents' ability to solve successfully the expressive aspects of their new role will influence profoundly their ability to perform the instrumental tasks necessary for the child. Conversely, the ease with which parents are able to solve the instrumental tasks will influence their emotional response to the handicap. A parent counselor must deal with both the instrumental or technical and the expressive or emotional components of parental roles if he is to be successful in gaining cooperation and in contributing to the socialization process.

THE AGENTS OF PARENT SOCIALIZATION

There are many persons who come into contact with families with handicapped children who are not trained to do counseling or psychotherapy, but who nevertheless serve as agents of parent socialization by virtue of their participation in the process.

Physicians

In terms of the chronological sequence of events experienced by families with handicapped children, the general practitioner is the person who often begins the process of socializing parents to their new role. Whether or not he seeks this function, whether he is prepared to perform it effectively, or whether parents accept what he has to say, he gives the signal that parents must embark on a search for a new identity.

The general practitioner is at a particular disadvantage in that he may have inadequate knowledge about a specific handicap. There are a number of factors inherent in the diagnostic situation which may lead to an unsatisfactory relationship between the doctor and his patient (the family, in this case). He is often unprepared or actually unable to give parents the support and/or the information they desire most at the time of crisis. The realistic "medical ambiguities" of a particular condition may mean that the physician is unable either to give a firm etiological report or a "prescription" which can reverse the child's condition (Meadow, 1968).

In a recent study of deafness in England, parent respondents were asked whether they felt their doctor was very knowledgeable about hearing problems in young children. Ninety-seven percent responded negatively. Parents were also asked how much time had elapsed before a firm diagnosis of their child's deafness was made. Twenty-three percent said "almost immediately"; 11 percent said "within 6 months"; but the remaining 65 percent replied that diagnosis had taken anywhere from 6 months to more than 2 years (Meadow and Meadow, 1969). Parents of handicapped children seem universally to express dissatisfaction with their physician, whether he has diagnosed mental retardation (Waskowitz, 1959), cystic fibrosis (Blumenthal, 1969), brain damage (Barsch, 1961), or deafness (Meadow, 1968).

It is true that parents may tend to project their own feelings of shame and guilt and deal with them by blaming the physician (Begab, 1966). On the other hand, it seems that parents' complaints are often justified. Their descriptions of medical experiences, even allowing for distortion and expansion, too often reflect the fact that physicians have little training for recognizing the symptoms of childhood disabilities (the technical or instrumental task for which they should be equipped) and even less preparation for dealing with the feelings of parents during the diagnostic crisis (the emotional or expressive aspect of parental socialization).

Teachers, Audiologists, and Physical Therapists

The special educator, the audiologist, and the physical therapist are all essential members of the team working with handicapped children and their parents. The defined function of these professionals is an instrumental one. They must help parents to understand the reasons for particular regimes and to learn the techniques required for putting them into effect. Often, these professionals consider *only* the instrumental needs of parents and children. Attempting to motivate parents to work hard for their child's future technical competence, they may make demands or set standards which parents find difficult or impossible to fulfill. This can set up a cycle of discouragement and despair which can lead to parental paralysis. To strike a balance between motivation and overexpectation, between optimism for the future and false hope doomed to disappointment is a real and difficult problem.

Although the expertise of these professionals lies in the technical, instrumental areas, it is inevitable that they will be asked to help provide for parents' expressive or emotional needs. Although it is neither feasible

nor desirable for these technical professionals to become qualified counselors or therapists, it would certainly be beneficial if they were to have
an increased understanding of the expressive needs of their clients. It is
also important for these professionals to be able to recognize the limits of
their competency in meeting parents' emotional needs. Sometimes family
problems may be sufficiently intense to require referral to psychiatric or
psychological resources elsewhere in the community. At other times, these
professionals may be able to deal with family concerns with the guidance
of a mental health consultant (Schlesinger, 1971).

"Old" Parents as Socialization Agents for "New" Parents

Most conceptions of socialization include orientation by those who are
presently fulfilling the role. For example, the socialization of children by
their agemates or those only slightly older is important for understanding
childhood (Cooley, 1922). Socialization in professional schools is partially
performed by older students who orient newcomers to the expectations
of individual teachers and the everyday routine. The same process occurs
in the socialization of the parent of the handicapped child when he meets
other parents either individually or in groups and learns about the
feelings and experiences which he can expect from this new and exacting
role.

Parents often report that their contacts with others have enabled
them to accept their new duties and responsibilities and to find creative
ways of accomplishing necessary tasks. Others stress the emotional comfort found in sharing their feelings. Some gain hope or a more realistic
appraisal of their child's possibilities from more experienced parents.

Those who have coped with their own emotional reactions to their
child's handicap can be helpful in bridging the gap between the instrumental role socialization performed by some professionals (i.e., the physician, teacher, physical therapist, and audiologist) and the expressive role
socialization performed by professional therapists. Some of the most
useful contacts between "old" and "new" parents have taken place in
group settings where the mental health expert or professional therapist
is available to interpret or moderate the encounter. Hence, parents who
may be generally suspicious of, frightened by, or uncomfortable with
professionals are helped to relate to and accept the kinds of assistance
which can be offered.

Not all professionals believe that contact and questions between
parents should be encouraged. One teacher, for example, advises parents
of deaf children "not to keep asking other people for advice, especially
parents of other deaf children [because] all children are different, and
their deafness is unlikely to affect them in exactly the same way [Ling,
1968, p. 319]." Cooperation between parents and professionals would

alleviate the danger of one family's taking the experiences of another as a literal model for its own. It sometimes happens that parents who are the most willing to act as agents of socialization for others may appear threatening to those parents most in need of someone to bridge the gap between instrumental and expressive agents. They may be better educated, have different child rearing values, and come from a different socioeconomic background. Generally however, "old" parents can be of great potential value to "new" parents as agents of socialization, especially if they work with professionals.

Handicapped Adults

The handicapped adult can be seen in two different ways by the parents of a newly diagnosed handicapped child. He can be seen as a reassuring person, as someone who has succeeded in the face of his handicap and therefore as a person who lessens the intensity of the parents' anxiety and sense of despair. A blind man who through his business acumen has become a millionaire, a deaf-blind person who achieved worldwide fame and respect, a polio victim who became President of the United States all are very reassuring figures. The handicapped adult who is functioning adequately and has overcome the debilitating effects of his condition can serve as a positive image for the parent.

Unfortunately, a handicapped adult can also serve as a negative image. The worst anxieties of the new parent may be confirmed when he comes into contact with a poorly adjusted handicapped adult. At the beginning of the process of their socialization to the parental role many new parents are not ready to face the consequences of their child's handicap. They may be unwilling or unable to accept the possibility that their child may not be completely "normal" when he reaches adulthood. It would seem to be good practice to help parents to come gradually to an acceptance of this possibility fairly early in the child's life. Although parents find it encouraging to hear about only the Helen Kellers and the Franklin Roosevelts of the world of the handicapped, they should include ordinary handicapped people among their acquaintances. This will aid parents in formulating realistic goals for their child.

In the area of deafness, the situation of constant controversy regarding communicative modes (oral vs manual) has discouraged some hearing parents from meeting the many nonoral deaf adults who have made successful adjustment to life within a deaf community. They are afraid to face the reality that their child may not be able ever to communicate adequately by oral means. The stigma placed by society on disabled persons can be overcome by parents, but first they must overcome their own feelings of nonacceptance.

Professional Therapists

Theoretically, the professional therapist should be well equipped to counsel the parent of the handicapped child. The psychological problems, although different in focus, should be amenable to traditional therapeutic techniques. Many therapists do meet the multiple needs of the new parents. However, there are some who are hindered by their traditional approach to therapeutic problems. Many times the new parent requires emergency "first aid" and a flexible approach involving prolonged contact may not be necessary. Some recent research (Reid and Shyne, 1969; DeVos, Elliott, and Schlesinger, 1971) has indicated that short-term therapy for crisis intervention can produce dramatic and effective results.

The professional therapist needs specialized knowledge in addition to his generic training in order to counsel parents of children with varying handicaps. In addition, he may need to examine his own feelings about physical disabilities if he has had no direct personal experience in this area. For example, many trained social workers and other helping professionals meet the crisis of family deafness with a "shock-withdrawal-paralysis" syndrome, The *shock* of the encounter may cause the professional to *withdraw* from the situation and display a *paralysis* which prevents him from utilizing professional skills (Schlesinger, 1971).

THE EFFECTS OF PARENT AND CHILD STATUS ON THE SOCIALIZATION PROCESS

A status, in the abstract, is a position in a particular social pattern and consists of a collection of rights and duties (Linton, 1936). These social categories are important for the individual in terms of any new role he is called upon to play, including that of parent of a handicapped child. Factors which seem to have the most direct effect on the socialization process—socioeconomic status, age, religion, and physical disability for the parent and sex and birth order for the child—are discussed below.

Parents' Socioeconomic Status

The social and economic status of the parents of a handicapped child has a far-reaching effect on both their initial and their long-term response to disability. For example, the higher the social and occupational level of the family, the higher are the expectations for comparable achievement by their children and the greater their disappointment with a child who is incapable of realizing their hopes.

A number of authors have noted this discrepancy among parents of mentally retarded children. For example, mothers with high socioeconomic status were found to respond to the diagnosis of mental retardation as if to bereavement, whereas mothers of low socioeconomic status were found to respond as if to a role crisis (Farber, 1960). Downey (1963) found that families with more education demonstrated less interest in their institutionalized mentally retarded child and also placed these children in an institution at an earlier age.

> These families have great hopes and aspirations for their children stressing not only socialization as an internalization of norms but also socialization as preparation for entering the higher levels of formal education. The diagnosis of retardation quickly shatters these hopes and aspirations [Downey, 1963, p. 192].

The same general pattern has been noted among parents of deaf children. Those with higher socioeconomic status had greater expectations for the achievements of their children and were more disappointed when these expectations were not met. That these feelings are communicated to the child is suggested by the fact that deaf children from families with higher socioeconomic status have lower levels of self-esteem than do other deaf children (Meadow, 1969).

In a society where upward mobility and occupational-economic achievement are important norms, it is no wonder that parents of handicapped children "suffer a loss of self-esteem," "experience a feeling of shame," "anticipate social rejection," and "show feelings of guilt and self-reproach" when they give birth to a child who cannot be expected to meet their expectations (Roos, 1963). The greater the gap between parental expectations and the child's ability to meet them, the more difficult the process of socialization to the new role as parent of a handicapped child.

The family's lack of economic resources may be a source of additional worry in terms of their handicapped child. One study of families with child polio victims found that "the presence in the family of a handicapped child placed some fathers under greater compulsion to find a better-paying job [Davis, 1963, p. 110]." The cost of caring for a handicapped child may place an economic strain on many families. Recent advances in social legislation which provides aid for families with disabled children and in efforts to remove the stigma from requests for such aid are encouraging. There is little doubt that lack of economic resources in the families of handicapped children increases the difficulties of socialization.

Parents' Age and Child's Sex and Birth Order

The age of the parents may well relate to the handicapped child's sex and his birth order in creating family problems which need counseling.

Having a first child in any family disrupts previous family routines and modifies the values of the parents. The parents, however, can usually maintain most of their occupation, friendship and kinship commitments. In contrast, having a severely mentally retarded child frequently creates a situation of utter chaos [Farber, 1960, p. 5].

There is a greater chance that an older mother may give birth to a handicapped child, and the psychological problems of child rearing may be accentuated for this group as well. There is also evidence to suggest that the child born to an older mother frequently may not be as planned or welcomed as is the child born to a younger family. Older parents may worry more about providing for the needs of the handicapped child in later life. These problems in addition to the usual ones accompanying handicap may interfere with a smooth socialization process in relation to the parents' new role.

Where the handicapped child is the first-born, there may be need for genetic counseling for the family. When other normal children have already been born into the family, parental concern with and guilt about possible hereditary factors may be less critical. Also, the handicapped firstborn son of a young couple may create a more severe crisis of disappointed expectations than that of a firstborn daughter, or of a later-born son. Interviews with parents of deaf children have shown this to be the case in a great many instances. (For a general discussion of the influence of these variable of family structure on socialization, see Clausen, 1966.)

Parents' Religious Orientation

The influence of religious orientation on parental acceptance of handicap has been a subject for speculation and occasional research but the findings are somewhat contradictory. One study, for example, found that Catholic families were more likely to accept their handicapped child, compared to families with differing religious orientations (Zuk, 1959). A study of families of polio victims notes that:

One Catholic family . . . chose to regard [their child's handicap] as a stigma indicative of their son's blessedness and calling to the cloth. It is doubtful whether the parents ever completely resolved their conjectures about their responsibility for the child's illness [Davis, 1963, p. 38].

The large number of studies which cite examples of guilt, stigma, reduced self-esteem, and shame on the part of parents with handicapped children suggests that the influence of differing religious orientations might be a fruitful one for additional research on exceptional children and their families (Babbit, 1964; Cummings, Bayley, and Rie, 1966; Liberthson, 1968; Meadow, 1971; Thurston, 1960).

Parents' Physical Disability

A final characteristic which differentiates groups of parents and influences the socialization process is their own status as handicapped or nonhandicapped individuals. Research on the reactions of deaf and hearing parents to a diagnosis of their child's deafness indicates that deaf parents adjust relatively easily and quickly to the diagnosis. Their definition of their situation was much different from that of hearing parents who responded with denial, trauma, grief, or sometimes relief when they had suspected a different even less acceptable handicap (Meadow, 1968). In regard to families of mentally retarded children,

> . . . clinical observations and findings have focused primarily on the severely impaired or on the less handicapped with central nervous system damage. In nearly all instances, the intellectual disparity between parents and retarded child is marked. The reactions noted bear little resemblance to those in families in which the child's mental endowment approximates that of other members [Begab, 1966, p. 72].

Deaf families with deaf children seem to need particularly sensitive counseling if they are to accept and cooperate wholeheartedly with plans for the child's habilitation. Downs (1967) reports that of the five infants definitely identified as deaf in the Colorado program of early identification of hearing loss, two were the children of congenitally deaf parents and did not participate in the habilitation program because the parents did not cooperate.

Understanding the influence of a wide range of social positions, both ascribed and achieved, should be helpful to those who are professionally involved in the socialization of parents of handicapped children to their new role. The parents and children, in turn, should benefit from this increased understanding on the part of the agents of socialization.

REFERENCES

Babbit, P. H. Appraisal of parental attitudes. *Journal of Rehabilitation,* 1964, *30* (1), 20–21.

Barsch, R. H. Counseling the parent of the braindamaged child. *Journal of Rehabilitation,* 1961, 27 (3), 26–27, 40–42.

Barsch, R. H. *The parent of the handicapped child.* Springfield, Ill. : Charles C. Thomas, 1968.

Begab, M. J. Factors in counseling parents of retarded children. *American Journal of Mental Deficiency,* 1956, *60,* 515–524.

Begab, M. J. The mentally retarded child and the family. In I. Philips (Ed.), *Prevention and treatment of mental retardation.* New York : Basic Books, 1966. Pp. 44–58.

Blumethal, M. Experiences of parents of retardates and children with cystic fibrosis. *Archives of General Psychiatry,* 1969, *21,* 160–171.

Clausen, J. A. Family structure, socialization and personality. In M. Hoffman and L. Hoffman, (Eds.) *Review of child development research.* Vol. 2. New York : Russell Sage Foundation, 1966. Pp. 1–53.

Cooley, C. H. *Human nature and the social order.* (Rev. ed.) New York : Charles Scribner, 1922.

Cummings, S. T., Bayley, H. C., and Rie, H. E. Effects of the child's deficiency on the mother : A study of mothers of mentally retarded, chronically ill and neurotic children. *American Journal of Orthopsychiatry,* 1966, *36,* 595–608.

Davis, F. *Passage through crisis. Polio victims and their families.* Indianapolis : Bobbs-Merrill, 1963.

DeVos, W., Elliott, H., and Schlesinger, H. S. Mental health services for the deaf : Patients, therapeutic procedures, and evaluation. In H. S. Schlesinger and K. P. Meadow (Eds.), *Deafness and mental health: A developmental approach.* Final Report, Social and Rehabilitation Service Grant No. 14 P 55270/9–03, 1971. Pp. 37–69.

Downey, K. J. Parental interest in the institutionalized, severely mentally retarded child. *Social Problems,* 1963, *11,* 186–193.

Downs, M. P. Testing hearing in infancy and early childhood. In F. McConnell and P. Word (Eds.), *Deafness in childhood.* Nashville : Vanderbilt University Press, 1967. Pp. 25–33.

Farber, B. Family organization and crisis : Maintenance of integration in families with a severely mentally retarded child. *Monograph of the Society for Research in Child Development,* 1960, No. 25.

Liberthson, E. Helping families live with and for the mentally retarded child. *Journal of Rehabilitation,* 1968, *34,* 24–26.

Ling, A. H. Advice for parents of young deaf children : How to begin. *The Volta Review,* 1968, *70,* 416–419.

Linton, R. *The study of man.* New York : Appleton-Century, 1936.

Mantell, H. B. Pediatric evaluation of the deaf child. In F. McConnell and P. Word (Eds.), *Deafness in childhood.* Nashville : Vanderbilt University Press, 1967. Pp. 34–41.

Meadow, K. P. Parental response to the medical ambiguities of congenital deafness. *Journal of Health & Social Behavior,* 1968, *9,* 299–309.

Meadow, K. P. Self-image, family climate, and deafness. *Social Forces,* 1969, *47,* 428–438.

Meadow, K. P. Deafness and mental health : A residential school survey. In H. S. Schlesinger and K. P. Meadow (Eds.), *Deafness and mental health:* A developmental approach. Final Report, Social and Rehabilitation Service Grant No. 14–P–55270/9–03, 1971, Pp. 24–36.

Meadow, L. and Meadow, K. P. Dealing with deafness. *Talk,* 1969, *52,* 10–13.

Parsons, T. and Bales, R. F. *Family, socialization and interaction process.* Glencoe, Ill. : The Free Press, 1955.

Reid, W. J. and Shyne, A. W. *Brief and extended casework.* New York : Columbia University Press, 1969.

Ross, P. Psychological counseling with parents of retarded children. *Mental Retardation,* 1963, *1,* 345–350.

Schiller, E. J. Creative habilitation of parents of the cerebral-palsied child. *Journal of Rehabilitation,* 1961, *27* (6), 14–15, 39, 42.

Schlesinger, H. S. The preventive aspects of community psychiatry : Mental health consultation and education. In H. S. Schlesinger and K. P. Meadow (Eds.), *Deafness and mental health: A developmental approach.* Final Report, Social and Rehabilitation Service Grant No. 14–P–55270/9–03, 1971. Pp. 70–87.

Thurston, J. R. Attitudes and emotional reactions of parents of institutionalized cerebral palsied, retarded patients. *American Journal of Mental Deficiency,* 1960, *65,* 227–235.

Waskowitz, C. The parents of retarded children speak for themselves. *Journal of Pediatrics,* 1959, *54,* 319–329.

Zuk, G. H. The religious factor and the role of guilt in parental acceptance of the retarded child. *American Journal of Mental Deficiency,* 1959, *64,* 139–147.

7

Multidiscipline Experience: A Fresh Approach to Aid the Multihandicapped Child

William A. Hawke
Aaron Auerbach

In handicapped children, the handicaps are seldom single.[5,8,7,4,2]

The more handicaps the child has, the more people he needs to look after him. One professional cannot be everything to him. As Shephard[6] puts it :

> I suppose we all feel at times that nothing short of a God-like com-
> bination of knowledge—medical, neurological, psychiatric, psycho-
> logical, social and educational—could be adequate to these children's
> needs. But we have to face the fact that no one of us can hope to have
> more than a small part of this knowledge. It is for this reason that a
> "multi-disciplinary approach" is a phrase increasingly heard nowadays.

Such an approach is time-consuming and expensive : each case can involve physicians, an orthopedic surgeon, an opthalmologist, an otologist, physiotherapists, occupational therapists, speech therapists, a psychologist, and a social worker.[3]

The multidisciplinary approach also requires a tremendous amount of communication and cooperation. If these are not present, therapy may be fragmented, each discipline dealing with its own area of competence and its own disability. This could lead to duplicated or conflicting programs, gaps in therapy, or emphasis on physical programs to the detriment of educational and social programs.

We make a plea for the team approach and agree with Wolf and Anderson[9] that there is a need for more precise definitions, terminology,

From *Journal of Rehabilitation*, January/February 1975 (Vol. 41, No. 1), 22–24. Copyright © 1975 by the National Rehabilitation Association. Reprinted by permission of the Editor and authors.

and nomenclature and for an educationally conceived classification scheme for exceptional children, leading to more appropriate programming.

As multihandicapped children survive into adulthood, their problems become more difficult for them and more challenging for the professionals responsible for their care.

The substitution of a mosaic approach to therapy for the traditional diagnostic or analytic approach would benefit these children enormously.

Who Determines Social Control?

The purpose of social control of the rehabilitation process is defined as the maintenance of an effective chain of control for the purpose of minimizing the handicap.

With learning-disabled children, Auerbach[1] has said that the parents are the key group responsible for the social control of the learning disabilities and have relegated teachers, school officials, and professionals to a secondary role. In a rehabilitation center for multihandicapped children, however, the social control is determined first by the physicians, secondly by paramedical staff, and thirdly by the children themselves as all join forces to control the disability. The key role played by the physician is often determined as much by the faith of child and parents in his ability as by his real ability.

We have found that the success of the social control in a rehabilitation center depends on seven factors: (1) the social relations between staff members and between staff and children; (2) the adaptability of the child; (3) the orientation of staff toward the child's problems; (4) the concept the experts have of themselves; (5) the rehabilitation program; (6) the attitudes of therapist and child toward the prognosis; and (7) the acceptance of the child's sexuality.

Constant Dynamic Tension at Work

The staff lives in a state of constant dynamic tension between "working" and "relating to the child or other staff." The physiotherapist is under pressure to do so many treatments per day and yet must find time to relate to other members of the therapy team. The psychologist must assess and report on many children while also relating to other staff and assisting in patient management; the nurses must get their work done on the ward, yet must relate to the children by sitting and talking with them. The recreation staff have to justify their existence in the hospital by demonstrating that they actually work and *do not merely play with the children.* The physicians have children to examine, reports to dictate, and responsibilities in the hospital that limit the time they can spend with the children; also their social relations with staff are of prime importance for the smooth functioning of the hospital.

This tension between working and relating to others is not an unhealthy one, and most staff handle it well, but some do find it difficult and become extremely involved in work, to the detriment of their social contacts.

The quality of social relations between children and staff in a rehabilitation hospital is unique. Multihandicapped children are often charming, pleasant, and easy to get along with. It is common to see a child wheeling himself or pushing himself with the aid of a walker, smiling pleasantly as he goes along the corridor, where, incidentally, some of the most meaningful events take place in terms of his personality development and social adaptation. In a rehabilitation center, communication can take place virtually anywhere within the building. Considerable staff interaction takes place in wards, lounges, corridors, doorways, and the cafeteria, and many of the key human relationships that develop are initiated in these informal conversations.

Social contacts between children and staff are an integral part of the rehabilitation process. Staff members should allow time for such "socializing" in their busy schedule and should have no feelings of guilt over time spent in this way.

Latency-Age vs Adolescents

Too often adaptability is seen as an unblemished virtue; a child who has settled in well relieves the staff of many concerns. Staff members tend to feel more comfortable with latency-age children (7–12 years), because children of this age usually adapt well to rehabilitation centers, enjoy the programs, and present few problems. Adolescents, however, have needs which the staff find difficult to handle. Although the problem is often recognized by the staff, they cannot do much about it unless a separate unit is available, and the adolescents may be maladapted through no fault of their own. Some adolescents feel pressured by the staff to do things they do not want to do. They have had to follow doctors' and nurses' orders most of their lives, and they want some independence even with their limited capacity for independent activities.

From our experience, we find that the adolescent patient needs adolescent-oriented people to look after him. Such individuals are more adaptable to the demands of the adolescent.

In a center dealing predominantly with latency-age children, adolescent-oriented staff may find that differences of opinion with the latency-age oriented staff are often resolved to the advantage of the latter.

Health-Oriented vs Illness-Oriented

Physicians, nurses, physiotherapists, and occupational therapists are usually illness-oriented, often because of their training with physically ill children. Psychologists, social workers, educators, and child-care workers are usually health-oriented because of their training with physically normal children. The health-oriented staff, who want more or less normal activities, may feel restricted by the illness-oriented staff. Each side feels their viewpoint is valid. The health-oriented staff try to prepare the child for life in the outside world. The conservative position taken by the illness-oriented staff is based on the knowledge of what might go wrong if the child doesn't follow orders. A rehabilitation center, by definition, is a hospital for chronically disabled patients who are being prepared to cope as well as they can with the outside world, and so a balance must be sought between an illness-oriented program and a health-oriented program. We have found that as a child progresses in such a center, the program often shifts from an illness-oriented one to a health-oriented one. Some staff members have difficulty adjusting to this shift. When a child is ill, his dependency needs are regarded as sound, and his cry for help is considered genuine. Once he is judged to be healthy, his requests may be considered as manipulation, and his motives devious and crafty.

What Is Teamwork?

Many rehabilitation centers are staffed by "experts" who work on a 9 to 5 basis and then leave the patient to the nurse and child-care worker until the next morning. During the day the child is seen by physiotherapists, occupational therapists, prosthetic and orthotic personnel, nurses, psychologists, social workers, recreation staff, teachers, and physicians. During the evening, the hospital turns into a ghost town as most of the experts leave. It would seem that the time-utilization in the various disciplines involved, particularly psychology and social work, should be reexamined to determine whether the child can be given more extended attention, dependent on his needs rather than on the 8-hour availability of the experts.

Although each discipline should set up its own optimal treatment goals for the children, each of these goals must be modified by the goals of the other disciplines. The physiotherapist, the occupational therapist, the psychologist, the nurse, and the teacher must organize themselves so that the child can get what he needs the most. The goals of treatment are usually set by the physician, who usually confers with the other experts since their knowledge in a particular field often exceeds his own. The final decision is the outcome of teamwork, and in staff meetings, one may hear a physician's goals challenged by other experts. Often a long period of cooperation between staff members has led to respect for each other's competence. Since the children need so much help, there is an appreciation of what each discipline can contribute to their well-being. Where no individual believes that he has the ultimate answer, a spirit of relativism prevails.

Although individuals with special areas of competence carry out activities that cannot be done by people from other disciplines, the therapeutic program might be improved if the areas of function of the various disciplines overlapped. For example, in the classroom the teacher could not only teach the curriculum but could assist in the physical program of the child while he is being treated by a physical therapist, who in turn could assist the teacher in the educational program at other times.

The Child's Point of View

In many centers a child does not decide whether or not he will participate in a particular program. He is sent to certain departments and expected to perform at a reasonable level and to make sufficient progress to be discharged. The decisions as to when he comes and goes are made by the staff, who in turn obey the physician's directions. These directions are usually carried out to the letter. The chain of command is clear from the physician to staff to child. Both staff and children have decisions affecting their daily lives made for them by the physician, and they may well resent this pattern of dependence. Explanations may take the edge off the resentment, but a residue of dissatisfaction tends to remain.

Sometimes a patient refuses to accept prescribed medical treatment. His negative attitude may be considered a suitable reason for a psychological or psychiatric referral, but in some instances the child has merely set his own treatment goals. For example, a child may resist getting out of a wheelchair if it requires too much effort and if he has made a satisfactory adjustment to the wheelchair. A girl may not want to have an operation on her legs if she feels she would not be able to wear short skirts. To the therapeutic staff the functional aspects may be more important than the cosmetic, but teenage girls may not see it that way. Every effort should be made to see the child's point of view, and to communicate to him the reasons for his program.

Unspoken Fear Masked

An optimistic approach to rehabilitation on the part of staff and child often masks an unspoken fear, namely, that the child will not improve. The children often deny this fear; the staff are reluctant to discuss it.

They feel that the children will "get the message" and need not be told. Although bluntly telling a child that he is not improving may be a poor approach, evasiveness in discussing poor outcomes of therapy can permit the development of undesirable fantasies and fears.

Adolescent Sexuality Considered

Staffs of rehabilitation centers should accept the children's sexual drives, particularly in adolescence when sexual interest and activities are inevitable.

Multihandicapped adolescents are often over-protected from the outside world, including the outlets for aggressive drives and sexual behavior. Their sexual life should not be ignored; where possible they should be encouraged to anticipate a normal adult sex life. The sexual orientations of older children in rehabilitation centers may, however, be limited because of long-term, deeply nurtural relationships with adults which may restrict ultimate sexual development.

Multitrained Individuals Needed

Multihandicapped children need multitrained individuals who understand each other's jobs. Many gains could be made by abandoning the specialist model of education. This model is probably based on the medical profession with its need to specialize, a defense against the ever-increasing amount of information.

A different model of education based on the concepts of rehabilitation by team effort would benefit the children, the physicians, and the staff. Physicians, nurses, psychologists, physical therapists, occupational therapists, speech therapists, teachers, and social workers should have a common course of lectures and training so that when they start to work in rehabilitation, they will have had experiences as a team, be trained to function with greater awareness of the competency of other disciplines, and have a greater capacity to work together in a combined program. They will be trained not only as physiotherapists, occupational therapists, or speech therapists, and so on, but as rehabilitation therapists, combining the skills of a particular profession with increased knowledge of the social and emotional factors involved in an adequate rehabilitation program. One person, for example the physician, will be the leader of the team as *first amongst equals*, for the rehabilitation team, while moving toward democracy, must still have a line of control : one individual must coordinate the opinions and determine the basic principles of therapy for the individual child.

We have found that staff of rehabilitation centers are often thirsty for knowledge; they attend educational programs, participate enthusiastically, and evaluate these programs in terms of relevancy, interest, and potential applicability to their own activities.

CONCLUSIONS

I. The importance in the rehabilitation process of the social relationship that exists between staff and children is often minimized. There is a tendency to emphasize the professional activities of the staff as the main role in therapy, but both the professional and social relationships have therapeutic value.

II. Adaptability to the rehabilitation program, usually considered desirable by staff, may not in fact be desirable, particularly for the older child. It may indicate too great a dependency, too much acceptance of external controls, and too little initiative. A child's resistance to the program, with indications of independence and a desire to initiate activities on his own, may be healthy.

III. The concepts of illness orientation and health orientation are perhaps unavoidable because of present methods of training staff. However, the optimal program would be one blending these two concepts to a degree dependent upon the severity of handicap and the expectations for life outside the rehabilitation center. For the less handicapped child and for the older child, health orientation should be emphasized and illness orientation deemphasized, since too much of the latter could lead to limitations in initiative and foster dependence.

IV. Greater tolerance for diversity of programs would allow for greater flexibility, and the resulting programs could be better for the children.

V. One individual should be responsible for the overall program and the integration of the various professions in it.

VI. The therapeutic programs of the future should be carried out by individuals not trained in specific disciplines such as physiotherapy, occupational therapy, education, and so on, but rather trained in the broad area of rehabilitation as rehabilitation therapists. Fewer individuals would be involved in the therapeutic program and cooperation between those individuals would be increased.

VII. The therapeutic program should be provided throughout the whole day rather than intensively for short periods of time. For some children the focus of the rehabilitation program should be in the classroom activities with the other programs woven in.

VIII. There is often a tendency to avoid discussing with these children such things as their failure to improve, their sexual drives, etc. These topics should not be ignored but, where possible, should be dealt with by the staff. The timing of the discussion is important and should be based on the needs of the patient to discuss these problems.

REFERENCES

1. Auerbach, A., "The Social Control of Learning Disabilities." *Journal of Learning Disabilities.* 1971, *4*, p. 369.
2. Fouracre, M. H. "Educational Abilities and Needs of Orthopaedically Handicapped Children." *Elementary School Journal.* 1950, *51*, pp. 331–338.
3. Illingworth, R. S., "The Increasing Challenges of Handicapped Children." In Wolf, J. and Anderson, R., eds. *The Multiply Handicapped Child.* Springfield, Ill. : Charles C. Thomas, 1969.
4. Quibell, E. C., *et al.* "A Survey of a Group of Children with Mental and Physical Handicaps Treated in an Orthopaedic Hospital." *Arch. Vis. Child.* 1961, *36*, pp. 58–64.
5. Richardson, W. P. and Higgings, A. C., "A Survey of Handicapping Conditions and Handicapped Children from Alamance County, North Carolina." *American Journal of Public Health.* 1964, *54*, pp. 1817–1830.
6. Shepherd, J., "Intelligence Testing of the Multiply Handicapped Child with Communication Difficulties." *Spastics Quarterly.* 1965, *14*, p. 28.
7. Stiller, J. R., Wollin, E., and Kraus, A., "Follow-up Study of Children Seen in Diagnostic Centers for Handicapped Children." *American Journal of Public Health.* 1963, *53*, pp. 1743–1750.
8. Wishik, S. M., "Handicapped Children in Georgia : A Study of Prevalence, Disability, Needs, and Resources." *American Journal of Public Health.* 1956, *46*, pp. 195–203.
9. Wolf, J. and Anderson, R., *The Multiply Handicapped Child.* Springfield, Ill. : Charles C. Thomas, 1969.

Part III

The Personal Impact
of Disability

The personal response to disability can vary on a continuum from denial of its existence to exaggeration of its consequences. This response is dependent upon the environmental, social, and psychological characteristics of the respondent.

In applying personality theory to the study of psychological reactions to physical disability, English reviews psychoanalytic, Adlerian, body-image, and social role theories and discusses the contributions that each of these has made in understanding personal response to disability.

In the most thorough review of the literature to date, Schontz concludes that there is no evidence to support the hypotheses that different physical disabilities are related to particular personality types or that there is a relationship between severity of disability and the extent of psychological impact of disability. Schontz suggests that rehabilitation workers focus on understanding the personal meanings of disability rather than upon psychological processes assumed to be constant from patient to patient.

In this analysis of the impact of disability, Geis focuses upon the problem of personal worth. He discusses the importance of self-definition and the necessity, for rehabilitation workers, of changing the self-definition of their clients from a self-defeating to a self-benefiting one.

8

The Application of Personality Theory to Explain Psychological Reactions to Physical Disability

R. William English

In spite of a considerable increase, in recent years, in efforts to research many areas of rehabilitation psychology, virtually nothing has been done to relate salient personality theories to a developing psychology of disability. Although a little is known as to "why" physically disabled persons react as they do to disablement (McDaniel, 1969), even less is known about "why" the physically disabled are stigmatized (Yuker, Block, and Campbell, 1966, and English, 1971).

In this sense, the paper that follows is something of a pioneering effort, where precedents are lacking. Because this is a theoretical study, the goal will be to develop a manuscript that is basically descriptive and hypothesis-generating.

SALIENT THEORIES IN THE PSYCHOLOGY OF DISABILITY

Certain major theoretical principles and positions have obtained popularity in the psychology of chronic illness and disability and have more potential value than others. Occasionally these theories have been used to try and explain the impact of disablement on disabled persons per se; however, it seems possible to apply the same constructs to explain stigma. The theories that will be examined are: (1) Psychoanalytic Theory; (2) Individual Psychology; (3) Body Image Theory; and (4) Social Role Theory.

Psychoanalytic Theory

The earliest theory of personality which has applicability to explaining a psychology of disability is that of psychoanalytic theory developed by

From *Rehabilitation Research and Practice Review*, 3 (1971), 35–47. Reprinted by permission of the author and editor.

Sigmund Freud in the late 1800s and early 1900s. Freud conceptualized a duality of existence, where people are humans and animals. Within this model, he believed that people exist at different levels of growth and development, the lowest levels corresponding to the basic animal side of man. At lower maturational levels, psychoanalytic theory suggests that man operates in accordance with basic instinctual drives involving sex and security needs where only the fittest individuals survive. A central tenet of psychoanalytic theory seems to be that "competition" rules the lives of men. Where there is little if any security, the struggle between men may be very physical, resulting in the death or injury of combatants. However, even when physical security is virtually assured, as has generally been the case since the industrial revolution, men continue to compete for "psychological superiority." Psychoanalytic theorists believe that most behavior is unconscious and that learned behavior occurs in the formative preschool years.

If this bird's-eye view of psychoanalytic theory is applied to stigma, we might hypothesize that a nondisabled person who is prejudiced toward the disabled is a relatively immature individual with unexpressed hostilities and a need to feel psychologically superior. In terms of the disabled themselves, psychoanalytic theories would believe that disablement almost always has an adverse effect on personality, especially if it occurs in early childhood. They are likely to be immature and passive-aggressive types. Persons disabled after school begins probably would not experience any substantial change in personality, according to psychoanalytic thinking.

Individual Psychology

A neo-psychoanalytic theory of personality which is often mentioned by students of disability is termed "individual psychology." Its author was Alfred Adler (1927), who studied psychiatry with Freud after practicing ophthalmology and general medicine in Vienna. Adler's personality theory departed from Freud's psychoanalytic theory in its emphasis on social motivation and individuality, rather than sexual impulses.

The most relevant of Adler's constructs that relate to the stigmatization of the physically disabled are "striving for superiority," "inferiority," "compensation" and the idea of the "life style." Adler believed that all people possess an innate drive to strive for superiority. He felt this drive evolved into a pattern or life style from early childhood and that it was motivated to compensate for certain innate feelings of inferiority. Stigma, in the view of individual psychology, is part of the life style to achieve superiority—even at others' expense—by nondisabled persons.

Proponents of individual psychology believe that physically disabled persons attempt to compensate for a defective organ by strengthening it. In their view, physical or mental deformities are principal causes of a "faulty" life style. Individual psychology theorists probably believe there is a higher incidence of emotional disturbance among the disabled than the nondisabled (McDaniel, 1969).

Body Image Theory

Another neo-psychoanalytic system prominent in explaining the psychology of disability is "body image theory." The idea of the body image and its disruption due to chronic illness and physical disability has become nearly as popular a construct among rehabilitation practitioners as the construct of "inferiority" (McDaniel, 1969).

The individual who has contributed more than anyone else to body image theory is Paul Schilder (1950), as far back as 1935. Schilder and others believe that people respond to each other substantially in terms of nonverbal and physical cues and images.

Followers of Gestalt Psychology believe that, over time, most people have come to recognize that there is frequently an inconsistency between verbal and cognitive behavior and nonverbal body behavior (Köhler, 1947). This aspect of our humanness seems recognized both within ourselves and in others. To illustrate, we know there are times we have told companions we are very satisfied, while at the exact same moment our gestures and expressions communicated something else. As an aside, it is interesting to note that frequently we are less sensitive to our own incongruence than are others. Based on self-perceptions, it is usually the rule that we place most of our faith in what we see and not what we hear.

Related to this, body image theorists believe that the attitudes individuals have towards themselves and others are viewed as being shaped substantially in terms of their perceptions about physique. Although it is somewhat oversimplified, "body image" can be viewed as a construct existing on a continuum, where those who are most acceptant of their own bodies will be most acceptant of the bodies of others and vice versa.

Theoretically, the construct "body image" is of course closely related to that of the "self-concept," although proponents of Body Image Theory believe they are not equivalent concepts, but, rather, that body perceptions reflect generalized feelings of self (Wapner and Warner, 1965). In Freud's early writings he argued that the body image is closely related to the development of the ego. Freud thought the self-core followed first and foremost from a body ego, that the ego is derived from bodily sensations which can be thought of as a mental projection of the surface of the body (Fisher and Cleveland, 1968).

Many body image theorists believe that body attitudes are often the result and reflection of interpersonal relationships. Cleveland (1960) discovered that body attitudes appear to change during psychotherapy, and Popper (1957) showed that body images are differentially affected by previous success and failure experiences. In related research, Cleveland and Fisher (1965) have observed that body feelings are often correlated with various personality measures. Abel (1953) discovered that more severely facially disfigured persons make more distorted figure drawings. Abel's (1953) findings, however, are contradicted by a study by Silverstein and Robinson (1965), who found that judges were unable to distinguish between the self-figure drawings of paralytic and normal children.

Some objective data has come forth with regard to persons' objective body image, that is, how they are viewed by others, and attitudes toward physically disabled persons. In one study, English and Oberle (1971) had psychiatrists identify the extremes in occupational groups believed to employ women with a high and low emphasis on physique. Using the Attitude Towards Disabled Persons Scale, they found that the high-physique group, airline stewardesses, were significantly more rejecting of disabled persons than the low-physique group, typists. In another study, Witkin, Lewis, Hertzman, Machover, Meissner, and Wapner (1954) demonstrated fairly convincingly that body image is important in determining perceptual functioning. They observed that persons who produced more field-dependent figure drawings reflected a lower evaluation or confidence in their own bodies, whereas persons who drew less field-dependent figures had more self-body confidence.

Social Role Theory

A relatively recent trend of thought which is valuable to the study of psychological responses to disability and rehabilitation is social role theory. The major contributor in this area has been Talcott Parsons, a sociologist (1951 and 1958).

A basic construct in role theory is that of a "status," which is simply a collection of rights and duties (Linton, 1936). A role represents the dynamic aspect of a status where individuals put the rights and duties which constitute a particular status into effect. Obviously roles and statuses are quite interdependent, there being no statuses without roles or roles without statuses (Davis, 1949 and Gordon, 1966).

The basic notion underlying Role Theory is that people interact according to learned expectations of behavior. This represents the individualized side of Role Theory which is of greatest interest to psychologists, counselors, and other students of disability. Whereas the rights and duties attributed to statuses are generally well understood, role expectations are not as well understood. This seems attributable to the fact that there are many more roles than statuses to learn and that people are exposed to differential socialization experiences for role learning.

The fact that individuals enact roles in different ways is not completely understood but seems attributable to a number of factors : First is that people are exposed to an unequal number of roles, which influences the knowledge of role expectations; Second, people learn role expectations with a relative degree of accuracy, depending primarily on the relative teaching abilities of significant role models; Third, people possess differential role-taking skills, dependent on learning and heredity and constitution; Finally, role enactment is influenced by unknown factors, "X" if you will, such as motivation or personality.

Related to successful role enactment is the concept of role reciprocity (Sarbin, 1954). This is the construct that every role is closely interwoven with one or more others, e.g., girl-woman, father-son, winner-loser, and so on. It is believed therefore that people must understand role reciprocity if they are to accurately act out individual roles. In a general frame of reference, it might be argued that the most successful people in life are those who accurately know the expectations for the greatest number of roles and have the most outstanding role skills and the greatest drive to engage in role-taking activities.

In terms of disability, it has been hypothesized that persons primarily enact roles according to their expectations, or role set, for and about the so-called "sick-role" (Gordon, 1966). Parsons (1951) believed that Role Theory affords an ideal model for evaluating the reciprocal interaction of disabled and nondisabled persons. In Parsons' view, the major dyadic relationships influencing disability roles are between the physician and the patient and the patient and his family. Parsons (1951) goes on to state that these relationships must be viewed in terms of four behavioral presumptions of the sick role. First is the presumption that sick persons are exempt from social responsibility. Second is the presumption that the sick person cannot be expected to take care of himself. Illness or disability produces incapacity and consequently limits or inhibits the performance of routine duties. In this sense the sick person is viewed as incompetent and not accountable for his actions. That is, he is in a condition that must be cared for. Parsons' third behavioral presumption is that sick persons should wish to get well because health is viewed as necessary for the optimal performance of most important life tasks. Fourth, there is the presumption that society demands that sick persons should seek medical advice and cooperate with medical experts.

A psychological construct that is closely related to Parsons' behavioral presumptions about the sick role is that of "the requirement of mourning" developed by Barker, Wright, and Gonick (1946) and Wright (1955). They feel that there is an expectation or demand made on disabled persons to act sick, like it or not, for a time following disablement. This expectation, to be depressed over his loss of functionality and to brood or mourn, is believed to be almost universally imposed on the disabled person. The role demands represented by the "requirement of mourning" can be considered to be infectious and applicable to nearly all disabled and nondisabled persons. On the part of the disabled persons, mourning has frequently been observed, especially closely after disablement, along with such related affective dimensions as self-devaluation and spread or the generalization of dysfunctional anxiety (Wright, 1960). Significant others, that is, those persons who are closest to and psychologically most important to the disabled also experience the "mourning" response in what can be viewed as a sympathetic response due to a case of overidentification with the disabled person. Finally, some nondisabled persons who are not significant others—they may, in fact, not even personally know the disabled person—may require the disabled individual to mourn his loss because they are personally threatened by the person's medical condition or have a pathological need to feel psychologically superior.

In addition to the statements already made, Role Theory can be extended still further to explain the psychological impact of disability on so-called disabled and nondisabled individuals. In terms of the disabled themselves, it has been hypothesized that the response to disablement is quite individualized (Gordon, 1966). It has further been hypothesized (Parsons, 1958) that illness or disability disrupts established role patterns and leads to a reorganization of roles, which is also applicable to rehabilitation treatment or service which is designed to restore or maximize the person's ability to enact roles appropriately. These hypotheses have all been studied to some extent and are generally supported by research findings (McDaniel, 1969, and Wright, 1960).

As might be anticipated, given the embryonic development of a psychology of disability, not all hypotheses put forth by role theorists have been supported by research findings. For example, Parsons (1958) predicted that the severity of disability or illness would be directly related to the degree of individual psychopathology expressed by a disabled person. The conclusions of English (1968), McDaniel (1969), and Wright (1960), who have all written extended literature reviews on this topic, dispute this hypothesis.

Apart from those hypotheses, derived from Role Theory, which have or have not found support, there are many which apply to both the reciprocal disabled and nondisabled actors which simply have not been researched sufficiently to allow for definitive conclusions. It is assumed, for example, that disablement promotes a higher incidence of role conflict among the disabled and the nondisabled with whom they interact. The disabled, for example, are believed to be placed in the ambiguous situation of having to choose between acting "as if" they were healthy or sick, and the nondisabled encounter similar problems in wrestling with the question of how to treat the so-called disabled person. Related to this, it is believed, without substantiation as yet, that much of the negative interaction that has been observed as taking place between disabled and nondisabled persons, after traumatic disablement, can be ascribed to uncertainty about what are appropriate role expectations and role enactments. Theoretically, again this hypothesis has yet to be adequately tested, this explains why the disabled and nondisabled have unsatisfactory interactions and why the disabled promote "prejudice by invitation" and why the nondisabled inadvertently stigmatize the disabled (Wright, 1960). As a final example, more research needs to be forthcoming with regard to the concept of "stigma by association." This refers to the notion, developed by Olshansky (1965), that nondisabled persons—especially nonfamily members such as counselors or teachers—are often themselves victims of prejudice and are devalued simply because of their interaction with the disabled.

OVERVIEW

Up to this point, the focus of this article has been on presenting in rather straightforward terms the relative merits of four prominent and, I believe, promising personality theories as they apply to a psychology of disability. At this juncture, all the theories will be cast into a common conceptual model and briefly analyzed. The article will end after some succinct concluding remarks.

Table I.   The Effect of Heredity and Early Childhood on the Psychological Adjustment of the Physically Disabled

Personality Theories	(1) Heredity influences the psychological adjustment of the physically disabled	(2) Early childhood education influences the psychological adjustment of the physically disabled
Psychoanalytic Theory	Very Definitely	Very Definitely
Individual Psychology	Very Definitely	Very Definitely
Body Image Theory	Definitely	Definitely
Role Theory	Slightly or Not at All	Somewhat

In Table 1, the relative effects of two etiological conditions are considered, within the framework of four personality theories, as they apply to the psychological adjustment of the physically disabled. The subjective judgments that are made, in this table and in three others that follow, are solely those of the author. Evaluations made involved analysis on a five-point scale : very definitely; definitely; probably; somewhat; and slightly or not at all.

The theoretical data contained in Table I suggest that heredity and early childhood are believed to be very critical factors influencing the psychological adjustment of physically disabled persons by psychoanalytic theorists and Adlerians, while Body Theorists believe they are only critical and Role Theorists believe they are relatively inconsequential.

Conceptually these differences reflect the basic character of these theories. That is, they range on a continuum from the most pure psychological theory (psychoanalytic) to refined psychological theories (individual psychology and body image theory) to one of the most pure of sociological theories (role theory). These differences are, of course, only logical, given their historical origins. Considering that Freud and his protege Adler were medical men most active around the turn of the twentieth century, it is hardly surprising that they developed basically psychogenic theories of personality. In related fashion, Body Image Theory and Role Theory reflect the times in which they were written as well as the backgrounds of their major protagonists. Most body theorists have been psychologists, and nearly all of their work has been done since 1930. Most role theorists are sociologists or social-psychologists, and nearly all of their work is post–World War II.

Table II.   *The Psychological Impact of Disablement*

Personality Theories	(3) Disablement adversely affects the psychological adjustment of the physically disabled	(4) Disablement adversely affects the psychological adjustment of the significant others of the physically disabled
Psychoanalytic Theory	Somewhat	Somewhat
Individual Psychology	Very Definitely	Definitely
Body Image Theory	Definitely	Probably
Role Theory	Somewhat	Somewhat

The theoretical conclusions offered in Table II suggest that all the personality theories considered here believe that disablement has a negative effect on the psychological adjustment of the physically disabled. This seems not to be very important to psychoanalytic theorists and role theorists, but very important to Adlerians and body image theorists. In part, this interpretation of theory is based on the relative permanence of the personality core in early childhood according to psychoanalytic theorists and the relative optimism of role theorists in believing that adversity can be adjusted to. Because physique per se is such a central construct in the other two theories, it is logical to predict that they believe that disablement will have a serious negative effect on personality.

The conclusions about the influence of disablement on the psychological adjustment of the nondisabled significant others of the disabled is fairly consistent with the preceding interpretations. Because the people affected are secondary figures, however, the effects should not be as great.

Table III. *The Sociological Impact of Disablement*

Personality Theories	(5) Disablement adversely affects the life style of the physically disabled	(6) Disablement adversely affects the life style of the significant others of the physically disabled	(7) Disablement results in stigmatization of the physically disabled
Psychoanalytic Theory	Definitely	Definitely	Very Definitely
Individual Psychology	Very Definitely	Very Definitely	Very Definitely
Body Image Theory	Definitely	Probably	Probably
Role Theory	Definitely	Definitely	Somewhat

The construct examined in Table III (5) is related to the construct previously examined in Table II (3). The difference lies in the fact that the first analysis focuses on the psychological impact of disablement on the disabled person's interpersonal adjustment, while the second considers the sociological impact of disablement on the disabled person's life style, i.e. how one lives his life, where, and doing what with whom. A core component of "life style" is the notion that an individual's subjective and objective life chances are adversely changed by traumatic setbacks such as disablement (English, 1968).

In regard to these two dimensions, proponents of two personality systems, psychoanalytic theory and role theory, would seem to be prepared to argue that "disablement" does greater damage to a disabled person objectively—sociologically—than it does subjectively—psychologically. Proponents of two other theories, Adlerians and body image theorists, would seem not to see clear distinctions in the psychological and sociological consequences of disablement for disabled persons, while viewing the general impact as more handicapping than would Freudians or role theorists.

These theoretical conclusions are substantially the same when the relative psychological and sociological consequences of disablement are considered as they might apply to disabled persons' nondisabled "significant others." An examination of Table II (4) and Table III (6) reflects the attitude on the part of psychoanalytic theorists and role theorists that disablement is a more handicapping condition (Hamilton, 1948) sociologically than psychologically. Body image theorists view the impact as consistent, although individual psychologists might believe that disablement realistically affects the life styles of the disabled person's able-bodied friends and family more than it affects these significant persons psychologically.

These theoretical conclusions are relatively consistent with empirical data (English, 1968, McDaniel, 1969, and Wright, 1960) and may perhaps best be explained by two factors. First is a belief in the relative stability or permanence of personality beyond the most formative preschool years. Second is a belief that life style and socioeconomic statuses are somewhat tenuous realities which are indeed subject to change by major events, both good and bad. Comparatively, then, it seems that psychological conditions are somewhat more stable or permanent than are sociological conditions.

One additional construct has relevance for a discussion of the sociological impact of disablement according to personality theory. This is the notion that disablement contributes to the stigmatization of physically disabled persons (Table III [7]). Each of the four personality theories considered would appear to see some link between disablement and stigmatization, but only Freudian and Adlerian theorists seem likely to see the relationship as very substantial.

Assuming this theoretical analysis is accurate, it may best be attributed to the basic assumption that each of these theories makes with regard to the nature of man. It is generally conceded (Hall and Lindzey, 1957) that psychoanalytic and Adlerian personality theorists take a dim view of man and his basic motivations for interpersonal interactions. These theories tend to portray man as basically hedonistic and self-oriented, with definite needs to dominate others. In contrast, most body theorists would seem to hold a fairly neutral to neutral-negative view of man, while most role theorists have the attitude that man's character is basically neutral to neutral-positive.

The last set of constructs to be considered in a general conceptual model, as they relate to a psychology of disability, have to do with the rehabilitation of the physically disabled, their significant others and the likelihood of reducing stigma toward physically disabled persons. The theoretical conclusions which relate to these dimensions are presented in Table IV (8, 9, 10, 11, 12).

Table IV.   The Prognosis for Rehabilitative Treatment and Attitude Change

Personality Theories	(8) Physically disabled persons can recover from adverse psychological effects of disablement	(9) The significant others of the disabled can recover from the adverse psychological effects of disablement	(10) Physically disabled persons can recover from the adverse sociological effects of disablement	(11) The significant others of the disabled can recover from the adverse sociological effects of disablement	(12) Stigma toward the physically disabled can be reduced
Psychoanalytic Theory	Probably	Definitely	Somewhat	Probably	Slightly or not at all
Individual Psychology	Somewhat	Definitely	Somewhat	Probably	Slightly or not at all
Body Image Theory	Probably	Probably	Probably	Probably	Somewhat
Role Theory	Very Definitely	Very Definitely	Definitely	Very Definitely	Probably

The conclusions presented in Table IV (8) clearly suggest that physically disabled persons can recover from the adverse psychological effects of disablement. Individual psychologists would be most likely to be pessimistic in this regard, given the centrality of "organic inferiority" in their theory, while role theorists would be most optimistic because of their far greater emphasis on social causality. The presumption of all four theories, however, is that personality development is relatively complete at an early age, generally well before disablement occurs. All four theories would further presume that, while disablement may force a psychological setback, it is very unlikely to lead to a total personality change. Finally, all four theories, to some degree, place a considerable degree of confidence in counseling and psychotherapy and in therapeutic environmental manipulation. In this sense, they all believe that personality is malleable and that psychological adjustment can be improved.

Consistent with earlier conclusions on the impact of disablement, Table IV (9) suggests a more positive prognosis for recovery from the psychological effects of disablement for significant others than for the disabled themselves. The differences between the theories may best be attributable to their differential belief about the nature of man and the differential commitment people have to preserve interpersonal relationships and to help each other. Because psychoanalytic and Adlerian theorists believe man is basically motivated by self-gain, their judgment that the psychological effects of disablement for nondisabled persons will be slight is absolute. In contrast, the similar conclusion by role theorists is conditional and requires qualification. Their conviction that significant others will rebound from the negative effects of disablement is based on the same conviction for the disabled themselves. These roles are symbiotic and because they are, most role theorists would argue that, where physically disabled persons do not psychologically recover from the adverse effects of disablement, their significant others probably will not either.

The theoretical conclusions presented in Table IV (10, 11) regarding the prognosis for recovering from the sociological effects of disablement by the disabled and their significant others is consistent with the data presented in Table III (5 and 6) regarding the sociological impact of disablement. The prognosis is generally more pessimistic for recovering from the sociological effects than the psychological effects of disablement, as presented in Table IV (8 and 9). As before, we see more optimism among the newer and more sociological theories, Body Theory and Role Theory.

Finally, Table IV (12) presents conclusions about the chances of reducing stigma toward physically disabled persons. As would be expected, it was suggested that psychoanalytic and Adlerian theorists would be very pessimistic about changing negative attitudes towards disabled persons, while Body and Role theorists would hold some medium degree of optimism.

CONCLUDING REMARKS

In this theoretical article, attention has been paid to the relative value of four personality theories for explaining psychological reactions to physical disability. The theories considered (psychoanalytic, individual psychology, body image, and social role) are not exhaustive, but do appear to be among the most promising for explaining a general psychology of disability. Similarly, the conclusions reached in this article should be considered as tentative, challengeable, and hypothesis-generating in nature. Last, although the article's contents focused on physical disability, it appears to have substantial relevance to other disability groups.

All of the theories considered here, but especially those developed by Freud and Adler, can be faulted for having very little meaningful empirical research to back them. In fact, on some issues their hypotheses are in direct conflict with research findings. For example, all the theories suggest that disablement has a slight to profound impact on psychological adjustment, but several fairly exhaustive literature reviews suggest that there are few if any real personality differences between disabled and nondisabled persons (English, 1968, McDaniel, 1969, and Wright, 1960).

Early in this article certain positive attributes of each theory were presented. However, each has certain liabilities as well as systems to comprehensively relate to a psychology of disability. Psychoanalytic theory seems to place a disproportional emphasis on sex, heredity, early childhood, and the negative side of man. Some of these same criticisms appear applicable to Individual Psychology, regarding over-emphasis on heredity, early childhood, and projecting a very pessimistic image of man. Moreover, Adlerian theorists can be faulted for indiscriminately applying some concepts, e.g. compensation and inferiority (McDaniel, 1969).

The most damaging criticisms applicable to Body Image Theory seem to relate to a general feeling that it is too oblique and lacks comprehensiveness to such an extent that it may not be a theory at all. Furthermore, it may be faulted for failure to clearly discriminate the constructs of body image and self-concept. Finally, role theory seems inadequate to completely explain a psychology of disability because it is too sociological and does not attribute enough importance to personality and psychological variables.

At the present time, Role Theory seems to have a slight edge over the other three theories, but what is obviously needed is more research, both theoretical and empirical, on the application of theory to a developing psychology of disability. It is, frankly, appalling that rehabilitationists have not made more use of theory in their efforts to assist the disabled. Hopefully this article will ameliorate this situation to some degree.

REFERENCES

Abel, T. A. Figure drawing and facial disfigurement. *American Journal of Orthopsychiatry,* 1954, *23,* 253–264.

Adler, A. *The practice and theory of individual psychology.* New York: Harcourt, Brace, 1927.

Barker, R., Wright, B., and Gonick, M. *Adjustment to physical handicaps and illness: A survey of the social psychology of physique and disability.* New York: Social Science Research Council, 1946.

Cleveland, S. E. Body image changes associated with personality reorganization. *Journal of Consulting Psychology,* 1960, *24,* 256–261.

Davis, K. *Human society.* New York: Macmillan Co., 1949.

English, R. W. Assessment of change in the personal-social self-perceptions of vocational rehabilitation clients. Unpublished doctoral dissertation, University of Wisconsin, Madison, 1968.

————Correlates of stigma towards physically disabled persons. *Rehabilitation Research and Practice Review* (Accepted for publication, Fall, 1971).

————& Oberle, J. B. Toward the development of new methodology for examining attitudes toward disabled persons. *Rehabilitation Counseling Bulletin* 1971, *15* (2), 88–96.

Fisher, S. and Cleveland, S. E. *Body image and personality.* New York : Dover Publications, Inc., 1968.

Gordon, G. *Role theory and illness.* New Haven, Conn. : College and University Press Services, Inc., 1966.

Hall, C. S. and Lindzey, G. *Theories of personality.* New York : John Wiley and Sons, 1957.

Köhler, W. *Gestalt psychology.* New York : Mentor, 1947.

Linton, R. *The study of man.* New York : Appleton-Century-Crofts Co., 1936, pp. 113–114.

McDaniel, J. W. *Physical disability and human behavior.* New York : Pergamon Press, 1969.

Olshansky, S. S. Stigma : Its meaning and some of its problems for vocational rehabilitation agencies. *Rehabilitation Literature,* 1965, *26,* 71–74.

Parsons, T. *The social system.* Glencoe, Illinois : The Free Press, 1951.

————Definitions of health and illness in the light of American values and social structure. In E. G. Jaco (Ed.) *Patients, physicians and illness.* Glencoe, Illinois : The Free Press, 1958. Chapter 20, pp. 165–187.

Popper, J. M. Motivational and social factors in children's perception of height. Doctoral dissertation, Stanford University. Palo Alto, California, 1957.

Sarbin, T. R. Role theory. In G. Lindzey (Ed.) *Handbook of social psychology.* Cambridge, Massachusetts : Addison-Wesley Publishing Co., 1954, p. 223.

Schilder, P. *The image and appearance of the human body.* New York : John Wiley and Sons, 1950.

Silverstein, A. B. and Robinson, H. A. The representation of orthopedic disability in children's figure drawings. *Journal of Consulting Psychology,* 1965, *20,* 333.

Wapner, S. and Werner. H. (Ed.) *The body percept.* New York : Random House, 1965.

Witkin, H. A., Lewis, H. B., Hertzman, M., Machover, K., Meissner, P. B., and Wapner, S. *Personality through perception.* New York : Harper and Row, 1954.

Wright, B. *Physical disability: A psychological approach.* New York : Harper and Row, 1960.

————The period of mourning in chronic illness. In R. Harrower (Ed.) *Medical and psychological teamwork in the care of the chronically ill.* Springfield, Illinois : Charles C. Thomas, 1955.

Yuker, H. E., Block, J. R. and Younng, J. H. *The measurement of attitudes toward disabled persons.* Human Resources Center, Albertson, New York, 1966.

9

Physical Disability and Personality: Theory and Recent Research

Franklin C. Shontz

Opinion about the relationship between disability and personality has generally reflected uncritical acceptance of two assumptions. The first assumption is that specific forms of somatic disorder commonly are associated with specific types of personality. The second is that some types or degrees of disability constitute sufficient causes of psychological maladjustment.

Psychologists with an objective interest in the study of disability and personality have expended a good deal of effort to assess the merits of these entrenched and appealing notions. It is not generally realized how firmly and with what consistency the notions have been discredited by the evidence.

The first comprehensive reviews were published by Barker, Wright, and Gonick in 1946 and by Barker, Wright, Meyerson, and Gonick in 1953. These monographs (especially the 1953 revision) surveyed the available psychological literature, supplied critiques of research, and summarized findings to date. In her later book on the psychology of disability, Beatrice A. Wright (1960) credited these sources for her conclusions that there is no evidence that particular personality characteristics are associated with particular disabilities or that severity of disability is correlated with level of psychological adjustment. (No authority claims that disability never affects personality; individual reactions frequently are profound and intense. What is denied is the systematic and universal correlation of type or degree of disability with type or degree of personality adjustment.)

Disenchantment with the two hypotheses was not confined to those who dealt broadly with the issues. It was evident in the writings of experts on particular disabilities as well. Specific personality characteristics were not found to be associated with paraplegia (Berger, 1953), amputation (Fishman, 1962), epilepsy (Tizard, 1962), tuberculosis (Harris, 1953), or coronary heart disease (Whitehouse, 1962; Mordkoff and Parsons, 1967). Even when authorities claimed some degree of similarity of personality in persons with a particular form of disability, they carefully qualified their claims by noting that reactions are by no means identical, individual differences are marked, and maladjustment is far from universal.

What has been uniformly regarded as crucial is the personal meaning of his disability to each individual client. Such conclusions have been drawn for patients with ophthalmic conditions (Young, 1953), for the deaf (Levine, 1953; 1962) and hard of hearing (Lane, 1953), for patients with facial disfigurement (Abel, 1953; Madam, 1962), for the blind (Lowenfeld, 1953; Raskin, 1962), for patients with cerebral palsy (Garrett, 1953; Allen, 1962), poliomyelitis (Seidenfeld, 1953), multiple sclerosis (Harrower, 1953), cancer (Cobb, 1962), rheumatoid arthritis (Seidenfeld, 1962), language disorders (Wepman, 1962), and hemiplegia (Diller, 1962), and for exceptional children in general (Kaplan and Lotsof, 1968; Pringle, 1964). Virtually all these authors have cautioned that psychological treatment must be directed toward individual situations and reactions rather than toward psychological processes that can be assumed to be constant from patient to patient.

The negative character of disability effects. \Physical disability is commonly supposed to inflict only negative, disruptive, and disturbing psychological consequences. Wright (1960) has pointed out, however, that disability may generate opportunities and gratifications as well as frustrations and grievances. In an analysis of the contents of 31 first-person accounts of disability experiences, Shontz (unpublished) found that statements describing satisfactions occurred slightly more frequently than statements describing dissatisfactions. Wright and Shontz (1968) have shown how hope exerts a strong counterforce against despair. Such positive phenomena are all but ignored in most studies of the psychological aspects of disability.

THEORETICAL ALTERNATIVES

Fault-finding alone does not solve the theoretical problem. Discredited hypotheses must be replaced eventually by more attractive possibilities. Several such possibilities have been proposed. Some of these are considered briefly in the following discussion.

Interpersonal Theory

Probably the best developed theoretical ideas are those that have grown out of the work of Barker and his colleagues (Barker, Wright, and Gonick, 1946; Barker, Wright, Meyerson, and Gonick, 1953; Meyerson, 1955; Dembo, Leviton, and Wright, 1953; 1956; Barker and Wright, 1953; Wright, 1960). These theorists regard the body as a value-impregnated stimulus to the self and others. They trace the self-concept and personal values back to a primary source in interpersonal relations, particularly to evaluations by others. This group of theorists has generated and applied a number of useful descriptive concepts, such as spread, value loss, containment of disability effects, comparative and asset values, expectation discrepancy, new and overlapping situations.

Body Image Theory

Typically, body image theory applies psychoanalytic or psychoanalytically-derived principles to explain the development in each individual of a conception of, and set of attitudes toward, himself as a bodily entity (Schilder, 1935; Frank, 1959; Menninger, 1953; Fisher and Cleveland, 1968). The oral, anal, phallic, latency, and genital stages of psychosexual development work their effects through the body image, and it is by way of the body image that castration anxiety, arising initially during the Oedipal conflict, influences personality in persons with physical disabilities (Murphy, 1957).

The concept of the body image is not specific to the explanation of disability effects, but it serves a useful purpose by enabling practitioners in rehabilitation to express in a few words the nature of a client's difficulties and by providing a rational basis for making decisions about treatment (Shontz, 1969).

Motivation Theories

Maslow's (1954) theory of motivation has led to the distinction between lower level (hygiene or security) needs for physiological satisfactions and safety, and higher level (growth) needs for interpersonal gratifications and self-esteem. Motivational distinctions such as those proposed by Maslow are implied in discussions of disability reactions by Shontz (1962) and by Shontz, Fink, and Hallenbeck (1960). Barry and Malinovsky (1965) used Maslow's theory for organizing their comprehensive review of the literature on client motivation. Patterson (1964) expressed a preference for a unitary theory of motivation in the counseling situation. For Patterson, the unitary motive is self-actualization, a term used by Goldstein (1959) as well as by Maslow.

Keith (1968) called for greater emphasis on autonomous activity in theories of motivation in rehabilitation. He objected to the assumption that disability is equivalent to illness and that the proper role for the person with a disability is therefore the sick role (Parsons, 1954; Parsons and Fox, 1952) in which dependency and childlike behavior are expected and fostered by the environment.

McDaniel (1969) has suggested that the concept of achievement motivation (Atkinson and Feather, 1966) might be useful in rehabilitation, especially in work-oriented settings.

Attitudes Toward Disability

The idea that attitudes of others affect attitudes toward self is succinctly expressed by Siller, Chipman, Ferguson and Vann (1967):

> A person with a handicap reflects prevalent social attitudes of self-depreciation and self-hate. In the newly disabled, on the other hand, negative attitudes previously focused on members of a devalued out-group may refocus on the self with devastating results.

The interests of many investigators have been directed most clearly toward attitudes held by the nondisabled (Kleck, 1966; Yuker, et al., 1960; 1966; Wright, 1968). However, MacDonald and Hall (1969) have correctly pointed out that evidence of consistency in attitudes of others toward people with disabilities does not tell what the attitudes of the disabled themselves are. Nor does knowledge that a person holds certain attitudes toward disability prove that these attitudes would determine his reaction to personal disability. The study of devaluating attitudes toward disability is important in its own right, but it does not tell the whole story of disability and personality.

Crisis Theory

Several authors have expressed the view that disability may be considered a crisis-inducing event. Davis (1963), Cohn (1961), and Fink (1967) have provided analyses of the crisis experience into stages (e.g., shock, defensive retreat, acknowledgment, and adaptation—Fink, 1967). Fink tied his analysis to motivational theory by specifying that the early stages of reaction involve primarily security needs, while the last stage is growth oriented and can result in increased self-actualization. Shontz (1965) simplified the analysis by describing the adjustment process as a succession of approach–avoidance cycles. In the early stages of reaction, these cycles recur rapidly and reach high levels of emotional intensity. With time, a dampening process reduces both their frequency and intensity until, in adjustment, the cyclical nature of the process becomes virtually unnoticeable.

Crisis theory is not fully developed. It needs more careful and elaborate delineation of the stages of reaction and ways to determine in individual cases where the client is in the process of adjustment and how he can be best helped through it.

Miscellaneous Specific Proposals

Comparison level. The comparison level (CL) is the level of payoff or reinforcement a person experiences as neutral in value, i.e., as appropriate and reasonable. Outcomes exceeding the CL are experienced as good and satisfying. Outcomes below the CL are experienced as bad and dissatisfying (Thibault and Kelley, 1959). In disability, mourning occurs when outcomes drop below the CL. If the CL changes appropriately, or if outcomes return to their previous level (e.g., as a result of rehabilitation), adaptation takes place and mourning ceases. If outcomes are not grossly affected by disability, or if the CL was chronically below outcome level before disability (if the person always underestimated his own potential), mourning does not occur at all (Kelley, Hastorf, Jones, Thibault, and Usdane, 1960).

Comparison level theory points out that adjustment is a joint function of the actual situation (outcomes) and the way in which the situation is experienced (CL). Unfortunately, few investigators have used comparison level theory in actual research on personality and disability.

Stress. Cowen (1960) suggested that recent research on psychological stress might provide leads that would enable us to understand reactions to disability. Unfortunately, again, little seems to have come of this suggestion. Perhaps this is partly because adequate summaries of the complex literature on the subject of stress have not been available until recently (Appley and Trumbull, 1967; Lazarus, 1966). Certainly, no coherent psychological theory of stress response existed before Lazarus' book appeared. Perhaps the future will see a more significant application of stress theory to the explanation of relations between disability and personality.

Traditional theories of personality. Few traditional theories of personality have had much to say specifically about the impact of physical disability. Adlerian theory is most explicit, because Adler was concerned about the person's attempts to compensate for somatic defect (organ inferiority). However, the problem of reaction to disability seems far too complicated to be explained by a few sweeping concepts like inferiority complex and style of life. At the same time, Adler's theory does not lend itself to research because the theory is so strongly individualistic that it makes definitive empirical investigation of general laws applying to groups of subjects seem impossible.

The contributions of psychoanalytic theory appear largely in concern for the concept of the body image and for personality defenses (especially denial). Psychosomatic medicine has been strongly influenced by psychoanalytic thought, and some contributions to the study of disability and personality have been made by investigators of psychosomatic phenomena. However, despite its claim to concern for all aspects of organismic functioning, only a small percentage of psychosomatic research deals with the process of adaptation to disability once it has occurred.

AN EXAMINATION OF RECENT LITERATURE

Subsequent sections of this report summarize a review of the recent literature on personality and disability. The sources examined were primarily recognized psychological journals (such as the *Journal of Abnormal Psychology, Clinical Psychology,* and the *Journal of Personality*), although several medical-psychiatric sources were also reviewed (such as the *American Journal of Psychiatry,* and the *Journal of Nervous and Mental Disease*). In addition, certain specialized publications, such as the *Journal of Chronic Diseases* and the *Archives of Physical Medicine and Rehabilitation,* were examined for relevant articles. Most of these sources were surveyed for five years of publication, from 1965 through 1969.

In the following sections, examples from this literature are used to demonstrate that evidence in support of the two popular hypotheses described above is still lacking (though the hypotheses themselves seem not to have been abandoned), and that interpretations of findings continue to be dominated by the preconceived idea that disability is a source of psychological maladjustment. Useful by-products of this demonstration are the proposal of some rather important generalizations about disability effects and the opportunity to comment on methodological issues.

Kidney and Heart Disease

Published reports on the psychological aspects of illness and disability tend to reflect developments in the field of medicine. Consequently, several reports have described the psychological effects of kidney and heart failure and responses to treatment of these conditions with artificial or transplanted organs. Although specific behavioral responses are associated with renal or cardiac failure, these are toxicity or deficiency effects (fatigue, anorexia, cognitive disturbances) which generally disappear when normal body functioning has been restored (Kemph, 1966). Emotional responses to treatment are varied and individualized, but many patients experience fantasies of rebirth as well as guilt over taking advantage of the death of the donor, when transplant is involved (Kemph, Bermann, and Copolillo, 1969). Patients sometimes think of themselves as zombies who have returned from the dead and are therefore not quite human (Abram, 1968; 1969). The most common postoperative psychiatric complication is depression (Kemph, 1967).

Lunde (1969) expressed the fear that personality disturbances will be frequent as transplants become more common. However, it has been observed that most psychiatric symptoms in such cases either can be prevented by adequate preoperative preparation and sympathetic postoperative care (H. R. Lazarus and Hagens, 1968) or successfully treated with psychotherapy or drugs (Kemph, 1967) when they do occur. Even catastrophic responses with severe behavioral effects have been found to last but a few days. They are replaced by mild depression which tends to lift spontaneously after a period of time (Abram, 1965).

Preoperatively, anxiety or denial are common (Abram, 1969). Weiss (1966) found that, in general, high preoperative scores on the MMPI correlated with poor reactions to open heart surgery, although no specific standard MMPI scales (except the Barron Ego Strength Scale) correlated significantly with postoperative reaction. Henricks, MacKenzie, and Almond (1969) found that preoperative MMPI data from survivors of open heart surgery generally resembled MMPI profiles of patients with other medical diagnoses. (The almost universal MMPI profile associated with medical illness of any type shows elevations on Hs, Hy, and D). Men who did not survive were more agitated than men who did. Women who did not survive were more overcontrolled and more concerned with bodily complaints. To some investigators (Kimball, 1969; Eisendrath, 1969) it appears that the best predictor of favorable response to radical surgery is a history of previously successful adjustment and coping.

The coronary personality. A large number of studies has attempted to determine whether a specific personality is associated with predisposition for, or presence of, coronary heart disease. The "coronary" (or type A) personality is usually described as aggressive, competitive, ambitious, and prone to a sense of urgency or time pressure. Some instruments have been devised for detecting this type of personality (Bortner and Rosenman, 1967; Jenkins, Rosenman, and Friedman, 1967), and a few studies have revealed differences in massed data between appropriately selected groups on personality test scores (Caffrey, 1968; 1969; Keith, Lown, and Stare, 1965; Ibrahim, Jenkins, Cassell, McDonough, and Hames,

1966; Miller, 1965; Klein and Parsons, 1968; Mordkoff and Golas, 1968; Mordkoff and Rand, 1968). Nevertheless, nearly all investigators who found such differences in grouped data placed heavy qualifications on their interpretations. Keith et al. (1965) noted that more than half their coronary patients did *not* show pattern A behavior. Mordkoff and Rand (1968), Klein and Parsons (1968), and Miller (1965) observed that many patients with heart disease gave responses that are typical of responses given by patients with other illnesses (i.e., elevation of Hs, D, and Hy on the MMPI). Some investigators (Klein et al., 1965; Ludwig and Wysong, 1969) found discriminations among groups to be statistically significant only for younger persons. Others noted that personality test data usually correlate at least as well with social class measures as with the presence or absence of coronary disease (Keith et al., 1965; Mordkoff and Golas, 1968). However, Antonovsky (1968) reviewed 56 studies and concluded that, if there is a relationship between heart disease and social class, it is not a simple one and its presence has not been convincingly demonstrated.

Rheumatoid Arthritis

The list of personality attributes ascribed to patients with arthritis is long. They have been said to have weak egos, to repress hostility, to be compliant and subservient, to be potentially psychotic, to be depressed, dependent, conscientious, masochistic, emotionally labile, compulsive, introverted, conservative, perfectionistic, moody, nervous, worried, tense, overconcerned about personal appearance, and prone to express psychopathology in physical symptoms.

Evidence exists that patients with rheumatoid arthritis behave differently from people who are not physically ill (Moos and Solomon, 1964; 1965a; 1965b), although even these findings have not gone uncontested (Nalven and O'Brien, 1968). Geist (1969) reported finding differences between arthritics and patients with other illnesses, but none of the differences was statistically significant. Warren and Weiss (1969) studied MMPI scores of patients in nine disability groups (including arthritis) and found no way to classify subjects into meaningful disability clusters.

Obesity

Atkinson and Ringuette (1967) found no distinguishing MMPI features in the records of 21 obese persons, nor was there evidence of homogeneous psychological, biographical, or familial factors that distinguished these subjects from any others. Crumpton, Wine, and Groot (1966) found that obese subjects produced generally flat MMPI profiles and showed less psychopathology than neuropsychiatric patients. Werkmann and Greenberg (1967) characterized the obese as self-satisfied and concerned with giving socially acceptable responses. High suggestibility (Glass, Lavin, Henchy, Gordon, Mayhew, and Donohoe, 1969) and field dependence (Karp and Pardes, 1965) have been reported in obese subjects. Glass et al. found, however, that underweight subjects also were highly suggestible. It is likely therefore that the critical factor in these studies is deviance rather than obesity per se.

Overview

The results summarized above are typical. Similar conclusions are justified by studies of asthma (Aaron, 1967; Green, 1965; Knapp, 1969), hemophilia (Mattsson and Gross, 1966), Huntington's chorea (Werner and Folk, 1968), leprosy (Ponomareff, 1965; Weigand and Dawson, 1967), systemic lupus erythematosus (Guze, 1967), epilepsy (Ferguson and Rayport, 1965; Kleck, 1968; Schwartz, Dennerll, and Lin, 1968; Meier and French, 1965; Small, Small, and Hayden, 1966), cancer (Fras, Litin, and Pearson, 1967; Goldfarb, Driesen, and Cole, 1967; Koenig, Levin, and Brennan, 1967), pulmonary emphysema (DeCencio, Leshner, and Leshner, 1968), Wilson's disease (Goldstein, Ewert, Randall, and Gross, 1968), ileostomy and colostomy (Dlin, Perlman, and Ringold, 1969), hemicorporectomy (Frieden, Gerther, Tosberg, and Rusk, 1969; DeLateur, Lehmann, Winterscheid, Wolf, Fordyce, and Simons, 1969), mastectomy (Jarvis, 1967), deafness (Fiebert, 1967), multiple sclerosis (Hovey, 1967), brain damage (Krug, 1967; Lansdell, 1968; Shaw and Matthews, 1965; Watson and Thomas, 1968), blindness (Zunich and Ledwith, 1965), gastric ulcers (Thoroughman, Pascal, Jarvis, and Crutcher, 1967; Wolowitz, 1967), diabetes (Swift, Seidman, and Stein, 1967), cleft palate (Gluck, McWilliams, Wylie, and Conkwright, 1965; Palmer and Adams, 1962; Ruess, 1965), essential hypertension (Hardyk, Chun, and Engel, 1966), paraplegia and quadriplegia (Kunce and Worley, 1966; Mitchell, 1970).

The recent literature provides no support for the hypothesis that particular disabilities are associated with particular personality characteristics or for the hypothesis that disability is a sufficient cause of maladjustment. Such group differences as have been found are weak and are usually subject to interpretation in terms of contaminating factors. In massed data, the somatically ill consistently show higher levels of depression and concern for body functions than do the somatically healthy or the psychiatrically disturbed. However, the somatically ill show no evidence of marked or enduring psychopathology.

IMPORTANT GENERAL ISSUES

Stability of Personality

Radical changes in body structure frequently have little or no prolonged effect on personality. Procedures such as hemicorporectomy (Frieden, et al., 1969; DeLateur, et al., 1969), bilateral hip disarticulation (Hirschenfang, Cosla, and Benton, 1966), ileostomy and colostomy (Dlin, et al., 1969), and the introduction of cardiac pacemakers (Gladstone and Gamble, 1969) involve gross alterations of the body. Yet, investigators report little or no evidence of radical, permanent personality change as a result of these interventions. Stone, Rowley, and MacQueen (1966) found that MMPI data from adolescents with physical symptoms having an organic (as opposed to a functional) basis were virtually the same as those from the normative sample for the test. Even patients with intractable cancer (Koenig, et al., 1967) or pulmonary emphysema (DeCencio, et al., 1968) show no signs of serious disorders of behavior. Personality structure may be temporarily disorganized by somatic crisis, but it seems capable of reestablishing itself by drawing on preexisting resources for integration of the crisis experience into the self.

Depression and Somatic Improvement

Ferguson and Rayport (1965) described five persons with epilepsy whose seizures had been arrested. In all five cases, a crisis followed improvement and depression set in. In the preceding discussion of surgery for kidney and heart disorder, it was noted that depression is a common postoperative reaction. Depression and guilt have also been observed in survivors of atomic bombings (Lifton, 1967) and concentration camps (Krystal, 1968).

The commonsense view of disability as a negative psychological experience does not prepare us for the possibility that improvement from illness or that removal of disability or threat to life may produce depression. Neither does it prepare us to accept the fact that personality disturbance is more likely to occur when disability is mild or marginal than when it is severe; yet, such seems to be the case (Cowen and Bobgrove, 1966).

DeWolfe, Barrell, and Cummings (1966) found that older patients with more severe illnesses expressed less discomfort than younger patients with milder disabilities. Schwab, Marder, Clemmons, and McGinness (1966) found that patients with psychiatric diagnoses were more anxious than patients with somatic illnesses and that lower anxiety was generally associated with more severe medical conditions. These findings were substantially confirmed in a related study by Goldman and Schwab (1966).

A balance theory of expectations (Heider, 1958) may be devised to explain these and related findings. According to this view, severe pain or suffering is subjectively equated with punishment or trial by ordeal, while the expectation of relief is subjectively equivalent to purification, exoneration, rebirth, or release from confinement. Negative explanations for suffering are balanced by positive expectations for states of relief. When relief actually occurs, and the person who has suffered finds himself basically unchanged, no more free of problems than he was before (indeed, he may have more problems than he did previously), the expected balance is disconfirmed and disruption of behavior follows.

Denial

The concept of denial is used in two distinctly different ways in the literature. On the one hand, it is used in the traditional way, to refer to a pathological defense against overwhelming affect, which is avoided by distorting or rejecting the harsh facts of reality. On the other hand, denial is sometimes regarded as an effective mode of adjustment, in which a person becomes capable of realistic present action by refusing to allow himself to anticipate necessary sufferings of the future. Thus, for example, when investigators find that families of children with cardiac pacemakers are well adjusted and realistic, the interpretation of denial is offered in explanation (Gladstone and Gamble, 1969). Similarly, when patients with myelopathy are found to be better adjusted on a test of personality than the normal population on which the test was standardized, it becomes "evident that some form of psychologic denial is in operation" (Weiss and Diamond, 1966, p. 75). Investigators do not seem to consider the possibilities that absence of anxiety may sometimes be taken as a sign of good adjustment, that suffering may be concealed without being denied, that hope is as real as despair, or that suffering may produce genuine psychological growth and maturity. This is a serious lack in virtually all studies of personality and disability.

COMMENTS ON RESEARCH METHODS

Case Studies and Impressionistic Reports

Several new ideas have been suggested by case studies. The case study also provides the investigator with a vehicle for describing rare and unusual patients or conditions. As might be expected, most of the work on the effects of radical surgery is reported in case study or impressionistic form.

The least impressive case studies are those in which intuitions are offered as if they were something more than suggestive evidence or illustrations of a theoretical position. It is not possible to prove that disability and personality are related or that psychiatric symptoms are more frequent in people with disabilities than in other groups, by simply communicating clinical impressions in a professional journal. Unfortunately, much of the literature still attempts to do this.

Test-Based Studies

A large number of studies employ psychological tests. However, many such studies do not provide contemporaneously obtained data from comparison groups. It cannot be assumed that test norms (which have usually been obtained from persons without disabilities, tested months or years previously under quite different examination conditions) or that data obtained by others, who have tested subjects in different institutions, provide satisfactory standards for comparison of results obtained with a given sample at a given time and place.

One notes the lack of factor analytic research in this literature. Properly replicated, basic, intensive and extensive multivariate research, using a variety of psychological measures with subjects having a variety of somatic conditions, could go a long way toward clarifying the descriptive problem and identifying the most important variables for future study.

Evidence and inference.   What evidence ultimately would be needed to show that personality and disability are, in fact, related in some systematic way?

First, groups of patients with virtually nothing in common except the disability in question must be shown to differ in performance on some measure of behavior from persons without disabilities.

Second, patients with one disability must be shown to differ from groups of patients with other disabilities.

Third, within groups of persons who have the disability, degree of manifestation of relevant personality characteristics must be shown to correlate appropriately with severity, duration, or some other medical feature of the disability.

None of the studies cited in the literature comes anywhere close to meeting any (except, perhaps, the first) of these requirements.

Even a satisfactory demonstration that personality and disability are correlated cannot establish the existence or directionality of a cause–effect relationship between them (Keith, 1966; Lahav, 1967; McFarland and Cobb, 1967). Cause–effect relationships can be established only by longitudinal study of the same subjects over a period of time.

Longitudinal data also must be interpreted with caution. If a third factor (say, malnutrition) produces, first, personality changes and only later produces bodily disease, longitudinal tests would show predictive validity for personality tests and still fail to reveal the true cause of the illness. Similar cautions apply to the study of somatopsychological relations, in which the demonstration that given personality follows the onset of a particular disability must be accompanied by evidence that other factors cannot be adduced to explain them both.

Psychological variables. Future research will be more productive if it concentrates more heavily on relations between psychological variables than on relations between somatic variables and behavior. An instance of the type of research that ought to be done more often is a study which found that dogmatism (Rokeach, 1960) in blind subjects correlated positively with denial and negatively with depression (Hallenbeck, 1967). These findings suggest that denial of illness is not an isolated defense mechanism but is embedded in the matrix of the whole personality structure. Findings such as these can provide useful leads to counselors and therapists, who are in a position to influence belief systems in ways that will promote favorable client reactions.

Naturalism. In conjunction with increased emphasis on psychological variables, it would be highly desirable for investigators to develop more naturalistic techniques. In this respect, one of the most interesting studies in the literature was conducted by Belmont, Benjamin, Ambrose, and Restuccia (1969). These investigators observed patients' task-oriented activities in the presence of and in the absence of the therapist. Level of activity was found to remain high when the therapist was absent from patients without cerebral damage but to drop significantly when the therapist was absent from patients with hemiplegia.

This study operationally defined motivation as "continuing to work when the therapist leaves." The definition is naturalistic, easily objectified, and intuitively appealing. With it, one can study motivation in a variety of behavior settings and can look for correlations between motivated behavior and a variety of measures, including those derived from psychological tests. The investigator can be sure his results will reveal something of interest not only to himself but also to those who work directly with clients. The naturalistic approach (Willems and Raush, 1969) offers many possibilities for fruitful research on disability, nearly all of which remain open to exploitation by ingenious investigators.

Experimental Methods

If the word *experiment* is taken to mean only research in which a carefully operationized independent variable is manipulated under rigidly controlled laboratory conditions, there are practically no experimental studies in the literature on disability and personality. Given a broader conception of the term, however, it is possible to identify a few (though not many) investigations that can be called experimental in spirit, if not in actual design.

An example of experimentation using naturally occurring events as the independent variable is a study by Riklan, Levita, and Cooper (1966) of the psychological effects of bilateral subcortical chemosurgery and cryosurgery for Parkinson's disease. These investigators administered a battery of cognitive, perceptual, and personality tests to 22 patients who had undergone surgery from five to 23 months before testing. A comparison group consisted of patients with the same disease who had not experienced surgery. Lack of significant differences between groups led the investigators to conclude that these forms of surgery have no lasting effects on cognitive or perceptual functioning, on body image or personality.

In a more obviously contrived investigation, Roberts, Dinsdale, Matthews, and Cole (1969) used operant methods to modify undesirable self-care behavior in a hemicorporectomized patient. The patient was successfully taught to prevent decubitus ulcers by being given reinforcement for proper care of his own skin. Operant methods are deservedly becoming more popular in rehabilitation settings (Michael, 1970; Shontz, 1970) as a means for managing client behavior. Whether these methods exert a significant influence on personality processes as well as on overt behavior remains to be seen.

The overall lack of experimental research is a serious deficiency in the literature on personality and disability. Investigators must ask less often "what are people with disabilities like?" and more often "what effects do specific events have upon the behavior of people with disabilities?" This requires an experimental attitude.

SUMMARY AND CONCLUSIONS

Two hypotheses dominate the literature on disability and personality. One hypothesis is that many (if not all) forms of somatic disability are associated with particular forms of personality. The other hypothesis is that the extent of the effects of disability on personality are proportional to the severity of disability. Both hypotheses are derivable from the assumption that all psychological effects of disability are negative, i.e., disruptive, dissatisfying, and disorganizing.

Previous reviews of the literature have concluded that there is virtually no support for these hypotheses or for the assumption with which they have so much in common. The present survey discloses no evidence to challenge that conclusion.

Several generalizations are suggested by the recent literature :

First, basic personality structure appears to be remarkably stable even in the face of serious somatic change. Such disorganization as occurs is generally transient, even though it may be severe in many cases.

Second, illness and disability (regardless of type) produce general increases in depression and somatic concern, but they do not necessarily raise the level of manifest anxiety. Absence of anxiety is often a sign of good adjustment and is not always presumptive evidence of the operation of the mechanism of denial.

Third, negative emotional experiences, such as depression and despair, are sometimes associated with improvement in somatic status as well as with the onset of disability or disease. The crucial factor seems to be sudden change in an enduring somatic state rather than illness or health, per se.

Methodologically, there is a need for descriptive research that is sufficiently comprehensive in scope to provide necessary information in compact and usable form. More attention should be paid to relations among psychological variables, and less effort should be devoted to the search for correlations between somatic variables and behavioral responses. Few studies are sufficiently naturalistic in design to permit ready application of findings to the rehabilitation situation. There is a paucity of needed experimental research with a psychological orientation.

Studies of disability and personality often appear to be investigations of convenience, rather than programs of investigation designed to pursue to the end the answer to some particular question. As a result, much valuable time and talent is wasted, not only in the conduct of unproductive research, but also in the rapid accumulation of uninstructive reports which others must periodically take the time to review.

REFERENCES

Aaron, N. S. Some personality differences between asthmatic, allergic, and normal children. *Journal of Clinical Psychology*, 1967, 23, 336–340.

Abel, T. M. Facial disfigurement. In J. F. Garrett (Ed.) *Psychological aspects of physical disability*. (Rehabilitation Service Series No. 210.) Washington, D.C. : Office of Vocational Rehabilitation, Department of Health, Education and Welfare, 1953. Pp. 112–124.

Abram, H. S. Adaptation to open heart surgery : A psychiatric study of response to the threat of death. *American Journal of Psychiatry*, 1965, 122, 659–667.

Abram, H. S. The psychiatrist, the treatment of chronic renal failure, and the prolongation of life : I. *American Journal of Psychiatry*, 1968, 124, 1351–1358.

Abram, H. S. The psychiatrist, the treatment of chronic renal failure, and the prolongation of life : II. *American Journal of Psychiatry*, 1969, 126, 157–162.

Allen, R. M. Cerebral palsy. In J. F. Garrett and E. S. Levine (Eds.) *Psychological practices with the physically disabled.* New York : Columbia University Press, 1962. Pp. 159–196.

Antonovsky, A. Social class and the major cardiovascular diseases. *Journal of Chronic Diseases*, 1968, 21, 65–106.

Appley, M. H. and Trumbull, R. *Psychological stress.* New York : Appleton-Century-Crofts, 1967.

Atkinson, J. and Feather, N. *A theory of achievement motivation.* New York : Wiley, 1966.

Atkinson, R. M. and Ringuette, E. L. A survey of biographical and psychological features in extraordinary fatness. *Psychosomatic Medicine*, 1967, 29, 121–133.

Barker, R. G. and Wright, B. A. The social psychology of adjustment to physical disability. In J. F. Garrett (Ed.) *Psychological aspects of physical disability.* (Rehabilitation Services Series No. 210.) Washington, D.C. : Office of Vocational Rehabilitation, Department of Health, Education and Welfare, 1953. Pp. 18–32.

Barker, R. G., Wright, B. A., and Gonick, M. R. *Adjustment to physical handicap and illness: A survey of the social psychology of physique and disability.* New York : Social Science Research Council, Bull. 55, 1946.

Barker, R. G., Wright, B. A., Meyerson, L., and Gonick, M. R. *Adjustment to physical handicap and illness: A survey of the social psychology of physique and disability* (rev. ed.) New York : Social Science Research Council, Bull. 55, 1953.

Barry, J. R. and Malinovsky, M. R. *Client motivation for rehabilitation: A review.* Gainesville, Fla. : Regional Rehabilitation Research Institute, University of Florida, 1965.

Belmont, I., Benjamin, H., Ambrose, J., and Restuccia, R. D. Effect of cerebral damage on motivation in rehabilitation. *Archives of Physical Medicine and Rehabilitation*, 1969, 50, 507–511.

Berger, S. Paraplegia. In J. F. Garrett (Ed.) *Psychological aspects of physical disability* (Rehabilitation Service Series No. 210.) Washington, D.C. : Office of Vocational Rehabilitation, Department of Health, Education and Welfare, 1953. Pp. 46–59.

Bortner, R. W. and Rosenman, R. H. The measurement of pattern A behavior. *Journal of Chronic Diseases,* 1967, 20, 525–533.

Caffrey, B. Reliability and validity of personality and behavioral measures in a study of coronary heart disease. *Journal of Chronic Diseases,* 1968, 21, 191–204.

Caffrey, B. Behavior patterns and personality characteristics related to prevalence rates of coronary heart disease in American monks. *Journal of Chronic Diseases,* 1969, 22, 93–103.

Cobb, B. Cancer. In J. F. Garrett and E. S. Levine (Eds.) *Psychological practices with the physically disabled.* New York : Columbia University Press, 1962. Pp. 231–260.

Cohn, N. Understanding the process of adjustment to disability. *Journal of Rehabilitation,* 1961, 27(b), 16–18.

Cowen, E. L. Personality, motivation, and clinical phenomena. In L. H. Lofquist (Ed.) *Psychological research and rehabilitation.* Washington, D.C. : American Psychological Association, 1960. Pp. 112–171.

Cowen, E. L. and Bobgrove, P. H. Marginality of disability and adjustment. *Perceptual and Motor Skills,* 1966, 23, 869–870.

Crumpton, E., Wine, D. B., and Groot, H. MMPI profiles of obese men and six other diagnostic categories. *Psychological Reports,* 1966, 19, 1110.

Davis, F. *Passage through crisis: Polio victims and their families.* New York : Bobbs-Merrill, 1963.

DeCencio, D. V., Leshner, M., and Leshner, B. Personality characteristics of patients with chronic obstructive pulmonary emphysema. *Archives of Physical Medicine and Rehabilitation,* 1968, 49, 471–475.

DeLateur, B. J., Lehmann, J. F., Winterscheid, L. C., Wolf, J. A., Fordyce, W. E., and Simons, B. C. Rehabilitation of the patient after hemicorporectomy. *Archives of Physical Medicine and Rehabilitation,* 1969, 50, 11–16.

Dembo, T., Ladieu-Leviton, G., and Wright, B. A. Acceptance of loss— amputations. In J. F. Garrett (Ed.) *Psychological aspects of physical disability.* (Rehabilitation Service Series No. 210.) Washington, D.C. : Office of Vocational Rehabilitation, Department of Health Education and Welfare, 1953. Pp. 80–96.

Dembo, T., Leviton, G. L., and Wright, B. A. Adjustment to misfortune— a problem of social psychological rehabilitation. *Artificial Limbs,* 1956, 3, 4–62.

DeWolfe, A. S., Barrell, R. P., and Cummings, J. W. Patient variables in emotional response to hospitalization for physical illness. *Journal of Consulting Psychology,* 1968, 30, 68–72.

Diller, L. Hemiplegia. In J. F. Garrett and E. S. Levine (Eds.) *Psychological practices with the physically disabled.* New York : Columbia University Press, 1962. Pp. 125–158.

Dlin, B. M., Perlman, A., and Ringold, E. Psychosexual response to ileostomy and colostomy. *American Journal of Psychiatry*, 1969, 126, 374–378.

Eisendrath, R. M. The role of grief and fear in the death of kidney transplant patients. *American Journal of Psychiatry*, 1969, 126, 381–387.

Ferguson, S. M. and Rayport, M. The adjustment to living without epilepsy. *Journal of Nervous and Mental Disease*, 1965, 140, 26–37.

Fiebert, M. Cognitive styles in the deaf. *Perceptual and Motor Skills*, 1967, 24, 319–329.

Fink, S. L. Crisis and motivation : A theoretical model. *Archives of Physical Medicine and Rehabilitation*, 1967, 48, 592–597.

Fisher, S., and Cleveland, S. E. *Body image and personality* (rev. ed.) New York : Dover, 1968.

Fishman, S. Amputation. In J. F. Garrett and E. S. Levine (Eds.) *Psychological practices with the physically disabled.* New York : Columbia University Press, 1962. Pp. 1–50.

Frank, L. K. Image of the self. In G. Leviton (Ed.) *The relationship between rehabilitation and psychology.* Washington, D.C. : U.S. Department of Health, Education and Welfare, 1959. Pp. 26–35.

Fras, I., Litin, E. M., and Pearson, J. S. Comparison of psychiatric symptoms in carcinoma of the pancreas with those in some other intra-abdominal neoplasms. *American Journal of Psychiatry*, 1967, 123, 1553–1562.

Frieden, F. H., Gertler, M. Tosberg, W., and Rusk, H. A. Rehabilitation after hemicorporectomy. *Archives of Physical Medicine and Rehabilitation*, 1969, 50, 259–263.

Garrett, J. F. Cerebral palsy. In J. F. Garrett (Ed.) *Psychological aspects of physical disability* (Rehabilitation Service Series No. 210.) Washington, D.C. : Office of Vocational Rehabilitation, Department of Health, Education and Welfare, 1953. Pp. 60–67.

Geist, H. Psychological aspects of rheumatoid arthritis. *Proceedings, 77th Annual convention, American Psychological Association*, 1969, Pp. 769–770.

Gladston, R. and Gamble, W. J. On borrowed time : Observations of children with implanted cardiac pacemakers and their families. *American Journal of Psychiatry*, 1969, 126, 104–108.

Glass, D. C., Lavin, D. E., Henchy, T., Gordon, A., Mayhew, P., and Donohoe, P. Obesity and persuasibility. *Journal of Personality*, 1969, 37, 407–414.

Gluck, M. R., McWilliams, B. J., Wylie, H. L., and Conkwright, E. A. Comparison of clinical characteristics of children with cleft palates and children in a child guidance center. *Perceptual and Motor Skills*, 1965, 21, 806.

Goldfarb, C., Driesen, J., and Cole, D. Psychobiologic aspects of malignancy. *American Journal of Psychiatry*, 1967, 123, 1545–1552.

Goldman, J. and Schwab, J. J. Medical illness and patients' attitudes: Somatopsychic relationships. *Journal of Nervous and Mental Disease*, 1966, 141, 678–683.

Goldstein, K. What can we learn from pathology for normal psychology. In G. Leviton (Ed.) *The relationship between rehabilitation and psychology.* Washington, D.C.: U.S. Department of Health, Education and Welfare, 1959. Pp. 36–61.

Goldstein, N. P., Ewert, J. C., Randall, R. V., and Gross, J. B. Psychiatric aspects of Wilson's disease (hepatolenticular degeneration): Results of psychometric tests during long-term therapy. *American Journal of Psychiatry*, 1968, 124, 1555–1561.

Green, R. Asthma and manic-depressive psychosis—simultaneously incompatible or coexistent? *Journal of Nervous and Mental Disease*, 1965, 140, 64–70.

Guze, S. B. The occurrence of psychiatric illness in systemic lupus erythematosus. *American Journal of Psychiatry*, 1967, 123, 1562–1570.

Hallenbeck, P. A. *Dogmatism and visual loss.* (Research Series No. 17.) New York: American Foundation for the Blind, 1967.

Hardyk, C. D., Chun, K., and Engel, B. T. Personality and marital-adjustment differences in essential hypertension in women. *Journal of Consulting Psychology*, 1966, 30, 459.

Harris, D. H. Psychological aspects of tuberculosis. In J. F. Garrett (Ed.) *Psychological aspects of physical disability.* (Rehabilitation Service Series No. 210.) Washington, D.C.: Office of Vocational Rehabilitation, Department of Health, Education and Welfare, 1953, Pp. 97–111.

Harrower, M. R. Psychological factors in multiple sclerosis. In J. F. Garrett (Ed.) *Psychological aspects of physical disability.* (Rehabilitation Service Series No. 210.) Washington, D.C.: Office of Vocational Rehabilitation, Department of Health, Education and Welfare, 1953. Pp. 68–79.

Heider, F. *The psychology of interpersonal relations.* New York: Wiley, 1958.

Henrichs, T. F., MacKenzie, J. W., and Almond, C. H. Psychological adjustment and acute response to open heart surgery. *Journal of Nervous and Mental Disease*, 1969, 148, 158–164.

Hirschenfang, S., Cosla, H. W., and Benton, J. G. Anxiety in a patient with bilateral hip disarticulation: Preliminary report. *Perceptual and Motor Skills*, 1966, 23, 41–42.

Hovey, H. B. MMPI testing for multiple sclerosis. *Psychological Reports*, 1967, 21, 599–600.

Ibrahim, M. A., Jenkins, C. D., Cassell, J. C., McDonough, J. R., and

Hames, C. G. Personality traits and coronary heart disease. *Journal of Chronic Diseases,* 1966, 19, 255–271.

Jarvis, J. H. Post-mastectomy breast phantoms. *Journal of Nervous and Mental Disease,* 1967, 144, 266–272.

Jenkins, C. D., Rosenman, R. H., and Friedman, M. Development of an objective psychological test for the determination of the coronary-prone behavior pattern in employed men. *Journal of Chronic Diseases,* 1967, 20, 371–379.

Kaplan, M. F. and Lotsof, E. J. Are the principles of behavior of "exceptional children" exceptional? *Psychological Reports,* 1968, 23, 1207–1213.

Karp, S. A. and Pardes, H. Psychological differentiation (field dependence) in obese women. *Psychosomatic Medicine,* 1965, 27, 238–244.

Keith, R. A. Personality and coronary heart disease : A review. *Journal of Chronic Diseases,* 1966, 19, 1231–1243.

Keith, R. A. The need for a new model in rehabilitation. *Journal of Chronic Diseases,* 1968, 21, 281–286.

Keith, R. A., Lown, B., and Stare, F. J. Coronary heart disease and behavior patterns. *Psychosomatic Medicine,* 1965, 27, 424–434.

Kelley, H. H., Hastorf, A. H., Jones, E. E., Thibault, J. W., and Usdane, W. M. Some implications of social psychological theory for research on the handicapped. In L. H. Lofquist (Ed.) *Psychological research and rehabilitation.* Washington, D.C. : American Psychological Association, 1960. Pp. 172–204.

Kemph, J. P. Renal failure, artificial kidney and kidney transplant. *American Journal of Psychiatry,* 1966, 122, 1270–1274.

Kemph, J. P. Psychotherapy with patients receiving kidney transplants. *American Journal of Psychiatry,* 1967, 124, 623–629.

Kemph, J. P., Berman, E. A., and Coppolillo, H. P. Kidney transplant and shifts in family dynamics. *American Journal of Psychiatry,* 1969, 125, 1485–1490.

Kimball, C. P. Psychological responses to experience of open heart surgery : I. *American Journal of Psychiatry,* 1969, 126, 348–359.

Kleck, R. Emotional arousal in interaction with stigmatized persons. *Psychological Reports,* 1966, 19, 1226.

Kleck, R. Self-disclosure patterns of the nonobviously disabled. *Psychological Reports,* 1968, 23, 1239–1248.

Klein, H. P. and Parsons, O. A. Self descriptions of patients with coronary disease. *Perceptual and Motor Skills,* 1968, 26, 1099.

Knapp, P. H. The asthmatic and his environment. *Journal of Nervous and Mental Disease,* 1969, 149, 133–151.

Koenig, R., Levin, S. M., and Brennan, M. J. The emotional status of cancer patients as measured by a psychological test. *Journal of Chronic Diseases,* 1967, 20, 923–930.

Krug, R. S. MMPI response inconsistency of brain damaged individuals. *Journal of Clinical Psychology*, 1967, 23, 366.

Krystal, H. (Ed.) *Massive psychic trauma*. New York : International Universities Press, 1968.

Kunce, J. T., and Worley, B. H. Interest patterns, accidents and disability. *Journal of Clinical Psychology*, 1966, 22, 105–107.

Lahav, E. Methodological problems in behavioral research on disease. *Journal of Chronic Diseases*, 1967, 20, 333–340.

Lane, H. S. The hard of hearing. In J. F. Garrett (Ed.) *Psychological aspects of physical disability*. (Rehabilitation Service Series No. 210.) Washington, D.C. : Office of Vocational Rehabilitation, Department of Health, Education and Welfare, 1953. Pp. 147–161.

Lansdell, H. Effect of extent of temporal lobe surgery and neuropathology on the MMPI. *Journal of Clinical Psychology*, 1968, 24, 406–412.

Lazarus, H. R., and Hagens, J. H. Prevention of psychosis following open-heart surgery. *American Journal of Psychiatry*, 1968, 124, 1190–1195.

Lazarus, R. S. *Psychological stress and the coping process*. New York : McGraw-Hill, 1966.

Levine, E. S. The deaf. In J. F. Garrett (Ed.) *Psychological aspects of physical disability*. (Rehabilitation Service Series No. 210.) Washington, D.C. : Office of Vocational Rehabilitation, Department of Health, Education and Welfare, 1953. Pp. 125–146.

Levine, E. S. Auditory disability. In J. F. Garrett and E. S. Levine (Eds.) *Psychological practices with the physically disabled*. New York : Columbia University Press, 1962. Pp. 279–340.

Lifton, R. J. *Death in life: Survivors of Hiroshima*. New York : Random House, 1967.

Lowenfeld, B. The blind. In J. F. Garrett (Ed.) *Psychological aspects of physical disability*. (Rehabilitation Service Series No. 210.) Washington, D.C. : Office of Vocational Rehabilitation, Department of Health, Education and Welfare, 1953. Pp. 179–195.

Ludwig, E. G. and Wysong, J. Work, heart disease and mental health. *Journal of Chronic Diseases*, 1969, 21, 687–689.

Lunde, D. T. Psychiatric complications of heart transplants. *American Journal of Psychiatry*, 1969, 126, 369–373.

MacDonald, A. P. and Hall, J. Perception of disability by the nondisabled. *Journal of Consulting and Clinical Psychology*, 1969, 33, 654–660.

Madan, R. Facial disfigurement. In J. F. Garrett and E. S. Levine (Eds.) *Psychological practices with the physically disabled*. New York : Columbia University Press, 1962. Pp. 261–278.

Maslow, A. H. *Motivation and personality*. New York : Harper, 1954.

Mattson, A. and Gross, S. Adaptational and defensive behavior in young hemophiliacs and their parents. *American Journal of Psychiatry*, 1966, 122, 1349–1356.

McDaniel, J. W. *Physical disability and human behavior.* Elmsford, N.Y. : Pergamon Press, 1969.

McFarland, D. D. and Cobbs, S. C. Causal interpretations for cross-sectional data. *Journal of Chronic Diseases,* 1967, 20, 393–406.

Meier, M. J. and French, L. A. Some personality correlates of unilateral and bilateral EEG abnormalities in psychomotor epileptics. *Journal of Clinical Psychology,* 1965, 21, 3–9.

Menninger, K. A. Psychiatric aspects of physical disability. In J. F. Garrett (Ed.) *Psychological aspects of physical disability.* (Rehabilitation Service Series No. 210.) Washington, D.C. : Office of Vocational Rehabilitation, Department of Health, Education and Welfare, 1953. Pp. 8–17.

Meyerson, L. Somatopsychology of physical disability. In W. M. Cruickshank (Ed.) *Psychology of exceptional children and youth.* Englewood Cliffs, N.J. : Prentice-Hall, 1955, 1–60.

Michael, J. L. Rehabilitation. In C. Neuringer and J. Michael (Eds.) *Behavior modification in clinical psychology.* New York : Appleton-Century-Crofts, 1970.

Miller, C. K. Psychological correlates of coronary artery disease. *Psychosomatic Medicine,* 1965, 27, 257–265.

Mitchell, K. R. The body image variable and level of adjustment to stress induced by severe physical disability. *Journal of Clinical Psychology,* 1970, 26, 49–52.

Moos, R. H. and Solomon, G. F. MMPI response patterns in patients with rheumatoid arthritis. *Journal of Psychosomatic Research,* 1964, 8, 17–28.

Moos, R. H. and Solomon, G. F. Psychologic comparisons between women with rheumatoid arthritis and their nonarthritic sisters : I. Personality tests and interview rating data. *Psychosomatic Medicine,* 1965, 27, 135–149. (a)

Moos, R. H. and Solomon, G. F. Psychologic comparisons between women with rheumatoid arthritis and their nonarthritic sisters : II. Content analysis of interviews. *Psychosomatic Medicine,* 1965, 27, 150–164. (b)

Mordkoff, A. M. and Golas, R. M. Coronary artery disease and responses to the Rosenzweig Picture-Frustration Study. *Journal of Abnormal Psychology,* 1968, 73, 381–386.

Mordkoff, A. M. and Parsons, O. A. The coronary personality : A critique. *Psychosomatic Medicine,* 1967, 29, 1–14.

Mordkoff, A. M. and Rand, M. A. Personality and adaptation to coronary artery disease. *Journal of Consulting and Clinical Psychology,* 1968, 32, 648–653.

Murphy, W. F. Some clinical aspects of the body ego, with special reference to phantom limb phenomena. *Psychoanalytic Review,* 1957, 44, 462–477.

Nalven, F. B. and O'Brien, J. F. On the use of the MMPI with rheumatoid arthritic patients. *Journal of Clinical Psychology*, 1968, 24, 70.

Palmer, J. M. and Adams, M. R. The oral image of children with cleft lips and palates. *Cleft Palate Bulletin*, 1962, 12, 73–76.

Parsons, T. *Social structure and personality*. New York: Free Press of Glencoe, 1964.

Parsons, T. and Fox, R. Illness, therapy, and the modern urban American family. *Journal of Social Issues*, 1952, 8, 31–44.

Patterson, C. H. A unitary theory of motivation and its counseling applications. *Journal of Individual Psychology*, 1964, 20, 17–31.

Ponomareff, G. L. Phenomenology of delusions in a case of leprosy. *American Journal of Psychiatry*, 1965, 121, 1211.

Pringle, M. L. K. The emotional and social readjustment of physically handicapped children : A review of the literature between 1928 and 1962. *Educational Research*, 1964, 6, 207–215.

Raskin, N. J. Visual disability. In J. F. Garrett and E. S. Levine (Eds.) *Psychological practices with the physically disabled*. New York: Columbia University Press, 1962. Pp. 341–375.

Riklan, M., Levita, E. and Cooper, I. S. Psychological effects of bilateral subcortical surgery for Parkinson's disease. *Journal of Nervous and Mental Disease*, 1966, 141, 403–409.

Roberts, A. H., Dinsdale, S. M., Mathews, R. E. and Cole, T. M. Modifying persistent undesirable behavior in a medical setting. *Archives of Physical Medicine and Rehabilitation*, 1969, 50, 147–153.

Rokeach, M. *The open and closed mind*. New York: Basic Books, 1960.

Ruess, A. L. A comparative study of cleft palate children and their siblings. *Journal of Clinical Psychology*, 1965, 21, 354–360.

Schilder, P. *The image and appearance of the human body*. New York: International Universities Press, 1950. (Orig. publ. 1935.)

Schwab, J. J., Marder, L., Clemmons, R. S., and McGinnis, N. H. Anxiety, severity of illness and other medical variables. *Journal of Psychosomatic Research*, 1966, 10, 297–303.

Schwartz, M. L., Dennerll, R. D., and Lin, Y. Neuropsychological and psychological predictors of employability in epilepsy. *Journal of Clinical Psychology*, 1968, 24, 174–177.

Seidenfeld, M. A. Psychological problems of poliomyelitis. In J. F. Garrett (Ed.) *Psychological aspects of physical disability*. (Rehabilitation Service Series No. 210.) Washington, D.C.: Office of Vocational Rehabilitation, Department of Health, Education and Welfare, 1953. Pp. 33–45.

Seidenfeld, M. A. Arthritis and rheumatism. In J. F. Garrett and E. S. Levine (Eds.) *Psychological practices with the physically disabled*. New York: Columbia University Press, 1962. Pp. 51–84.

Shaw, D. J., and Matthews, C. G. Differential MMPI performance of brain-damaged vs. pseudo-neurologic groups. *Journal of Clinical Psychology*, 1965, 21, 405–408.

Shontz, F. C. Severe chronic illness. In J. F. Garrett and E. S. Levine (Eds.) *Psychological practices with the physically disabled.* New York : Columbia University Press, 1962. Pp. 410–445.

Shontz, F. C. Reaction to crisis. *Volta Review*, 1965, 67, 364–370.

Shontz, F. C. *Perceptual and cognitive aspects of body experience.* New York : Academic Press, 1969.

Shontz, F. C. The problems and promises of psychological research in rehabilitation. In E. P. Trapp and P. Himelstein (Eds.) *The exceptional child: Research and theory.* New York : Appleton-Century-Crofts, 1970.

Shontz, F. C., Fink, S. L. and Hallenbeck, C. E. Chronic physical illness as threat. *Archives of Physical Medicine and Rehabilitation*, 1960, 41, 143–148.

Siller, J., Chipman, A., Ferguson, L., and Vann, D. H. *Studies in reactions to disability. XI: Attitudes of the nondisabled toward the physically disabled.* New York : New York University, School of Education, 1967.

Small, J. G., Small, I. F., and Hayden, M. P. Further psychiatric investigations of patients with temporal and nontemporal lobe epilepsy. *American Journal of Psychiatry*, 1966, 123, 303–310.

Stone, F. B., Rowley, V. N. and MacQueen, J. C. Using the MMPI with adolescents who have somatic symptoms. *Psychological Reports*, 1966, 18, 139–147.

Swift, C. R., Seidman, F. and Stein, H. Adjustment problems in juvenile diabetes. *Psychosomatic Medicine*, 1967, 29, 555–571.

Thibault, J. W. and Kelley, H. H. *The social psychology of groups.* New York : Wiley, 1959.

Thoroughman, J. C., Pascal, G. R., Jarvis, J. R., and Crutcher, J. C. A study of psychological factors in patients with surgically intractable duodenal ulcer and those with other interactable disorders. *Psychosomatic Medicine*, 1967, 29, 273–283.

Tizard, B. The personality of epileptics : A discussion of the evidence. *Psychological Bulletin*, 1962, 59, 196–210.

Warren, L. W. and Weiss, D. J. Relationship between disability type and measured personality characteristics. *Proceedings, 77th Annual Convention, American Psychological Association*, 1969. Pp. 773–774.

Watson, C. G. and Thomas, R. W. MMPI profiles of brain-damaged and schizophrenic patients. *Perceptual and Motor Skills*, 1968, 27, 567–573.

Weigand, E. L. and Dawson, J. G. Response patterns of Hansen's disease patients on the perceptual reaction test. *Journal of Clinical Psychology*, 1967, 23, 452–454.

Weiss, A. J. and Diamond, M. D. Psychologic adjustment of patients with myelopathy. *Archives of Physical Medicine and Rehabilitation*, 1966, 47, 72–76.

Weiss, S. M. Psychological adjustment following open-heart surgery. *Journal of Nervous and Mental Disease*, 1966, 143, 363–368.

Wepman, J. M. The language disorders. In J. F. Garrett and E. S. Levine (Eds.) *Psychological practices with the physically disabled*. New York : Columbia University Press, 1962. Pp. 197–230.

Werkman, S. L. and Greenberg, E. S. Personality and interest patterns in obese adolescent girls. *Psychosomatic Medicine*, 1967, 29, 72–80.

Werner, A. and Folk, J. J. Manifestations of neurotic conflict in Huntington's chorea. *Journal of Nervous and Mental Disease*, 1968, 147, 141–147.

Whitehouse, F. A. Cardiovascular disability. In J. F. Garrett and E. S. Levine (Eds.) *Psychological practices with the physically disabled*. New York : Columbia University Press, 1962. Pp. 85–124.

Willems, E. P. and Raush, H. L. (Eds.) *Naturalistic viewpoints in psychological research*. New York : Holt, Rinehart and Winston, 1969.

Wolowitz, H. M. Oral involvement in peptic ulcer. *Journal of Consulting Psychology*, 1967, 31, 418–419.

Wright, B. A. *Physical disability—A psychological approach*. New York : Harper and Row, 1960.

Wright, B. A. The question stands : Should a person be realistic? *Rehabilitation Counseling Bulletin*, 1968, 11, 291–296.

Wright, B. A. and Shontz, F. C. Process and tasks in hoping. *Rehabilitation Literature*, 1968, 29(11), 322–331.

Young, M. A. C. The partially seeing. In J. F. Garrett (Ed.) *Psychological aspects of physical disability*. (Rehabilitation Service Series No. 210.) Washington, D.C. : Office of Vocational Rehabilitation, Department of Health, Education and Welfare, 1953. Pp. 162–195.

Yuker, H. E., Block, J. R., and Campbell, W. J. *A scale to measure attitudes toward disabled persons*. Albertson, N.Y. : Human Resources Foundation, 1960.

Yuker, H. E., Block, J. R. and Younng, J. H. *The measurement of attitudes toward disabled persons*. Albertson, N.Y. : Human Resources Foundation, 1966.

Zunich, M. and Ledwith, B. E. Self-concepts of visually handicapped and sighted children. *Perceptual and Motor Skills*, 1965, 21, 771–774.

10

The Problem of Personal Worth
in the Physically Disabled Patient

H. Jon Geis

In the spring of 1963 I presented a convention paper on the subject of personal worth as a psychological problem in the rehabilitation of physically disabled patients. For the several years prior to this time I had worked intensively and exclusively with such patients at major rehabilitation centers in the New York City area, and I had become convinced of the importance of this problem as it existed in the core of the psychodynamic blockages, which, I felt, held the key to the individual's successful physical and emotional rehabilitation.

Since 1963 I have been heavily engaged in a more than full-time private psychotherapy practice in which I have seen many hundreds of patients in a wide variety of diagnostic categories. I have found the problem of personal worth to be the central psychodynamic problem of all patients, not just those with physical disabilities, and I have spent a good deal of time developing techniques and theory appropriate for its full consideration. This material, not appropriate for inclusion here, is presently being integrated into a lengthy consideration of counseling and psychotherapy for eventual presentation in book form.

However, in the years since 1963 I have had increasing misgivings about my failure to make my original convention paper available to a wider public, particularly to rehabilitation professionals. I have therefore decided to publish it. Although nine years have passed since it was written, it is my judgment that the material is more relevant and timely than ever. The passages that follow constitute, with the exception of some editorial changes, the same paper as that originally presented to an audience of professional rehabilitation workers at the 1963 convention.

From *Rehabilitation Literature*, *33* (1972), 34–39. Copyright © 1972 by the National Easter Seal Society for Crippled Children and Adults. Reprinted by permission of the Editor.

The Person, Personal Worth, and Value

What is a person worth? This is a simple yet searching question. It is a question every man consciously directs toward himself at one time or another, in some form such as "Am I worth it?" or "Am I worthwhile?" At times it is expressed in the negative: "I am worthless, no good, a nothing." More often the person is aware of his negative self-appraisal as a feeling of worthlessness or inadequacy, rather than a clear cognitive idea. Beyond these relatively conscious expressions, however, the sense of one's own worth, high or low, appears to be a relatively stable and ongoing aspect of one's identity or self-concept, lying for the most part out of awareness.

We might ask whether "worth" is really anything more than just another term that is used to stand for self-esteem or a related self-description, whether it is really a phenomenon in its own right and justifies inquiry. Many investigators apparently do not view self-worth as an important aspect of one's self-evaluation. In Wylie's[13] review of studies dealing with the self-concept there are only 2 studies dealing specifically with "self-worth" out of a list of approximately 480 references. However, to those who work closely with the physically disabled there is strong clinical evidence that the term is meaningful in its own right: Our rehabilitation centers and agencies are filled each day with persons who express in direct or hidden ways the feeling of being worthless. Depression, self-blame and self-hatred, blocked motivation, slowed behavior or pathological compensatory activity, and difficulties progressing on the rehabilitation program and in community adjustment—these are all concomitants of feelings of low worth. It therefore seems crucial that we, as professional helping persons in the rehabilitation field, try to understand the nature of the problem of personal worth and its implications for the distressed people with whom we work.

Let us begin by defining the term *worth*. English and English,[3] in their *Dictionary of Psychological and Psychoanalytical Terms*, define worth essentially as follows: "The value placed by a given person upon something." This tells us that worth has to do with value, for our purposes, the value a disabled person places upon himself. The logical aspect of our problem, then, falls within the scope of axiology, which is the scientific study of values and evaluation. The study of values has, of course, been pursued for thousands of years as a specialty within philosophy.

Our question now is: What does it mean when we say that a physically disabled patient values or does not value himself?

If something is of value it is a positive thing for us—that is, we have an approach valence regarding it—and it is so because it is actually or potentially capable of giving satisfaction to us. The physically disabled patient values himself positively, or feels worthwhile, when he perceives himself as giving or being capable of giving satisfaction to himself now or at some future time. Beyond the simple requirement that a thing be satisfying to us for it to be of value, the value problem gets more complex.

Here it is important to be aware of what is continually a controversy among value theorists, namely the location of values—whether value resides in the object valued (e.g., an automobile), in the object valued and also in the person doing the valuing (i.e., in the relationship between the automobile and the person), or only in the person doing the valuing.

Smith,[11] in his monograph on *Value Convictions and Higher Education*, warns against confusing the three locations and says that at any one time "value" may mean one or more of these: "Value may mean *what* is chosen, the fact *that* something is an object of choice and is preferred, and *why* it is chosen." The third location—the *why*—is value as it resides in the personality or in the character structure of the person; it is, as Smith refers to it, "a criterion or standard for decision-making." When we speak of a value in the personality we refer to a basic, emotionally embedded disposition of the person to behave in terms of some abstract concept of worth. A collection of these basic values may be referred to as a value orientation, as for example Erich Fromm's marketing orientation, Holland's[5] motoric orientation, or one's orientation toward oneself, often called the self-concept.

The first location, value residing in the object, is called a value preference when it is indicated as an object of value by the person. When a patient states a preference for himself, as, for example, when a paraplegic young man says he likes himself when he ambulates on crutches, he may say this because being on crutches makes him feel more independent, more powerful, or more attractive. That is, any one of a number of values in the patient's personality may account for the same value preference, liking oneself as a person who ambulates.

Smith's analysis is based on an examination of what he calls "the human capacity for evaluation" as it is represented in the act of valuing. He says[11] that "the ability to respond . . . in a critical way . . . is at the basis of all discussion concerning what has come to be called *value*" (p. 8). The critical response has three essential components: (a) awareness of a contrast in experience, so that we may be able to say that one alternative is better than another; (b) a criterion, or standard for decision-making, so that we may be able to make a judgment; (c) relevant knowledge of the situation. The most important component of the critical response—the part that, for Smith, is value—is the criterion: "Unless the critical question is raised concerning the criterion of the preference or choice and its *binding force* upon us, we are as far from the center of value as we can be" (p. 14). *"For the value aspect resides in the criterion determining the critical response."*

Hartman[4] has made the same point in a different way. In asking how we know what is good, which is another way of talking about what is of positive value, he concludes that Good is a property not of objects but of concepts. . . . whenever the word 'good' is used, a logical operation is performed : we combine the properties of the concept of the thing with the idea of the particular thing that is said to be good (of value) . . . . The logical operation is the meaning of the word 'good' (or value'). . . . A thing is 'good' (of 'value') . . . if it has the qualities that define its concept. What Hartman is saying, in terms of our problem, is that the patient values himself to the extent that he fulfills his idea of the kind of person he should be. As we have seen earlier, this idea is rooted in one's basic value orientation toward oneself. Therefore, we may conclude, in agreement with the psychotherapy terminology of Ellis,[2] that it is the patient's definition of himself, as it is rooted in his basic value orientation toward himself, that allows him to feel of worth or of value to himself. If he basically defines himself as worthwhile or valuable to himself only when he fulfills his own values regarding the kind of person who is worthwhile and valuable—then he cannot feel worthwhile or valuable until he is that person.

Personal Worth Depends upon the Self-Definition

The paraplegic young man who focuses only on complete physical return, the once-beautiful actress who was disfigured by scalding water and continues to yearn for her former beauty, the teenage boy with the congenital limp who idealizes the normal physical status of his peers— these are people who continue to define their worth—that is, their value to themselves—in terms of a self-image that can never be, and necessarily, then, they cannot feel worthwhile. It is true, of course, that physical and social realities are ever-present reminders to the person that he is not getting and cannot get the same satisfactions from the environment and, hence, cannot give himself the same satisfactions that he was able to get with his former status. Yet the problem is still basically one of the individual's definition of himself, whatever the realistic opportunities for objective environmental benefits. The patient's definition of himself is the crucial factor determining in what ways he does or does not satisfy himself; that is, things outside of the patient do not satisfy the patient, but he satisfies himself in terms of these things. He is the arbiter of his satisfactions, and he determines his satisfactions by the way he defines or conceives of himself.

It might be argued, for example, that the patient may be made to feel worthwhile if he is told that God loves him or if others act toward him as if he is worthwhile. From a technical point of view, sometimes these techniques may work, but only if the patient first believes in God and defines himself in such a way that he values himself positively because he is loved by God. Similarly, he basically has to define himself as worthwhile because others treat him as worthwhile. His belief in the importance of being loved by God or being thought of as worthwhile by others permits him to feel satisfaction or, more correctly, to give himself satisfaction and thereby to value himself positively.

Let me pause a moment to note that the problems of value change have of course been dealt with by others in the rehabilitation field.[1] The present discussion is somewhat different, I think, because it focuses not only on the person as an object of his own value, but on the relationship between the notion of value and personal worth.

If, then, the patient's feelings of high or low worth, and the accompanying benefits and difficulties in adjustment, reality adaptation, and so on are contingent on his definition of himself, the problem is: What kind of definition of himself might the patient acquire so as not to feel worthless? Moreover, what can we do to help him toward a less self-defeating and more self-enhancing definition of himself?

To help us in thinking about ways to change the patient's self-definition, let us consider two other aspects of the personal worth experience, namely, the psychological meaning of feeling worthless and the problem of whether there is any such thing as intrinsic self-worth.

Our culture's great emphasis on the values of productivity and success on the one hand, and being attractive physically or in personality on the other, has been well documented by many writers. One might argue, with some success, I think, that any culture at least moderately encourages productivity and personal attractiveness because of the required nature of functioning in socially productive and esteemed roles —that is, as a worker and as "a person one would like to know." Our culture, however, emphasizes these goals so strongly that not to achieve them, or be on the way toward achieving them, tends to require feelings of worthlessness. These feelings are most dramatically noticeable in the traumatically injured patient whose ability to obtain satisfactions through productivity or attractiveness is suddenly cut off.

Operationally, as I have noted it in clinical work with patients, the basic ideational content, either openly expressed or thought, of feeling worthless as a result of the productivity value, appears to be: (a) I cannot be productive now; (b) I have always been unproductive; (c) I always will be unproductive and life is hopeless for me; (d) therefore, I am worthless and an awful person; (e) and, therefore, I might as well not exist. For the beautiful actress who is now disfigured the thinking is similar: (a) I am not attractive now; (b) I have always been unattractive; (c) I always will be unattractive; (d) therefore, I am worthless and an awful person; (e) and, therefore, I should not be living. Note here what is involved:

First, the patient's thinking that he cannot be productive or attractive now must undoubtedly be a distortion—there are very few cases where all of one's productivity or all of one's attractiveness is eliminated in all respects. A paraplegic may be productive in many ways, and an actress may be attractive in figure, dress, personality, and other ways. Feelings of low worth, like self-esteem, depression, and some other emotions, tend to be all-or-none in nature. That is, the emotion may be evoked by consideration of only one aspect of what is most often a complex situation, and the patient may feel, and conceive himself to be, "all" worthless. It is true that sometimes the attachment seems to be only to a particular aspect, such as productivity as a door-to-door salesman or attractiveness of face. But most often even these situations imply a general, more basic value orientation in terms of which assets related to productivity and attractiveness are still available. Here the notion of emphasis of new value areas, with consequent "value spread," as discussed by Wright,[12] is relevant.

Second, in our examples of the experience of feeling worthless, note that past and future time perspective is cut off or distorted: The patients are unable to conceive of themselves as ever having been productive or attractive in the past. They might provide themselves much satisfaction and feel more worthy in terms of what they did or were in the past, but they do not consider this. Further, they might derive satisfaction and worth from contemplation of possible changes in their condition in the future, that is, of their potential worth, but, similarly, they do not perceive this.

Third, the patients' conclusions, that they are worthless because they are unproductive or unattractive, in one sense are logically true because they are conclusions drawn from their arbitrary definitions of themselves. But this is a distortion because it assumes that worth is based only on the deficit feature, overlooking evidence about remaining assets and, perhaps, what might be called intrinsic worth. (I am worthwhile— I simply assert that I am—without the need to fulfill any conditions to be so.) Note also that the patients conclude that not only are they worthless but they are awful people, which implies that they expect rejection from other people and don't deserve anything else. Not only are they worthless but, to some extent, of negative value. Their thinking runs: "If I am not of value to myself, then I am not worth valuing, and others will reject me; that will be something terrible that I cannot stand. I must be an awful person." This kind of thinking may persist for long periods with great strength, and it may account for both withdrawal behavior and a frantic search for approval and love.

The last factor, where the patient feels that he should not exist, is a conclusion drawn from the patient's evaluation of himself as worth nothing, to himself or the world, and therefore his life is meaningless and empty. This is not to say that most or nearly all patients do not want to live, for I believe they do. However, the logical conclusion that the patient must draw from his irrational premises is that of ceasing to exist. I have seen this conclusion expressed at least partly in most patients, fully in many others, particularly soon after onset of the disability, and it is especially strong in those patients who have intense guilt feelings.

Intrinsic Worth—An Illusion?

Another important consideration is whether it is possible for one to value oneself intrinsically, that is, apart from any externally derived notion of what one should be. This notion is of course related to the concept of asset value, where a thing is valued for itself alone, versus comparative value, where a thing is valued according to whether it is better or worse than something else.[1] Here the object to be valued is the patient himself.

In general, people in our culture value themselves in extrinsic terms, that is, according to externally derived standards such as achievement, productivity, and attractiveness. As suggested earlier, intrinsic worth refers to the valuing of something simply in itself, without a criterion. Though desirable psychologically, this would appear to be an extremely difficult if not impossible goal to achieve in actuality. Perhaps it is a technical problem only. At this point I cannot be sure. But what it means is that the individual must be able to assert to himself that he is worthwhile or valuable without fulfilling any prior stipulated criterion. No conditions, no ifs, ands, or buts—he simply is worthwhile. At present (1963) the techniques for helping the patient achieve this state are, at best, unclear if not forever out of reach. For it does not appear possible for a person to value himself when there is no satisfaction-giving aspect of himself to value. On the other hand, it is hard to conceive of a patient who is completely unable to give himself satisfactions. But then this returns us to the framework of extrinsic or contingent value or worth. As we will see later on, I believe the psychology of Being may be employed to increase the patient's ability to get satisfactions from himself.

The Therapeutic Goal: Change the Self-Definition

Let us return now to the problem of changing the patient's self-definition from a self-defeating to a self-benefiting one. We have seen that the valuing aspect of the patient's definition of himself is anchored in his basic value orientation toward himself. Insofar as he yields himself satisfactions that meet his basic value standards, he values himself positively; when he does not, he tends to consider himself worthless or of negative value. The patient whose work productivity is limited by his recent disablement must learn to value productivity—or more correctly, to value himself as a productive person—as something desirable, preferred, and perhaps worth aspiring toward, but not as something necessary to his sense of worth. This is similar to the notion of asset value.

However, I think the therapeutic effort should be directed not only toward emphasizing the asset nature of the value, which seems to be the emphasis in the literature (e.g., B. A. Wright[12]), but it should also focus strongly on eliminating the need aspect of the value. That is, the patient should be taught, as Ellis suggests,[2] that he does not need or require fulfillment of his value orientation to live happily or to feel worthy. As Ellis points out, there are few if any things outside of the physiological needs that a person cannot do without, although he might not be as happy as he would be without these things as with them. The patient creates disturbance for himself when he believes—incorrectly— that he must produce at a certain level or that he must have an attractive face. He defines his situation so that he necessarily and inevitably feels worthless and an awful person because his requirement is fixed and absolute. Therapy involves showing the patient that he does not, actually, desperately need to attain a certain standard of productivity, that his dire need is really only a fixed belief, that this fixed belief necessarily causes him disturbance and prevents him from getting satisfactions that are attainable, and that he is better off valuing his goals, and thereby himself, preferentially rather than absolutely. When the patient learns to look at things this way, his basic value orientation will have changed and he will have defined himself differently.

We should remember, I think, that often it is a good idea for a patient to retain high standards for himself. Maladaptation and poor adjustment are promoted not by high standards per se, but by rigid, unrealistic, requirement-centered adherence to these standards, an adherence that by its very nature must result in feelings of low worth and self-blame when the goals generated by these standards are not attained.

The Psychology of Being in Rehabilitation Work

In addition to what we have already discussed, there would appear to be on the horizon a whole new set of ways to increase the patient's self-worth and promote good psychological adjustment. Due to space limitations I can go into this area only briefly.

When we look at ourselves as rehabilitation workers and when we look at our professional literature, it appears that we are wholly pre-occupied—often with as much intensity as our patients show—with helping the patient develop better ways of doing things; that is, to become more efficient at reaching goals (which is extrinsic valuing), rather than at least also setting out to help the patient learn simply to be, that is, to value things in themselves (which is intrinsic valuing). One notices no great emphasis in our field on techniques to facilitate asset or intrinsic valuing. However, in the last few years American psychology has begun to devote some concern to the psychology of Being, as for example in the writings of May[8] and Maslow.[7] Operations for attaining the Being state are rather vague, but it seems high time that these notions be thought through and tested out for application in work with the physically disabled.

Florence Kluckhohn,[6] in her schema of valued personality types, characterizes Mexican society as having a dominant Being orientation and the American culture as stressing Doing. Being is described as non-developmental, almost spontaneous activity which stresses the "isness" of the personality. This kind of activity is found, for example, in *fiesta* activities. Kluckhohn's Doing orientation has as its more distinguishing feature "its demand for action in the sense of accomplishment and in accord with standards which are conceived as being external to the acting individual," which is exemplified by the stock American phrases "getting things done" and finding ways "to do something." Kluckhohn describes a third value orientation, Being-in-Becoming, which she characterizes as a kind of self-actualization or self-development, a spontaneous yet somewhat controlled kind of activity that is carried out in the service of development of the individual's total integrated personality.

Henry Murray's[9] analysis is similar to Kluckhohn's yet more precise. His ungoverned or process activity appears to correspond to pure Being, "a state in which the mind moves in its own inherent manner for its own intrinsic pleasure" (p. 37). It is effortless and aimless, and marked by a continuous flow of ongoing activities. Close to Kluckhohn's Being-in-Becoming state is Murray's modal, or formal, activity. This, Murray notes, is closer to Being than to Doing. In modal activity satisfaction is concurrent with the activity. Illustrations are expressions and receptions of sensuous, dramatic, or comic patterns, such as ballet dancing and witnessing a ballet, or telling a funny story and laughing at it. A third type of activity, directional activity, corresponds to the Doing state, in that "satisfaction is linked with the ultimate effect (or goal) of the activity" (p. 14).

Maslow distinguishes Being behavior from Deficiency-motivated behavior. Being behavior, he says, "is released . . . expressive rather than coping" (p. 37), "non-striving, purposeless, self-validating" (p. 68). Being behavior is valued for its own sake and is concerned with end-experiences and end-values rather than with the means to reach them. Deficiency-motivated behavior is goal-oriented, instrumental behavior that seems to correspond to the Doing behavior described earlier.

A heightened state of Being is probably one of the results of psychotherapy, even though few therapists besides May and the existentialists write about it as such. Ellis's talk about helping the individual to "be himself" and Rogers'[10] therapeutic goal of "an increasing openness to experience," or having a less defensive and inhibited personality, suggest an implicit emphasis on Being in psychotherapy goals.

But what, you may ask, does all this have to do with promoting the patient's sense of personal worth? Simply this : There is no doubt that two, perhaps three, modes of behavior have been distinguished : Being, Being-in-Becoming or Becoming, and Doing. The physically disabled patient's definition of himself and therefore his sense of worth have been based, in most instances, exclusively on values attached to Doing behavior. When the patient is as a result of his disability less able to provide himself with satisfactions in terms of the Doing orientation, his sense of worth may be increased by helping him to derive satisfactions, and thereby to value himself more highly, by increasing his ability to have Being experiences.

There is not enough space remaining for me to explore some techniques for facilitating Being growth on the rehabilitation program. However, the following list of terms, which are aspects of the Being state, may stimulate you to think of your own techniques for facilitating Being : exploring, manipulating, experiencing, being interested, choosing, delighting, enjoying, organizing, simplifying, being truthful and experiencing truth, being playful, being unique, and being realistic. With what techniques, we might ask ourselves, could we increase our patients' capacities to behave in these ways?

In conclusion, I have tried to clarify the meaning of personal worth and to highlight it as a crucial problem in the rehabilitation of the physically disabled patient. I would hope that this paper has to some degree succeeded in these aims and that the related considerations will help to stimulate improved techniques for dealing with it.

REFERENCES

1. Dembo, Tamara, Leviton, Gloria Ladieu, and Wright, Beatrice A. Adjustment to Misfortune—A Problem of Social-Psychological Rehabilitation. *Artificial Limbs.* Autumn, 1956, 3 :2 :4–62.
2. Ellis, Albert. *Reason and Emotion in Psychotherapy.* New York : Lyle Stuart, 1962.

3. English, Horace B. and English, Ava Champney. *A Comprehensive Dictionary of Psychological and Psychoanalytical Terms.* New York : David McKay, 1958.

4. Hartman, Robert S. The Science of Value, p. 13–37, in : Maslow, Abraham H., ed. *New Knowledge in Human Values.* New York : Harper, 1959.

5. Holland, John L. A Theory of Vocational Choice. *J. Counseling Psychol.* Spring, 1959. 6 :1 :35–45.

6. Kluckhohn, Florence Rockwood. Dominant and Variant Value Orientations, p. 342–357, in : Kluckhohn, Clyde, Murray, Henry A., with collaboration of Schneider, David M., eds. *Personality in Nature, Society, and Culture.* (ed. 2) New York : Alfred A. Knopf, 1953.

7. Maslow, A. H. *Toward a Psychology of Being.* New York : D. Van Nostrand, 1962.

8. May, Rollo. The Existential Approach, chap. 66, p. 1348–1361, in : Arieti, Silvano, ed. *American Handbook of Psychiatry, Vol. II.* New York : Basic Books, 1959.

9. Murray, Henry A. and Kluckhohn, Clyde. Outline of a Conception of Personality, p. 3–49, in : Kluckhohn, Clyde, Murray, Henry A., with the collaboration of Schneider, David M., eds. *Personality in Nature, Society, and Culture.* (eds. 2) New York : Alfred A. Knopf, 1953.

10. Rogers, C. R. A Therapist's View of the Good Life. *The Humanist.* 1957. 17 :291–300.

11. Smith, John E. *Value Convictions and Higher Education.* New Haven, Conn. : Edward W. Hazen Foundation, 1958.

12. Wright, Beatrice A. *Physical Disability—A Psychological Approach.* New York : Harper, 1960.

13. Wylie, Ruth C. *The Self Concept: A Critical Survey of Pertinent Research Literature.* Lincoln, Neb. : University of Nebraska Press, 1961.

The Interpersonal Impact of Disability

In many instances, interactions between disabled and nondisabled persons are not constructive. These interactions have been described as strained or anxiety-provoking for both participants. In some cases, the persons who have disabilities are excluded socially from others. In others, they may be intruded upon through stares or questioned out of curiosity. In Part IV, the problems of these interactions are discussed, and suggestions for improvements are provided.

In a classical study focusing upon the social acceptance of persons with disabilities on the part of persons who are not disabled, Ladieu-Leviton, Adler, and Dembo focus upon three main issues: (1) the characteristics of acceptance versus nonacceptance, (2) some of the reasons for nonacceptance, and (3) ways in which some of these difficulties may be resolved. Their response to these issues provides useful, timely information to the rehabilitation practitioner.

Persons with disabilities sometimes lack the social skills necessary to communicate successfully with nondisabled people in the community, particularly about the stigmatizing effects of their disability, and they are rarely taught these skills. Cogswell, in her study of the problems of paraplegics in their self-socialization, reviews the problems and suggests the sequential ordering of social encounters by increasing difficulty as an alternative to these difficulties. In discussing the practical implications of her model, Cogswell provides useful suggestions for those who work with disabled people.

11

Studies in Adjustment to Visible Injuries: Social Acceptance of the Injured

Gloria Ladieu-Leviton
Dan L. Adler
Tamara Dembo

In exploring the social–psychological problems of the visibly injured, one sees the constant striving of the injured person to combat what he considers the negative implications of his injury. Among these he counts a variety of attitudes and behaviors which the noninjured direct toward him; e.g., they display unwarranted pity, and treat him as an object of curiosity. In general, the injured feels that as a person he is set apart from people at large. What he demands above all is social acceptance.

The gravity of the problem as seen by injured people is epitomized in the statement of one amputee:

> "You can't write an article about it. It can be said in one sentence— There is no acceptance."

Although this is an extreme instance, it reflects in nature, if not in degree, the general problem as seen by the injured man.

When he demands social acceptance, the injured may ask the noninjured to assess concomitants of the injury in a practical way, and to

From *Journal of Social Issues*, 1948, 4 (14), 55–61. Reprinted by permission of the publishers.

The work described in this paper was done partially under a contract between Stanford University and the Office of Scientific Research and Development, recommended by the Committee on Medical Research, partially under a contract between the Research and Development Board of the Surgeon General's Office of the Army and Stanford University. The Advisory Board of the project included: Ernest R. Hilgard (Chairman), Roger G. Barker, Paul R. Farnsworth, George S. Johnson, Donald E. King, Quinn McNemar and Calvin P. Stone.

behave accordingly. Thus, the noninjured are to avoid exaggeration and to eliminate misconceptions regarding the limitations set by the injury.

On the basis of interviews[3] with 125 visibly injured persons (see Table 1) we can summarize what, for them, constitutes social acceptance; what obstacles, in their opinion, stand in the way of such acceptance; and what procedures may alleviate or eliminate the negative implications of injury with respect to acceptance.

Table 1.   Distribution of Subjects with Regard to Type of Injury

Amputation:
Leg
below knee and Symes	30
above knee	25
bilateral	3

Arm
below elbow	12
above elbow	9
bilateral	3
One arm and one leg	1
Fingers	4

Plastic Surgery:
Facial Injuries	24
Hand Injuries	4
Other Visible Injuries:	10

Total:	125*

* Hospitalized Veterans	88
Nonhospitalized Veterans	22
Civilians	15

ACCEPTANCE VERSUS PARTICIPATION

First and foremost it is important to differentiate between what may be called nonparticipation and nonacceptance. *Nonparticipation* is seen by injured and noninjured alike as a reasonable abstinence from social activities which are limited by the reality of the handicap. Neither the injured nor the noninjured could expect, for example, to have a leg amputee play on a company baseball team which competes with other teams. This injured man might *miss* the activity keenly, but knowing that he cannot meet the physical requirements, he is not apt to see the situation as one of nonacceptance. *Nonacceptance*, from his point of view, is a one-sided affair, resting primarily upon the negative attitudes of the noninjured. It appears as a resistance or reluctance to admit him to various kinds and degrees of social relationship. Unlike those instances when actual physical limitations exclude him from an activity, it carries with it an aura of ostracism.

Frequently the injured feel that there is a discrepancy between what the noninjured see as the physical, social, and psychological limitations of the injury and the limitations actually present and acknowledged by the injured. Frequently when the noninjured judge that physical limitations preclude an activity, the injured know that some form of participation is possible—that the limitations are not really coextensive with the demands of the situation as seen by the noninjured.

The margin of difference between the two points of view may spell the difference between nonparticipation and nonacceptance of the injured person. Moreover, it often may give the appearance of willful avoidance of the injured on the part of the noninjured, even though this be not the case. If, however, the difference is resolved, the situation merely becomes an instance of nonparticipation, and the problem of acceptance does not arise.

REASONS FOR NONACCEPTANCE

The injured feel that they cannot be expected to shift *their* attitudes concerning their physical limitations in order to narrow this margin, since they feel that they are the ones who really know the actual reality limitations in their own cases. They feel that it is the noninjured who have to reexamine their attitudes for possible misconceptions, biases, and mistaken beliefs in order to reduce the discrepancy. In the following sections we shall give our attention to these misconceptions as they are pointed out by the injured. They will be discussed under three headings: namely, misconceptions which pertain to the physical limitations of the injured, to the appearance of the injury, and to evaluations of the worth of the injured as a person.

A. Physical limitations

A far-reaching misconception is the tendency on the part of the noninjured to overestimate physical limitations imposed by an injury. Some statements taken from the records exemplify this error:

> "Everyone was going dancing. Everyone had dates but I stayed home . . . The boys thought I couldn't dance. I was quite unhappy for a while."

> "It doesn't follow as night and day that a man with a high AK (above knee amputation) can't go on a hike . . . I would just invite him and if he declines, well, he will thank me for my kindness in inviting him."

The simplest remedy is clearly indicated in the quotation above. Since the noninjured cannot readily acquire information as to the variable capacities of the injured, they may indicate their willingness to have him participate, and leave to him the judgment of whether or not he will be able to do so. The noninjured may feel that in the event that participation is impossible, it will seem inconsiderate to have even suggested it. The danger of hurting the feelings of the injured, however, will be no greater than in other nonparticipation situations. At the same time the additional distress of apparent rejection will be avoided.

The manner of approach indicated is also of value in minimizing another kind of misconception. This is the failure on the part of the noninjured to realize the ability and willingness of the injured to participate socially by playing a role different from the usual one. Thus, the injured point out :

"I don't feel bad about not being a fisherman, and I got a kick out of going along and watching . . . A fellow who can't play basketball quickly resigns himself to being a spectator . . . I will go out and referee if the kids are playing."

"I played in *Pride and Prejudice.* Someone said, 'She limped just like an old person.' Ingenue parts—if you can't do that, that doesn't mean you can't do anything."

"In high school we had a baseball team. I would hit the ball and they would run for me. That was a tremendous thing they did. . . . When they put me on the baseball team that was great. Then I was in the group."

The implication is that the injured person, motivated by his changed circumstances, willingly restructures situations so that he may become a participant. The restructurizations may range from quite simple to rather extensive ones. Since the noninjured lack the strong motivation of the injured, they are less apt to think of such expedients. Accordingly, they are asked to forego any preconceived ideas of "possible" roles for the injured, and provide, instead, the opportunities for his social participation. In this way the injured person may determine the manner of participation which is compatible with both his interests and ability.

In addition to the misconceptions regarding injury-imposed limitations, there are special problems engendered by the reduced ease and speed of performance of the injured. Whether the injured are denied participation or not, they feel that the noninjured emphasize the inconvenience which they must endure. The injured attribute to the non-injured an apparent unwillingness to "bear with him and be patient and all that." A few examples suffice to make their point clear:

> "When you go in a public place you don't want to be fiddling around with your overcoat. They don't want to wait for you all the time."

> "And when you're hiking you tire out easy. People try to sympathize and wish you hadn't come on the trip and they don't want to associate with you."

Whether these attitudes are actually maintained by the noninjured, or only projections of the injured's fears, the result is the same—a feeling of nonacceptance on the part of the latter.

Assuming that the noninjured wish to include the injured person, it would be well to clarify the degree of inconvenience which the noninjured may be expected to bear. If the inconvenience is slight, they will take it as a matter of course—just as a man will slow his pace in the company of a woman. They will, too, be expected to make slight changes of plans to make easier or less awkward the participation of the injured. An arm amputee suggests, for example, the following:

> "Of course, if a person has one arm you don't want to invite him to a steak dinner. Arrange your menu accordingly. Have croquettes or something that can be handled with one hand nicely."

More can be expected of close persons than of casual acquaintances in both these respects. In the main, the performance of the injured may be judged not by their efficiency and smoothness of performance, but in terms of the end achieved—successful participation in a social group.

B. *Appearance of the Injury*

The discrepancy between the beliefs of the noninjured, and the facts as they exist, operates relative to the appearance of the injury just as it does relative to injury-imposed limitations. One of its forms seems to be an overestimation of the "unsightliness" of the injury, which prompts the noninjured to avoid the injured man lest they be forced inadvertently to view the injury. Even close family members may contribute to this kind of nonacceptance:

> "Mother and Dad were afraid to look. They thought it was wide open. They couldn't understand how it healed so soon."

The noninjured who himself has no "squeamishness" about seeing the injury is, nonetheless, careful to consider the feelings of others who might be more sensitive. He may, for example, hesitate to invite a visibly injured person to a social gathering because of the discomfort it might cause his guests, and, secondarily, the injured man. The tendency here is probably in the direction of overestimating the frequency and strength of such negative reactions.

Such generalizations appear to be more the product of anticipation than of realism. With reference to such feelings, the noninjured should remember that the "unsightliness" of the injury cannot be judged until seen. Further, familiarity and social contact with the injured may serve to lessen the feelings of aversion, whether they arise in anticipation or in actuality. Of such contacts the injured say :

> "You are conscious of the thing all the time and the public is too, more so than you are, until they are accustomed to it and then like us they don't even see it. After the public sees it it won't matter any more. I felt that way myself. After you are around them (other injured) a while you don't notice it. You think different and you see different."

> "Pity, repulsion, surprise, horror . . . they have a feeling of distaste— that's the first impression. After they have seen it a while they get used to it, and it doesn't bother them."

Limiting such contacts because of the expectation of aversion stops the educative process which the injured call "getting used to" the injury, and unnecessarily isolates them.

C. *Personal evaluation*

Another important consideration is felt by the injured to militate against their social acceptance. They believe that they are evaluated by the non-injured not only in terms of the physical aspects of their injury, but in terms of presumed psychological concomitants as well. There appears to be a spread of evaluation from characteristics actually affected by the injury, to other characteristics not necessarily so affected. This "halo" phenomenon is considered as generally devaluative or negative. Thus, the injured point out :

> "The majority think, in case a man is injured it throws him completely into another world or something, and it doesn't."

> "I think most people would think it would give a man an inferiority complex . . . I expect they'd think he'd be shy and sensitive. . . . The

people who came expected to see me in a much worse mental state than I was. I was pretty cheerful."

"If they could just see the morale of these fellows they would feel a lot different. They feel he is disabled and doesn't want to be around anybody."

In similar fashion the injured imply that the spread of evaluation may go so far that the injured person is considered in a position of lower status and unworthy of acceptance.

"Some people do condescend to the injured. I can't appreciate the basis for that attitude but it does happen."

"A lot of people feel sorry, think you're a cripple, and look down in a very severe way."

"You can just tell by the way a person looks. Some women will look at you as though they have a sorry look. Other people will look at you as if in contempt."

When the injured do not feel seclusive, or know that—aside from the injury—they are not "handicapped," it is the noninjured who must shift preconceived and erroneous attitudes. It is they who can best obviate the accusation of "willful" nonacceptance.

APPARENT VERSUS GENUINE ACCEPTANCE

Sometimes, though the injured person is given access to activities and relationships, he feels rejected nonetheless. These are instances in which he attributes to the noninjured unwelcome motivations such as duty or pity or the empty gestures of acceptance devoid of genuine pleasure in sharing the social situations with him. Such acceptance he interprets as "apparent," in contrast to the genuine acceptance which he seeks.

The anxiety of the injured in this regard makes him ascribe unwelcome motives when they do not exist, and to seek assurance of genuine rather than apparent acceptance. For example, a noninjured woman reported that a man with whom she had spent an enjoyable evening, remarked, "You'll probably be angry but I'll ask you anyway. Did you go out with me only because I am an amputee?"

An injured woman expresses anxiety about her acceptance in this way:

"There may be a feeling of superiority on the part of the other person, that he is patronizing you in being with you for that hour. It has never happened to me. I imagine it could happen. You would feel he didn't want to bother to be with a handicapped person. . . .

"I don't think this has ever happened, but I guess it has—they are doing you a favor being with you. It has never happened to me. They might pity you. . . .

"I would like to know if they feel superior to the other person, whether they realize it or not, and because of this feeling, if they have it, are they being with you because they feel they owe it to you, the less fortunate?"

Apparent acceptance is then not more welcome than nonacceptance —perhaps even more disturbing. In each, the injured see an underlying inability or unwillingness in others to know them as they actually are.

SUMMARY

This discussion of social acceptance of the injured is limited to the problems as seen by them. Three general questions are considered : (a) what characterizes social acceptance or nonacceptance, (b) what, according to the injured, are some of the reasons which account for their nonacceptance, (c) how may some of these difficulties be reduced or resolved?

In considering these questions we have indicated the distinction between *nonparticipation* and *nonacceptance*, and between *apparent* and *genuine* acceptance. The reasons for nonacceptance of the injured are developed mainly in terms of the misconceptions of noninjured persons relative to the injury and its effects. The discrepancies between points of view of the injured and noninjured are pointed out. Particular reference is made to the noninjured's evaluation of the physical limitations of the injury, its appearance, and its effect on the personality of the injured person. Remedies aimed at correcting misconceptions and reducing the indicated discrepancies are suggested.

NOTES

1. The research staff included : Dan L. Adler, Tamara Dembo, Eugenia Hanfmann, Helen H. Jennings, Gloria Ladieu, Milton Rose, Ralph K. White and Beatrice A. Wright. The three mentioned above are responsible for the writing of this paper.

We wish to acknowledge the help of Donald Glad, Research

Assistant. Special thanks are given to Alice Phillips Rose, Research Assistant, who volunteered to work on the project. We highly appreciate the cooperation of the staff and patients of Bushnell General Hospital and Dibble General Hospital.

2. For detailed account of the interview procedure, see : Studies in Adjustment to Visible Injuries : Evaluation of Help by the Injured. Ladieu, G., Hanfmann, E., and Dembo, T., *Journal of Abnormal and Social Psychology*, April, 1947.

Studies in Adjustment to Visible Injuries : Evaluation of Curiosity by the Injured. White, R. K., Wright, B. A., and Dembo, T., *Journal of Abnormal and Social Psychology*, Oct., 1947.

12

Self-Socialization:
Readjustment of Paraplegics
in the Community

Betty E. Cogswell

Paraplegics receive little or no professional help for one aspect of the rehabilitation process. In the first phase of rehabilitation, medical teams are available for teaching the physical skills necessary for independent mobility and for assisting patients to accept the reality of their disability. In the final phase, rehabilitation counselors are available to assist with occupational choice, training, and placement. No professional assumes explicit responsibility, however, for assisting paraplegics to learn the social skills necessary to relate successfully with nondisabled people in the community. Many of these skills are acquired during a middle phase of rehabilitation, after paraplegics leave the hospital and before they resume full-time student or work roles.

Physical disability is potentially stigmatizing, and the salience of stigma increases outside of the hospital. To become successfully rehabilitated, paraplegics must learn to diminish this effect. This, however, occurs through self-teaching, for paraplegics are left to chart their own course. This paper presents findings on one aspect of the process—the way paraplegics sequentially arrange their social encounters. It should be noted, however, that the paraplegics studied were essentially unaware that their experiences were sequentially patterned.

PROCESS OF SOCIALIZATION

Rehabilitation may be analyzed advantageously as a process of socialization. In fact, if rehabilitation had not been conceptualized in this way, the present findings might have been overlooked. A socialization model

From *Journal of Rehabilitation*, May/June, 1968 (Vol. 34, No. 3), 11–13. Copyright © 1968 by the National Rehabilitation Association. Reprinted by permission of the Editor and the author.

focuses attention on the processes by which individuals acquire new roles and leads to questions on the development of new self-definitions, skills, activities, and associations. Socialization proceeds through interaction among novices (individuals learning a new role) and agents (individuals responsible for training). In the research reported here, socialization was studied from the perspective of the novices, that is, paraplegics' learning the disabled role. Paraplegics were interviewed at repeated intervals about their experiences after leaving the hospital. They were asked what they did, whom they saw, how they responded to other people, and how other people responded to them. Comparison of the experiences of those studied reveals that the course of socialization was structured in a way that provided opportunities to develop and master social skills for relating to people in the normal world. Medical professionals may give patients gross indications that they will encounter interpersonal problems in the community, but paraplegics mainly discover these problems for themselves and proceed to handle them in their own way. They become their own socializing agents as well as agents for the many people they encounter who are uncertain about proper behavior toward a disabled person.

The data for this paper are taken from a more extensive study which followed paraplegics from the time of injury to the time they resumed roles in the community. Data were collected in a general teaching hospital over a five-year period by means of field observations and interviews with members of a rehabilitation team and with 36 young adult paraplegics. Eleven of these paraplegics were chosen for intensive study through a series of open-ended interviews with both patients and their families. Generalizations were abstracted primarily from the intensive study data. Data on the other 25 paraplegics, however, were used to refine initial hypotheses. The rehabilitation team was composed of physicians, nurses, physical therapists, occupational therapists, and social workers. The study group of paraplegics included both males and females, whites and Negroes, and private and staff patients. The subjects' social class ranged from lower class to upper middle.

MIDDLE PERIOD OF REHABILITATION

Paraplegics need a month or more after leaving the hospital to practice the physical skills necessary to function in the normal world. In theory, after this amount of time, they should be physically ready to resume a job or begin job training. A curious finding is that most paraplegics who do eventually resume full-time training or work roles delay for one to several years. The reasons for this delay are of particular concern for rehabilitation practitioners. Some medical professionals note differences in the way patients respond when they first go home and at that time in the future when they become ready to go back to work, but they are unable to give a clear description of these differences. Some suggest that this may be a necessary period of mourning that paraplegics cannot be rushed through.

Compared to pre-trauma life, all of the paraplegics upon returning home had a marked reduction in (a) number of social contacts with others in the community, (b) frequency in entering community settings, and (c) number of roles that they played. All of the paraplegics studied eventually showed some increase in these three activities; however, there is wide variation in the extent of increase. If one takes resumption of a work role as a final indicator of rehabilitation, only six of 26 followed regularly at this hospital had reached this level at the time of last contact. (Ten of the original 36 did not return to this hospital for their medical care after completing physical retraining. Of the 26 followed here, one died, two were remaining at home on the advice of their lawyer, and one developed a heart condition which prevented his return to work. All of the paraplegics had either worked or had been fulltime students prior to injury. The six subjects who did return to work, five men and one woman, are all from middle class families.) The others who arrested at lower levels along the way appear to have had common socialization experiences up to this point.

All paraplegics face problems which evolve from the stigma of disability. In the hospital, medical personnel help paraplegics develop a self-image of independence and personal worth. Although difficulties are encountered, it is easier to establish and maintain this self-image in the sheltered social environment of the hospital than in the world outside. When paraplegics return to their homes and communities, definitions of their disability as a social stigma reach the height of salience. This common problem apparently orders their course of socialization.

SELF-SOCIALIZATION INTO A DEVALUED ROLE

In our society the disabled role is socially devalued. Effective socialization results through learning to reduce the stigmatizing effects of disability. Paraplegics must learn the physical and social skills necessary to play the role with sufficient ease to prevent contamination of their identity as well as their performance of other roles. (See Goffman, 1963, for a sociological definition of stigma.) Physical disability, like most stigmas, is not equally stigmatizing in all social situations. Salience of disability as a stigma varies with the type of individual encountered and the type of social setting. It also varies with the paraplegic's definition and projection of self as worthy or demeaned and with his skill in managing others' definitions of his disability.

In learning the skills of stigma management, paraplegics become their own socializing agents. Change which occurs during this period is more apt to occur through day-to-day accommodation to problems rather than through systematic goal-directed behavior. Paraplegics have a diffuse image of a final goal—reintegration into the community as persons of independence and worth. This image was initiated in the hospital by rehabilitation practitioners. There is, however, no awareness of the intermediate steps necessary to attain this goal. There is no agent to spell out these steps nor to structure progress through the sequence.

Paraplegics, seemingly unaware of the long-range process, order their course of socialization in response to day-to-day problems by avoiding social situations where negative social response can destroy positive definitions of self, by seeking out social situations where demands are not beyond their current level of competence, and by manipulating social encounters to emphasize positive and minimize negative aspects of self. At first, when paraplegics have had little experience in dealing with disability as stigma, the threat of failure is great. Uncertain of what the responses of others will be, paraplegics tend to expect the worst. They are quick to interpret any questionable response as derogatory and rapidly withdraw if they perceive the slightest strain in a social encounter. They are apprehensive that the attention of others may be focused on the disability and that other aspects of self will be treated as irrelevant.

TIME-STRUCTURING OF SOCIALIZATION

The middle period of rehabilitation begins with a self-imposed moratorium during which paraplegics remain at home. Uncertain about how to proceed, they arrest momentarily. Re-entry into the community is gradual and is structured simultaneously in two ways : by sequential choice of social settings and sequential choice of associates. These two sequences begin with social situations which are easiest to handle and proceed to those more difficult. In essence, paraplegics search out the least threatening environments for the trial of new behavior.

Self-Imposed Moratorium

On returning home, paraplegics become aware that their once familiar community has become strange. One world is lost, and another is yet to be gained. They are unclear about their own identity, for they must establish new self-definitions for the spectrum of social relationships. These range from casual encounters with waitresses, clerks, barbers, filling station attendants, and dentists to more enduring relationships with friends, dates, teachers, and employers. New definitions of self grow through encounters with others, yet paraplegics are reluctant to resume social contacts. Instead they stay at home for a time in passive avoidance of the outside world. Pretrauma conceptions of self do not apply; new conceptions of self have not emerged; and action is arrested because paraplegics are unable to answer the question, Who am I?

During the first few weeks, a host of friends and neighbors come to visit, but this is not sustained. Very quickly, paraplegics find themselves alone. They describe this period as a time of social isolation and inactivity. When asked, "Whom do you see?" they reply, "Nobody." When asked, "What do you do?" they reply, "Nothing." Since there are few social expectations for the disabled role, paraplegics may stay at home for any length of time without arousing negative reactions from family or others in the community. Family and friends may encourage outings; but if the paraplegic is not responsive, these overtures tend to cease.

Sequential Selection of Social Settings

Paraplegics first enter those social settings which require the least amount of physical and social skill and proceed later to those more difficult. In selecting settings, patients used three criteria: (a) physical accessibility, (b) flexibility for leaving the scene, and (c) salience of stigma.

Physical accessibility may be considered in terms of four types of increasingly difficult settings: (a) those where the paraplegic can go and remain in his automobile; (b) those allowing easy wheelchair maneuvering, where surfaces are level and where there are wide doors and aisles; (c) those that can be easily entered by wheelchair but require the paraplegic to change seats, such as a dentist's office, barbershop, or theater; and (d) those where some physical assistance from another person is necessary, such as climbing long flights of stairs or crossing rough terrain.

Regarding flexibility for leaving settings, paraplegics want the option of leaving quickly if stigma should become salient. They are concerned with the socially acceptable length of time one must remain after entering a setting. Public streets provide the most flexibility. Following in order of decreasing flexibility are stores, places where one may have an appointment which lasts for thirty minutes or longer, visits, and parties. The most lengthy time-binding setting and the last to be reentered is place of work.

Settings vary in the degree to which each paraplegic feels his disability may become stigmatizing. One paraplegic mentioned that "People don't mind you on the street, but they don't like you in their intimate places like bars." Several mentioned that they began going to church and then to church parties long before they had the nerve to go to private parties. They seemed to feel that people in a religious setting had a greater obligation to accept them.

Sequential Selection of Associates

As paraplegics resume social relationship in the community, they choose individuals who will support definitions of them as individuals of independence and social worth. These relationships are sequentially timed. First, paraplegics phase-out and seldom resume relationships with pretrauma friends; second, they begin to associate with individuals of lower social status; and third, they begin to associate with new individuals of equal status.

The paraplegics maintained very few friendships that existed prior to their injuries, declaring that they did not like to be with people that they had known before the accident. Pretrauma friends are attached to a conception of the paraplegic as he once was and have difficulty relating to him as a disabled person. Paraplegics find it difficult to establish a new identity with those who view them from a pretrauma frame of reference. These paraplegics mentioned a number of problems which ensued when they tried to maintain old relationships: expressions of pity frequently contaminated the relationship, the sincerity of overtures made by old friends was questioned, old friends were inclined to offer unneeded physical assistance, and paraplegics felt that old friends made invidious comparisons between the pre- and posttrauma relationship. One of the more articulate paraplegics mentioned the added difficulty in assisting others to readjust to him. In discussing a breakup between him and his girl, he said, ". . . one person can fight it, but to try to carry somebody, to try to rehabilitate them to me at the same time and take the chance of its not working out, that would be a big loss and might make you tend to give up [in your own rehabilitation]."

As paraplegics begin to acquire new friends, they tend to choose people of lower social status than their pretrauma friends. (Fred Davis [1963] found that polio children on returning home established a close friendship with another child whose status and acceptance in the group was marginal.) These friends may be of lower social class, decidedly younger or older than the patient, or less attractive in other ways. By choosing friends of lower status, paraplegics are able to balance the negative definitions of disability against some negative characteristic of the other person. If, in these relationships, paraplegics become successful in projecting themselves as a person of worth and become skilled in eliciting this definition from others, they proceed to more difficult relationships eventually forming successful relationships with new individuals of equal status. Physical disability will always pose problems for relationships with others, but paraplegics learn to handle these problems with sufficient ease to maintain stable social relationships.

AWARENESS OF PERSONAL CHANGE

Incidents which are here cited as structured in time emerge in interviews as unrelated experiences. Paraplegics do not have a frame of reference for ordering these events into sequences which lead to mastery of the disabled role. Unlike many types of socialization, there were no agents to present the steps involved. Neither was there sufficient contact among paraplegics during this period for them to compare experiences and establish common benchmarks of progress (Julius A. Roth [1963] used the term "benchmarks of progress" to designate events which occur sequentially in a career and which are indicative of movement toward an end-point.)

From the perspective of the paraplegics, this period of time often lacked meaning : days often seemed wasted and empty and appeared to lead nowhere. It is useful to contrast this experience with socialization in the hospital. Here medical personnel repeatedly listed for paraplegics the sequence of events necessary to achieve physical independence. Accomplishments which are meaningless from a normal person's perspective—sitting balance, wheelchair maneouvering, transfer, standing balance, walking with braces and crutches—were symbolized by hospital staff as indicators of progress. Paraplegics accepted this symbolic definition and thereby derived tremendous self-satisfaction from mastery of steps which otherwise they might have considered inconsequential. Due to definitions of the situation presented by the rehabilitation practioners and accepted by the paraplegics, days had meaning and were filled with purposive activity. Paraplegics knew the steps to be mastered and could assess their own progress.

PRACTICAL IMPLICATIONS

Uncertainty is one of the most threatening experiences a person must face. Any framework for ordering expectations is perhaps better than none. Paraplegics now leave the hospital with only a vague impression of what to expect in their local communities. It would be naive to assume that this uncertainty could be eliminated; but it would appear that it could be reduced, and rehabilitation might be enhanced, if each paraplegic left the hospital with a planned sequence of socialization. Obviously this sequence should be geared to the individual life situation of the patient and to his individual goals. Activities appropriate to the life-style of a particular paraplegic could be ordered in terms of their increasing social difficulty, and each type of activity could be given symbolic meaning as an indicator of progress toward rehabilitation.

It is perhaps also important to maintain frequent contact with paraplegics during this period. Events since the last contact could be reviewed and assessed. Events for the coming period could be planned and encouraged. The symbolic meaning of social encounters could be reaffirmed. This procedure divides the middle period of rehabilitation into steps of small increments, reducing somewhat the degree of uncertainty. By presenting paraplegics with a framework for ordering this period of socialization and by guiding them through the steps, rehabilitation practitioners might be able to reduce the length of time between hospital discharge and resumption of training or work roles as well as to increase the number of paraplegics who complete the course. Claims for the merit of this procedure, however, must await experimental evaluation.

The findings presented here also have an important implication for present programs of rehabilitation. Rehabilitation counselors should take into consideration that initial stalling by paraplegics is in no way predictive of job success or failure. Some paraplegics stay at home for two to three years, yet eventually they make good social and work adjustments. This suggests that rehabilitation counselors should not despair if a paraplegic is at first unwilling to resume full-time work. It would seem important to maintain contact with this type of client for several years, giving him repeated opportunities for job training or job placement.

These notions on socialization, while applying to young adult paraplegics, may be equally pertinent to other age groups with other types of disabilities. Almost all physical disabilities are potentially stigmatizing, and successful adjustment to these conditions usually requires learning the skills of stigma management. The findings also may have some bearing on the resocialization of released prisoners and psychiatric patients as well as on alcoholics, drug addicts, and other types of deviants.

This paper has dealt with only one aspect of paraplegics' socialization career in the community—ordering social encounters by increasing difficulty. As paraplegics' social skills increased, they attempted to enter more difficult social situations. Further research is necessary to specify the skills which are important and to ascertain the manner in which these skills may be learned. Although our present knowledge of resocialization into the community is limited, it would seem worthwhile for the rehabilitation system to consider assuming greater responsibility for this period of adjustment. Research should be encouraged, and the potential role of rehabilitation workers should be evaluated to determine whether professional assistance might enhance rehabilitation.

NOTE

The author wishes to acknowledge the helpful suggestions of Professors Harvey L. Smith, Marvin B. Sussman, and Donald D. Weir, M.D. who read an earlier version of this paper.

REFERENCES

Davis, Fred, *Passage through Crisis: Polio Victims and Their Families.* New York : Bobbs-Merrill, 1963, pp. 147–148.

Goffman, Erving. *Stigma: Notes on the Management of Spoiled Identity.* Englewood Cliffs, N.J. : Prentice-Hall, 1963, p. 5.

Roth, Julius A. *Timetables: Structuring the Passage of Time in Hospital Treatment and Other Careers.* New York : Bobbs-Merrill, 1963.

Part V

Attitudes toward Disabled Persons

The societal response toward disability is a reflection of the attitudes of others toward disability and toward disabled persons. This attitude is often negative, and it affects the interpersonal relationship between nondisabled persons and disabled persons as well as society's attempt to rehabilitate persons with handicaps.

English examines the correlates of negative attitudes toward physically disabled people and suggests methods of combating this stigma. He supports a point of view that in many instances the stigma turns physical disabilities into personal, vocational, and social handicaps.

Based on his survey of the various means of changing societal attitudes toward persons with disabilities, Anthony suggests an experience combining both contact with and information about persons with disabilities. Anthony discusses ways in which broad societal rehabilitation programs might be implemented in the fields of education, employment, and public service.

The papers in Part V should enable the reader to have a clearer understanding of attitudes, how they affect the lives of disabled persons, and how they can be changed.

13

Correlates of Stigma toward Physically Disabled Persons

R. William English

The purpose of this basic research paper is to provide information about the anatomy of prejudice toward the physically disabled. "Stigma" refers to an attribute that is deeply discrediting, and a stigmatized person is one who is thought to be not quite human or normal (Goffman, 1963). In the final analysis, stigma might best be considered to be the negative perceptions and behaviors of so-called normal people to all individuals who are different from themselves. Though the present paper considers stigma in a limited frame of reference as it applies primarily to persons with physical disabilities, in reality most if not all of the content seems readily transferable to other stigmatized groups, e.g., the mentally retarded, mentally ill, socially disadvantaged, and religious and racial minorities.

Theoretically, it has been suggested (Barker, 1948; Gellman, 1959; and Wright, 1960) that physically disabled persons are a minority in much the same sense as traditional minority groups, such as Negroes and Jews. Barker was first to suggest that physically disabled persons, like traditional minorities, are subject to group stereotypes, overlapping situations—involving role conflict between acting normal versus disabled —and an underprivileged social status position. Empirically, this theoretical position has been examined, and it has been confirmed that there is a significant relationship between negative attitudes toward traditional minorities and negative attitudes toward the physically disabled. Although the absolute level of the correlation is moderate, approximately .40, the relationship is consistent over time and does suggest that there is credence in the belief that physically disabled

From *Rehabilitation Research and Practice Review*, 2 (1971), 1–17. Reprinted by permission of the author and Editor.

persons are perceived in much the same manner as traditional minority groups.

Although it is impossible to specifically document the number or percentage of nondisabled persons who stigmatize the disabled, there is little doubt that stigma does exist and that it is a basic fact of life for nearly all disabled persons. Informally, interpersonal relations between nondisabled and disabled persons tend to follow a superior–inferior model of social interaction or to be nonexistent. Numerous accounts (Wright, 1960) exist of disabled persons who have remarked that non-disabled persons treat them as if they were disabled in every way. That is, a blind person may feel that he is often treated as if he were also mentally retarded, socially immature, and without feelings, interests, or ideas. Results of research by Kleck, Ono, and Hastorf (1966) support the notion that nondisabled persons tend to be more emotionally incongruent with disabled persons than with other nondisabled persons. They discovered that nondisabled persons demonstrated stereotyped, inhibited, and overcontrolled behavior with the disabled. Further, nondisabled Ss interacting with a disabled person showed less variability than Ss interacting with a normal stimulus person, terminated the interaction sooner, and expressed opinions less representative of actual beliefs. In a companion study, Kleck (1968) simulated relations between normal–normal and disabled–normal persons. Normal actors interacting with a confederate playing an amputee role showed: greater motor inhibition, distorted positivism toward the disabled, and distorted cognitive agreement with the person acting disabled.

Informally, words exist within our language system which describe disabled persons in devaluating terms: words such as "retard," "psycho," "crip," and "dummy" connote stigmatization. Within formal institutional structures, words also exist which contribute to separating and stigmatizing the disabled. Instead of the word "retard" we hear the word "mentally retarded," and similarly we hear other words such as "emotionally ill," "psychologically disturbed," "schizophrenic," "orthopedically disabled," and "mentally deficient." Although these terms have professional value in that they are descriptive, and they are supposedly related to prescriptive rehabilitation planning, they often have a stigmatizing effect (English and Palla, 1971; Jaffe, 1966; Szasz, 1970; Blatt 1970). I believe that this is inherent in almost all instances, regardless of how well-intentioned the labeling process may be.

Behaviorally, a substantial amount of segregation takes place involving disabled persons. While the intent of such institutional segregation may well be to assist individuals, one of the clearest results is that the segregated person feels psychologically apart and inferior to his nondisabled peers, who interact in integrated surroundings (Blatt, 1970 and Dunn, 1968). Although a certain amount of segregation in special classes and institutions may be necessary, it should be minimized wherever possible. For example, orthopedically disabled children without learning disabilities do not need to be placed in special classrooms.

A final example of formal institutionalized stigma is the existence of restrictive legislation which denies disabled persons basic civil liberties such as the right to drive an automobile, vote in elections, marry, become a parent, and the right to secure employment (Schreiber, 1970). The basic premise upon which all this restrictive legislation has been passed, which is to protect society, itself is a foremost example of stigmatization. Furthermore, the fact that restrictive legislation continues to exist in many instances without any moral, philosophical, humanitarian, or scientific basis underscores the current American tragedy of stigmatization, within formal institutional structures.

In summary, stigma exist in the lives of most disabled persons, and generally represent the most salient and frustrating problem to be overcome in rehabilitation. Without negative community attitudes, disabled individuals and their families and human service agents could deal with the basic medical limitations of disabled individuals—what Hamilton (1950) called "disability." With negative community attitudes (stigma), the disabled individual, his family, and human service agents must deal with a host of other problems which severely restrict, "handicap," the life space of the disabled individuals and often contribute to severe problems of personal, social, and vocational adjustment.

Studies conducted on the attitudes of the general public toward physically disabled persons in general suggest that nearly half of the nondisabled public have primarily negative attitudes toward physically disabled persons. Although this statistic is interesting for practical purposes, it is almost useless as an aid to understanding the character and makeup of nondisabled persons who stigmatize the disabled.

Understanding the individuals and institutions that stigmatize the disabled most is an extremely complex problem which can only be arrived at by careful examination of numerous correlates or factors which contribute to overall attitudes. Specifically, there appear to be demographic, personality, attitudinal, and experimental and behavioral correlates of attitudes toward disabled persons. These numerous factors interact and account for a particular person's attitudes or tendency to stigmatize the disabled.

DEMOGRAPHIC CORRELATES OF STIGMA TOWARD PHYSICALLY DISABLED PERSONS

Sex

Consistently, females have displayed more favorable, accepting attitudes toward physically disabled persons than males (Chesler, 1965; Freed,

1964; Jabin, 1966; Lukoff and Whiteman, 1963; Siller, 1964; Titley and Vieny, 1969; and Yuker, Block, and Campbell, 1960). In contrast to these studies, nonsignificant differences were reported between males and females in studies by Bell (1962), Freed (1964), Siller (1964), and Siller and Chipman (1965). No studies reported nondisabled males to have more favorable attitudes toward the disabled than nondisabled females.

While the results of tests of sex differences in attitudes toward the disabled may be ego-inflating for women and ego-deflating for men, it is somewhat expected, given traditional role expectations for the two sexes and the different socialization processes to which men and women have been exposed. These findings are in fact consistent with personality test data which indicate that women are basically more nurturant and less evaluative than men. Perhaps a negative consequence of the current revolution in sexual identity will be that women will become less nurturant, more evaluative, and more stigmatizing of disabled persons.

Socioeconomic Status

Surprisingly, researchers have paid sparse attention to examining the relationship between socioeconomic factors and attitudes toward the disabled. The limited data that is available suggest that socioeconomic status is related to attitudes toward particular disability groups but unrelated to attitudes toward the disabled in general. Studies which have compared income groups suggest that higher income groups are more accepting of individuals with intellectual and emotional deficiencies (Farber, 1968 and Jabin, 1966).

It is theorized that this difference in attitudes toward types of disability by socioeconomic group is related to the basic values and life style of lower and higher income groups. Specifically, higher income groups value intellectual and social competence more highly than physique or physical prowess. These values appear to be reversed for a substantial number, if not a majority, of nondisabled persons from lower income groups.

Age

Another demographic variable which has frequently been examined as it related to attitudes toward the disabled is "age." Overall, studies of nondisabled subjects suggest that there is little or no relationship between age and attitudes toward disabled persons. Although significant relationships have been reported which would suggest that young adults hold slightly more favorable attitudes toward disabled persons than adults in general, the size of the correlation has been very low, under .20, and accounts for little of the variance (Auvenshine, 1962; Bell, 1962; Siller, 1963; and Siller and Chipman, 1965).

Education

Examination of the relationship between age and attitudes toward disabled persons is complex, for in the case of young persons the age variable is confounded with education. That is, high school and college students demonstrate more positive attitudes toward disabled persons at each higher grade level (Auvenshine, 1962; Elias, English, Moffet, Simon, and Tuker, 1965; Horowitz, Reese, and Horowitz, 1965; Jabin, 1966; Knittel, 1963; and Siller, 1964). The most obvious interpretation of this result is that education in general contributes to the development of more positive attitudes toward disabled persons. However, studies of adults who have completed their education and left school suggest that this relationship may be situation-bound. Bell (1962) found no significant differences between dichotomized educational levels and attitudes toward disabled persons, and Cohen (1963) discovered an inverse relationship between the level of employers' education and their willingness to hire mentally retarded persons. In related research, Palmerton and Frumkin (1969) discovered that the more college counselors knew about the physically disabled, the greater was their tendency to be prejudiced toward the disabled.

Because of the contradictions in the data it is hazardous to make inferences about the long-term effect of educational grade level on attitudes toward the disabled. However, the data are sufficient to permit the theoretical belief that generally there is greater tolerance of individuals who are different in educational settings than exists in noneducational atmospheres, and that probably there is a dissipation with regard to the degree to which disabled persons are tolerated once people leave school. In some respects this suggests that people are considerably suspect to being influenced by situational values and rhetoric, i.e., the liberal college atmosphere versus the more conservative noncollege atmosphere.

Disability

Another demographic variable which has received considerable attention by researchers as it relates to the attitudes of nondisabled toward the disabled is that of disability itself. Theoretically, it has been hypothesized by numerous writers that type of disability, extent or severity of disability, hereditary versus acquired disability, and age of onset of disability would be related to the attitudes of the nondisabled person toward the disabled. Although these relationships have been examined rather extensively (Alessi and Anthony, 1969; Wilson and Alcorn, 1969; Wright, 1960; and Yuker, Block, and Younng, 1966), results indicate that there is virtually no relationship between any of these disability variables and stigma. Empirically, this result is consistent with the results of studies which have examined the relationship between disability and the adjustment of disabled persons. While theoretically it has been conjectured that individuals with obvious and severe disabilities acquired after childhood would be more maladjusted, no empirical evidence has been found to support this view. In interpreting these data we can conjecture that each individual person has his own perceptions or hangups with regard to disability. When counseling and psychology students have been asked to enumerate the types of disability they would personally find to be most crippling, they consistently have stated quite different reactions and perceptions (English, 1970; and Wilson and Alcorn, 1969). For one person, the sensory loss derived from blindness may be the most adversive disability, and for another it may be a progressive disease like multiple sclerosis or loss of intellectual functioning as represented by brain damage.

Religion

Nondisabled persons from different religious groups have been found (Farber, 1968; Robinson and Robinson, 1965; and Stubblefield, 1965) to differentially accept the mentally retarded. Catholics are significantly more accepting than Protestants or Jews, who are generally approximately equally accepting. English (1971) reported somewhat contradictory results in that the attitudes of nondisabled college students from different religions were nonsignificantly related to attitudes toward blind persons.

These contrasting findings may possibly be explained by differences in dogma or theoretical beliefs, and a tendency toward less secularization in the Catholic faith. Conjointly, there may be a stereotypic tendency to attribute the etiology of mental retardation to prenatal and paranatal factors, versus blindness, which is generally associated with postnatal etiology. These inferences must be considered with great caution, however, given the relative sparseness that religion has been examined with regard to attitudes toward disabled persons.

Occupation

Investigators have begun to examine the relationship between the occupation of nondisabled persons and their attitudes toward the disabled. Jordan and Cessna (1969) successfully hypothesized that special educators and rehabilitation counselors, teachers, laborers, and managers would show a decreasing tendency toward a progressive and asset-value orientation. English and Oberle (1971) found that occupational emphasis upon physique was related to attitudes toward the physically disabled.

Specifically, that stewardesses (members of an occupation placing a high emphasis on physique) were significantly more negative, rejecting, of physically disabled persons than typists (members of an occupation placing a low emphasis on physique). Mean scores of the two occupational groups indicate that stewardesses fell at the 25th percentile and typists at the 75th percentile level on the Attitude Toward Disabled Persons (ATDP) standardization norms.

Although it is premature to draw extensive conclusions with regard to the relationship between occupations and attitudes toward the disabled, the findings of these two studies suggest that this is a promising area for further investigation. Part of the central focus of such future study should be on examining attitudes toward disabled persons as influenced by occupational choice per se versus values derived by the milieu and reinforced by that social structure. The interaction of occupational choice and occupational values should also be examined.

Nonsignificant Demographic Variables

Finally, a number of demographic variables have been found to be unrelated to attitudes of nondisabled persons toward the physically disabled. These include : marital status, urban–rural residence, nationality, and race (Brunswick, 1970; English, 1971; and Yuker, Block and Younng, 1966).

PERSONALITY CORRELATES OF STIGMA TOWARD PHYSICALLY DISABLED PERSONS

Current psychological theory has not yet been able to adequately explain the relationship between personality correlates of nondisabled persons and their attitudes toward the disabled, and relatively few such studies have been attempted. The most salient personality dimensions that have been studied are motivation; self-concept; anxiety; interests; and intelligence.

Motivation

Because it has seemed logical to assume that attitudes, of both nondisabled and disabled persons, toward the disabled are related to motivational factors, studies have been conducted relative to operationalizing Murray's (1938) 16 Psychogenic Needs and examining their relationship to attitudes toward the disabled. The instrument used in these investigations is a revision of the Gough Adjective Checklist which was developed by Heilbrun (1958 and 1959). Of the 15 motives that have been studied in various research pieces, only two, aggression and intraception, have been found to be significantly correlated with attitudes toward disabled persons.

Regarding "aggression," it has been hypothesized from theory that less aggressive persons would express more positive attitudes toward disabled persons. This theory has been confirmed and the hypotheses verified, in a study by Siller (1964) although nonsignificant results have been reported by Siller and Chipman (1965). No significant contradictory results have been reported by any known studies.

A second psychogenic need that appears to be associated with attitudes toward disabled persons is "intraception." Siller (1964) reported a significant correlation of .13, using a sample of 233 college students and Yuker (1962) reported a correlation of .25 with a sample of 66 college students. Although the correlations are significant, neither accounts for even ten percent of the variance and consequently can be considered as little more than statistical artifacts attributable to the use of relatively large samples. Although the tentative evidence on intraception suggests that persons who see themselves as insightful are predisposed to being empathic and understanding in their interactions with disabled persons, the data are very limited, and clearly more research is called for before any definitive inferences can be drawn.

Numerous motivational factors have been found to be statistically unrelated to the Attitudes Toward Disabled Persons scale. These include : nurturance; affiliation; affect; achievement; dominance; deference; succorance; dependency; need for endurance; order; change; heterosexuality; autonomy; or exhibitionism (Yuker, Block, and Younng, 1966).

Self-Concept

In some studies, scores from the ATDP Scale have been associated with various measures of self-concept, e.g. Semantic Differential Scale, and the Maslow Security–Insecurity Inventory. The results of these studies consistently show that there is a low but significant correlation between positive self-concept and a tendency to be more accepting of the physically disabled. The correlations coefficients reported in Yuker (1962) and Siller (1964) were .17, .19, .27, and .40, which yield a mean *r* of .26. Although no studies report contradictory findings, nonsignificant findings are reported in many studies when specific definitions of self-concepts were related to attitudes toward the disabled. For example, Epstein and Shontz (1961) found no relationship between prejudice and body cathexis, while Yuker (1962) found "abasement" unrelated to stigma, and Siller (1964) found "self-acceptance" to be nonsignificantly associated with attitudes toward the physically disabled.

Anxiety

It has been demonstrated (Jabin, 1966; Siller, 1964; and Yuker, Block, and Campbell, 1960) that attitudes toward disabled persons are significantly related to manifest anxiety. Correlations range from a low of .14 to a high of .53. That is, those who accepted the disabled most tended to be lower in manifest anxiety. These results are consistent with the data on self-concept and stigma, which is to be expected as nearly all prevailing theories of personality suggest that positive self-concept and low anxiety are highly related dimensions.

Although no studies report contradicting results, some investigators have reported a nonsignificant association between anxiety and attitudes toward the disabled (Arnholter, 1963; and Siller and Chipman, 1965).

Intelligence

Only one study involving disabled persons as subjects has shown there to be a significant positive relationship between higher intelligence and overall attitudes toward physically disabled persons (Yuker, Block, and Campbell, 1960). In contrast to this single study, Knittel (1963), Yuker (1962, 1964), and Block (1962) found no significant relationship between attitudes toward the disabled and intelligence. These results correspond to data in the area of mental retardation, which consistently shows intelligence to be predictive only to performance in educational situations (Farber, 1968; Koestoe, 1960; and Robinson and Robinson, 1965).

In addition to studies that have examined the relationship between intelligence and overall attitudes toward the physically disabled, some studies have been more exact and considered the relationship between intelligence and attitudes toward specific disability groups.

Because no studies using nondisabled persons as subjects are known related to this problem, it is necessary to extrapolate from studies with disabled *Ss*. In one such study, Bauman (1954) found a significant negative correlation (-.56) between attitudes toward blindness and Wechsler-Bellevue Verbal I.Q., using 443 blind persons as subjects. In subsequent research, Bauman, Platt, and Straus (1963) replicated this study and obtained a significant correlation of -.43. A tentative conclusion to be drawn from these studies is that persons of higher intellectual capacity tend to be more accepting of blind persons. However, because intelligence and attitudes have not been studied extensively, and because the results are contradictory to the data between intelligence and overall attitudes toward physically disabled persons, the preceding interpretation must be considered with great caution. It is possible, for example, that intelligence may function as a confounding factor in some specific attitude measures. That is, more intelligent individuals may be able to analyze the purposes of a specific attitudinal measure and answer in more socially desirable ways.

Social Desirability

Doob and Ecker (1970), Feinberg (1967), Helson, Blake, Mouton, and Olmstead (1956), and Jabin (1966) all found social desirability to be significantly related to positive attitudes of nondisabled persons toward the disabled. That is, nondisabled persons with higher needs for social approval were more accepting of the disabled. This is well illustrated by Doob and Ecker's findings, which showed that housewives were significantly more compliant to requests to fill out a 70-item questionnaire when the requestor wore an eyepatch. Interestingly, nonsignificant results were obtained when housewives submitted to 15- to 20-minute interviews. This discrepancy in results may perhaps be explained by the differential structural role demands of interviews vs. questionnaires. That is, the interview is acknowledged to demand more personal, direct interaction of persons, which may have been more threatening to the housewives studied (Kerlinger, 1965). This suggests that social desirability and anxiety may interact and that avoidance may increase as a response pattern if the possibility of interaction with a disabled person becomes more realistic for the nondisabled.

Tolerance of Ambiguity

Feinberg (1971) administered the Budner Scale of Tolerance—Intolerance of Ambiguity and the Attitudes Toward Disabled Persons Scale to 62 college students and tested for differences in ambiguity among those *Ss* most positive and negative toward the disabled. His results were significant, indicating that nondisabled persons who are better able to tolerate ambiguity are generally more accepting of physically disabled persons. These findings confirm part of role theory that suggests that a state of ambiguity exists in interactions between disabled and nondisabled persons (English, 1971; Feinberg, 1971; Rochester, 1971; and Wright, 1960), which demands that expectations be modified and new, appropriate role behavior be learned.

Summary

Overall, there does appear to be a significant relationship between certain personality constructs and attitudes toward the disabled. While the relationships that do exist are not extensive, they are sufficient to allow us to conclude that personality does play a part in the attitudes which nondisabled persons hold toward the disabled. Results imply that less aggressive persons, with higher self-concepts, lower levels of anxiety, higher needs for social approval, and greater ability to tolerate ambiguity are the most accepting of the disabled.

Interestingly, these results are consistent with the limited amount of information we have with regard to these variables as they relate to the personal and social adjustment of disabled persons. Although the correlational data is even lower in this regard, it is such as to suggest that the best-adjusted physically disabled persons are individuals who have more positive self-concepts, are less aggressive, less anxious, and have fewer needs for social approval along with a greater ability to tolerate ambiguity.

ATTITUDINAL CORRELATES OF STIGMA TOWARD PHYSICALLY DISABLED PERSONS

Overall and Specific Attitudes

Correlational research has shown that overall attitudes toward physically disabled persons, as measured by instruments such as the Attitudes Toward Disabled Persons Scale (ATDP), are closely related to attitudes toward specific types of disabled persons. Siller and Chipman (1965) correlated Attitudes Toward Disabled Persons scores with scores from the Feeling Check List (FCL). They found that overall attitudes, of adults and young adults, were significantly related to attitudes toward these specific disability types: Amputation (.31), Skin Disorder (.36), Cerebral Palsy (.31), Blindness (.34), and Body Deformations (.34). When Attitudes Toward Disabled Persons scores were correlated with scores from the Social Distance Scale (SDS), the following correlations were found between overall attitudes toward the physically disabled and opinions about these specific disability types: Amputation (.26), Skin Disorders (.28), Blindness (.29), and Body Deformation (.31). These correlations were lower than those obtained associating Attitudes Toward Disabled Persons data with data from the Feeling Check List, but all were significant. Overall attitudes toward the physically disabled appeared unrelated to opinions about deafness and paralysis based on correlations between the Attitudes Toward Disabled Persons Scale and the Feeling Check List, and the Attitudes Toward Disabled Persons Scale and the Social Distance Scale (Siller and Chipman, 1965).

Overall attitudes toward the physically disabled are also significantly associated with attitudes toward the aged (Human Resources, 1962, 1964; and McCourt, 1963). McCourt (1963) administered the Attitudes Toward Disabled Persons Scale and the Attitudes Toward Old People Scale (AOP) to a sample of 360 professional and paraprofessional geriatric workers. He made nine statistical tests and found significance in each case, with correlations ranging from .33 to .68. Yuker (1964) also correlated scores from the Attitudes Toward Disabled Persons Scale and the Attitudes Toward Old People Scale. The tests were administered to three different samples of disabled employees of Abilities, Inc., and three significant correlations were obtained (.26, .27, .44).

In two studies (McCourt, 1963 and Yuker, 1962) Attitudes Toward Disabled Persons scores and Attitudes Toward Old People scores were nonsignificantly associated. While the results are not entirely consistent, the weight of the evidence reinforces the belief that there is a significant positive relationship between overall attitudes toward the physically disabled and attitudes toward the aged.

If future researchers derive the same result, they will confirm the theoretical view that the greatest amount of public acceptance is extended to severely disabled persons. In one pertinent theoretical study, Farber (1968) conjectured that there is considerably more tolerance of the severely intellectually deficient, with IQ's under .50, than of the moderately and mildly retarded. Farber believes that such differential tolerance is based on the belief that lower-level retardates are basically incompetent and should not be held responsible for their behavior or their intellectual deficiencies. In contrast, higher level retardates are perceived as socially deviant persons who deliberately use their intellectual deficiency in a manipulative fashion to obtain secondary gain(s). Another explanation for differential stigma by severity of disability is that more mildly impaired individuals are more psychologically and economically threatening to nondisabled persons (Doctor and Sieveking, 1970).

Disability Type Preferences:
Attitudes toward Physical versus Mental Disabilities

Some differences do appear to exist among the attitudes of the nondisabled toward persons with physical versus mental disabilities, but the relationships are complex and difficult to analyze. The critical variable that appears to be interacting with disability type, to account for attitudinal differences, is the "context situation."

When a context situation is not specified, nondisabled persons express more positive attitudes toward the physically disabled. Freed (1964) reported this finding when he modified the Attitudes Toward Disabled Persons Scale to study attitudes toward the physically disabled versus the "mentally ill' and the "alcoholic." Bates (1965) used similar methodology and had similar, though less striking, results concerning attitudes toward the physically disabled persons who suffered a nervous breakdown. On a continuum this suggests that a generic household label, like nervous breakdown, may be a less adversive symbol of stigma than a more definitive professional label, like "mental illness" or "alcoholic."

Consideration of stigma toward the disabled in terms of social and occupational context situations produces more definitive information. Although most research that has related disability type preferences to social context situations has not reported results of statistical tests, the accumulation of data suggest that nondisabled persons find physically disfigured persons less "socially" acceptable than persons who are functionally handicapped by difficulties such as mental illness, alcoholism, and diabetes. Present research (English and Palla, 1971; MacDonald and Hall, 1969; Macgregor, 1967; Richardson, Hastorf, Goodman, and Dornbush, 1961; Siller, 1963; and Whiteman and Lukoff, 1965) suggests that an "aesthetic" factor strongly influences social and personal preferences of nondisabled persons for the disabled. This is well illustrated by a study (English and Palla, 1971) involving the attitudes of nondisabled clerical workers toward a photograph of a mildly and severely retarded adolescent boy. Results demonstrated that nondisabled persons hold much more positive attitudes toward persons with intact, so-called normal, body images. The most salient Semantic Differential Scale accounting for individual responses was the "potency" dimension, which involved constructs such as weakness, sickness, dependency, and ugliness.

In occupational context situations, nondisabled persons, especially employers, appear to choose disabled persons primarily in terms of functional ability or productivity, versus reliance on physical appearance and style in social situations. Data suggests that vocationally the orthopedically disabled, e.g. amputees and paraplegics, are generally preferred as workers over persons with sensory disabilities, e.g. deaf and blind, who in turn are generally more preferred as workers than persons with brain-related disabilities, e.g. brain injured, cerebral palsied, epileptic, and mentally retarded (Appell, Williams, and Fishell, 1963; Bates, 1965; Barker, 1964; Baxt, David, Jaffey, and Wang, 1959; Kvaraceus, 1956; Murphy, Dickstein, and Dripps, 1960; Nikoloff, 1962; and Rickard, Triandis, and Patterson, 1963).

·Although definitive data does not appear to be available relevant to the work productivity of different disability groups, it may be that many employers prefer persons with organic versus functional limitations because the actions of organically disabled persons may appear to be more predictable, and therefore they might be considered to be more reliable, dependable employees. Certainly the degree of ambiguity increases along a continuum from organic to functional disability, and this is likely to contribute to adverse reactions among many nondisabled persons.

Prejudice and Authoritarianism

For some time, it has been theoretically believed that attitudes toward disabled persons are part of a broader constellation of attitudes toward persons who are demographically or psychologically different from prevailing social norms. That is, attitudes toward the physically disabled may be part of a larger constellation of attitudes toward people who are different in any way. To evaluate this concept, some investigators have correlated scores of nondisabled persons on measures of attitudes toward disabled persons with scores on measures of general prejudice. In a study conducted at Human Resources, Inc., Chesler (1965) correlated Attitudes Toward Disabled Persons scores with four locally constructed measures of prejudice toward various minority groups. The correlations for the four subscales ranged from -.40 to -.46, and the median correlation was -.44. The overall correlation which included all of the four subgroups was -.52. All five coefficients of correlation were in the predicted direction, and all of them were statistically significant beyond the .01 level. These results correspond to those reported in previous research by Cowen, Underberg, Verrillo (1958), and Kogan (1959). Cowen et al. reported significant correlations between attitudes toward blindness and scores on the California anti-minority and anti-Negro scales using a sample of college students. In closely related research, Kogan (1959) reported significant relationships between ethnocentrism and prejudice towards the aged among college students.

In summary, the results of these studies confirm the theoretical belief that prejudice is a general and pervasive attitudinal characteristic of certain nondisabled individuals which is reflected in a tendency to reject whatever groups they perceive as different from themselves rather than only one or two specific outgroups. Graphically, the results suggest that individuals who reject disabled persons also tend to reject other distinctive groups which may be identified by racial, religious, or ethnic terms. In light of the extensiveness and saliency of stigma among certain persons, it is easy to comprehend the complexity involved in changing prejudice toward the physically disabled and the different.

Other related studies have been conducted: English (1971) found that the expressed ethnocentrism of college students was significantly associated $(r=.41)$ with attitudes toward blind persons; Cowen, Rockway, Babrone, and Stevenson (1967) reported a significant association between antideafness and authoritarian, anti-Negro and antiminority attitudes; and Jabin (1966) indicated that authoritarianism was significantly related to attitudes of pity, hostility, and repulsion of nondisabled high schoolers toward the disabled.

In addition to the authoritarianism construct, measures of attitudes toward disabled persons have been correlated with various measures of personal and mental rigidity. The latter have included constructs such as Machiavellianism; Intellectual Pragmatism; and Dogmatism. The results of these studies are somewhat contradictory; however, the data appear to suggest that low mental and personal rigidity is associated with positive attitudes toward the disabled (Genskow and Maglione, 1965; Rickard, Triandis, and Patterson, 1963; Yuker, 1962, 1964; and Yuker and Block, 1964).

Experiential and Behavioral Correlates of Stigma toward Physically Disabled Persons

Theoretically it has been assumed (Wright, 1960) that the attitudes that nondisabled persons have toward disabled persons are learned and are a function of their past experiences interacting with disabled persons. Yuker, Block, and Younng (1966) summarized over 40 studies in this area and report that in general increased amount of contact time between nondisabled and disabled persons is related to an improvement in attitude. However, far more important than the mere extent of contact appears to be a consideration of the type or quality of contact that takes place between the two groups. Studies have demonstrated that close and intimate contact produces far more significant and positive changes in attitudes than relatively superficial contact. Particularly in instances where nondisabled persons have had the opportunity to interact with the disabled in relatively equalitarian statuses, not as a superior relating to an inferior, there has been an improvement in attitudes toward the disabled. In summary, more positive attitudes have been found to be related to close interpersonal contact with disabled persons in personal, social, educational, and vocational settings.

Although the data are inconclusive, tentatively it may be speculated that certain types of contact between the nondisabled and the disabled may actually result in the development of more negative attitudes (stigma) on the part of the nondisabled. Research (Yuker, Block, and Younng, 1966) has shown that some hospital and medical workers develop more negative attitudes toward the physically disabled over time. This finding might be explained by the fact that interaction between the nondisabled and the disabled in a hospital setting tends to be generally superficial and involves individuals of unequal status position. Furthermore, hospitalization implies that the disabled person is placed in a dependent position, where materially he contributes less to the nondisabled person than that person does to him. Such a situation could create resentment and hostility toward the disabled if close contact did not take place.

Research by Palmerton and Frumkin (1969) further illuminates the relationship between contact, between helpers and helpees, and attitudes. They found that college counselors had more favorable attitudes toward the disabled when they enjoyed interacting with the disabled, when it was difficult to avoid contact, and when they had alternative job opportunities available with the nondisabled.

In related research, Farber (1968) reviewed studies that indicate that on occasion persons have developed more negative attitudes toward the disabled and disadvantaged after visiting them within an institution setting. Thus, the institutional visit which often has been established as a means to improve community attitudes toward the disabled appears in many instances to backfire and result in general repulsion and rejection of the disabled. These feelings may be explained by the psychological reaction people experience at seeing other humans, and themselves as well if they evoke projection, in a dependent status within a total institution. Further, negative reactions may result from the physical conditions of the institution, in addition to unreasonable restrictive policies governing the lives of residents and the perception that staff hold negative and devaluating attitudes toward the residents.

Vocationally, it appears that persons in certain occupational areas hold more positive attitudes toward the disabled than others. English and Oberle (1971) found that occupations that place a low emphasis on physique, e.g. typists, are more accepting of physically disabled persons in general than occupations which place a high emphasis on physique, e.g. stewardesses. Related to this finding are studies which have shown that individuals employed in human service occupations are likely to hold more positive attitudes toward the disabled than individuals in other occupational areas (Jordan, 1969).

Finally, research (Skellhaus, 1966) has shown that preprofessional educational training contributes to a reduction in negative attitudes, and vocational studies (Yuker, Block, and Younng, 1966) indicate that stigma is reduced when nondisabled persons work closely with disabled persons over a long time period.

Work should be regarded as a humanizing experience which provides individuals with dignity and prestige. Specifically in work individuals have the opportunity and responsibility for displaying competence. Since one of the most prevailing stereotypes of the disabled persons is that they are basically incompetent, work can be associated with improving positive attitudes toward the disabled and different.

REFERENCES

Alessi, D. F. and Anthony, W. A. The uniformity of children's attitudes toward physical disabilities. *Exceptional Children,* 1969, *35(7),* 543–545.

Appell, M. J., Williams, C. M., and Fishell, K. N. Interests of professionals in fields of exceptionality. *Vocational Guidance Quarterly,* 1963, *12(1),* 43–45.

Auvenshine, C. D. The development of a scale for measuring attitudes toward severely disabled college students. Unpublished doctoral dissertation, University of Missouri, 1962.

Barker, D. G. Concepts of disabilities. *Personnel and Guidance Journal,* 1964, *43(4),* 371–374.

Barker, R. C. The social psychology of physical disability. *Journal of Social Issues.* 1948, *4,* 29–38.

Bates, R. E. Meaning of "disabled" and "handicapped" : their relationship to each other and specific defects. Unpublished doctoral dissertation, University of Houston, 1965.

Bauman, M. K. *Adjustment to Blindness: A study as reported by the committee to study adjustment to blindness.* Harrisburg, Division of Documents, Department of Property and Supplies, Commonwealth of Pennsylvania, 1954.

————, Platt, H. and Strauss, S. A measure of personality for blind adolescents. *International Journal for the Education of the Blind,* 1963, *13(1),* 7–12.

Baxt, R., David, P., Jaffe, A., and Wang, D. Survey of employers' practices and policies in the hiring of physically impaired workers. *Bulletin of the Federation of Employment and Guidance Service,* May, 1959.

Bell, A. H. Attitudes of selected rehabilitation workers and other hospital employees toward the physically disabled. *Psychological Reports,* 1962, *10(1),* 183–186.

Blatt, Burton. *Exodus from pandemonium.* Boston : Allyn and Bacon, Inc., 1970.

Block, J. R. Motivation, satisfaction and production of handicapped workers. Unpublished doctoral dissertation, New York University, 1962.

Bradley, P. A. Generalized rejection : Content or artifact. *Proceedings of the American Psychological Association Convention,* Miami, Florida, 1970, *5(2),* 699–700.

Brunswick, A. F. What generation gap? A comparison of some generalized differences among blacks and whites. *Social Problems*, 1970, *17(3)*, 358–371.

Chesler, M. A. Ethnocentrism and attitudes toward the physically disabled. *Journal of Personality and Social Psychology*, 1965, *2(6)*, 877–882.

Cohen, J. Employer attitudes toward disabled persons. *American Journal of Mental Deficiency*, 1963, *67*, 705–713.

Cowen, E. L., Underberg, R. P., and Verrillo, R. T. The development and testing of an attitudes to blindness scale. *Journal of Social Psychology*, 1958, *48*, 297–304.

———, Rockway, A. M., Babrone, P. H., and Stevenson, J. Development and evaluation of an attitudes to deafness scale. *Journal of Personality and Social Psychology*, 1967, *6(2)*, 183–191.

Doctor, R. M. and Sieveking, N. A. Survey of attitudes toward drug addiction. Proceedings of the *Annual Convention of the American Psychological Association*, 1970, *5(2)*, 795–796.

Doob, A. N. and Ecker, B. P. Stigma and compliance. *Journal of Personality and Social Psychology*, 1970, *14(4)*, 302–304.

Dunn, L. M. Special education for the mildly retarded : is much of it justifiable? *Exceptional Children*, 1968, *35*, 5–24.

Elias, J., English, R. W., Moffet, J., Simon, W., and Tucker, W. Popular conceptions of the civil rights movement. *Proceedings of the Midwest Sociological Association Convention*, Minneapolis, April 4, 1965.

English, R. W. Differential perceptions of the seriousness of a disability. (Unpublished manuscript, Syracuse University, 1970).

——— Assessment and modification of attitudes toward blind persons. (Accepted for publication by *Psychological Aspects of Disability*, 1971).

——— and Oberle, J. Towards the development of new methodology for examining attitudes toward disabled persons. *Rehabilitation Counseling Bulletin*, Fall, 1971, *15(1)*.

English, R. W. and Palla D. B. Attitudes of non-disabled persons toward a photograph of a mildly and severely mentally retarded adolescent. *Training School Bulletin*, May, 1971, *68(1)*, 55–63.

Epstein, S. and Shontz, F. Attitudes toward persons with physical disabilities as a function of attitudes toward one's own body. Paper presented at *American Psychological Association*, New York, September, 1971.

Farber, B. *Mental Retardation: its social context and social consequences.* Boston : Houghton, Mifflin Company, 1968.

Feinberg, L. B. Social desirability and attitudes toward the disabled. *Personnel and Guidance Journal*, 1967, *46(4)*, 375–381.

——— Tolerance of ambiguity as a variable in attitudes toward disabled persons. Unpublished manuscript, Syracuse University, 1971.

Freed, E. X. Opinions of psychiatric hospital personnel and college students toward alcoholism, mental illness and physical disability : an exploratory study. *Psychological Reports*, 1964, *15(2)*, 615–618.

Gellman, W. Roots of prejudice against the handicapped. *Journal of Rehabilitation*, 1959, *25(1)*, 4–6, 25.

Genskow, J. K. and Maglione, F. D. Familiarity, dogmatism and reported student attitudes toward the disabled. *Journal of Social Psychology*, 1965, *67*, 329–341.

Goffman, E. *Stigma*. Englewood Cliffs, New Jersey : Prentice-Hall, Inc., 1963.

Hamilton, K. W. *Counseling the Handicapped in the Rehabilitation Process.* New York : Ronald Press, 1950.

Heilbrun, A. B. Relationship between the Adjective Check List, Personal Preference Schedule and desirability factors under varying defensiveness conditions. *Journal of Clinical Psychology*, 1958, *24(3)*, 283–287.

——— Validation of a need scaling technique for the Adjective Check List. *Journal of Consulting Psychology*, 1959, *23*, 347–351.

Helson, H., Blake, R. R., Mouton, J. S., and Olmstead, J. A. Attitudes as adjustments to stimulus background and residual factors. *Journal of Abnormal and Social Psychology*, 1956, *52*, 314–322.

Horowitz, L. S., Rees, N. S., and Horowitz, M. W. Attitudes toward deafness as a function of increasing maturity. *Journal of Social Psychology*, 1965, *66*, 331–336.

Jabin, N. Attitudes toward the physically disabled as related to selected personality variables. *Dissertation Abstracts*, 1966, *27(2-B)*, 599.

Jaffe, J. Attitudes of adolescents toward the mentally retarded. *American Journal of Mental Deficiency*, 1966, *70(6)*, 907–912.

Jordan, J. E. and Cessna, W. A comparison of attitudes of four occupational groups toward education and physically disabled persons in Japan. *Journal of Social Psychology*, 1968, *78*, 283–284.

Kerlinger, F. N. *Foundations of Behavioral Research*. New York : Holt, Rinehart and Winston, Inc., 1965.

Kleck, R. Physical stigma and nonverbal cues emitted in face to face interaction. *Human Relations*, 1968, *21(1)*, 19–28.

———, Ono, H. and Hastorf, A. H. The effects of physical deviance upon face to face interaction. *Human Relations,* 1966, *19(4)*, 425–436.

Knittel, M. G. A comparison of attitudes toward the disabled between subjects who had a physically disabled sibling and subjects who did not have a physically disabled sibling. Unpublished doctoral dissertation, University of South Dakota, 1963.

Koelstoe, O. P. Employment evaluation and training program. *American Journal of Mental Deficiency*, 1960, *65*, 17–31.

Kogan, N. Attitudes toward old people : The development of a scale and examination correlates. *Journal of Abnormal and Social Psychology*, 1959, *59*, 44–55.

Kvaraceus, W. C. Acceptance-rejection and exceptionality. *Exceptional Children*, 1956, *22*, 328–331.

Lukoff, I. F. and Whiteman, M. A summary of attitudes and blindness : components, correlates, and effects. Unpublished manuscript, Human Resources Library, 1963.

MacDonald, A. P. and Hall, J. Perception of disability by the nondisabled. *Journal of Consulting and Clinical Psychology*, 1969, *33(6)*, 654–660.

MacGregor, F. C. Social and cultural components in the motivation of persons seeking plastic surgery of the nose. *Journal of Health and Social Behavior*, 1967, *8(2)*, 125–135.

McCourt, J. F. A study of acceptance of the geriatric patient among selected groups of hospital personnel. Unpublished doctoral dissertation, Boston University, 1963.

Murphy, A. T., Dickstein, J., and Dripps, E. Acceptance, rejection and the hearing handicapped. *Volta Review*, 1960, *62(5)*, 208–211.

Murray, H. A. *Exploration in Personality*. New York : Oxford University Press, 1938.

Nikoloff, O. M. Attitudes of public school principals toward employment of teachers with certain physical disabilities. *Rehabilitation Literature*, 1962, *23*, 344–345.

Palmerton, K. E. and Frumkin, R. M. College counselors' attitudes toward education considered a determinant of attitudes toward disabled persons. *Perceptual and Motor Skills*, 1969, *28(2)*, 441–442.

Parsons, T. Definitions of health and illness in the light of American values and social structure, in E. Gartly Jaco (Ed.) *Patients, physicians and illness*, Glencoe, Illinois : The Free Press, 1958, 165–187.

Richardson, S. A., Hastorf, A. H., Goodman, N., and Dornbusch, S. M. Cultural uniformity in reaction to physical disabilities. *American Sociological Review*, 1961, *26*, 241–247.

Rickard, T. E., Triandis, H. C., and Patterson, C. H. Indices of employer prejudice toward disabled applicants. *Journal of Applied Psychology*, 1963, *47*, 52–55.

Robinson, H. B. and Robinson, N. M. *The mentally retarded child: A psychological approach*. New York : McGraw-Hill Book Company, 1965.

Rochester, R. K. A consideration of the role theorist's interpretation of mental illness. Unpublished masters thesis, Syracuse University, Summer, 1971.

Schreiber, M. (Ed.). *Social Work and Mental Retardation*. New York : The John Day Company, 1970.

Siller, J. Reactions to physical disability. *Rehabilitation Counseling Bulletin*, 1963, *7(1)*, 12–16.

———— Personality determinants of reaction to the physically disabled.

American Foundation for the Blind Research Bulletin, 1964, 7, 37–52.

—— and Chipman, A. Personality determinants of reaction to the physically handicapped : II. Projective techniques. Albertson, New York. Unpublished manuscript, Human Resources Library, 1965.

Skellhaus, M. SWEAT project evaluation. *Project News* of the Parsons State Hospital and Training Center, 1966, *2(10),* 10–17.

Stubblefield, H. W. Religion, parents and mental retardation. *Mental Retardation,* 1965, *3(4),* 8–11.

Szasz, T. *The manufacture of madness.* New York : Harper and Row, 1970.

Titley, R. W. and Virey, W. Expression of aggression toward the physically handicapped. *Perceptual and Motor Skills,* 1969, *29(1),* 51–56.

Whiteman, M. and Lukoff, I. F. Attitudes of the sighted toward blindness and physical handicap. Paper presented at the Eastern Psychological Association, New York, April, 1960.

Wilson, E. D. and Alcorn, P. Disability simulation and development of attitudes toward the exceptional. *Journal of Special Education,* 1969, *3(3),* 303–307.

Wright, B. A. *Physical Disability: a psychological approach.* New York : Harper, 1960.

Yuker, H. *Yearly psycho-social research summary.* Albertson, New York, Human Resources, Inc., 1962.

—— *Yearly psycho-social research summary.* Albertson, New York, Human Resources, Inc., 1964.

Yuker, H. E. and Block, J. R. Intellectual attitudes and college performance. Paper presented at American Psychological Association, Los Angeles, September, 1964.

——, Block, J. R., and Campbell, W. J. A scale to measure attitudes toward disabled persons. *Human Resources Study Number 5.* Albertson, New York. Human Resources, Inc., 1960.

——, Block, J. R., and Younng, J. H. *The measurement of attitudes toward disabled persons.* Human Resources Center, Albertson, New York, 1966.

14

Combating Stigma toward Physically Disabled Persons

R. William English

In recent years a substantial body of research literature has been accumulating pertinent to the attitudes of nondisabled persons toward physical disability and physically disabled persons. Summary reviews in this area (Barker, Wright, Meyerson, and Gonick, 1953; English, 1971a; McDaniel, 1969; Wright, 1960; and Yuker, Block, and Younng, 1966) clearly indicate that nearly all physically disabled persons are stigmatized to some extent and that for some physically disabled persons stigma is their most salient or basic fact of life. (Stigma in this research is defined as human depreciation and human devaluation. The term *stigma* (Goffman, 1963) refers to an attribute that is deeply discrediting and by definition a stigmatized person is one who is not quite human or normal.) In many instances stigma appears to be a basis of further limiting medically impaired persons by turning physical disabilities into vocational, personal, and social handicaps (Hamilton, 1950).

If we take a specific disabled person and isolate the tasks involved in assisting him, we can quickly see that the vast majority of professional effort at education and rehabilitation involve issues that have nothing to do with disability per se but are problems of handicap. For example, without stigma the task of rehabilitating an amputee would involve little more than surgery and prosthetic fitting. From a medical perspective, given modern surgical techniques and opportunity for prosthetic fitting immediately after surgery, physical restoration of amputees is a matter of weeks. Consider now the case of amputation as it usually exists in reality because of negative attitudes toward disability by the nondisabled. We still have a medical problem, but in addition there are concomitant psychological, social, family, and vocational problems. For instance,

From *Rehabilitation Research and Practice Review*, 2 (1971), 19–27. Reprinted by permission of the author and Editor.

persons who are traumatically disabled usually conform to societal expectations that demand that they enact a sick role and mourn their loss of functional ability. With the omnipresence of culturally induced handicap, most amputees require the assistance of numerous other human service helpers besides medical personnel, such as psychiatrists, psychologists, social workers, rehabilitation counselors, physical therapists, occupational therapists, recreational therapists, vocational educators, vocational evaluators, and placement specialists. Not surprisingly, the rehabilitation of amputees is usually considered in terms of months or years versus weeks.

Hopefully, this anecdote illustrates the importance of stigma in limiting the lifestyle of the disabled and suggests where the energies of professional helpers and citizen advocates should be exercised. Unfortunately, however, efforts to date to deal with stigma have been virtually nonexistent, and those efforts which have been attempted have largely been failures (English, 1971b). Important in this regard is the fact that human service professionals have been dealing with stigma superficially and avoiding most successfully any meaningful encounter with some of the most critical issues facing physically disabled persons. By this I refer to the fact that traditionally, and today, we have tended to implement a crisis model of rehabilitation by restricting our efforts to dealing exclusively with disability and disabled persons. Although in certain respects preoccupation with crisis intervention is defensible, given that harried rehabilitation personnel are constantly overburdened with the immediate personal and material needs of disabled clients, it must also be argued that it is incomplete. However difficult it is for us to accept the data, I believe it is a foregone conclusion that by itself direct client service is little more than holding action, if it is even that, and has limited long-term value for assisting masses of persons who are physically disabled. Clearly in my own mind the existence of social stigma, which changes disabled persons into handicapped persons, is symptomatic of a diseased society.

This clearly suggests that to significantly improve the quality of life for the disabled and culturally different, we must treat ourselves and society as a whole. Undeniably this is a major challenge, and history is not necessarily on our side. In spite of a great broadening in humanitarian rhetoric and increases in rehabilitation expenditures, the overall picture remains the same today as it was twenty-five years ago. Numerically and proportionately the incidence of disablement has not decreased, and attitudes among the nondisabled have not measurably improved. Worse still is the fact that even as our society has stayed in lockstep, the expectations of the disabled themselves for a new, equal, nonhandicapped life have increased.

The rest of this paper is devoted to delineating a methodology for reducing and eliminating prejudice toward the physically disabled. For the most part the suggestions offered operationalize the cumulative findings of numerous studies on attitudes toward the disabled into a plan of action.

ACTION METHODOLOGY

1. *Increase the amount of meaningful contact between the disabled and the nondisabled.* Interaction has been shown to contribute to a lessening of stigma when the contact is of an egalitarian nature where the two parties engage in a mutually rewarding activity (Yuker, Block, and Younng, 1966). Such interaction might take place in a variety of settings : Educational, Occupational, Religious, Recreational, Social, and so on.

2. *Provide the disabled with the facts about stigma and improve their behavioral skills in dealing with the nondisabled.* Although stigma is a basic fact of life for all people who are socially different, disabled persons especially are often sheltered, kept in the dark, and not appraised of the effect community attitudes may have on their lives. This results in ambiguity and contributes to increasing anxiety and further forces the disabled person to enact a sick role. Professionals, e.g. physicians, counselors, and educators, can help avoid perpetuating such a cyclical reaction by acquainting physically disabled persons with the facts, as we know them, about stigma.

    At the same time, disabled persons should be appraised, through individual and group sensitivity experiences, of the types of succumbing behaviors they personally display that particularly annoy and invite the prejudice of nondisabled persons (Wright, 1960). Furthermore, disabled persons should be helped to acquire greater finesse in interacting with nondisabled persons, so that the contact will be more pleasing and profitable to both parties. Simulation techniques, such as role playing, psychodrama, and sociodrama, can be of great value in this regard (English, 1966).

3. *Influence the mass media to present more realistic views of disability and disabled persons.* In spite of press coverage and advertisements which praise the abilities of disabled persons, it appears that a substantial amount of mass-media programming, particularly

television, is such as to contribute to the formation of negative attitudes among the nondisabled toward the disabled. In many shows, e.g. children's cartoon shows, adult adventure shows, and horror movies, nefarious characters are enacted by actors with obvious physical disabilities—the implication being that people are evil specifically because of physical deformities. In other shows, e.g. medical shows and soap operas, the negative consequences of disability are overdramatized. Disability is often presented in a context that is cloaked with exaggerated pity and sadness, and the disabled are characterized as being weak, dependent, immature, stupid, and emotionally unstable.

Specific examples of television shows that have unrealistically portrayed disabled persons on a regular basis are the "Wild, Wild West," "Medical Center," and "Ironside." The first of these was a western adventure series that consistently showed disabled persons to be sadistic criminals, the second is a medical drama that occasionally overplays the psychological effects of traumatic disablement, and the last is a detective drama that greatly underplays the psychological effects of disability by totally ignoring its existence, even though the fictional "Detective Robert Ironside" is a paraplegic, confined to a wheelchair.

Disability exists and should not be ignored by the mass media; however, programs in this area should be realistic and responsible. Conversely, mass-media merchants must be persuaded to stop exploiting disability for profit through characterizations that stereotype the disabled as psychological wrecks, their lives in ruin, or wicked persons who prey upon nondisabled persons.

4. *Design stimuli, to be presented via the mass media, to reduce stigma.* Experiments to manipulate attitudes toward the disabled via the mass media—through techniques such as videotapes, audiotapes, films, and typescripts—have largely failed to have import, because the stimuli have been too diffuse and the audience too heterogeneous. Some promise may exist for successfully reducing stigma if the results of the numerous studies on stigma are used to design specific and potent stimuli to be presented via the mass media to special interest groups, such as to occupational groups that place a high emphasis on physique (English, 1971b; English and Oberle, 1971).

5. *Include the disabled person's family and his significant others in his treatment program.* Often human service personnel fail to successfully assist the disabled, because they do not deal with the

environment within which he lives. The most important part of this environment are the individuals who are psychologically closest to the disabled person. Often they themselves stigmatize the disabled and need help. In turn, significant others often feel, sometimes justifiably, stigma by association. Wherever possible, they should be included in the treatment plan or at least persuaded to support it. Without the cooperation of the persons closest to the disabled, most of our efforts at education and rehabilitation will likely fail. The disabled person's rehabilitation program may also fail, if help is not extended to his closest associates who are having great difficulty accepting his disability.

6. *Organize the physically disabled politically.* In recent years, many racial minorities, e.g. Negroes, Indians, Mexican-Americans, have organized themselves politically and achieved considerable success in improving their basic material conditions of living. Such organization has also contributed to racial cohesion and to an increase in personal pride, dignity, and self-esteem among members of these stigmatized groups. Their success suggests that other stigmatized groups may wish to act in a more militant fashion.

Theoretically, any aggressive confronting action of an outgroup toward the dominant ingroup impedes ultimate social assimilation, even though the outgroup may force an improvement in their basic living conditions. Consequently, marginally and less physically observable stigmatized persons may wish to forego politically confronting the system in order to obtain assimilation into the dominant group of the so-called normal. The mentally retarded are a case in point (Blatt, 1970). By one estimate (Farber, 1968) approximately 80% of persons classified as mentally retarded have IQ's above 50, and the majority of these persons show no physical signs of retardation. Census data indicates that approximately 4.5% of the U.S. population under 18 years of age are mentally retarded; however, the incidence of retardation for persons over 18 is only 1.5%—the incidence irrespective of age is 3%. The interpretation of such data is that a majority of mildly mentally retarded persons are able to be assimilated into the dominant unstigmatized society after they complete their secondary education and leave school, at about age 18. Although some data (Edgerton, 1968) suggest that the assimilation of educably retarded persons may not ever be totally complete, nevertheless many persons who have been labeled as educable retardates may be better off attempting to assimilate themselves ("pass") than to acknowledge they are retarded for purposes of secondary gain, whereby they inadvertently perpetuate their stigmatization. The case of visibly stigmatized persons, however, may be different. Because of aesthetic appearance, many physically disabled persons, like the blind and orthopedically disabled, may find it impossible to completely assimilate themselves and escape stigma. This situation is analogous to nonwhite persons attempting to assimilate themselves among the white majority. In essence physically disabled individuals may have nothing to lose and everything to gain by politically organizing themselves to improve their life chances. Inadvertently, their involvement might contribute to a general improvement in the opportunities available to all stigmatized persons.

7. *Pressure elected officials to review and repeal legislation that is dysfunctional and unnecessarily restricts the lifestyle of disabled persons.* Local, state, or federal statutes which are especially suspected of having no therapeutic value to the disabled or the community should have highest priority, e.g. there are statutes in some states forbidding "all" epileptics from driving an automobile. Professional people, professional lobbyists, and concerned citizens can, and should, all contribute in this area.

8. *Promote and participate in citizen advocacy programs.* Nondisabled persons should be educated about the effect of stigma on the disabled and organized into cohesive community action groups dedicated to eradicating stigma. Free clinics or workshops should be established to help inform such groups of a priority of needs in their local community and to increase their understanding about meaningful, nonstigmatizing ways they can help the disabled. Depending on the community, the highest priorities will vary, for example, elimination of architectural barriers may take precedence in one community while institutional abuse in housing, education, employment, or some other area may take precedence in another community.

9. *Change the concept and design of institutions.* Documentary case material (Blatt, 1966; Blatt, 1970; Goffman, 1961; and Szasz, 1970) has demonstrated that institutionalization is frequently dysfunctional and nonrehabilitative from the patient's perspective. In some institutions rehabilitative services, for practical purposes, are nonexistent and the only thing differentiating institutionalization from incarceration in prisons is the fact that imprisonment carries a predetermined sentence and the period of institutionalization is indefinite.

Because the efficacy of institutional treatment has not been established, in spite of their existence for over one hundred years, it is appropriate to consider new directions regarding the residential treatment of the disabled and socially different. The following specific suggestions relate to such institutional reform :

a. *Close down older institutions with antiquated physical facilities.*

b. *Do not build any new massive "total" institutions.*

c. *Substitute smaller community facilities—hostels, half-way houses and group homes—for large institutions, to serve relatively small groups of persons—less than 50.*

d. *Relocate individuals who have received an inappropriate institutional placement.* Some individuals should have never been institutionalized and should be relocated. A clear example of this latter situation is represented by the great number of geriatric cases institutionalized in mental hospitals versus geriatric hospitals.

e. *Establish active rehabilitation programs in all institutions versus mere custodial care.*

f. *Establish a regular schedule, at least four times a year, for reviewing the rehabilitation status of all patients.* Depending on a particular resident's progress, he should be discharged or have his rehabilitation program modified.

10. *Further professionalize the human services.* Within the human services professions, there are numerous steps that should be taken to help eliminate stigma. These include :

a. *Engaging in sensitivity training to identify and deal with our own tendencies to stigmatize the disabled and the different.*

b. *End the demeaning financial exploitation of disability labels by community resources serving the disabled.* Nearly all agencies, particularly those in the private sector, tend to exaggerate the negative aspects of disability in well-meaning attempts to raise funds to meet budgets—the worst example of this seems to be the "poster campaigns." Unfortunately, this process bears a high price tag of its own in further stigmatizing disabled persons. That is, nondisabled persons who contribute to help people "because" they are too unhappy and too helpless to help themselves psychologically expect, almost demand, that such disabled persons be inferior to themselves. Correspondingly, they will find it most difficult to accept this person as a human equal later. Clearly these dangers should be considered so that fund raising can be conducted in a more honest and responsible manner.

c. *Establish professional standards which can be used as guidelines for controlling the quality of human service personnel.* Olshansky (1965) has indicated that human service personnel who serve the disabled are often stigmatized Undoubtedly, some of this stigma is a consequence of poor services. Maintaining incompetent human service personnel represents a kind of prejudice by invitation for all the human service professions, which can cost dearly in terms of public confidence and support. More important, such stigma must be avoided as it greatly hinders efforts to assist the disabled and disadvantaged. Incompetents should be purged and barred, and individuals whose skills are outdated should be required to take remunerative training.

d. *Make professional associations more political.* Professional groups, such as the American Personnel and Guidance Association (APGA) and the Council for Exceptional Children (CEC), have a greater responsibility than to meet once a year to present scholarly papers which do little more than academically catalog the problems of the human services and rarely lead to a meaningful consideration of solutions. Questions must be raised, but answers must also be actively sought and decisive actions taken. The amelioration of stigma should be one of the first responsibilities of every professional organization. Although some groups have already become more politically oriented, much more aggressive action is called for to meet the challenges before us.

e. *Actively follow-up disabled persons after formal termination of services.* Follow-up is the neglected child of the rehabilitation process in that few educators or clinicians actually consider the disabled person once he has completed his formalized program. Undoubtedly, many of our failure experiences can be traced to this neglect, as most disabled persons and their families continue to need some moral and financial support after regular services have been terminated.

f. *Reduce or eliminate local and national conflicts between human service personnel.* It is unnecessary to enumerate all the sources of personal and professional conflict within the human service professions, but there is no denying that serious divisions exist, and that the disabled and disadvantaged are the losers in such intramural battles. Examples could be cited in almost endless fashion: Two or more agencies serving the same client population may work in total isolation, not acknowledging each other's presence or considering avenues of cooperation; professionals and paraprofessionals may fail to develop ways to provide their consumer group with complementary services; organizations may rigidly cling to stereotyped and unrealistic requirements for staff positions and inadvertently hire less-qualified personnel.

    While occasionally there are legitimate differences of opinion—based on theory, training and experience—conflicts must be regarded as illegitimate in that they are only self-serving.

g. *Disseminate information on stigma.* All professional educators and practitioners have a responsibility to share their knowledge, experience, and research about stigma at every opportunity. Failure to disseminate such information to our colleagues, constituents, and the general public is a luxury which contributes to our deprofessionalization and which must end.

The ideas that have been presented for combatting stigma towards the disabled are diverse, although undoubtedly incomplete, and hopefully will motivate us to act more assertively on behalf of the disabled. At the same time readers are encouraged to consider their relevance as they apply to their own life situations, and if they decide to act they are advised to adopt the following strategy: *Choose a single suggestion or action project and devote all or most of your energies to completing it before starting something else.*

In its entirety, stigma is a problem of overwhelming proportions where realism blurs with pessimism and where it is easy to despair and lapse into a state of hopelessness. Functionally this can be avoided by developing a case of therapeutic tunnel vision including the identification and concentration of energies on single potentially realizable objectives.

REFERENCES

Barker, R. G., Wright, B. A., Meyerson, L., and Gonick, M. R. *Adjustment to physical handicap and illness: A survey of the social psychology of physique and disability.* New York, Social Science Research Council, 1953.

Blatt, B. *Exodus from pandemonium.* Boston : Allyn and Bacon, Inc., 1970.

———. Personal communication. Syracuse University, Workshop on Human Abuse : Protection and public policy, Syracuse, New York, July 22, 1970.

——— and Kaplan, F. *Christmas in purgatory.* Boston : Allyn and Bacon, Inc., 1966.

Edgerton, R. B. Anthropology and mental retardation : a plea for the comparative study of incompetence. In H. J. Prehm, L. A. Hamerlynck, and J. E. Crosson (Eds). *Behavioral research in mental retardation.* Eugene : University of Oregon, Rehabilitation Research and Training Center in Mental Retardation, 1968.

English, R. W. Correlates of stigma towards physically disabled persons. Manuscript accepted for publication by *Rehabilitation Research and Practice Review,* Fall, 1971a.

———. Assessment, modification and stability of attitudes toward blind persons. Manuscript accepted for publication by *Psychological Aspects of Disability,* Fall, 1971b.

———. The use of group dynamics in vocational rehabilitation counseling with the emotionally disturbed. Unpublished manuscript, University of Wisconsin (Madison), 1966.

——— and Oberle, J. B. Towards the development of new methodology for examining attitudes toward disabled persons. Manuscript accepted for publication by the *Rehabilitation Counseling Bulletin,* Fall, 1971.

Farber, I. *Mental retardation: its social context and social consequences.* Boston : Houghton, Mifflin Co., 1968.

Goffman, E. *Asylums.* New York : Doubleday and Co., Inc., 1961.

——— *Stigma.* Englewood Cliffs, New Jersey : Prentice-Hall, Inc., 1963.

Hamilton, K. W. *Counseling the handicapped in the rehabilitation process.* New York : Ronald Press, 1950.

McDaniel, J. W. *Physical disability and human behavior.* New York : Pergamon Press, 1969.

Olshansky, S. S. Stigma : its meaning and some of its problems for vocational rehabilitation agencies. *Rehabilitation Literature,* 1965, *26,* 71–74.

Szasz, T. *Manufacture of madness*. New York : Harper and Row, 1970.

Wright, B. A. *Physical disability: A psychological approach*. New York : Harper, 1960.

Yuker, H. E., Block, J. R., and Younng, J. H. *The measurement of attitudes toward disabled persons*. Albertson, New York, Human Resources Center, 1966.

15

Societal Rehabilitation:
Changing Society's Attitudes toward
the Physically and Mentally Disabled

William A. Anthony

Physically and/or mentally disabled individuals, who bear such labels as the mentally ill, physically handicapped, or mentally retarded, often are the targets of prejudice and discriminatory practices. Researchers have shown that this discrimination is least apparent in relatively impersonal situations and most blatant in contemplating either close interpersonal or business situations, such as marriage and employment (McDaniel, 1969; Rusk and Taylor, 1946; Whatley, 1959). It would appear that society is least tolerant of the disabled individual in areas of functioning which in our culture are of critical importance to mental health.

With the growing interest in preventive or community psychiatry, mental health professionals have increased their concern about the impact of the community's negative attitudes on the mental health of the mentally and physically disabled (Bindman and Spiegel, 1969; Caplan, 1964; Caplan, 1970; Iscoe and Spielberger, 1970; Lamb, Heath, and Downing, 1969). Various researchers have theorized that society's attitudes and expectations for the disabled may be of critical importance in maintaining the mental health of the physically handicapped and in restoring quickly the mental health of the mentally ill (Anthony, 1970; Centers and Centers, 1963; Roehrer, 1961; Scheff, 1963; Spitzer and Denzin, 1968; Yamamato, 1971). If society's attitudes are indeed so

Reprinted from *Rehabilitation Psychology*, 19 (1972), 117–126. Copyright © 1972 by the American Psychological Association. Reprinted by permission of the publisher and author.

crucial to the functioning of the physically and mentally disabled, it would seem incumbent upon mental health professionals to attempt to influence these attitudes in a positive direction.

In this survey *societal rehabilitation* refers to efforts which attempt to reduce the general public's prejudicial attitudes toward the disabled individual. *Societal rehabilitation* is to be distinguished from *individual rehabilitation*. The latter is designed to restore or reintegrate the disabled individual into society (Jacques, 1970).

Although efforts at societal rehabilitation have been varied, it seems both possible and legitimate to group these attempts into three broad categories on the basis of the procedures emphasized: (a) contact with the disabled individual, (b) information about the disabled individual, and (c) a combination of both contact and information.

CONTACT

One procedure designed to induce attitude change is to arrange contacts between the general public and members of a disabled group. Studies investigating the contact dimension do so in two different ways. One method is to divide the subjects into groups simply on the basis of their self-reports about the amount of contact which they have had with a member of a disabled group and determine if differences exist in the attitudes of subjects differing in amount of self-reported contact. The second method exposes the subjects to a specific contact experience and assesses the effects of this observable contact experience on the subjects' attitudes.

Results of studies of the first type are fairly divergent. If one struggles to find a consensus, it appears that individuals who report contact tend to have slightly more favorable attitudes than those who report no contact. Evidence of the facilitative effects of contact has been provided by Semmel and Dickson (1966), who found that as the amount of contact reported by college students increased, attitudes toward handicapped people became more positive. Another study also provided evidence of a moderate tendency toward more favorable attitudes by individuals who said they had had contact with the physically disabled (Gaier, Linkowski, and Jacques, 1968). A further example of the mild effects of contact was provided by Jaffe (1967). He found that high school students who reported some contact with the mentally retarded showed a more positive attitude on one of three attitudinal measures.

Slightly negative effects of contact also have been reported (Cowen, Underberg, and Verrillo, 1958). These researchers found that individuals who had had contact with the blind tended to have more negative attitudes than individuals reporting no contact.

A recent monograph summarized the results of over twenty studies of the relationship between reported contact with the physically disabled and attitudes toward physically disabled persons. Similar to the results presented previously, the studies exhibited a wide range of findings, but a slight majority of studies reported a significant relationship between amount of contact and favorableness of attitude (Yuker, Block, and Younng, 1966).

These retrospective contact studies are methodologically deficient in several important ways that may account for their conflicting results. First, it is the individual subject who defines what is meant by *contact* : the type of contact experience no doubt varies from subject to subject. Also, the contact experience for many subjects may have contained informational components as well, and the independent effects of contact and information may not be isolated.

These deficiencies are overcome in the more experimental type of contact study, and as a result the divergent findings disappear. Studies of the effects of specific contact experiences with a wide variety of disabled groups consistently have found no consistent changes in the subjects' attitudes as a result of their contacts with disabled persons.

Physically Disabled

Anthony and Cannon (1969) found no effect on physically normal chlidren's attitudes toward physical disability as a result of attendance at a 2-week summer camp with physically handicapped children. The findings indicated a nonsignificant tendency for children who had negative attitudes to become even more negative. Similarly, Centers and Centers (1963) found that children who attended class with amputee children had significantly more rejecting attitudes toward the amputee children than toward a matched group of nonhandicapped children. In a study of adult attitudes, Granofsky (1966) was unable to improve the attitudes of volunteer hospital workers toward the physically disabled by arranging eight hours of social contact between the volunteers and a group of physically disabled men.

Mentally Retarded

Studies which attempted to change attitudes toward the mentally retarded through contact experiences have met with equally discouraging results. These studies typically involve assessing the attitudes of school children toward mentally retarded classmates who have been integrated into the nonmentally-retarded children's class or school. The findings are unanimous in indicating that contact is not sufficient to produce positive attitudes toward mentally retarded children (Lapp, 1957; Rucker, Howe, and Snider, 1969; Strauch, 1970).

Mentally Ill

The unique effects of a contact-only experience with mental patients recently has been investigated (Spiegel, Keith-Spiegel, Zirgulis, and Wine, 1971). College students visited mental patients for 1–3 hours per week for a semester but received no supervision or information. At posttesting the students saw the typical mental patient as significantly more depressed and irritable, less neat, and less interested in socialization. Their scores on the Opinions about Mental Illness scale (OMI) changed on only two of the five scales—the students became significantly less authoritarian but also less benevolent toward the mentally ill.

Of peripheral interest is one other study which examined the specific effects of contact with the mentally ill (King, Walder, and Pavey, 1970). Rather than assessing attitude change, this investigation assessed pre-post personality changes in college students who volunteered for a semester-long companion program in a mental hospital. While some personality change did occur, it was more circumscribed than the changes brought about by a similar contact plus information experience to which it was compared.

In summary, while a dearth of experimental studies on the effects of contact exist, those that have been done are in general agreement—contact in and of itself does not significantly change attitudes toward persons with a disability. The unique effects of contact on changing attitudes toward the physically handicapped, mentally retarded, or mentally ill have yet to be demonstrated.

INFORMATION

Attempts also have been made to change attitudes by providing the nondisabled person with information about disabled people. This information may take the form of a book, a course lecture or discussion, or a film or institutional tour. General agreement seems to exist in the literature that regardless of the way in which the information is presented, the power of information alone to produce positive attitude change is negligible.

Several studies investigated the attitude change of college students enrolled in an abnormal psychology course (Altrocchi and Eisdorfer, 1961; Costin and Kerr, 1962). The first study compared students in classes of abnormal psychology, personality development, and industrial management. As would be expected, abnormal psychology students increased their information about mental illness; however, their attitudes toward mental illness as measured by a semantic differential did not change.

Costin and Kerr (1962) compared students in an abnormal psychology class with a comparable group of controls. They reported some changes for the abnormal psychology students on the OMI, but these changes appeared to reflect informational increases rather than attitudinal changes. For example, the students increased their belief that mental illness is caused by interpersonal experience (Interpersonal Etiology scale), but they did not change their opinion about how different the mentally ill are from normals (Mental Hygiene Ideology). Furthermore, their scores on a scale of benevolence toward mental patients decreased.

Semmel and Dickson (1966) compared seniors in elementary education who had taken a course in special education with those who had not. No significant difference was found in attitudes measured by the Connotative Reaction Inventory, a scale designed to assess how comfortable a person says he would be in 10 social situations with a physically disabled person. Two studies on the combined effects of contact plus information have used as a control group an information-only sample—typically psychology majors or introductory psychology students (Chinsky and Rappaport, 1970; Smith, 1969). Neither study reported significant, positive changes in attitudes as a result of didactic course-work in psychology.

Another way to present information about disabled people is by means of a film or institutional tour. Staffieri and Klappersack (1960) examined the effect of viewing a favorable film on cerebral palsy on college students' attitudes. The authors found no change in attitudes as measured by a social distance scale. An attempt to modify high school and college students' attitudes toward the mentally retarded by providing them with a tour of a state school for the mentally retarded did result in attitude changes, "but not necessarily of a positive nature" (Cleland and Chambers, 1959). While the students became more open in praise of the institution and employees, they tended to see the mentally retarded children as "better off in the institution."

Sarbin and Mancuso (1970) recently reviewed various educational programs designed by mental health professionals which attempted to influence the general public to consider mental illness with the same nonrejecting attitudes as somatic illness. Similar to the results of the informational studies reviewed in this survey, they concluded that mental health education campaigns have been notably unsuccessful in their objective.

In conclusion, it would appear that providing individuals with information about disabled people has demonstrated only the obvious effect—it increases a person's knowledge about disabled people. However, merely having more and more information about persons with a disability does not enable the nondisabled persons to evaluate the disabled person more positively. An as yet untested possibility remains that the information presented by the professionals is faulty and that some other kind of information would be effective in facilitating attitude change.

CONTACT PLUS INFORMATION

Many researchers have attempted to change attitudes toward disabled individuals by combining the contact experience with some type of information about the disability. The findings of these studies appear to be remarkably consistent: Regardless of the type of disability studied, and seemingly independent of the type of contact and information experience provided, all studies reported that a contact-plus-information experience had a favorable impact on the nondisabled person's attitudes.

Physically Disabled

Anthony (1969) studied the attitudes of counselors employed at a summer camp for handicapped children. The camping experience provided the counselors with information conveyed by the professionals on the camp staff as well as continuous contact. The findings indicated that at the beginning of the camping experience new counselors had significantly less positive attitudes than counselors who had worked at the camp previously, and that by the end of the summer the new counselors had significantly improved attitudes toward physically disabled persons.

In a cross-sectional study of the effects of rehabilitation counselor training, Anthony and Carkhuff (1970) found that advanced students, who generally had more contact and information about physical disability, had more positive attitudes toward physically disabled individuals than beginning students whose attitudes did not differ from graduate students in a nonhelping profession.

Rusalem (1967) attempted to change the attitudes of a group of high school girls toward the deaf-blind. A unique aspect of this study was that the students were preselected from a larger group to form two groups: one with the most positive attitudes and one with the least positive. In addition, the students did not volunteer but were required to participate in the research. The contact and information experience consisted of six 1-hour group sessions that involved information about deaf-blindness, instruction in the manual alphabet, and the opportunity to communicate with deaf-blind individuals. Measures of attitude change were self-reports, a sentence completion test, and behavior.

Results showed that students with the most positive attitudes did not change on the self-report or the sentence completion test, probably due to a ceiling effect, but that the group with the poorest attitudes improved on both the attitude and behavioral measures. Measures of behavioral change included self-initiated volunteer work and reading about deaf-blindness.

Mentally Ill

The studies concerned with changing attitudes toward mental illness have used only two groups of subjects—student nurses in psychiatric training and college students concurrently working part-time in a mental hospital and enrolled in courses which provided them with an opportunity to discuss their work. The college students were participants in programs which ranged from 30 hours (Chinsky and Rappaport, 1970) to 2 years (Smith, 1969) and varied in intensity from 40 hours per week (Kulik, Martin, and Scheibe, 1969; Scheibe, 1965) to several hours per week (Holzberg and Gewirtz, 1963; Keith-Spiegel and Spiegel, 1970). Using a variety of measures such as the Adjective Check List, Opinions about Mental Illness Scale, and the Custodial Mental Illness Ideology Scale, all of the above studies reported favorable effects on attitudes toward the mentally ill.

Of related interest some researchers also investigated the effects of contact-plus-information experiences on volunteers' descriptions of themselves. The results have been inconsistent. Both positive effects (Scheibe, 1965; Holzberg, Gewirtz, and Ebner, 1964) or no effects (Chinsky and Rappaport, 1970) as a result of the contact-plus-information experience have been reported.

The effects of psychiatric-nurse-training on the attitudes of student nurses have been investigated repeatedly (Altricchi and Eisdorfer, 1961; Hicks and Spaner, 1962; Lewis and Cleveland, 1966; Smith, 1969). Within a time span of 8–16 months, the psychiatric nursing experience provides the student nurses with extensive opportunities for contact as well as exposure to the professional literature in psychopathology. The research has shown consistently that this type of experience has positive effects on attitudes toward mental illness.

Mentally Retarded

A study of attitudes toward mental retardation, while not a pre- post-test design, compared a group of student teachers and teachers of the mentally retarded with teachers and students in general education and professionals in other fields. The findings indicated that student teachers and teachers of the mentally retarded had the most positive attitudes (Efron and Efron, 1967). If one can assume that training to teach the mentally retarded involves both contact and information, this result is consistent with the previously reported positive effects of a contact-plus-information experience.

CONCLUSIONS AND IMPLICATIONS

1. The attitudes of nondisabled persons toward persons with a disability can be influenced positively by providing the nondisabled individual with an experience which includes contact with disabled persons and information about the disability. Neither alone is sufficient, significantly and consistently, to have a favorable impact on attitudes toward disabled persons. It appears that without information contact has only a limited positive effect or may even reinforce existing negative attitudes. Similarly, information without contact increases knowledge about the disability only but appears to have little or no effect on attitudes.

The consistency of the research is all the more remarkable when one considers that the present survey examined attitudes toward three different disability groups assessed with a variety of attitudinal measures. In addition, the type of contact-plus-information experience varied from study to study. While it is conceivable that a researcher could deliberately arrange a destructive contact-and-information experience and obtain negative results, it is impressive that of the variety of contact-plus-information experiences which researchers have so far investigated, all have yielded positive results.

2. The research conclusions on the contact-plus-information experiences must be limited because almost all the studies have been done on either college students who volunteered to undergo a contact experience or trainees in the helping professions. A dearth of research exists on other age groups, nonhelping professionals, and nonvolunteers.

3. Little is known about how much time is needed to change attitudes. The programs presented in this survey varied in length from 6 hours to 2 years. Smith (1969) suggested that attitude change occurs early in a semester-long contact-plus-information experience. The fact that Rusalem (1967) was able to bring about both attitude and behavioral change toward the deaf-blind in only 6 hours suggests that an extremely short but intensive contact-plus-information experience is capable of producing favorable attitude change.

4. Professionals involved in community mental health and rehabilitation possess sufficient knowledge to begin to design broad societal rehabilitation programs based on a contact-plus-information experience. Mental health professionals who work in the schools could devise a societal rehabilitation program consisting of a required course, at the high school level, similar to the kind of program conducted by Rusalem (1967). Such courses should include contact with physically disabled and formerly mentally disabled individuals, as well as reading and discussions which facilitate student understanding of their reluctance to interact with

disabled persons. College instructors of abnormal psychology courses also might include a contact-plus-information experience as part of their course requirements.

Other professionals could run programs designed to change the attitudes of employers. Perhaps such a course could be required in-service training for personnel directors of government agencies. The attitudes of private employers might be changed by training disabled persons to conduct job development interviews, thus insuring a contact-plus-information experience for each employer interviewed.

All of these societal rehabilitation programs should be based on the principles of program development which emphasize the development of simple steps to achieve a complex goal such as attitude change (Carkhuff, Friel, and Berenson, 1972). In addition, such programs must evaluate their efforts not just in terms of attitude change but ultimately in terms of behavioral criteria. For example, if the attitude change program was directed at employers the real measure of success might be the number of disabled persons subsequently hired. Or, if the target population was high school and college students, behavioral measures might include variables such as the number of individuals who subsequently volunteered to work in agencies serving disabled persons, or the amount of information about disabilities obtained on the students' own initiative, or the frequency of contact with disabled persons.

REFERENCES

Altrocchi, J. and Eisdorfer, C. Changes in attitudes toward mental illness. *Mental Hygiene*, 1961, 45, 563–570.

Anthony, W. A. The effect of contact on an individual's attitude toward disabled persons. *Rehabilitation Counseling Bulletin*, 1969, 12, 168–171.

Anthony, W. A. The physically disabled client and facilitative confrontation. *Journal of Rehabilitation*, 1970, 36(3), 22–23.

Anthony, W. A. and Cannon, J. A. A pilot study on the effects of involuntary integration on children's attitudes. *Rehabilitation Counseling Bulletin*, 1969, 12, 239–240.

Anthony, W. A. and Carkhuff, R. R. The effects of rehabilitation counselor training upon trainee functioning. *Rehabilitation Counseling Bulletin*, 1970, 13, 333–342.

Bindman, A. J. and Spiegel, A. D. (Eds.) *Perspectives in community mental health*. Chicago : Aldine, 1969.

Caplan, G. *Principles of preventive psychiatry.* New York : Basic Books, 1964.

Caplan, G. *The theory and practice of mental health consultation.* New York : Basic Books, 1970.

Carkhuff, R. R., Friel, T., and Berenson, B. G. *The art of program development.* Amherst, Mass. : Human Resource Development Press, in press, 1972.

Centers, L. and Centers, R. Peer group attitudes toward the amputee child. *Journal of Social Psychology,* 1963, 61, 127–132.

Chinsky, J. M. and Rappaport, J. Attitude change in college students and chronic patients : A dual perspective. *Journal of Consulting and Clinical Psychology,* 1970, 35, 388–394.

Cleland, C. C. and Chambers, W. R. Experimental modification of attitudes as a function of an institutional tour. *American Journal of Mental Deficiency,* 1959, 64, 124–130.

Costin, F. and Kerr, W. D. The effects of an abnormal psychology course on students' attitudes toward mental illness. *Journal of Educational Psychology,* 1962, 53, 214–218.

Cowen, E. L., Underberg, R. P., and Verrillo, R. T. The development and testing of an attitude to blindness scale. *Journal of Social Psychology,* 1958, 48, 297–304.

Efron, R. E. and Efron, H. Y. Measurements of attitudes toward the retarded and an application with educators. *American Journal of Mental Deficiency,* 1967, 72, 100–107.

Gaier, E. L., Linkowski, D. G., and Jacques, M. E. Contact as a variable in the perception of disability. *Journal of Social Psychology,* 1968, 74, 117–126.

Granofsky, J. Modification of attitudes toward the visibly disabled. Unpublished doctoral dissertation, Yeshiva University, 1966.

Hicks, J. M. and Spaner, F. E. Attitude change and mental hospital experience. *Journal of Abnormal and Social Psychology,* 1962, 65, 112–120.

Holzberg, J. D. and Gewirtz, H. A method of altering attitudes toward mental illness. *Psychiatric Quarterly Supplement,* 1963, 37, 56–61.

Holzberg, J. D., Gewirtz, H., and Ebner, E. Changes in moral judgment and self-acceptance as a function of companionship with hospitalized mental patients. *Journal of Consulting Psychology,* 1964, 28, 299–303.

Iscoe, I. and Spielberger, C. D. (Eds.) *Community Psychology: Perspectives in training and research.* New York : Appleton-Century-Crofts, 1970.

Jacques, M. E. *Rehabilitation counseling: Scope and services.* New York : Houghton Mifflin, 1970.

Jaffe, J. Attitudes and interpersonal contact : Relationships between contact with the mentally retarded and dimensions of attitude. *Journal of Counseling Psychology,* 1967, 14, 482–484.

Keith-Spiegel, P. and Spiegel, D. Effects of mental hospital experience on attitudes of teenage students toward mental illness. *Journal of Clinical Psychology,* 1970, 26, 387–388.

King, M., Walder, L. O., and Pavey, S. Personality change as a function of volunteer experience in a psychiatric hospital. *Journal of Consulting and Clinical Psychology,* 1970, 35, 423–425.

Kulik, J. A., Martin, R. A., and Scheibe, K. E. Effects of mental hospital volunteer work on students' conceptions of mental illness. *Journal of Clinical Psychology,* 1969, 25, 326–329.

Lamb, H. R., Heath, D., and Downing, J. J. (Eds.) *Handbook of community mental health practice.* San Francisco : Jossey-Bass, 1969.

Lapp, E. A. A study of the social adjustment of slow learning children who were assigned part-time regular classes. *American Journal of Mental Deficiency,* 1957, 62, 254–262.

Lewis, D. L. and Cleveland, S. E. Nursing students' attitudinal changes following a psychiatric affiliation. *Journal of Psychiatric Nursing,* 1966, 4, 223–231.

McDaniel, J. W. *Physical disability and human behavior.* New York : Pergamon Press, 1969.

Roehrer, G. A. The significance of public attitudes in the rehabilitation of the disabled. *Rehabilitation Literature,* 1961, 22, 66–72.

Rucker, C. N., Howe, C. E., and Snider, B. The participation of retarded children in junior high academic and non-academic regular classes. *Exceptional Children,* 1969, 35, 617–623.

Rusalem, H. Engineering changes in public attitudes toward a severely disabled group. *Journal of Rehabilitation,* 1967, 33(3), 26–27.

Rusk, H. A. and Taylor, E. J. *New hope for the handicapped.* New York : Harper, 1946.

Sarbin, T. R. and Mancuso, J. C. Failure of a moral enterprise : Attitudes of the public toward mental illness. *Journal of Consulting and Clinical Psychology,* 1970, 35, 159–173.

Scheff, T. J. The role of the mentally ill and the dynamics of mental disorder : A research framework. *Sociometry,* 1963, 26, 436–453.

Scheibe, K. E. College students spend eight weeks in mental hospital : A case report. *Psychotherapy: Theory, Research, and Practice,* 1965, 2, 117–120.

Semmel, M. I. and Dickson, S. Connotative reactions of college students to disability labels. *Exceptional Children,* 1966, 32, 443–450.

Smith, J. J. Psychiatric hospital experience and attitudes toward "mental illness." *Journal of Consulting and Clinical Psychology,* 1969, 33, 302–306.

Spiegel, D., Keith-Spiegel, P., Zirgulis, J., and Wine, D. B. Effects of student visits on social behavior of regressed schizophrenic patients. *Journal of Clinical Psychology*, 1971, 27, 396–400.

Spitzer, S. P. and Denzin, N. K. *The mental patient: Studies in the sociology of deviance.* New York : McGraw-Hill, 1968.

Staffieri, R. and Klappersack, B. An attempt to change attitudes toward the cerebral palsied. *Rehabilitation Counseling Bulletin*, 1960, 3, 5–6.

Strauch, J. D. Social contact as a variable in the expressed attitudes of normal adolescents toward EMR. *Exceptional Children*, 1970, 36, 495–500.

Whatley, C. D. Social attitudes toward discharged mental patients. *Social Problems*, 1959, 6, 313–320.

Yamamato, K. To be different. *Rehabilitation Counseling Bulletin*, 1971, 14, 180–189.

Yuker, H. E., Block, J. R., and Younng, J. H. *The measurement of attitudes toward disabled persons: Human Resources Study No. 7.* Albertson, N.Y. : Human Resources, 1966.

Part VI

Sexuality and Disability

The sexual realities of persons with disabilities have traditionally been given little recognition by professionals, although currently this is a major area of concern. It has been suggested that sexual functioning, along with excretory functioning, is a subject area that is greatly avoided by professionals working with clients. Part of this neglect undoubtedly stems from taboos against the discussion of sex; another reason for avoidance is the lack of education and information about sex as it relates to people with physical disabilities. Part VI should help the reader in overcoming both attitudinal and informational problems.

In his general discussion of sexuality and disability, Diamond presents the views of the client, the professional, the agency, the family, and the person to whom the client's sexual attention is focused. Following a discussion of these perspectives, the author examines specific problems and issues related to sexual functioning and provides guidelines for improving the sexual relationship.

Special considerations in providing sex education for physically handicapped children are discussed by Bloom. Particular focus is upon assisting parents to recognize that their children are sexual beings, with the needs and desires of nonhandicapped children. Important issues related to marriage and parenting are also presented.

The psychosocial aspects of sexuality in disabled and nondisabled people and the role and reactions of the rehabilitation team in assisting to overcome problems related to sexual functioning of patients with cardiovascular disorders, spinal cord injury, and amputation are presented in the article by Griffith and his associates. The importance of understanding premorbid life style as it relates to sexual functioning is emphasized.

Singh and Magner look more specifically at spinal cord injury and its implications for sexual functioning. The importance of the self-concept, particularly the view of oneself as a sexual practitioner and object, is presented as a critical element in the adjustment of spinal cord-injured persons to their own status.

16

Sexuality and the Handicapped

Milton Diamond

Professional recognition of the sexual problems and concerns of the handicapped has been developing and expanding for the last several years. To date, however, little has been formalized in print and what has been done is primarily directed toward making the professional aware of the area as one of legitimate concern. For this presentation, I would like to formalize some specific matters to be considered, offer specific recommendations for handling problems, and develop a directness in dealing with some of the more controversial issues involved. This is now appropriate, since during the past several years many excellent people have contributed their knowledge and efforts to make the sexual probelms of the handicapped a respectable issue of concern and have awakened many to the disrespect that must be attached to ignorance and non-concern with the subject (e.g., Comarr; Gochros and Schultz; Kempton). These positive efforts have further engendered a desire for professionals to have working models and ideas to follow the general attitudinal changes stressed previously.

My presentation will be divided into several portions. First, I will indicate how the perspectives of various individuals or groups color the way this subject is treated. Then I will deal with some specific problems and issues in sexual expression and follow this with recommendations for handling problems that fall into associated areas. My concluding comments will contain several general rules for improving sexual functioning that are pertinent for all, able-bodied and handicapped, but more so for the handicapped.

First, I would like to make clear just how many levels I think are

From *Rehabilitation Literature*, 35 (1974), 34–40. Copyright © 1974 by the National Easter Seal Society for Crippled Children and Adults. Reprinted by permission of the Editor.

involved with sexuality and how these must be distinguished. It must be understood that when one considers sexuality, one must not think only of genitals or bedroom activity, although that is usually what first comes to mind. At least two broad areas must be considered : public and private sexuality.

Public.   How does the person act in public; what role is played by these actions? Will a handicap interfere with the individual's personal or public appraisal of his or her masculinity or femininity? For example, can a telephone lineman with a paralyzed leg accept, without loss of masculinity, the job of a telephone operator? Can the arthritic housewife accept the loss of her hands and deft touch without considering it a reflection of her femininity?

Sexual patterns and roles are our public demonstration of socially recognized sexual expressions. Public concerns may manifest themselves in the choice of how the individuals interact with society.

Private.   Here we refer to the genital sexual responses and those inner problems not usually discernible. This includes the ability to maintain an erection, have orgasm, receive and give genital and sensual pleasures, and reduce sexual tensions in oneself or partner.

Naturally, these public and private concerns might be combined.

Next, I would like to make clear that we must not confuse genital satisfaction, love, reproduction, and marriage. These four areas are quite distinct, although they may go together or be related. We must clearly keep them separate in our own minds and in the minds of our clients, certainly to insure just what is being communicated. The four areas of genital satisfaction, love, reproduction, and marriage offer different rewards and present different problems. For example, a client wanting genital satisfaction doesn't necessarily want marriage, and one wanting marriage doesn't necessarily want children or sex. If this seems like too radical a concept, just recall that it is only a few generations back when our ancestors had marriages that were arranged so sex and marriage were started without love, most present-day marriages are not entered into by virgins, and birth control and family planning are facts of life. In a very practical vein, we must insure that children are to be considered on their own merits not as visual proof of masculine or feminine abilities; reproduction is not sexual identity and neither is genital gratification. A handicapped person might be more disadvantaged than an able-bodied person in having a child who is not wanted for himself but rather as an affirmation of masculinity or femininity.

It is appropriate here to distinguish between the different stages during which persons may become handicapped. These may be considered : prepubertal, adolescent, marriageable, married, separated, divorced, widowed, and senescent. A teenager is obviously involved with different concerns than is a senior citizen, and obviously the attendant concerns of one with memories of the past and lost demonstrated abilities would differ from those of one who never had experiences to draw from. While this will not be dealt with in detail now, it is well to reflect on how each stage has its specific concerns.

PERSPECTIVES AND ISSUES

At least five different perspectives have to be considered in any professional situation. These viewpoints are those of : (1) the client; (2) the professional dealing with the client; (3) the agency represented by the professional; (4) the family in which the client resides; and (5) the "second person" involved, i.e., the individual to whom the client's attention is or might be focused.

These five different perspectives all have a similar focus, but they may differ quite markedly. There may even be many areas of wide disagreement and friction among these five factions, although theoretically they should all be working together.

Client

The client generally looks at his or her problem as quite personal and private. The client may consider the sexual situation as separate from the handicap or part of the handicap but generally thinks it's a problem to be borne in silence and one that should not concern the professional. This is doubly so for the handicapped compared to the able-bodied. Both the able-bodied and handicapped have, first of all, been taught that sexual matters are private and not to be honestly discussed, so this is a common problem. But the handicapped also has or is given the feeling that any interest or effort that doesn't focus most directly on the handicap should be considered minor. For example, the blind should worry only about seeing and the paralyzed only about walking.

Professional

The professional quite often looks at sexual problems as outside both the professional's scope and the client's area of legitimate concern. The professional's training has generally been toward getting the individual back on the job, capable of caring for a family and generally self-supporting. Regardless of whether the professional has been trained as a physician, psychologist, social worker, or other type of therapist, until quite recently sexual counseling was never considered as within the legitimate scope of activities. Therapists were not taught the clues to which to attend in this area. Often, even if the client does bring up concern regarding the subject, the professional quite often avoids the issue entirely by not replying to the clues or defends himself by saying words to the effect of, "You should be worried about not being able to walk or not being able to see or not being able to hear rather than worrying about your sexual concerns." It's as if the sexual concerns have to be of lower magnitude than the other abilities. The professional more than anyone must realize that meeting an individual's sexual concerns can go a long way in reestablishing or establishing a general feeling of self-worth conducive to general rehabilitation.

It must be mentioned here, in contrast with what I've just said, that an overzealous professional should in this area, as in others for which he has been trained, be careful to be attuned to client sensitivities. One should not project concerns on patients that are not there, since many handicapped handle their sexual concerns quite well.

Agency

Agencies, most often, are interested only in those factors that they consider leading to job placement or getting the person functioning in the home. They think in terms of productivity or income, and their distance from the client makes them even less aware than the professional counselor of some of the human sexual concerns of the client. Agencies change even more slowly than do individual professionals. So, even though the professional (physician, social worker, counselor, or psychologist) might be interested in the individual client's sexual abilities, the agency frequently takes a dim view of these concerns. Often, the agency is most concerned with image and thinks that being concerned with an individual's sexual problems is inappropriate for a state, foundation-supported, or religion-affiliated organization. Again, I think these views are changing, and it's slowly becoming apparent, to both the professional and the agency, that, once an individual's worth as a complete person is reestablished, he or she is much more apt to be educable, hireable, and self-content with himself and his situation.

Family

Next, we have the family perspective. Here the issue is quite different. To be sure, the family, too, thinks the sexual problems are private and not to be discussed in public. They think they are also outside the province of the agency or professional dealing with the client, yet the family is quite often ambivalent about the situation. While they recognize that these are valid issues, they generally wish the sexual concerns to be ignored; they want them to sort of "go away," since they are ill at ease dealing with them, and don't really know how to handle the issues. They, too, are beset with the societal value that sex is private and not to be discussed in public.

Quite often, the family would imagine that if, especially in younger people, sex is not discussed, it would never come up in a person's experiences. As with the able-bodied, they don't know how to deal with overt sex, whether it be masturbation or displays of affection toward possible sexual partners. They have strong conflicts. On the one hand, they want to consider the handicapped family member like everyone else and thus allow all opportunities. On the other hand, they don't want to, as they consider it, raise false expectations and hopes. Lastly, it is difficult for the family to recognize that children or parents can be sexual. Regardless of age, elderly parents are often considered "beyond it" and children "not yet ready."

Second Person

Last is the "second person." This is the perspective of the one on whom the client focuses his or her sexual attention. This is also considered to be personal and private, but here the individual definitely is concerned with how the handicap may be involved, although the concern may not be shown. There is the question of just what the partner can do or not do, and can this be discussed openly, or will the issue be too sensitive for probing? Often both of the parties involved seek advice and counsel from others, lay and professional, instead of speaking with each other about sexual feelings, concerns, capabilities, and expectations.

SPECIFIC ISSUES

With my broad introduction and talk of perspectives, I will now present three specific issues that must and can be dealt with within these perspectives. These issues are: (1) performance and expectations, (2) guilt, and (3) communication. While my remarks are directed mainly toward dealing with the concerns of the handicapped, it will be obvious that they apply equally as well to the able-bodied.

Performance and Expectations

Too many individuals view their sexual expression as a performance to be rated and graded on some sort of consensually agreed-upon scale. It is as if there were a "right" and a "wrong" way to be sexual and anything less than "right" is to be criticized. Our society certainly fosters these expectations and we live with them in Archie Bunker fashion every day.

For our clients, in a realistic and nonjudgmental manner, we have to realign the performance expectations with performance capabilities, so that the only allowable criteria for concern are based on what the couple or the individuals prefer within their abilities. The capabilities naturally will limit the expectations, but it must be made clear that the value systems that an individual puts on a particular type of love relation, or sexual relation, or reproduction relation, or marriage relationship, should be on an individual level or a couple level, so long as public society is not disturbed. Private acts have no standards that are immutable or written in stone. As we ourselves don't ask society's blessings on our private activities, let's help our clients to be encouraged in arriving at their own acceptable solutions with our blessings. Not only should we sanction their solutions, regardless of how novel, but we must encourage experimentation so that many possibilities are attempted to achieve a maximum of satisfaction.

Guilt

Here it is appropriate to introduce the issue of guilt. Too often the clients have enough problems with considering themselves different. In the area of sexuality, we must honestly stress that being different may be of small actual matter, because what one does in the privacy of the bedroom is of concern only to the individuals involved. If the function of sexual expression is private genital satisfaction, then that takes precedence over public approval, and, if the purpose is to give or receive love, then that is not dependent upon certain formulas of performance or public acceptance.

With these concepts, the client should realize that guilt is an inappropriate feeling, not because the individual is less able, but because no standards for anyone, able-bodied or not, are legitimately imposed. One needn't worry about being different sexually, because anything goes that is functional and mutually acceptable. Oral-genital stimulation, manual stimulation, anything that the couple or the individual can find satisfaction in doing is okay, and we as professionals and agencies have to make our permission and sanction (because we have the power to grant such) very clear. We must not put a negative value on any practice found acceptable, whether it involves masturbation, oral-genital relations, a female superior position, or anything else that satisfies the couple.

For this we have to train ourselves against being judgmental and considering some practices preferable to others. This doesn't mean that we have to force on any client any practice he or she may find objectionable. We also shouldn't force our own or society's guilt-laden values on the person or couple. We may encourage experimentation into previously personal or societally taboo areas. We should do all we can to help remove whatever inappropriate guilt feelings may exist in the achievement of sexual satisfaction.

Communication

Lastly, here it is appropriate to talk about communication. There are practically no sexual concerns or situations that cannot benefit from increased communication by and between the individuals involved. Expectations and performance capabilities can be more realistically appraised with good communication, and false impressions can be minimized. The handicapped, as do many able-bodied, often attach a magnified value to certain suspected deficiencies without ever testing the reality of the situation with the "second person." For example, in the realm of sexuality, most of us are concerned with something in our physical makeup. In this regard the handicapped and able-bodied again are alike. Consider that an individual may be concerned personally with being bald, having small breasts, or being deaf, blind, or elderly. Only by communication with the "second party" can one find out if the concern is mutual or the magnitude of the concern. Communication between the individuals involved will reduce hesitancy in finding out just what is and is not possible and what is or is not acceptable.

As professionals, we must thus encourage open, frank discussions of sexual matters as legitimate topics of conversation (often this means removing guilt in talking about sex). We must realize, parenthetically, that communication may be nonverbal as well as verbal. A touch, glance, smile, or grimace may speak loudly. However, for most, an adequate vocabulary still provides the best means of transmitting ideas and feelings. Regrettably, not everyone has an adequate vocabulary and we as professionals may help in providing one. For the deaf, for example, we might remedy the lack in acceptable universal signs for many sexual and reproductive ideas. We hope a satisfactory vocabulary is available soon.

We then come full circle. Good communication can help the other issues, linking performance and expectations and reducing guilt as well as helping in its own way. With this brief introduction, I'd like to present a dialogue and see how it exemplifies some of the issues at hand. (See Note)

JERRY: Well, I don't really think that I had any idea that things were going to be so different after the operation on my back. I thought my sexual life was going to be the same as it always was, and it turned out to be completely different.

MICKIE: I think at first I felt a sense of desolation that the emotional side of my life was all over with and that I've been condemned to the life of a robot or a zombie.

FRANCIS: I feel embarrassed when I talk to girls, because I drool a lot, and I spit when I talk. And during the conversation, I keep on drooling; I feel like a waterfall.

GEORGE: A heart attack is a massive insult to the body, and to myself as a person. And because of this, the relationship between myself and others—the alienation, the depression—is a whole area of related phenomena that we ought to study very carefully; an area of which we know very little about.

BILL: I've been paralyzed for over 20 years and it's been so long ago that I've forgotten what "normal" sex was. But as I recall, it had to do with sex being pretty much equated with an orgasm. But since I've been paralyzed and had a few chances of sex, I've realized that orgasm is not so important in sex; in fact, it actually hinders the enjoyment of it, because when you don't worry about the orgasm and don't think about the orgasm, sex just continues on and on, and it's never over.

DR. DIAMOND: When we think of the functions that sex serves, we have to think in terms of giving and getting pleasure, of reducing tension, of sharing intimacies. If we keep that in mind we can remove ourself from the stereotype that "good" sex involves only an erect penis in a vagina; that that's the only way or right way. Do you feel that the value of an orgasm is part of the myth, Bill?

BILL: Well, very much so. In fact, before, you kinda work up to something, and then it's over. This way, you just keep going on and on.

DR. DIAMOND: What do you find the most pleasurable thing now?

BILL: Well, still touching the penis, but just touching the nipples and breasts and the sides. I'm very sensitive under the arms.

DR. DIAMOND: So you could find your own way of giving and getting pleasure and that solves your own needs.

BILL: Yeah, but it's much better when somebody else does it.

DR. DIAMOND: Well, that's what I assumed.

BILL: You just have to try—find the right partner, and I guess the right partner is just about anyone who shares your feelings toward each other.

DR. DIAMOND: Mickie, how about yourself?

MICKIE: Well, since being paralyzed and getting out of the more severe part of it, I find that I am perfectly normal except that the mechanics of the thing are different. My legs and back are totally paralyzed. As far as feelings are concerned, if anything, they're heightened because the type of polio I had made me hypersensitive. I find that it's just mostly the mechanics that interfere. And, of course, the preconceived idea that, because you're in a wheelchair, "Don't bother with her—she can't do anything anyway."

DR. DIAMOND: Well, we find that even able-bodied persons begin to find that there is more than one way to skin a cat and probably the handicapped find this out a lot quicker. George, how about you and your heart condition?

GEORGE: Well, I feel like there isn't that comfort that I'm getting from the rest of the people here about my relationship with sexuality. When I had my heart attack, the doctor told me to stop having sex for awhile, but he never told me when to come on again. I feel a profound kind of lack of knowledge and hesitancy . . .

MICKIE: George, do you feel a sense of fear in this area?

GEORGE: Oh, yeah. I think that the fear that accompanies this kind of activity is very profound because it's a deep insult to the body. There's a great hesitancy and I think this leaves a feeling of separation.

DR. DIAMOND: How about with your wife? Obviously, you can look at it both ways. You may want love, but she doesn't want to lose you. Francis, how about yourself with cerebral palsy? How do you see your condition now?

FRANCIS: Well, I'd like to be like any normal guy. I had this cerebral palsy since back in my preschool years. There came a time when the doctors over there wanted me to progress and I didn't progress rapidly. Now, I could do almost anything any normal person could do.

DR. DIAMOND: But now, are you dating now? Are you married now?

FRANCIS: Oh, no. I'm still dating girls.

DR. DIAMOND: Jerry, how about yourself with your back condition?

JERRY: With me, it was a problem, I believe, of creating a new self-image. I thought that I had to be the virile male and live up to my wife's expectations (which she didn't have) of me. She was perfectly satisfied with what I was able to give her after the accident, but I was always trying to do more, and finally I just sat back and enjoyed it, and it was great!

DR. DIAMOND: Why couldn't it have been this way before?

JERRY: Yeah, why did I have to go through all this misery of thinking that I wasn't performing and that I had lost my capabilities.

DR. DIAMOND: Isn't that a problem with all of us—we become spectators, rather than participants. We ask, "What am I supposed to be doing?" rather than, "What can I do?" Shouldn't we concentrate on what we have, rather than on what we don't have?

BILL: This business about fear—it can be emotional fear, too. With fear that, once you are handicapped, you're not going to be able to live up to the expectation that you've been taught in the past other people have of you and you have of yourself. Being in a wheelchair, they don't have the same expectations; they kind of wonder if you can or you can't. Once you show that you can have intercourse, you can also show them what would normally be progressing steps to intercourse. You can show them that you've had good experiences and pleasurable experiences, and the orgasm doesn't become important anymore—or the typical intercourse methods.

DR. DIAMOND: Did you have different experiences as you went through different ages? Many of you have had your handicaps for quite some time.

MICKIE: I've had a rather different type of life. I lost my first husband because of my illness. He couldn't face up to having a disabled wife and two small children. The second time around, it was great. However, before my husband died, he was, for the last two or three years, so very ill that for us there was no more sex as most people think of it. But there was still a deep affection between us. I built my life around different types of activities, so I can't say that I really felt too great a lack in my life, because he was still very affectionate, very sweet to me, and showed me lots of love and attention, and I tried to do the same for him. That was important. The fact that we no longer had typical sexual relations just ceased to be of any importance to either one of us.

DR. DIAMOND: Do any of you get the feeling that either the spouses or lovers, or what have you, are hesitant in initiating sex because of the handicap? How do you overcome that?

GEORGE: I feel that one of the greatest difficulties with my whole family is lack of being able to say it's all right. We begin to have a profound doubt of our own feedback mechanism. You know what I mean—an acceptance. That I'm okay where I'm at is kind of cut off because of this regression. You know, when you're on your own, you lose that trust in yourself.

DR. DIAMOND: Is there anybody that you can communicate with? Your physician or your spouse?

GEORGE: Somewhat; I think more would be helpful.

DR. DIAMOND: Francis, whom do you talk to when you have problems?

FRANCIS: I sometimes talk to my parents, counselors, or probably with the girl I'm dating. I find that the girls are understanding. I talk about the problems that I have, and they feel compassion about my problems, and I feel that they understand.

DR. DIAMOND: What is your biggest problem that you think you've had and overcome? Jerry, how about that?

JERRY: I really believe that the biggest problem was living up to an expectation that wasn't expected at all.

DR. DIAMOND: But now you don't worry about it at all?

JERRY: No, I don't worry about it. That's just the way it is. My wife is a wonderful woman. She's very loving and we've established a new relationship on a different level.

DR. DIAMOND: You just don't have the movements.

JERRY: Right.

DR. DIAMOND: Bill, how about yourself?

BILL: I agree with that. That the most important thing is to get your own self-confidence and just do what comes naturally when you're with your girl.

DR. DIAMOND: How do you do that?

MICKIE: Well, you throw your inhibitions out the window and let it all hang loose.

DR. DIAMOND: How do you do that though? How do you throw out your inhibitions if you've got them?

BILL: It's just a matter of confidence. The first time you may not take advantage of what you later perceive to be the girl's willingness, then you verbally kick yourself in the rear end. The next time, by God, you're not going to make the same mistake twice! You're going to go ahead and do it.

DR. DIAMOND: Mickie, you said something I think is crucial about getting rid of your inhibitions. How about those feelings with guilt? That you may be doing something that somebody else says is not normal?

MICKIE: That is a very hard thing to overcome, but you've got to make up your mind; either you're going to take happiness now while it's there waiting for you or forget it because you're not going to come back and do it again. You know—it's that simple. It isn't like having a piece of cheese in the "refrig" and a week later going and getting it out. There's no way that you're going to be able to do that. So you've got to say—maybe we'll try something else.

DR. DIAMOND: Sex, in terms of genitals, is important but, in terms of personal worth, getting along with somebody and self-worth are perhaps more important.

MICKIE: Oh, I think so!

What does the discussion illustrate? The dialogue demonstrates how the separation of expectations and capabilities is narrowed when guilt feelings are lessened. It goes further, as we must, in reducing guilt and lessening the gap between expectations and capabilities by legitimately doing away with false expectations. For example, we do away with the "myth," which, in essence, states that the only satisfactory means of expressing oneself sexually and achieving satisfaction is with an erect penis in a well-lubricated vagina. For the able-bodied as well as the handicapped, sexual satisfaction is possible without these practices and, in fact, may even be more satisfying. Hands, mouth, feet, any body part may be used any way to achieve satisfaction, and one means is not, a priori, to be preferred over another. Presenting this concept in a positive way can be very helpful to clients.

Further, we should do away with the "marriage manual" formula and concept, which views some activities as foreplay, some as afterplay, and only coitus as "the real play," each "play" with a prescribed time allotment and sequence. We must advocate that anything goes, for however long or in whatever sequence. This is as true for those whose motor functions are compromised as for those with a sensory loss. Persons should be encouraged to maximize the use of those functions that remain, rather than bemoan the nonuse of those functions that are lost.

We can do even more to lessen the gap between capabilities and expectations by suggesting the use in sexual expression of some of the same types of devices we would offer to lessen the gap in job performance between capabilities and expectations. I'm referring to the use of prostheses. We certainly encourage the use of and recommend artificial arms, legs, or eyes where they will serve a function, even a cosmetic one. We can do similarly in a sexual situation. While the use of false breasts has become common for women with mastectomies, we might encourage or at least recommend the use of dildos, vibrators, or anything that the client might find usable, functional, or cosmetic in his or her sexual relationships.

While this might strike some as inappropriate, I think we have to realize that the same reasons other prosthetics are used in normal, everyday life apply to their sexual use. This actually should be seen as quite appropriate for the handicapped, since many able-bodied use them routinely; in fact, the able-bodied provide the major market for their present use. The aged and arthritic and hand amputees can certainly use vibrators where they have lost hand function, and an artificial penis or vagina also has its use, for either solitary or mutual pleasure. While it may take some education on the part of both the client and the partner to accept these devices, with professional encouragement they can accept or reject them without the connotations of guilt that might otherwise go along with their use of consideration. It is to be emphasized that these devices are presently available and are most often used by the able-bodied, so they should not carry a special stigma for the handicapped.

These should legitimately be sold in surgical supply stores as freely as in the porno supply shops, where they are presently sold.

Prostheses help those with motor problems. For those with a sensory loss, I will offer a suggestion that is also helpful for those with reduced motor abilities, i.e., maximize the use of all possible senses. If a person is deaf or blind, then obviously maximal use is made of other input means. A soft touch or caress or kiss on a sensitive area may be quite stimulating, and we can increase or multiply the use of available senses by reading or viewing explicit, sexually orientated material or pornography, by the use of perfume, good food, fancy candles, music, and the like. Certainly it should be reiterated here that talking and touching, the most basic means of communicating, must be increased. Eye contact and language are to be encouraged. Novelty and spontaneity also have erotic overtones that should be exploited for maximum sexual satisfaction.

The dialogue also stressed another major point made earlier. That is, satisfaction is quite different from orgasm. Further, sex is, itself, usually used as a means of communicating deep feelings. These feelings can be provided with simple touches, glances, and personal interchanges, which don't require elaborate gymnastics or idealized anatomy. Satisfaction is most often a result of good sexual communication and shared intimacy and is independent of orgasm. Satisfaction and orgasm may be simultaneously sought after but separately achieved. If we make this idea acceptable to our clients, I think we will have helped them in a major way.

In conclusion, I would like to apologize for not discussing, in detail, special problems associated with pregnancy or contraception, or dealing with the special issues and concerns of the mentally retarded. These must await a subsequent publication. What I did hope to do, however, is alert your attention to: (1) the difference between public and private sexuality; (2) the separate concerns attendant to genital satisfaction, love, reproduction, and marriage; (3) these aspects as different, dependent upon the client's life stage; and (4) sexuality as viewed from various perspectives. Further, I tried to show how to deal conceptually with several overriding issues for the handicapped, i.e., expectations and performance, guilt, and communication. Lastly, I tried to provide some specific ideas to help meet these issues.

I would reiterate that everyone's sexual life can be improved by (1) increased communication; (2) decreased guilt with anything mutually satisfying; and (3) education and ease in dealing openly with sexual issues, so that expectations are more realistically in line with performance capabilities. All of this serves the human need for satisfaction in self-assessment and interpersonal relationships. This satisfaction is seen as the first stage in a person's successful road to rehabilitation specifically, but contentment with life's lot generally.

What I am offering for you to master are concepts that don't take a large budget or special, elaborate training. What it does take is empathy, and those in rehabilitation, by virtue of the career choice, have usually demonstrated an ample supply of this.

NOTE

At the 1973 regional National Rehabilitation Association conference in Hawaii, a half-hour video recording of various participants discussing sex and the handicapped, made with the aid of the Rehabilitation Association of Hawaii, was presented. This dialogue is a slightly modified portion of the tape. A full copy of the tape is available from the Public Television Library, 512 E, 17th St., Bloomington, Ind. 47401, under the title *When Illness Strikes, Program 21* of the *Human Sexuality Series*, moderated by Dr. Milton Diamond.

17

Sex Education for the Physically Handicapped

Jean L. Bloom

Parents of severely physically handicapped children are preoccupied with the tasks of helping them to become self-sufficient within their physical limitations.

As a result, it is often most difficult for them to accept the fact that their children are sexual beings. Although handicapped, these youngsters have needs and desires that are not really different from those of a normal child. Most of them can—and should—look forward to marriage. The job of the parents is to help create in the handicapped child a desire to live as full a life as possible.

Essentially, the groundwork for the development of sexuality in both the physically handicapped and the physically normal child is the same. If the parents have played their role well, they will have contributed a sound basis for an adequate sexual adjustment. The handicapped child will be emotionally healthy and be able to cope with the adult world.

There will, of course, be special adjustments to be made at all ages and special problems to be solved. Here are examples of some of these problems facing severely handicapped couples about to be married.

Lucy and Norman were two eighteen-year-old post-polio victims who had been dating and were considering marriage. Norman, in a wheel-chair, was more severely disabled than Lucy who was able to walk with braces and crutches. Norman's concern was whether he would be able to perform the sex act adequately because of severe muscle weakness in his lower extremities.

During discussion of this problem with his counselor, he learned that it was quite acceptable for Lucy to assume the more active role during intercourse. This young man was quite relieved to learn that he would not be less a man for his adaptation to his physical problem.

Bob, on the other hand, had hemophilia (a condition where the blood does not clot when any bleeding occurs) which ran in his mother's family. He was quite angry with her for bearing him, knowing this disability to run in the family. Bob was a good-looking nineteen-year-old who wanted to marry when he finished junior college.

He wanted children but stated that he definintely would want to practice birth control and fulfill his need to be a father by adopting children. These factors he had discussed with his fiancée who agreed to the practice of birth control and to the adoption of children.

Judy had been injured in an automobile accident when she was ten years old and was paralyzed from the waist down. She wanted to live a normal life as a woman, wife, and mother. Her parents encouraged her courtship and engagement to a young, mildly disabled man.

When they married, Judy's parents paid for modification of kitchen facilities so that Judy would be able to do her homemaker's chores comfortably and efficiently from her wheelchair. When the baby came along, they contributed a small amount each week for the care of the child until Judy's husband received a promotion in his work and could assume the additional financial burden.

Although handicapped people may marry a physically normal mate, this goal is not a very realistic one for the more severely disabled. Parents, too, must accept the child's disability if they are to help in the realistic selection of a marriage partner. Therefore, they must encourage their child to meet and date handicapped individuals.

Another consideration will be how much, if any, financial aid the young married couple will need. The couple should be encouraged to become self-supporting if possible. They should be encouraged to live by themselves rather than with their parents. However, modifications of the physical surroundings in which they live may be one of the ways parents can be of assistance.

If either or both have problems in walking, a car (with modified controls) would help them by facilitating movement and enabling them to broaden their environment both for work and pleasure. If the occupational skill level of the couple is low, parents may have to assume some responsibility for supplementing their income.

Parents will be faced with seeking information about whether the disability is hereditary and whether physical adjustments will need to be made in performing the sex act. Again these are questions and problems which will require some adjustment and acceptance on the parents' part if they are to give the child adequate guidance.

A physician can explain whether the disability is hereditary. The parents' task will be to explain that many people marry and have satisfying lives but should not or cannot have children. Often these people adopt children in order to fulfill their need to become mothers and fathers.

Parents of handicapped children will find—just as do parents of normal children—that their children will masturbate more frequently as sexual desire increases prior to and during adolescence. Because physically handicapped children have limited physical outlets, masturbation is usually the major sexual outlet until the person dates or marries.

Parents can help the child most by letting him know in suitable ways that this practice is a normal part of the development of all children and will have no adverse effect. They should not make the child feel that the practice is in any way dirty or abnormal. However, they can let him know clearly that it is a private activity that is not to be carried on in public.

To function successfully as an adult sexual being requires important learning experiences which are not directly sexual in the early years. These include, for example, learning to identify oneself as a member of the male or female sex and acquiring a sense of personal worth.

When the family praises the handicapped child's small accomplishments, this helps him to begin to feel that he is a useful human being. A feeling of personal worth is related also to achieving independence and becoming self-sufficient.

These tasks of development can be fostered by teaching the child to dress himself, feed himself, and toilet himself as soon as he is physically capable of doing so. Bathing, walking, and traveling independently are tasks which must be encouraged also.

When children who are perfectly capable of assuming these activities are still being cared for by their parents, they are made to feel very inadequate and a terrible burden on the family.

The result is that the child devaluates himself as a person and begins to carry these feelings into school and work performance as well as into his everyday relationships with others and into his feelings as a sexual person.

Adequate social development is a parental responsibility also. The child must learn to relate to and play with both physically normal and physically handicapped children of the same age. Through testing out meaningful ways of relating to others, the child learns how to gain friends and to be a friend and to learn to depend on people other than the family members.

Such experiences enable the individual to learn to evaluate how he can and should fit into and contribute to the community and should help him gain the strength to evaluate himself and life realistically.

The task of allowing the child to become independent is usually quite a difficult one for parents of handicapped children. However, it is important that they become physically and emotionally independent by late adolescence. By that time, the child should be able to select and buy his own clothes, be permitted to travel as independently as possible, have friends of both sexes, participate in teenage activities, and have dates.

Along with increasing freedom the child must learn how to assume increasing responsibility. This applies also to sexual behavior. Young people must be helped to understand that learning sexual control is a part of the maturation process. If a boy only uses girls for sexual outlet, he does not respect the rights of these girls as people and learns to devalue women in general. So, too, the girl who allows herself to be used only as a sexual outlet loses respect for herself as a person and as a woman.

In summary, parents of handicapped children should realize that their job of sex education is not essentially different from that of parents of normal children, although their problems will be greater. Only if they accept the fact that their children are sexual beings can they help to lay a sound foundation for an adequate sexual adjustment in later life.

18

Sexual Dysfunctions Associated with Physical Disabilities

Ernest Griffith

Roberta B. Trieschmann

George W. Hohmann

Theodore M. Cole

Jerome S. Tobis

Victor Cummings

This paper is an abridgement of six addresses, the first three of which are concerned with the psychosocial aspects of sexuality in normal and physically disabled individuals and with the reactions of a rehabilitation team to sexual problems of patients. The remaining three addresses outline principles of management of sexual dysfunctions associated with three types of physical disability: cardiovascular disorders, spinal cord injury and amputation.

Sex, Sex Acts, and Sexuality

Roberta B. Trieschmann

Sexual function is a complex matter; therefore, it is important to distinguish among sex, sex acts, and sexuality.

Sex is one of the four primary drives, the others being hunger,

From *Archives of Physical Medicine and Rehabilitation*, 56 (1975), 8–13. Copyright © 1975 by the American Congress of Rehabilitation Medicine and the American Academy of Physical Medicine and Rehabilitation. Reprinted by permission of the Managing Editor.

thirst, and avoidance of pain. These drives originate in the subcortex but are modified by learned responses originating in the cortex. Thus the cortex governs the methods, occasions, opportunities, and expressions of the primary drives. A majority of these learned patterns are regulatory, inhibitory, or prohibitory, deriving historically through church and state laws.

Sex acts are behaviors involving the secondary erogenous zones and genitalia, sexual intercourse being only one kind of sex act. The term *sex act* does not indicate the relationship of the people involved, their emotions, or their attitudes.

Sexuality is the combination of sex drive, sex acts, and all those aspects of personality concerned with learned communications and relationship patterns. This learned, regulated communication and relationship process occurs at many levels, for example, conversation, shared activities and interests, and various expressions of affection, including sexual intercourse.

Learning of controls, prohibitions, and regulations may produce many attitudes, anxieties, and misconceptions about sexuality which interfere with communication and relationships among people. Attitudes vary according to age, race, sex, social class, and religion. Some examples of the prohibitory, regulatory attitudes that influence the expression of sexuality include :

Sex before marriage is wrong, or sinful, or both.
A good woman is sexually innocent before marriage.
It is acceptable for men, but not women, to be sexually experienced before marriage.
Sex for other than procreation is sinful.
Masturbation is sinful, harmful, destructive.
Genital-genital contact is the only proper form of sexual contact.
Perversion is anything other than genital-genital contact.

Such attitudes are complex interactions of an intellectual concept with an attached emotion; therefore, they are not always easily changeable through reasoning alone. These attitudes can create anxiety and guilt about having sexual urges and about how those urges are to be expressed. They may inhibit communication and the genuine expression of love. Functional sexual dysfunctions occur because certain of these attitudes inhibit behavior sufficiently so that the person is unable to experience pleasure, satisfaction, and relaxation during sexual interactions.

Some of these attitudes may inhibit the effectiveness of any member of a treatment team who deals with individuals who have a sexual dysfunction. These attitudes may hinder the adaptations that a disabled individual must make if he (she) is to regain a reasonably satisfactory relationship with the partner.

The communication process during sexual activity may be considered in the context of the sexual response cycles of men and women described by Masters and Johnson. Men and women differ somewhat in the timing, intensity, and duration of their sexual excitement, a situation requiring communication if mutual satisfaction is to be experienced.

A man can reach the plateau phase and orgasm fairly rapidly. After the orgasm, he is incapable of further sexual reaction until a period of time has elapsed, the time varying according to the individual and his age. This one pattern is fairly typical of most men. But a woman's sexual response is more complex, less predictable, and more susceptible to interruption. One pattern is that of gradual progression from excitement and plateau phases to a series of orgasms. Other women progress to the plateau stage and hover at that level without achieving an orgasm. And some women progress rapidly to the plateau phase, attain an orgasm, and rapidly lose sexual interest.

During the excitement and plateau phases, communication becomes critical because interruptions or other changes can alter the level of sexual excitement of either partner and interfere with satisfaction. A comfortable couple, sensitive to one another, will coordinate these response cycles for their mutual enjoyment. By superimposing upon his normal situation the attitudes and inhibitions that may be learned, one can appreciate how difficult the communication process can be. If an individual has a large number of inhibiting attitudes, there is a higher probability that he will have a less satisfactory sex life than one who does not have as many of these attitudes. Furthermore, a physical disability may introduce additional complications of mobility limitations, neurological impairment of the sex organs, and chronic pain or discomfort.

Therefore, we must recognize that the onset of a physical disability does not eliminate sexual feelings any more than it eliminates hunger or thirst; there are many different kinds of sex acts available for satisfaction, and a disability may interfere with only a certain number of these; and the sexuality of the disabled individual must be evaluated in terms of his particular pattern of relating to others. We must consider this human being in terms of who he is, what attitudes he has learned about sexuality, and what his premorbid sexual functioning was. Therapeutic efforts must include the disabled individual's partner since both must learn new patterns of behavior. Thus, evaluation of the partner in terms of his or her concept of sexuality and attitudes toward sexual functioning is essential.

Reactions of the Individual with a Disability Complicated by a Sexual Problem

George W. Hohmann

The many taboos and prohibitions surrounding all three aspects of sex (sex drive, sex acts, and sexuality) intensify the threat imposed by assault on the sexual ability of the physically disabled person. This generates a severe and immediate anxiety in the person. The assumption is generally made by the patient, his family, and the professional staff that his sex drive and sexuality are essentially nonexistent. Anxiety is intensified by attitudes, misapprehensions, and misunderstandings in several areas on the part of these same people. The patient's anxiety is further increased by a lack of responses to his questions, an unwillingness to listen to his problems, a postponement of discussion of his anxiety, an inability to perceive his unasked questions. He is met by innuendos communicating to him that he is an asexual being, that neither he nor anyone else should be concerned about any aspect of his sexual functioning.

What then does the disabled person expect from the staff in helping him deal with feelings, anxieties, and attitudes about his sexuality? He has a right to expect a lack of judgmental attitudes on the part of the staff. He expects the staff to be relatively free from enforcing on him the major prevailing cultural attitudes. He expects assistance in overcoming his misapprehensions regarding his sexuality and taboos of things that he would like to do. He has a right to expect a willingness to provide the information requested in a spirit of comfort, sensitivity, and truthfulness.

The person expects to discuss sexuality with someone with whom he has a meaningful relationship. It is someone with adequate knowledge about sexual function in the normal person, and sexual function in the particular disability state (and associated medical disorders) which the individual has. It is someone who, if not free of sexual hangups, does not impose them on the disabled person.

The patient wants counseling that will help him and his partner establish a meaningful relationship in the area of sexuality, sex acts, and sex drive and enable them to come to some decision as to how they will function in their sexual relationship. In order to discuss what a person is to be told about sexuality, several definitions of sex can be considered:

1. A buildup of striated and autonomic muscle activity culminating in orgasm.
2. A method of procreation.
3. A way of building flagging self-esteem.
4. A way of manipulating and controlling other people.
5. An expression of tenderness, mutual concern, love and affection.

The patient wants to develop attitudes so that he is free to engage in whatever sexual behavior is organically possible and psychologically acceptable to him and his partner.

What can the patient expect to do? Genital intercourse is possible for an overwhelming majority of disabled people. Foreplay of various types can be an extremely gratifying experience. Body contact is possible for most individuals. Stimulation of the secondary erogenous zones may prove gratifying and pleasurable whether or not genital function is possible. The use of prosthetic appliances has been acceptable to many people. Many marriages have been based on casual expressions of self-esteem, affection, and love.

The patient may ask about what he can expect in the way of gratification from his sexual life. Regardless of type and degree of disability or physical condition, his sexuality can be used to weld a relationship with another human being. He can please a partner; he can experience empathic gratification. He can enjoy the excitement of stimulating the secondary erogenous zones and achieve feelings of adequacy from giving pleasure to another person.

A few precautions should be considered in counseling:

1. Do not put a person in conflict with his God.
2. Avoid extreme pressure on the patient to discuss sexuality.
3. Avoid forcing your morality and convictions on the patient.
4. Do not threaten the patient with your own sexuality.
5. Do not make sex an all-or-none sort of experience.
6. Do not assume that once the topic is discussed that you can leave it alone.
7. Do not conclude that there is only one way to convey information.
8. Be sure that the conjoint nature of sexual relationships is held parallel.
9. Do convey the notion that all relationships, including the sexual one, are a matter of compromise.

Help the patient understand and work on this kind of premise in negotiating his sexual relationships.

Reaction of the Rehabilitation Team to Patients with Sexual Problems

Theodore M. Cole

In considering the title of this discussion, most rehabilitation professionals would first focus on the word *sexual.* To them, it may mean that they are being asked to reveal something of themselves, perhaps to deal with their own sexuality, to yield some of their own preciously guarded privacy. A second reaction may be to the word *problems.* What are this patient's problems, his physiological and anatomic limitations, the things he can and can't do? Only on the third time around may we finally consider the patient, his partner, and especially their feelings. These three reactions are often overcast with the morality of the professionals on the rehabilitation team. There may be a sense of rightness and wrongness about human sexuality. For most of us, these reactions are also overcast with a general ignorance about human sexuality. For many, these reactions are weighted with sexual guilt, fear, and titillation.

Some of the reactions of the rehabilitation team to patients with sexual problems include :

1. I will leave the discussion of sex to someone who is effective because I don't want to hurt the disabled person.
2. I will leave the discussion of sex to the specialists because I do not know enough about it myself.
3. My primary responsibility is to help people achieve a better state of health, and sex is separate from health.
4. I will deal with sexuality in people who became employed and act responsibly because they need the information more than the homebound person.
5. If I introduce the discussion of sexuality, it may become unmanageable.
6. There should be hospital rules about sexuality; and if patients break these rules, they should be reprimanded or dismissed.

In contrast to the above, it is time to consider sexuality as a legitimate part of the rehabilitation process. Team members should try discussing sexuality with colleagues and with disabled patients. Disabled people can take it and will appreciate your sensitivity and interest. Sexuality is a proper dimension of health care delivery and thus should be discussed with the appropriate information given. In this manner, professionals can play a meaningful role by endorsing the concept of sexuality to disabled patients. Rather than equating sexuality with employability, information on sexuality should be made available to all physically disabled patients since it is a part of us all and should not have to be earned through work. Furthermore, hospitals should provide the opportunity for privacy in addition to the opportunity to interact with others. We should encourage sexual rehabilitation in the hospital as well as outside of it.

There is a need for practical information which can help people develop the competence which is an important part of human sexual expression. But much more important is the inherent permission to be sexual. If sexual confidence can be reestablished, more will feel that they dare try reentry into the world of vocation, self-respect, and responsibility. A frank and personal approach helps to desensationalize the sensitive aspect of physical disability. It humanizes the disabled in the eyes of the able-bodied treator or counselor, for it is difficult for the treator to regard his client as less than he if he knows that the client has access to and skills with one of the most powerful aspects of human behavior, human sexuality.

Cardiovascular Patients and Sexual Dysfunctions

Jerome S. Tobis

It is questionable whether the findings that Masters and Johnson obtained in a somewhat laboratory-type situation have validity to cardiac stress. Their estimates of pulse rates rising to 170 and 180 per minute must have been influenced by the fact that the partners were being monitored. This certainly must have influenced the emotional and autonomic responses of the participants. One of the really valuable contributions made in this area is that of Hellerstein and Friedman. They reported on 91 male subjects who had participated in a YMHA physical fitness program. These 91 individuals, 48 of whom had myocardial infarctions and 43 of whom were healthy but coronary-disease prone, were subjected to an extensive questionnaire concerning their sexual behavior. Eighteen of 43 respondent subjects with coronary artery disease indicated that they developed one or more symptoms during sexual relations. Most common of these symptoms was excessively fast heartbeat. In some 20% of those with coronary disease, there were symptoms suggestive of angina. The interval between the coronary event and resumption of sexual activity was approximately 14 weeks. The impact of a coronary event on sex was great during the first six months after the acute episode but by the end of the first year was minimal.

Curiously, this finding is at odds with other reports in the literature. Tuttle reports that some 10% of people who were involved in a work-evaluation unit were totally impotent long after their acute episode and Weiss stated that some 30% of his subjects reported impotence. Whether this represents a skewed population that Hellerstein and Friedman were dealing with, that is, a predominantly Jewish population of middle-class businessmen, or whether the physical fitness program improved their sexual performance, is open to question and deserves further study. It was the impression of Hellerstein and Friedman that those who participated in the exercise program improved relative to their sexual behavior in terms of quality and frequency of sexual activity. These authors found that the physiological cost for sex in the middle-aged male, married approximately 20 years or longer, was less than the requirement for carrying out the Master's Two Step Test. They estimated that approximately 6 kilocalories per minute was required for a maximum of perhaps 30 seconds, with a heart rate of less than 120 beats. Obviously, these variables depend on who the partners are; those involved in extramarital relationships presumably require considerably higher energy costs. The frequency of the occasional cardiovascular catastrophies during extramarital intercourse has never been well established. If the cardiac patient is capable of climbing one or two flights of stairs or walking a block briskly without difficulty or complaint, he is likely able to participate in the sex act.

Another factor that should be considered is the wife's attitude. Often her fear and anxiety that sexual activity may be disastrous for the patient will mitigate against a normal relationship. Many of the antihypertensive drugs may contribute to some degree of impotence. Serious depression associated with fear and anxiety concerning the disease may be a factor. Another consideration is the effect of exercise. Isometric exercise has been shown by Donald and his colleagues to raise blood pressure significantly and produce additional stress on an already impaired heart. Under such circumstances, the person with significant heart disease should avoid the prone position, and instead use the side-lying position or other postural modifications. Certainly the cardiac patient should avoid heavy eating, or heavy imbibing of alcohol prior to participation in sex.

Spinal Cord Injury Patients and Sexual Dysfunction

Theodore M. Cole

What do we know about how a paraplegic or quadriplegic person responds to sexual stimulation? The research on paraplegic women is abominably lacking. We know of no literature that describes the secretions from the wall of the vagina during sexual arousal in a woman with complete cord transection. Nor does the literature tell us what happens to the swelling and opening of the labia, contracting of the uterus, and ballooning and expanding of the vagina. We know that the clitoris may become reflexly tumescent; the nipples may indeed swell, as may the breasts. Breathing, blood pressure, and pulse rate may increase. Muscles may go into spasm, and a characteristic sex flush can occur.

What about the paraplegic or quadriplegic man with complete cord transection? His penis may become erect; his nipples may erect. His muscles may develop spasms; his blood pressure, pulse, and respiration may increase. The skin of his scrotum may tense. He may develop a skin flush. However, it is unusual for him to have an emission or ejaculation. Thus, the spinal cord patient is capable of most of the sexual responses of the able-bodied.

Still, we tend to think of the paraplegic or quadriplegic person as somehow drastically different from the able-bodied. Coupled with that is the fact that we tend to regard information about the sexuality of spinal cord-injured people as drastically different from other medical information we may obtain. We have divided medical information into at least two packages: general medical information and sexual information. Masters and Johnson have suggested that the reason the sexual history has been separated from routine history-taking is that all of us take sexual functioning out of its natural context of everyday living. Our difficulty in assigning sexual function an honorable role as a basic physiological process stems from a physical characteristic unique to this form of physiology. Sexual functioning can be delayed indefinitely or even denied for a lifetime. One cannot say the same for other natural functions.

I talk with a patient about his spinal cord injury and his sexuality together within the context of the total problems faced by him or her. Several principles guide me : I am no longer frightened or put off by the person in the bed; most people can take what I am going to say. I try to be understanding and to use a lot of eye contact. I sanction sexuality as a positive aspect of life. I set expectations for activity and gratification, and that I will return for further discussion. Shortly after the patient's injury, when there is still concern about his survival, is not an opportune time to begin the discussion. However, when the time comes that you would consider appropriate for such discussion, you can be assured that the patient has already been thinking about it.

What do I talk about? First, I talk about his losses : I ask about physical, occupational, recreational, and self-image types of losses. As he responds, I learn what he considers to be a loss. I must remember that those things I consider losses may not be so to him. Then I talk about activity or performance. What can he do, not just sexually, but also in regard to other kinds of activities? I inquire about his or her partner : "Do you have a partner? Do you have a relationship going? How is this person going to interact with you in your home life, your work life, and in your sex life?" I talk about the future. "What kinds of adjustments do you think are necessary, sexual and other than sexual?" I talk about communication : "How are you going to communicate with people? How are you going to communicate with your sexual partner?" Then I end an interview by coming back to the present with discussion of general concerns such as nursing procedures. Finally, I set the expectation that I will be back to talk later. I am not done; I will return to continue discussion of this subject.

Amputees and Sexual Dysfunction

Victor Cummings

Those of us in the health professions who treat patients with major limb amputation, either congenital or surgical, ordinarily do not include sexual problems when considering the functional problems that they must face during and after prosthetic rehabilitation. One can guess at the reasons that little attention has been given to sexual problems among amputees. First of all, the majority of amputees who find their way to organized clinics are usually in the older age group. Even if they were not amputees, many physicians would feel that probing into their sex lives would be a waste of time, and a source of irritation and embarrassment. Secondly, if the amputee is younger and in good health, one might assume that he or she has no sexual problems, so why bother asking? It is the rare amputee who will spontaneously imply that he or she has sexual problems, and it is very rare that he or she will ask direct questions about sex problems. Finally, it is only relatively recently that the health professions have become sensitized so that some attention is paid to the physiology, pathology, and psychology of sex. Unfortunately for the amputee, it is the patient with emotional, cardiac, and neurological problems who receives the most attention. Speaking about the surgical amputee then, what kind of problems does he or she face with regard to sex? There is the obvious emotional trauma: the depression and mourning period, the distortion of body image, and the perception of self as not whole, or as ugly, or as no longer feminine or masculine.

Although an amputation obviously creates a profound psychological impact, there may be quite a difference between the sexes with regard to the kind of impact it produces. In the male, the impact is usually similar to castration: that is, the loss of limb is equated to the loss of manhood. But the impact on a female psyche may be quite another thing. In their study, Weinstein and associates have demonstrated that the bodily part preference of men and women differs considerably. They reported that the largest majority of men between the ages of 20 to 40 years rated the penis as the part of the body to be most valued, while the majority of women between the ages of 20 to 70 years rated the tongue as the most important organ.

Phantom sensation, whether painful or not, can present problems. This phenomenon is almost always present in patients who have undergone amputation. A painful phantom can be disturbing or disastrous when performing the sex act.

The mechanics of body positioning during sex play and intercourse have presented difficulties. Balance, movement, or lack of either may be a problem. Some problems can be solved simply, for example by suggesting to the upper extremity amputee to switch sides of the bed with the partner so they have their normal arm free in the side-lying position. Change of position during the sex act might be necessary. In some cases, change from the male superior to the female superior position might be indicated.

Often the disease causing the amputation causes additional problems. The male patient with a diabetic neuropathy may be unable to ejaculate, or have an erection, or both. Similarly, the male who has undergone bilateral lumbar sympathectomy may be unable to ejaculate, or may ejaculate retrogradely. Vascular disease can add to the difficulties. Erection can be interfered with due to inadequate blood flow. The most classic example of this is the Leriche syndrome, which causes impotence and high intermittent claudication. Enforced isolation because of limited mobility can impose added difficulties. If a man and woman who are not amputees do not get along, and cannot resolve their differences, one or the other can walk out and find another mate. But in many instances, a severely handicapped amputee cannot walk out, or for that matter cannot walk anywhere, particularly if living in a walk-up apartment or tenement.

Another aspect of sexuality of the amputee is somewhat unusual in nature. It concerns the nonamputee who is sexually aroused by an amputee of the opposite sex. This sexual variance, which is a form of fetishism, occurs, to my knowledge, in men only. These men have gone so far as to form organizations. They look down upon the female amputee who covers her stump with a prosthesis, referring to such a woman as one who "tries to pass." They call themselves hobbiests, and write stories or draw pictures about their fantasies.

There is far less known about congenital amputees, and much clinical research must be done to identify their problems so that we in the health professions can sort them out and go about finding some answers.

SUMMARY

Those who treat sexual dysfunctions of the physically disabled should be aware of the distinctions among sex drive, sex acts, and sexuality. Although a disability may impose alterations in sex acts, sex drive and sexuality remain intact. Before initiating treatment, the therapist should know both patient and sexual partner as people whose sexuality and sexual function have been shaped by previous specific experiences, attitudes and beliefs.

Anxiety is a frequent early reaction of the patient. He may share the assumption of family and staff that his sex drive and sexuality cease to exist. Patient expectations of counseling include lack of judgmental attitudes and provision of readily accessible, accurate information. Various types of gratification are possible. Precautions in counseling are enumerated.

Early reactions of rehabilitation team members may be concerned with the need to deal with their own sexuality and ignorance, limitations which the disability imposes upon sexual acts and the morality of sex. Examples of conventional approaches in managing sexual problems are presented. Suggestions of alternate strategies and their rationale are offered.

Management of sexual dysfunction in cardiac patients requires familiarity with the study by Hellerstein and Friedman of men with coronary artery disease. Cardiac patients capable of one–two flights of stair-climbing should be able to participate in sex acts. Significant variables affecting sexual activities in these patients are the attitude of the spouse, drugs, depression, exercise, positioning, and dietary intake.

Most of the physiological sexual responses seen in the able-bodied remain in spinal cord-injured subjects. History-taking and discussions of sexuality should be done in context of the patient's total problems. Principles of interview technique and topics of discussion are reviewed.

Sexual problems of amputees may be related to emotional trauma such as depression and distortion of body image. Additionally, phantom sensations, difficulties in balance and positioning, and associated disease states may alter sexual performance. Immobility may enforce physical isolation.

19

Sex and Self:
The Spinal Cord-Injured

Silas P. Singh
Tom Magner

Introduction

Paraplegia is paralysis of both legs and the lower part of the body, resulting from injury or disease of the spinal cord at the level of the chest or lower back. *Quadriplegia* or *tetraplegia* ("four-paralysis") is paralysis of both legs and both arms resulting from injury or disease involving the spinal cord at the level of the neck. In the informal friendliness of a spinal cord injury hospital ward, the patients often call each other "paras" if they have paraplegia, and "quads" if they have quadriplegia. For simplicity in this paper, *cord-injured patients* means paraplegics, quadriplegics, or both.

The spinal cord is a bundle of nerve fibers and cells about 17 inches long, the length depending upon the height of the adult. It connects the brain with the muscles, skin, and internal organs. The level, or location, of injury or damage is a key factor in symptoms and in activities of daily living for the person with spinal cord injury, whether from accident or disease. The central nervous system consists of the brain and spinal cord.

Description of the level of the injury or damage involves a kind of medical shorthand for the vertebra (one) or vertebrae (two or more) where the spinal cord damage occurs. The vertebrae are the 33 bones of the spinal column that surround and partially protect the spinal cord. A typical neck (cervical) injury is at C5 level. C stands for cervical, 5 means the 5th vertebra (back bone) counting downward from immediately below the skull.

From *Rehabilitation Literature*, 36/1 (1975), 2–10. Copyright © 1975 by the National Easter Seal Society for Crippled Children and Adults. Reprinted by permission of the Editor.

The chest vertebrae are called thoracic or dorsal, and their abbreviation is T or D, for example, T8 or D8 level. The lower back vertebrae are called lumbar, and their abbreviation is L. The spinal cord ends between L1 and L2.

The symptoms of spinal cord injury depend upon the level or injury of the spinal cord, not the level of bone injury. The spinal cord is soft and easily squeezed and damaged by pressure from the surrounding bones. Cord damage sometimes occurs above or below the level of bone injury. Hence, two patients with a C6 vertebra injury will have different capabilities if their points of spinal cord injury differ.

Whatever the accident or disease that leaves both legs paralyzed, spinal cord injury or damage is a major and increasing problem today. Automobile accidents are the leading cause of spinal cord injury in America, but motorcycle and motor scooter accidents are increasing alarmingly. Falls from heights and sports such as football, diving (into shallow water), and skiing cause many spinal cord injuries in young people. In employed men, industrial accidents contribute to the number of spinal cord injuries. Older persons are prone to injury from falls or from not being cautious enough as a pedestrian. Combat injuries cause a relatively small percentage of spinal cord injury but have been highly significant in inspiring improvements in care for patients.

Diseases leading to paraplegia, for which causes or cures are as yet undiscovered or are incomplete, include cancer and other tumors of the spinal cord, infections and abscesses of the spinal cord, multiple sclerosis, congenital defects, including severe forms of spina bifida, and other rarer neurological disorders.

Estimates from various sources of the number of Americans with paraplegia range from 60,000 to 100,000. New cases per year have been estimated at 4,500 to 10,000.

Approximately 78 out of 100 persons with traumatic spinal cord injuries are males, since they engage in more dangerous sports and occupations.

Sexual Function

Injuries to the spinal cord or cauda equina frequently cause partial or complete loss of sensory and motor function below the lesion. Paralyzed patients have to face many difficult physical and psychological problems, including the belief of the patient or his family that he has completely lost his sexual function. Up until several years ago, the view held by most physicians was that the less said about sexual function, the better. Paraplegics and quadriplegics were encouraged to substitute another interest for their sex drive.[20] Today, after a great deal of research, it has been determined that most people with spinal cord injuries can have sexual activity; however, it probably will be limited to some extent, depending on the level and extent of the injury.[109]

Lesions can occur at one of four levels: cervical, upper thoracic, lower thoracic, and lumbar. Generally, the higher the lesion, the better the chances for the male's being able to have erections and to ejaculate; however, with a high level of injury, often there is more neural damage and it is more difficult to carry out coitus.[22]

In a study at Hines Veterans Hospital in Chicago in 1957, of the 100 patients, 33 had cervical lesions. Of these 33, 27 (82%) were able to have complete erections, 2 (6%) were not able to have any type of erection, 14 (42%) attempted intercourse, and 11 (33%) were successful. Of the total of 100, 21 had upper thoracic lesions. Of these 21, 15 (71%) had complete erections, 4 (19%) had incomplete erections, 2 (10%) had no erection at all, 8 (38%) attempted intercourse, and 6 (29%) were successful. In the next group, 39 with lower thoracic lesions, 18 (46%) had complete erections, 12 (31%) had incomplete erections, 9 (23%) had no erection, 12 (31%) attempted intercourse, and 6 (15%) were successful. In the last group, 7 with lumbar lesions, 4 (57%) had incomplete erections, 2 (29%) had incomplete erections, 1 (14%) had no erections, 4 (57%) attempted intercourse, and 3 (43%) were successful.[114]

These figures show that, in general, the lower the injury, the less the chance for the spinal cord victim to have erections and ejaculate; however, each individual is so unique in his injury that it is nearly impossible to predict the extent to which a person can have sex.

A spinal cord victim may have a complete or an incomplete lesion. If the lesion is complete, the cord is transected and there is no feeling below the level of the transection.[91] With this type of injury, there is a possibility of erection, but very little chance of ejaculation. With an incomplete lesion, there still may be partial feeling beneath the level of injury, and both erection and ejaculation are possible.[94]

For the male, the sex act consists of three major occurrences, desire, erection and ejaculation.[89] Desire can be built up in a number of ways, one of which is through fantasy. The male may have dreams in which he is fully functioning sexually; to many this will give sexual desire. The need to prove to himself or to his mate that he can perform is another factor in building up desire.[72] Erection occurs when the blood vessels of the cavernous bodies actively dilate by parasympathetic stimulation to engorge and stiffen the penis. The center for erection is located in the sacral portion of the cord and may be activated reflexly by sensory impulses reaching the center over the pudenal nerve from the numerous sensory nerve endings in the glans and prepuce. Erection is also often activated by psychic stimuli descending from the cerebral cortex through the spinal cord.[89]

A male should be able to have erections and ejaculate if the sacral cord, cauda equina, and thoracolumbar sympathetic outflow are intact. Because these two centers are far apart, a lesion may affect one and leave the other intact, which means that many times the injured man can have erections but cannot ejaculate.[89]

In the female, the problem of sex has not been studied as extensively as in the man. In a woman, the problem is not so traumatic. She plays the passive role in sexual relations usually.[109] The penis enters the vagina and, with the contraction of her sphincter muscles, the male is able to reach ejaculation. It can be a relatively simple process for the woman; therefore, with a spinal cord injury, it is still possible for her to have coitus. She may lack feeling but not function. She may even become pregnant and deliver a child normally.[79]

While it has been proved that up to 70 percent of all spinal cord patients are capable of having some degree of sexual activity,[114] many do not indulge in any type of sex and actually have a poor attitude toward the whole idea of a person with this type of injury engaging in sex. There are many reasons for this attitude, all of which go back to the idea of self-concept, which is : (1) how a person perceives himself, (2) what he thinks, (3) how he values himself, and (4) how he attempts through various actions to enhance or defend himself.[98] In spinal cord injury, the self-concept many times is low.[43] Many factors account for this. Physical disability is one. Loss of bladder and bowel control and inability to walk causes great shame and feelings of inferiority. Increased dependency is another factor, and body image is the final and most important one. The concept of body image or body schema refers to the mental idea and/or basic attitudes a person has toward his own body and reflects how he perceives himself physically, esthetically, and socially. It also provides a clue as to how he sees himself in relation to his world and hence reflects his style of life[74] and

> . . . in working with disabled individuals, one is frequently impressed not with their depression, as one would imagine, but with their complete inability to understand what the disability is all about. . . . There is a veritable struggle that takes place. . . . They cannot find a place in their body image for the deformity.[74]

The study of sexual abilities in spinal cord injury is relatively new, but its importance cannot be overly stressed. The main concern of a spinal cord patient after the frustration and bitterness of the first few months is the ability to live as a functioning person in society. For so long, society was interested solely in the physical rehabilitation of these people, but that is not enough. They need help in accepting what has happened to them and learning to live with it; hence the creation of a "whole-man concept."[81] Sex is a major part of this acceptance because it involves marriage and raising a family, which is both normal and fulfilling to most. Cord-injured patients today are not willing to settle for physical rehabilitation. Many are demanding to know what their sexual limitations are and how to realize their full sexual capacity.[90] Most physicians are educated to handle the physical problem of sex with the spinal cord-injured, but they are not educated to handle the emotional problems going along with them. This constitutes a major problem. Patients very much need counseling in this area.

It is especially important to correlate the positive relationship between self-concept and sexual attitudes in the spinal cord-injured. If a counselor were to know a person's self-concept, there is a greater chance he could learn how that person feels about himself and the world around him. With this knowledge, the counselor should be better equipped to handle the recovery problem. If problematic sexual attitudes are a result of self-concept, the counselor would assist in solving a person's sexual problem through encouraging gradual acceptance of a positive self-concept by the client.

Self-Concept: Social Interaction

The self-concept of a person summarizes all that he is and serves as a supermoderator of his functioning.[30] It is the type of vital and relevant data about a person that supersedes other things in importance to the individual and thereby expresses his true raison d'être. What an individual feels, how he acts or reacts, and how others react to him is a direct result of his individual self-concept.

James[53] described the infant without a self at birth. He suggested that the self develops to become the sum total of "I," the knower or experiencer, and "Me," the self that is known or experienced.

Charles Horton Cooley,[25] in considering the meanings of "I" described a social self since labeled the "Looking Glass Self." Cooley's basic premise was that the self imagines a perception of itself in the mind of another and this affects behavior. Cooley's self idea has three basic elements: (1) the imagination of one's appearance to the other person; (2) the imagination of the other person's appraisal of that appearance; and (3) some kind of self-value feeling such as pride or shame.

Later, George Herbert Mead[71] described the features of self-conception from the stance of a social interactionist. Mead's theory proposed that an individual will conceive of himself as he believes significant others conceive of him and that he will tend to act in accord with expectations he projects to significant others. He will act the way "people like him" should act. Thus, Mead departed from the single notion of self-as-experienced and placed the emphasis on social interaction as an integral part of the development of self-concept.

Self has figured prominently in social control, economic behavior, social deviance, personal aspirations, psychological development, interpersonal attraction, social influence, psychopathology, and psychotherapy.

John Kinch[56] offers a general theory of self-concept in one sentence : "The individual's conception of himself emerges from social interaction and, in turn, guides or influences the behavior of that individual." The following are implicit in most considerations of the self-concept that take this stance and are suggested as basic postulates of the theory : (1) the individual's self-concept is based on his perception of the way others are responding to him; (2) the individual's self-concept functions to direct his behavior; and (3) the individual's perception of the responses of others toward him reflects the actual responses of others toward him.

The self is a very unique phenomenon. It can be divided into three types of self : (1) the identity self, (2) the behavioral self, and (3) the judging self.[30]

The identity self is perhaps the most basic aspect of the self-concept. This includes the labels he places on himself. As a young child, the labels are few and simple. "I am John"; "I am cute"; "I am ugly." These elements of identity continue to expand with the growth and broadening of the individual's abilities, activities, group memberships, and services for identification.

The behavioral self probably precedes the identity self. It is the action of the individual. An example of this would be riding a bike. The actual riding of the bike is the action or behavior. If a child masters it, he becomes a "bike rider," this becoming part of the identity self.

The third type of self is the judging self. The interaction between identity self and behavioral self and their integration into the total self-concept involves the judging of self. This self functions as an observer, standard setter, dreamer, comparer, and, most of all, evaluator. It also serves as mediator between the two selves and ultimately judges the self and determines the self-concept.

Self-concept is a complicated term that includes many different ideas of self, two of which are self-esteem and self-actualization. Self-esteem is essential for any individual.[30] He must feel he has worth. Self-esteem is derived from two main sources : the self and other persons. Esteem is earned as one achieves certain goals, operated by certain values, or measures up to certain standards. These goals, standards, and values may be internal, external, or both. They may be established, regulated, and applied by the judging self, by others, or by both.

Maslow[69] assigns a position of central importance to self-esteem. In his hierarchy of needs, a positive level of self-esteem is the final prerequisite for self-actualization; once self-esteem is achieved, the individual is free to concentrate on actualizing his potentials.

Maslow perceives self-actualization as the striving of man to become in actuality what he is potentially—to become everything he is capable of becoming—to do what he is best suited for.

Another area of self vital to self-concept is the body image. The body image is the composite picture the individual has of his own body. The picture is a multiply determined, continuously developing, and constantly changing condensed representation of the individual's current and past experiences of his own body. Berger,[7] in reference to paraplegic patients, emphasizes the necessity for the integration of the disability into the body image and further hypothesizes that the long period of withdrawal, depression, and lack of interest following the bodily insult is due to the great amount of psychic energy needed for this reintegrative process. Similarly, Grayson wrote : The image has to be reorganized so that the deformed, absent, or useless member of the body can somehow fit itself into the individual's image of himself.[43] He states that many patients who display a complete inability to understand what the disability is all about do so because they cannot find any place in their body image for the deformity. He attributes such symptoms as depersonalization, feelings of unreality, and resistance to the use of orthopedic appliances to a defense the ego unconsciously sets up to maintain its integrity in the face of body-image disturbance.

In the spinal cord-injured, self-concept is very important. It influences whether he will desire, seek, cooperate with, participate in, or successfully utilize rehabilitation services.[74] After the trauma, the patient goes through a series of changes. He changes from a state of independence to one of almost helpless dependence. He is dependent on others for movement, nourishment, and bodily care. Physically he has regressed to the level of an infant. He experiences three types of pain in the early stages of his paralysis—root pain, which is sharp, is excruciating, and radiates along the distribution of nerve roots; burning pain, which is poorly localized and diffuse and does not follow any root distribution; and visceral pain, which is dull and poorly localized and has a sickening quality.[74]

Because his mind is not affected by the injury, he is acutely aware of his disabilities. This awareness results in temporary or situational depression. This is natural; in fact, if the spinal cord-injured does not go through this depression, many times he is denying the injury, and this could be a severe problem. Along with feelings of depression, he also goes through such a phase where he is very dependent. Such patients are forced to become dependent for their bodily needs, but sometimes they become dependent on others for all their needs, physical and emotional.

Autistic thinking can obstruct rehabilitation. Facing reality regarding loss of function is most difficult for the paraplegic patient. Every paraplegic patient, it is safe to say, believes that sooner or later he will recover his lost functions and will walk again. Frustration can also be a result of the trauma. These frustrations may vary from trivial slights to absolute blocking of goals.[74]

These phases can make the cord-injured person feel abnormal and not at all accepting of himself. It is believed one who is not self-accepting will also have a poor self-concept. The sexual limitation of a spinal cord victim is probably the most frustrating and serious of all his disabilities.[94]

It has been established that sex is important to spinal cord victims, as well as to walking persons; in fact it is so important to one with cord injury that he would rather have this function than walk.[94] It is important, however, that he learn the extent and limitations of his abilities and desires. This takes much adjustment. He must accept a rather passive role in sexual relations. The female mate must be the aggressor.[89] It is up to her to stimulate the penis to erection and ejaculation.

The spinal cord-injured person also must make adjustment to a change in sexual desire. In a study by Weiss and Diamond[110] on sexual desires and activities, prior to disablement, 92 percent of the male population reported desire, and 96 percent of them reported some form of sexual activity. After disablement, 81 percent reported desire, and 69 percent of them reported sexual activity—a decrease in both desire and activity. In the same study, of the female population, 48 percent reported desire before disablement and 52 percent reported some sexual activity. After disablement, 62 percent reported desire and 62 percent reported sexual activity. These reactions show an increase in both desire and activity in the female, and compared to the results of the male study all the reactions show a "convergence effect."[110]

Another adjustment that is difficult for the spinal cord victim lies in his continued sexual interest and fantasy. It has been reported that, while his sexual abilities have been limited somewhat, his drive is as strong as ever.[110] Obviously, this is frustrating to the individual. This drive is many times fulfilled through fantasy and dreams. Usually the dream or fantasy is on a par with the type of sex life before trauma. If the individual had an extremely active, fulfilling sex life before trauma, his dreams tend to follow that trend.[72] In a study by Bors and others[12] of 35 patients, 10 remembered complete, dry dreams; 14 remembered incomplete, dry dreams; and only 10 remembered no dreams (no correlation between dream and type of injury). In an overall study, 46 percent of paraplegic males have some type of sexual dreams, and in none of them did the paraplegic see himself disabled in any way.

Another obvious obstruction that most spinal cord victims find difficult to overcome is inability to discuss the problem of sex openly. For many it is an embarrassing topic, and, instead of discussing it, they ignore the matter entirely, and whatever sexual ability there might be goes unrealized.

For many paraplegic males to engage in sex, the penis must be forced to an erection by either manual or oral manipulation. Many find the latter "dirty" and against their moral principles and therefore will not engage in this type of sex. But after talking and learning more about sex, many realize it is natural and necessary for sex.

It is the author's belief that attitudes toward sex will undoubtedly revert to the upbringing of the individual and are extremely difficult to change. If a child is raised in an atmosphere where there is little affection shown between parents or between parents and children, chances are a child will begin to feel that sex is a "dirty" thing. On the other hand, if a child is raised in a home where there is love shown all around, he will acquire an attitude that sex between people who love each other is good.

Those from the first group, who believe that sex is "dirty," feel this way because they have a rather negative view of themselves in a sex role. They cannot function on a sexual level because their attitude toward themselves is poor. A spinal cord victim will sometimes take a dim view of himself because he has not integrated his disability into his body image. His handicapped body looks ugly to him, so he feels that a person as unattractive as he is should forego any type of sex activity.[7]

Research

Although the cultural trend has been toward a more open, less inhibited outlook on sexual material, the scientific aspect of that same culture has, with some exceptions, remained chastely distant from investigating things remotely connected with sexuality.

Gebhard[37] notes that, prior to World War II, almost no research had been done in the area of human sexuality. He comments on the problems that arose, mentioning the fact that the stigma attached to such research not only dissuaded some scholars from undertaking it but also at times prevented the publication of work already completed.

With today's society so much more open to sex it is impossible to repress it; spinal cord victims want to know and are entitled to know, since their own sexual functioning must be altered. It can be asserted that the job of properly rehabilitating patients is impossible without giving full cognizance to the impelling psychosocial problems that they face.

Adjusting to sexual limitations is an important part of the rehabilitation of the patient to his maximal physical and emotional level. Any effective rehabilitation program must consider the whole person, for the greatest resource in the rehabilitation of any individual is that individual himself.

At a workshop conducted by Dr. Theodore Cole from the University of Minnesota[94] the great need for research was expressed. Dr. Cole's goal was to change attitudes of physicians and hospital staff as well as spinal cord patients and their mates about prospects for sexual fulfillment. Dr. Cole and his wife, Sandy, stressed that spinal cord victims have many sexual problems and that physicians are often handicapped by their own taboos and fears but that solutions can be found with research.[94]

Bucy[15] emphasizes that attitudes of members of the medical profession and the ignorance and indifference of the general public have made the United States the most backward, negligent major civilized country of the world in providing adequate care for civilians who have been paralyzed by spinal cord injury. England has had a spinal cord center for over 25 years.

Mueller,[74] as cited previously in this article, has pointed out that one is impressed less often with the disabled's depression than with their complete inability to understand what the disability is all about. The most intelligent persons, even those having medical training, frequently are genuinely puzzled as to what the disability means to them. In their struggle to comprehend, these disabled persons need an explanation, or some form of counseling.

Counseling about sex should include positions, special techniques of foreplay, and stimulation and feeling by couples on such matters. Cole and his wife Sandy tried to explain what paraplegics and quadriplegics can and cannot do sexually and stimulated the open and honest exchange of views and feelings.

Talbot has outlined in philosophical-historic terms the necessity for dealing with psychological aspects of sexuality in cord-injured patients, but little has been written about the actual counseling of the cord-injured man regarding his sexual function.

Hohmann[51] has worked for 30 years in accumulating information in relation to counseling about sex. Hohmann states the most effective counselor is one with warmth, gentleness, and personal interrelationships. The counselor should know all about the neurological urology and psychology of sex relationships before taking this on. The counselor should be relatively free of sex hangups; if not, he could exploit the patient with this feeling. The counselor must know something about typical male and female sex attributes in our society.

The ideal research setting would be a cord center that would provide both physical and emotional rehabilitation. This cord center could provide prompt and adequate care and also an atmosphere of hope, initiate a demand for research, and provide a clearinghouse for the exchange of information about existing curricula or those being planned in medical school for counselors.

REFERENCES

1. Ashcraft, Carolyn and Fitts, William H. Self-Concept Change in Psychotherapy. *Psychother.* May, 1964. 1 :3 :115–118.
2. Auerback, Alfred. The Battle of the Sexes. *Medical Aspects of Human Sexuality.* Dec., 1967. 1 :4 :6–11.
3. Barker, Roger G., and others. *Adjustment to Physical Handicap and Illness: A Survey of the Social Psychology of Physique and Disability.* New York : Social Science Research Council, 1953.
4. Baum, William C. Neurogenic Vesical and Sexual Dysfunction Attendant on Trauma to the Spinal Cord : Observations on Management. *J. Michigan Med. Soc.* Mar., 1962. 61 :5 :574–584.
5. Bell, Robert R. Some Emerging Sexual Expectations Among Women. *Medical Aspects of Human Sexuality.* Oct., 1967. 1 :2 :65–67, 72.
6. Bensman, Alan and Kottke, Frederic J. Induced Emission of Sperm Utilizing Electrical Stimulation of the Seminal Vesicles and Vas Deferens. *Arch. Phys. Med. & Rehab.* July, 1966. 47 :7 :436–443.
7. Berger, Stanley. The Role of Sexual Impotence in the Concept of Self in Male Paraplegics. *Dissertation Abstracts.* 1952. 12 :4 :533.
8. Bolles, M. Marjorie and Landis, Carney. *Personality and Sexuality of the Physically Handicapped Woman.* New York : Paul B. Hoeber, 1942.
9. Bors, Ernest. Spinal Cord Injuries. *Veterans Administration Tech. Bul. TS10–503.* Dec. 15, 1948. p. 26–27.
10. Bors, Ernest. The Spinal Cord Injury Center of the Veterans Administration Hospital, Long Beach, California, U.S.A. : Facts and Thoughts. *Paraplegia.* Nov., 1967. 5 :3 :126–130.
11. Bors, Ernest and Comarr, A. Estin. Neurological Disturbances of Sexual Function with Special Reference to 529 Patients with Spinal Cord Injury. *Urolog. Survey.* Dec., 1960. 10 :6 :191–222.
12. Bors, Ernest, and others. Fertility in Paraplegic Males. *J. Clinical Endocrinol.* Apr., 1950. 10 :4 :381–398.
13. Boyarsky, S. Management of the Genito-Urinary Problems of the Paraplegic. *Alabama J. Medical Sciences.* Apr., 1967. 4 :119–122.
14. Brady, John Paul, *moderator.* Roundtable : Frigidity. *Medical Aspects of Human Sexuality.* Feb., 1968. 2 :2 :26–27, 30–31, 36–37, 40.

15. Bucy, Paul C. Paraplegia : The Neglected Problem. *Physical Therapy.* Mar., 1969. 49 :3 :269–272.

16. Caprio, Frank Samuel. *Variations in Sexual Behavior.* New York : Citadel Pr., 1955.

17. Cavanagh, John R. Rhythm of Sexual Desire in Woman. *Medical Aspects of Human Sexuality.* Feb., 1969. 3 :2 :29, 34–35, 39.

18. Cibeira, Jose B. Some Conclusions on a Study of 365 Patients with Spinal Cord Lesions. *Paraplegia.* Feb., 1970. 7 :4 :249–254.

19. Coflin, T. *The Sex Kick: Eroticism in Modern America.* New York : Macmillan, 1966.

20. Colbert, James N. Philosophia Habilitatus : Towards a Policy of Human Rehabilitation in the Post-Institutional Phase of Disability. *J. Rehab.* Sept.-Oct., 1969. 35 :5 :18–20.

21. Comarr, A. E. Sexual Function Among Patients with Spinal Cord Injury. *Urologia Internationalis.* 1970. 25 :2 :134–168.

22. Comarr, A. Estin. Sexual Concepts in Traumatic Cord and Cauda Equina Lesions. *J. Urol.* Sept., 1971. 106 :375–378.

23. Comarr, A. Estin and Bors, Ernest. Spermatocystography in Patients with Spinal Cord Injuries. *J. Urol.* Jan., 1955. 73 :1 :172–178.

24. Congdon, C. S. *Self-Theory and Chlorpromazine Treatment.* (Unpublished doctoral dissertation) Vanderbilt Univ., Nashville, Tenn. : 1958.

25. Cooley, Charles Horton. *Human Nature and the Social Order.* New York : Charles Scribner's Sons, 1902.

26. Desmond, John. Paraplegia : Problems Confronting the Anaethesiologist. *Canadian Anaesthetists' Soc. J.* Sept., 1970. 17 :5 :435–451.

27. Ellis, Albert. *The American Sexual Tragedy.* New York : Twayne, 1954.

28. Ellis, Havelock. *Psychology of Sex: A Manual for Students.* New York : Emerson Books, 1964.

29. Fitts, W. H. *Manual for the Tennessee Self Concept Scale.* Nashville, Tenn. : Counselor Recordings and Tests, 1965.

30. Fitts, William H. *The Self Concept and Self-Actualization. (Research Monograph 3)* Nashville, Tenn. : Dede Wallace Center, 1971.

31. Ford, Amasa B. and Orfirer, Alexander P. Sexual Behavior and the Chronically Ill Patient. *Medical Aspects of Human Sexuality.* Oct., 1967. 1 :2 :51, 57–61.

32. Fordyce, W. E. Psychological Assessment and Management, chap. 6, p. 168–195, in : Krusen, Frank H.; Kottke, Frederic J.; and Ellwood, Paul M., Jr., eds. *Handbook of Physical Medicine and Rehabilitation.* Philadelphia : W. B. Saunders, 1971.

33. Frankel, Alan. Sexual Problems in Rehabilitation. *J. Rehab.* Sept.-Oct., 1967. 33 :5 :19–21.

34. Fried, Edrita. *The Ego in Love and Sexuality.* New York : Grune & Stratton, 1960.

35. Friedland, Fritz. Rehabilitation in Spinal Cord Injuries, chap. 17, p. 460–535, in : Licht, Sidney, *ed.: Rehabilitation and Medicine.* New Haven, Conn. : Elizabeth Licht, Publ., 1968.

36. Gagnon, John H. and Simon, William. *The Sexual Scene.* Chicago : Aldine Publ. Co., 1970.

37. Gebhard, Paul H. Human Sex Behavior Research, Chap. 23, p. 391–410, in : Diamond, Milton, *ed. Perspectives in Reproduction and Sexual Behavior.* Bloomington, Ind. : Indiana Univ. Pr., 1968.

38. Goldberg, M. Viewpoints : What Do You Tell Patients Who Ask about Coital Positions? *Medical Aspects of Human Sexuality.* Dec., 1968. 2 :12 :43, 46–48.

39. Goldberg, Martin, *moderator.* Roundtable : When Patients Ask About Various Sex Practices. *Medical Aspects of Human Sexuality.* Feb., 1969. 3 :2 :54–55, 58–61.

40. Goldman, George D. and Milman, Donald S., *eds. Modern Woman: Her Psychology and Sexuality.* Springfield, Ill. : Charles C. Thomas, 1969.

41. Göller, Herta and Paeslack, Volkmar. Our Experiences About Pregnancy and Delivery of the Paraplegic Woman. *Paraplegia.* Nov., 1970. 8 :3 :161–166.

42. Gorer, Geoffrey. *Sex and Marriage in England Today: A Study of the Views and Experience of the Under 45's.* London, Eng. : Nelson, 1971.

43. Grayson, Morris, in collaboration with Ann Powers and Joseph Levi. *Psychiatric Aspects of Rehabilitation.* New York : Inst. of Med. and Rehab., N.Y. Univ-Bellevue Med. Center, 1952.

44. Gross, Mortimer D. Marital Stress and Psychosomatic Disorders. *Medical Aspects of Human Sexuality.* Jan., 1969. 3 :1 :22, 24–25, 30, 32–33.

45. Guttmann, Ludwig. The Married Life of Paraplegics and Tetraplegics. *Paraplegia.* Oct., 1964. 2 :182–188.

46. Guttmann, Ludwig and Walsh, J. J. Prostigmin Assessment Test of Fertility in Spinal Man. *Paraplegia.* May, 1971. 9 :1 :39–51.

47. Henry, J. *The Self-Concept of Paraplegics and Quadriplegics: A Counseling Variable.* (Master's dissertation) Carbondale, Ill. : Southern Illinois University, 1972.

48. Herman, Myron. Role of Somesthetic Stimuli in the Development of Sexual Excitation in Man : A Preliminary Paper. *Arch. Neurol. & Psychiat.* July, 1950. 64 :1 :42–56.

49. Hetrick, William Robert. Sexuality Following Functional Transection of the Spinal Cord. *Dissertation Abstracts.* June, 1968. 28 :12 :5206B–5207B.

50. Hohmann, George W. Considerations in Management of Psychosexual Readjustment in the Cord Injured Male. *Rehab. Psychol.* Summer, 1972. 19 :2 :50–58.

51. Hohmann, George W. Some Effects of Spinal Cord Lesions on Experienced Emotional Feelings. *Psychophysiol.* Oct., 1966. 3 :2 :143–156.

52. Horne, Herbert W., Paull, David P., and Munro, Donald. Fertility Studies in the Human Male with Traumatic Injuries of the Spinal Cord and Cauda Equina. *New England J. Med.* Dec. 16, 1948. 239 :25 :959–961.

53. James, William. *The Principles of Psychology.* New York : H. Holt & Co., 1890.

54. Jochheim, K.-A. and Wahle, H. A Study on Sexual Function in 56 Male Patients with Complete Irreversible Lesions of the Spinal Cord and Cauda Equina. *Paraplegia.* Nov., 1970. 8 :3 :166–172.

55. Kessler, Henry H. *Rehabilitation of the Physically Handicapped.* New York : Columbia Univ. Pr., 1953.

56. Kinch, John W. Experimental Factors Related to Self-Concept Change. *J. Social Psychol.* Apr., 1968. 74 : 2nd half : 251–258.

57. Kinsey, Alfred, and others. *Sexual Behavior in the Human Female.* Philadelphia : W. B. Saunders, 1953.

58. Kinsey, Alfred C., Pomeroy, Wardell B., and Martin, Clyde E. *Sexual Behavior in the Human Male.* Philadelphia : W. B. Saunders, 1948.

59. Kuhn, Robert A. Functional Capacity of the Isolated Human Spinal Cord. *Brain.* Mar., 1950. 73 :Pt.1 :1–51.

60. Labenne, Wallace D. and Greene, Bert I. *Educational Implications of Self-Concept Theory.* Pacific Palisades, Calif. : Goodyear Publishing Co., 1969.

61. Levy, Ronald B. *Self-Revelation Through Relationships.* Englewood Cliffs, N.J. : Prentice-Hall, 1972.

62. Lewis, J. M. Impotence as a Reflection of Marital Conflict. *Medical Aspects of Human Sexuality.* June, 1969. 3 :6 :73–75, 78.

63. Lief, Harold I. New Developments in the Sex Education of the Physician. *J. Am. Med. Assn.* June 15, 1970. 212 :11 :1864–1867.

64. Lindner, Harold. Perceptual Sensitization to Sexual Phenomena in the Chronic Physically Handicapped. *J. Clin. Psychol.* Jan., 1953. 9 :1 :67–68.

65. Lipkin, K. Michael and Daniels, Robert S. The Role of Seduction in Interpersonal Relationships. *Medical Aspects of Human Sexuality.* June, 1969. 3 :6 :79, 82–83, 86, 88.

66. Long, Charles, II. Congenital and Traumatic Lesions of the Spinal Cord, chap. 25, p. 566–578, in : Krusen, Frank H.; Kottke, Frederic J.; and Ellwood, Paul M., Jr., eds. *Handbook of Physical Medicine and Rehabilitation.* Philadelphia : W. B. Saunders, 1971.

67. MacDowell, Fletcher H. Sexual Manifestations of Neurologic Disease. *Medical Aspects of Human Sexuality.* Apr., 1968. 2 :4 :13, 16–17, 20–21.

68. Marshall, Donald S., ed. and Suggs, Robert C. *Human Sexual Behavior: Variations in the Ethnographic Spectrum.* New York : Basic Books, 1971.

69. Maslow, Abraham Harold. *Motivation and Personality.* New York : Harper, 1954.

70. Masters, William H. and Johnson, Virginia E. *Human Sexual Response.* Boston : Little, Brown, 1966.

71. Mead, George Herbert. *Mind, Self, and Society, from the Standpoint of a Social Behaviorist.* Edited by Charles W. Morris. Chicago : Univ. of Chicago Pr., 1934.

72. Money, John. Phantom Orgasm in the Dreams of Paraplegic Men and Women. *AMA Arch. Gen. Psychiat.* Oct., 1960. 3 :373–382.

73. Morgan, Clifford T. and Stellar, Eliot. Subcortical Centers and Pathways, in : Morgan, Clifford T. *Physiological Psychology. (ed. 2)* New York : McGraw, 1950.

74. Mueller, Alfred D. Psychologic Factors in Rehabilitation of Paraplegic Patients. *Arch. Phys. Med. & Rehab.* Apr., 1962. 43 :4 :151–159.

75. Munro, Donald. Clinical Problems in Paraplegia : Paraplegia Then and Now and What Can Be Learned from the Comparison, chap. 5, p. 196–205, in : French, John D., and Porter, Robert W., eds. *Basic Research in Paraplegia; A Conference Sponsored by the California Spinal Cord Research Foundation under the Auspices of Los Angeles Society of Neurology and Psychiatry.* Springfield, Ill. : Charles C. Thomas, 1962.

76. Munro, Donald, Horne, Herbert W., and Paull, David P. The Effect of Injury to the Spinal Cord and Cauda Equina on the Sexual Potency of Men. *New England J. Med.* Dec. 9, 1948. 239 :24 :903–911.

77. Nagler, Benedict. Psychiatric Aspects of Cord Injury. *Am. J. Psychiat.* July, 1950. 107 :1 :49–56.

78. Nickerson, Eileen Tressler. Some Correlates of Adjustment of Paraplegics. *Dissertation Abstracts.* Aug., 1961. 22 :2 :632–633.

79. Oppenhimer, William M. Pregnancy in Paraplegic Patients : Two Case Reports. *Am. J. Obstet. & Gynecol.* July 15, 1971. 110 :6 :784–786.

80. Pfeiffer, Eric. Geriatric Sex Behavior. *Medical Aspects of Human Sexuality.* July, 1969. 3 :7 :19, 22–23, 26, 28, 81. *Physician's World.* Nov., 1973. p. 24.

81. *Physician's World.* Nov., 1973. p. 24.

82. Popenoe, Paul. *Sexual Inadequacy of the Male.* Los Angeles : Am. Inst. of Family Relations, 1950.

83. Powys, J. C. *Psychoanalysis and Morality.* San Francisco : Jessica Colbert, 1924.

84. Riddoch, George. The Reflex Functions of the Completely Divided

Spinal Cord in Man, Compared with Those Associated with Less Severe Lesions. *Brain.* 1917. 40 :264–402.

85. Rossi, Romolo and Conforto, Carmelo. 3rd Annual Convention on the Subject : Sexual Impotence : Psychotherapeutic Problems in Organic Sexual Impotence. *Rivista di Psichiatria.* 1969. 4 :4 :326–329.

86. Rossier, A. Problems Raised by the Rehabilitation of Spinal Cord Injury Patients. (French) *Schweiz. Arch. Neurol. Neurochir. Psychiat.* 1969. 103 :1 :117–136.

87. Rossier, A. B., Ruffieux, M., and Ziegler, W. H. Pregnancy and Labour in High Traumatic Spinal Cord Lesions. *Paraplegia.* Nov., 1969. 7 :3 :210–216.

88. Rusk, Howard A. *Rehabilitation Medicine.* St. Louis : C. V. Mosby, 1964.

89. Rusk, Howard A., *moderator.* Roundtable : Sex Problems in Paraplegia. *Medical Aspects of Human Sexuality.* Dec., 1967. 1 :4 :46–50.

90. Ryan, James H. Dreams of Paraplegics. *Arch. Gen. Psychiat.* Sept., 1961. 5 :3 :286–291.

91. Salzman, Leon, *moderator.* Roundtable : Female Orgasm. *Medical Aspects of Human Sexuality.* Apr., 1968. 2 :4 :37–38, 42–43, 46–47.

92. Saunders, Douglas and Yeo, John. Pregnancy and Quadriplegia— The Problem of Autonomic Dysreflexia. *Austral. & New Zealand J. Obstet. & Gynaecol.* Aug., 1968. 8 :3 :152–154.

93. Schimel, John L. The Fallacy of Equality in Sexual Relations. *Medical Aspects of Human Sexuality.* Aug., 1969. 3 :8 :15–22, 24.

94. Sex and the Paraplegic. *Medical World News.* Jan. 14, 1972. 13 :2 :35, 38.

95. Sherman, Julia A. What Men Do Not Know About Women's Sexuality. *Medical Aspects of Human Sexuality.* Nov., 1972. 6 :11 :138, 141–142, 144–147, 151.

96. Siller, Jerome. Psychological Situation of the Disabled with Spinal Cord Injuries. *Rehab. Lit.* Oct., 1969. 30 :10 :290–296.

97. *A Survey of Medicine and Medical Practice for the Rehabilitation Counselor.* Washington, D.C. : U.S. Vocational Rehabilitation Administration, 1966.

98. Symonds, Percival M. *The Ego and the Self.* New York : Appleton-Century-Crofts, 1951.

99. Talbot, Herbert S. A Report on Sexual Function in Paraplegics. *J. Urol.* Feb., 1949. 61 :2 :265–270.

100. Talbot, Herbert S. Sexual Function in Paraplegia. *J. Urol.* Jan., 1955. 73 :1 :91–100.

101. Talbot, H. S. The Sexual Function in Paraplegics. (Society Transactions) *AMA Arch. Neurol. & Psychiat.* 1951. 66 :650–651.

102. Thom, Douglas A., VonSalzen, Charles F., and Fromme, Allen. Psychological Aspects of the Paraplegic Patient. *Med. Clin. North Am.* Mar., 1946. 30 :473–480.

103. Thompson, Warren. *Correlates of the Self Concept. (Research Monograph 6)* Nashville, Tenn. : Dede Wallace Center, 1972.

104. Trainer, Joseph B. Emotional Bases of Fatigue. *Medical Aspects of Human Sexuality.* Jan., 1969. 3 :1 :59, 63–65.

105. Tsuji, I., and others. The Sexual Function in Patients with Spinal Cord Injury. *Urologia Internationalis.* 1961. 12 :4–5 :270–280.

106. Van Stolk, Mary. *Man and Woman.* Toronto, Can. : McClelland and Stewart, 1968.

107. Wahle, H. and Jochheim, K.-A. Studies on Neurogenic Disorders of Sexual Functions in 56 Paraplegic Men and Complete Irreversible Injuries of the Spinal Cord or the Cauda Equina. (German) *Fortschr. Neurol. Psychiat. und ihrer Grenzgebiete.* Apr., 1970. 38 :4 :192–201.

108. Warter, C. and Gonzáles, J. On Sphincteric and Sexual Disturbances in Paraplegics. (Spanish) *Neurocirugia.* Jan.–June, 1970. 28 :72–76.

109. Weber, Doreen D. and Wessman, Henry C. A Review of Sexual Function Following Spinal Cord Trauma. *Physical Ther.* Mar., 1971. 51 :3 :290–295.

110. Weiss, Aaron J. and Diamond, M. David. Sexual Adjustment, Identification, and Attitudes of Patients with Myelopathy. *Arch. Phys. Med. & Rehab.* Apr., 1966. 47 :4 :245–250.

111. Whitelaw, George P. and Smithwick, Reginald H. Some Secondary Effects of Sympathectomy with Particular Reference to Disturbance of Sexual Function. *New England J. Med.* July 26, 1951. 245 :4 :121–130.

112. Williams, J. G. Sex and the Paralyzed. *Sexology.* 1965. 31 :453–456.

113. Winston, Arnold, and others. Patterns of Psychological Decompensation in Patients with Spinal Cord Syndromes. *Diseases of Nerv. System.* Dec., 1969. 30 :12 :824–827.

114. Zeitlin, Austin B., Cottrell, Thomas L., and Lloyd, Frederick A. Sexology of the Paraplegic Male. *Fertility and Sterility.* July–Aug., 1957. 8 :4 :337–344.

Part VII

The Rights, Contributions, and Problems of Disabled Consumers

Until recently, persons with disabilities were involved little or not at all in the programs that shaped their lives. Today, however, many clients participate actively in their rehabilitation through self-help groups and as advisory group members, directors, or staff members in rehabilitation agencies. In addition, many rehabilitation workers currently espouse the concept of comanagement with clients.

Wright discusses the brief history of the development of human and civil rights for handicapped persons. She presents explicit principles and ideals as set forth in various Bills of Rights for disabled people and discusses their implications for practice.

In reaffirming its faith in human rights in December 1975, the United Nations proclaimed a Declaration of the Rights of Disabled Persons. This Declaration calls for national and international action to insure a common frame of reference for the protection of the rights, and assuring the welfare and rehabilitation of, the physically and mentally disabled. Those who work with disabled persons, as well as disabled persons themselves, should be fully aware of the rights contained in this Declaration in addition to the other social and legal rights of disabled persons.

Self-help groups are organized by peers who share a common problem. Jaques and Patterson discuss the development of self-help and its implications for rehabilitation. The self-help service model is compared to the professional service model, and the unique but complementary contributions of each are discussed.

In a moving presentation concerning an international application of a self-help group, L'Arche Movement, Vanier focuses upon the contribution that handicapped people make to humanity. His firsthand experience as founder of the Movement, which now encompasses nearly fifty communes of handicapped persons throughout the world, has provided Vanier with an understanding and philosophy of life that he sensitively and emotionally shares with the reader.

In an attempt to better understand the nature of a rehabilitation hospital, French had himself admitted in one as a patient. In their discussion of this admittance and the transition to the patient role with its accompanying boredom and strain, French, McDowell, and Keith provide rehabilitation workers with new insights into the patient's role.

20

Changes in Attitudes toward People with Handicaps

Beatrice A. Wright

Attitudes toward people with handicaps are not isolated phenomena that stand apart from the general sweep of social change. Two of the most vital general developments since World War II have been the increased emphasis on human and civil rights for all people and the determination on the part of disadvantaged groups to speak out and act on their own behalf. Many instances could be reported illustrating these developments in the case of race, religion, sex, prisoners, ethnic groups, and the poor. The present review cites examples that apply to people with physical and mental handicaps.

Affirmation of Human Rights

A most important document appeared in 1948 when the General Assembly of the United Nations adopted the Universal Declaration of Human Rights. That Declaration not only affirmed that it is possible for all of humanity to agree in general on what is important to every human being, but, more than that, it forthrightly stated that "every individual and every organ of society" has a responsibility to promote the matters contained in the Declaration.

Since then, in fact, different persons and organs of society have formulated principles to serve as guidelines for action to insure the fuller realization of human dignity. In 1973, the American Hospital Association published a "Patient's Bill of Rights" consisting of 12 points. These rights are considered to be so fundamental that every patient in a hospital setting is to be informed of them. The rights include such items

From *Rehabilitation Literature*, *34* (1973), 354–368. Copyright © 1973 by the National Easter Seal Society for Crippled Children and Adults. Reprinted by permission of the Editor.

as the right of the patient to respectful care and to consideration of privacy, the right to receive information necessary to give informed consent to any procedure or treatment, and the right to be advised if the hospital proposes to engage in human experimentation affecting his care. The document concludes with this significant emphasis. "No catalog of rights can guarantee for the patient the kind of treatment he has a right to expect. . . . [For such treatment] must be conducted with an overriding concern for the patient, and, above all, the recognition of his dignity as a human being."[3]

In addition to the rights of patients in general, a formulation of the basic rights of the mentally ill and the mentally retarded was published in 1973.[8] These rights are articulated in three broad categories, namely, the right to treatment, the right to compensation for institution-maintaining labor, and the right to education. Prototype court cases are presented to show that litigation can be a valuable tool and catalyst in protecting the rights of the mentally handicapped.

A set of 18 value-laden beliefs and principles published in 1972 provides guidelines for rehabilitation of people with disabilities.[12] The general tenor of these principles may be conveyed by citing a few of them :

1. Every individual needs respect and encouragement; the presence of a handicap, no matter how severe, does not alter these fundamental rights.
2. The assets of the person must receive considerable attention in the rehabilitation effort.
3. The active participation of the client in the planning and execution of his rehabilitation program is to be sought as fully as possible.
4. The severity of a handicap can be increased or diminished by environmental conditions.
5. Involvement of the client with the general life of the community is a fundamental principle guiding decisions concerning living arrangements and the use of resources.
6. All phases of rehabilitation have psychological aspects.
7. Self-help organizations are important allies in the rehabilitation effort.

For each of these principles, implications for action are elaborated. For example, principle 1 further asserts that "A person is entitled to the enrichment of his life and the development of his abilities whether these be great or small and whether he has a long or short time to live."

"A Bill of Rights for the Disabled,"[1] published in 1972, highlights 16 rights that apply to such areas as health, education, employment, housing, transportation, and civil rights. To take transportation as an example, it is resolved that programs and standards be established for the "modification of existing mass transportation systems and the development of new specially designed demand-schedule transportation facilities."

"A Bill of Rights for the Handicapped" was recently adopted by the United Cerebral Palsy Association.[11] Among the 10 rights listed are the right to health and educational services, the right to work, the right to barrier-free public facilities, and the right to petition social institutions and the courts to gain such opportunities as may be enjoyed by others but denied the handicapped because of oversight, public apathy, or discrimination.

Also in accord with the stress on civil rights is the recent declaration of intent by the Canadian Rehabilitation Council for the Disabled, which delineates 14 areas to which these rights pertain.[4] These areas include treatment, education, recreation, transportation, housing, spiritual development, legal rights, and economic security.

Accepting the handicapped person as a full human being means accepting him as having the full range of human needs, including those involving the sexual areas of life. The past few years have witnessed a much greater awareness of the importance of this matter. A brief summary of specialized studies and conferences in a number of countries was presented at the Twelfth World Congress of Rehabilitation International in 1972.[5] In this enlightening presentation, Chigier listed six rights with regard to sexual behavior of individuals in general and then traced the extent to which persons with disabilities are assisted or prevented from achieving these rights. Among the rights examined were the right to be informed about sexual matters, the right to sexual expression, the right to marry, and the right to become parents. While recognizing certain problems that come with greater freedom in these areas, the thrust of the analysis is directed toward constructive solutions that will enable severely disabled and mentally retarded persons to realize these rights more fully. Also in 1972, a beautiful article appeared on management of psychosexual readjustment in the cord-injured male.[7] It deals specifically with the kinds of sexual activities open to the cord-injured person and how the possibilities for sexual fulfillment can be enhanced between two people who care for each other.

Legislation helps to give reality to principles of human rights by making provision for the financing and administration of relevant services. The First International Conference on Legislation Concerning the Disabled was held in 1971. The principles guiding the recommendations reflect changing attitudes toward people with handicaps. For example, it is pointed out that "the ultimate objective of all legislation for the disabled is complete integration of the disabled in the community and to enable the disabled person to lead as normal a life as possible regardless of productive capacity."[6] The conference further emphasized that real progress can be achieved only when legislation is designed to foster "respect for the personality and human rights of the individual."[6]

Manifestations in Practice

Fortunately, the explicit expression of principles and ideals set forth in the aforementioned documents is increasingly becoming manifest in practice. Let us consider, as an example, the concept of integration, which has been regarded as a principle that can more fully insure the realization of human rights for most people. What is necessary to appreciate is that, once integration becomes a guiding principle, certain matters were not at issue until they quickly assume vital importance. The location of institutions and the houses in which handicapped people can live becomes important, because their location within communities enables participation of the handicapped in community offerings. Architectural barriers become an issue, because their elimination enables people with a wide range of physical abilities to have access to events within buildings at large. The organization of services becomes a challenge, because integration rather than segregation is fostered when special needs can be met within general community facilities, such as hospitals, comprehensive rehabilitation centers, schools, recreation areas, churches, and community centers. Transportation assumes special significance, because integration requires that the person have a way to get to the integrated facilities that exist. And, when these issues receive sufficient attention, ways to improve the situation become apparent.

A case in point is the increasing accommodation of handicapped children within regular schools. Helping to make such integration a reality are special classes, resource teachers, and teacher aides. The following conclusion, based on a review of children with hearing impairments, is also applicable to children with other handicapping conditions : "Recent experience indicates that children can manage in the ordinary school with more severe hearing impairments than has been generally considered possible."[9] Lest there be a too-ready overgeneralization, however, I hasten to add that this conclusion does not obviate the need for special groupings of children in particular instances and for special purposes.

Integration is not an answer for all circumstances. It will ill serve handicapped children unless their special needs are met through necessary accommodations within the community setting that nurtures a climate of full respect for the dignity of each individual. Nor must integration imply that, where handicapped people are integrated within general community settings, there is no need for handicapped people to get together. Sharing and solving mutual problems, participating in specially designed activities together, and finding needed companionship are some of the rewards that can be provided by self-help, recreation, and other groups. This does not mean that people should be forced to join such groups, that the groups are appropriate for all people with handicaps, or that these groups should preempt association with people who are not handicapped. But it does mean that such groups should not be discredited as fostering segregation, as limiting adaptation to a nonhandicapped world, or as implying overconcern with personal problems. It does mean that groups like these should be valued for providing the opportunity for people to meet together, have fun together, and to affirm and assert themselves together.

A second example of change in practice is the greater involvement of people with handicaps in leadership positions in agencies working on their behalf. Agencies are increasingly recognizing that handicapped people themselves have special contributions to make in the development of services directed toward meeting the needs and enriching the lives of clients. The United Cerebral Palsy Association (UCPA), for example, has enumerated the kinds of roles that adults with cerebral palsy are especially equipped to fill by virtue of their special vantage point.[10] It is explicitly pointed out that adults with cerebral palsy should serve on boards of directors and on *all* committees, that they can help with educating parents, that they can provide constructive role models and share personal experiences with young cerebral palsied children and teenagers, and that in-service training programs for such leadership roles are important just as are other in-service training efforts. A recent survey conducted by UCPA of New York on "The Status of the Cerebral Palsied Adult as a Board, Committee, or Staff Member in UCP Affiliates" revealed that one or more cerebral palsied adults were on the Board of Directors in 24% of the 227 local agencies who replied and served as staff members in 16 percent.[10] It was urged that these percentages be increased.

A third reflection in practice of the affirmation of human dignity is the enormously significant effort on the part of people with handicaps to speak out and act on their own behalf, an effort that so clearly parallels the efforts of other minority groups. Sometimes the effort has taken the form of individual action, as in the case of a blind woman who, in 1964, filed a complaint in criminal court against being refused restaurant service because of her seeing-eye dog. Sometimes the protest involved civil disobedience, as in 1967 when a group of seven persons were refused restaurant service because four of them were blind and had guide dogs. They refused to leave the premises until, after the owner contacted the Health Department, they were allowed to remain. Sometimes the effort involved street demonstrations, as in 1970, when a group of university paraplegic students undertook a 100-mile wheelchair trek to promote employment of the handicapped.

Sometimes the effort was extended beyond a single issue to include wide-ranging problems of concern to large numbers of people with handicaps. Thus, in 1970, after winning the case of a young woman confined to a wheelchair who had been refused a teaching license, the Law institute that was involved extended its services to all cases of infringement of civil rights of the handicapped. Among these new cases were a bedridden man who was refused an absentee ballot in a federal election and a blind man who was denied a teacher's license. Recently a National Center for Law and the Handicapped was established. Sometimes the effort on the part of the handicapped solicited the support of an entire community as in the case of the Committee for the Architecturally Handicapped, organized by two University of Kansas students. Curb cuts in town and on campus, the remodeling of buildings, the revamping of architectural plans for new construction, and the appearance of the international symbol of access attest to the success of this effort.

Parent groups have had a long and impressive history of involvement on behalf of children with disabilities; currently people with handicaps themselves are gaining the sense of strength and accomplishment that comes from actively participating in advancing their own cause. The number of self-help and mutual aid groups keeps growing. There are publications by people with handicaps for people with handicaps, such as *Accent on Living, Rehabilitation Gazette* (formerly *Toomey j Gazette*), *Paraplegia News,* and *The Braille Technical Press. Stuttering,* published for specialists in the field of speech pathology, primarily consists of papers presented at an annual conference by speech pathologists who stutter. All of these efforts reflect a greater readiness on the part of people with handicaps to acknowledge their own handicaps and to become actively involved with improving their circumstances and increasing understanding of their problems.

Prospects

Attitudes toward the handicapped have seen such marked change since World War II that I believe the reader will be able to guess whether the article from which the following is quoted was published before 1950 or after. It deals with the birth of a child with Down's syndrome (mongolian mental retardation):

> The problems presented by the arrival into a family of one of these accidents of development are many. . . . Because the mongolian is so incompetent in the ordinary technics of living, his mother soon becomes a complete slave to his dependency. As a result, she devotes all of her time to his necessary care, neglecting her other household duties, her other children . . . , and inevitably, her husband. The effect

of all this is that all other satisfying areas of living are blotted out
. . . . With the passing years, . . . [the mongol's] brothers and sisters
refuse to bring other children into the house, . . . and are obsessed
with a feeling of family shame no matter how unjustifiable it may be.
. . . There is only one adequate way to lessen all this grief, fortunately
a measure which most experienced physicians will agree to, and that
is immediate commitment to an institution at the time of diagnosis.
. . . When the diagnosis has been made in a newborn the mother is
told that the baby is not strong enough to be brought to her at present.
. . . Next, the father is asked to meet the physician immediately,
bringing with him any close relatives . . . the nature of the problem
is explained, . . . emphasizing its seriousness . . . and that immediate
placement outside the family provides the only hope of preventing
a long series of family difficulties. . . . [The mother] is asked, not to
make the decision, but to accept the one which has already been
made by the close relatives. . . . It means that the physician must take
the lead in precipitating an immediate crisis in order to prevent much
more serious difficulties later on. This is preventive medicine.[2]

The cues that one had in guessing correctly? There were many. In that
article the emphasis was on institutionalizing the child rather than on
seeking ways to make it feasible for him to remain with his family, at
least during his early years; the main responsibility for deciding the
issue rested with the physician rather than with those directly concerned,
i.e., the family; gross devaluating generalizations were made concerning
the devastating effects of having such a child; no consideration was given
the capacity of families, with the help of community resources, to be
able to accept and adapt to new circumstances. It is not likely that the
article in question could be published in a responsible professional
journal today, an indication of how attitudes have changed in the past
quarter of a century even though, to be sure, there continue to be
frequent breeches of the new directions in actual life settings.

We have seen how the ideals of human dignity and basic civil
rights are being reflected in what is being said and done regarding people
with handicaps. But how much can we count on continued progress?
Not very much, I would argue. To assert otherwise would be to invite
apathy. There is no guarantee that the right of each individual to respect
and encouragement in the enrichment of his life will increasingly be
honored, or that people with handicaps will increasingly have an
important voice in influencing conditions that affect their lives. Although
we can affirm that the changing attitudes described above are durable
insofar as they are regarded as expressions of basic human rights, we
must also recognize that they are fragile insofar as they are subject to
the vicissitudes of broad-sweeping social and political circumstances. The

lives of handicapped people are inextricably a part of a much wider socio-economic-political and ethical society affecting the lives of all people. It is therefore essential for all of us to remain vigilant to protect and extend the hard-won gains of recent decades and to be ready to counter undermining forces. Vigilance requires thoughtful action guided by continuing reevaluation of the effectiveness of present efforts and alertness to needs of changing conditions.

REFERENCES

1. Abramson, Arthur S. and Kutner, Bernard. A Bill of Rights for the Disabled. *Arch. Phys. Med. and Rehab.* Mar., 1972. 53 :3 :99–100.
2. Aldrich, C. Anderson. Preventive Medicine and Mongolism. *Am. J. Mental Deficiency.* Oct., 1947. 52 :2 :127–129.
3. American Hospital Association. *A Patient's Bill of Rights.* Chicago : 1973. Also published as : Statement on a Patient's Bill of Rights; Affirmed by the Board of Trustees, Nov. 17, 1972. *Hospitals.* Feb. 16, 1973. 47 :4 :41.
4. Canadian Council for Rehabilitation of the Disabled. A Declaration of Intent. *Rehab. Digest.* Spring, 1973. 4 :4 :4–5.
5. Chigier, E. Sexual Adjustment of the Handicapped, p. 224–227, in : *Proceedings Preview: Twelfth World Congress of Rehabilitation International, Sydney, Australia.* 1972, vol. 1.
6. First International Conference on Legislation Concerning the Disabled. *Internatl. Rehab. Rev.* Second Quarter, 1972. 23 :2 :18–19, 23.
7. Hohmann, George W. Considerations in Management of Psychosexual Readjustment in the Cord Injured Male. *Rehab. Psychol.* Summer, 1972. 19 :2 :50–58.
8. Mental Health Law Project. *Basic Rights of the Mentally Handicapped.* Washington, D.C. : Mental Health Law Project (*1751 N St., N.W., 20036*), 1973.
9. Telford, Charles W. and Sawrey, James M. *The Exceptional Individual.* (ed. 2) Englewood Cliffs, N.J. : Prentice-Hall, 1972.
10. United Cerebral Palsy Associations. Survey Shows Few CP Adults Involved in UCP Decision Making. *Crusader.* No. 6, 1971. p. 2.
11. United Cerebral Palsy Associations. A Bill of Rights for the Handicapped. *Crusader.* No. 3, 1973. p. 1, 2, 3, 4, 5, 6. Also published separately.
12. Wright, Beatrice A. Value-Laden Beliefs and Principles for Rehabilitation Psychology. *Rehab. Psychol.* Spring, 1972. 19 :1 :38–45.

21

United Nations
New York
General Assembly Resolution 3447 [XXX],
Adopted 9 December 1975

Declaration on the Rights of Disabled Persons

The General Assembly,

Mindful of the pledge made by Member States, under the Charter of the United Nations, to take joint and separate action in co-operation with the Organization to promote higher standards of living, full employment and conditions of economic and social progress and development,

Reaffirming its faith in human rights and fundamental freedoms and in the principles of peace, of the dignity and worth of the human person and of social justice proclaimed in the Charter,

Recalling the principles of the Universal Declaration of Human Rights,[9] the International Covenants on Human Rights,[10] the Declaration of the Rights of the Child[11] and the Declaration on the Rights of Mentally Retarded Persons,[12] as well as the standards already set for social progress in the constitutions, conventions, recommendations and resolutions of the International Labour Organisation, the United Nations Educational, Scientific and Cultural Organization, the World Health Organization, the United Nations Children's Fund and other organizations concerned,

Recalling also Economic and Social Council resolution 1921 (LVIII) of 6 May 1975 on prevention of disability and rehabilitation of disabled persons,

Emphasizing that the Declaration of Social Progress and Development[13] has proclaimed the necessity of protecting the rights and assuring the

[9] General Assembly resolution 217 A (III).
[10] General Assembly resolution 220 A (XXI), annex.
[11] General Assembly resolution 1386 (XIV).
[12] General Assembly resolution 2856 (XXVI).
[13] General Assembly resolution 2542 (XXIV).

welfare and rehabilitation of the physically and mentally disadvantaged,

Bearing in mind the necessity of preventing physical and mental disabilities and of assisting disabled persons to develop their abilities in the most varied fields of activities and of promoting their integration as far as possible in normal life,

Aware that certain countries, at their present stage of development, can devote only limited efforts to this end,

Proclaims this Declaration on the Rights of Disabled Persons and calls for national and international action to ensure that it will be used as a common basis and frame of reference for the protection of these rights :

1. The term "disabled person" means any person unable to ensure by himself or herself wholly or partly the necessities of a normal individual and/or social life, as a result of a deficiency, either congenital or not, in his or her physical or mental capabilities.

2. Disabled persons shall enjoy all the rights set forth in this Declaration. These rights shall be granted to all disabled persons without any exception whatsoever and without distinction or discrimination on the basis of race, colour, sex, language, religion, political or other opinions, national or social origins, state of wealth, birth or any other situation applying either to the disabled person himself or herself or to his or her family.

3. Disabled persons have the inherent right to respect for their human dignity. Disabled persons, whatever the origin, nature and seriousness of their handicaps and disabilities, have the same fundamental rights as their fellow-citizens of the same age, which implies first and foremost the right to enjoy a decent life, as normal and full as possible.

4. Disabled persons have the same civil and political rights as other human beings; article 7 of the Declaration of the Rights of Mentally Retarded Persons applies to any possible limitation or suppression of those rights for mentally disabled persons.

5. Disabled persons are entitled to the measures designed to enable them to become as self-reliant as possible.

6. Disabled persons have the right to medical, psychological and functional treatment, including prosthetic and orthetic appliances, to medical and social rehabilitation, education, vocational education, training and rehabilitation, aid, counseling, placement services and other services which will enable them to develop their capabilities and skills to the maximum and will hasten the process of their social integration or reintegration.

7. Disabled persons have the right to economic and social security and to a decent level of living. They have the right, according to their capabilities, to secure and retain employment or to engage in a useful, productive and remunerative occupation and to join trade unions.

8. Disabled persons are entitled to have their special needs taken into consideration at all stages of economic and social planning.

9. Disabled persons have the right to live with their families or with foster parents and to participate in all social, creative or recreational activities. No disabled person shall be subjected, as far as his or her residence is concerned, to differential treatment other than that required by his or her condition or by the improvement which he or she may derive therefrom. If the stay of a disabled person in a specialized establishment is indispensible, the environment and living conditions therein shall be as close as possible to those of the normal life of a person of his or her age.

10. Disabled persons shall be protected against all exploitation, all regulations and all treatment of a discriminatory, abusive or degrading nature.

11. Disabled persons shall be able to avail themselves of qualified legal aid when such aid proves indispensible for the protection of their persons and property.
    If judicial proceedings are instituted against them, the legal procedure applied shall take their physical and mental condition fully into account.

12. Organizations of disabled persons may be usefully consulted in all matters regarding the rights of disabled persons.

13. Disabled persons, their families and communities shall be fully informed, by all appropriate means, of the rights contained in this Declaration.

22

The Self-Help Group Model:
A Review

Marceline E. Jaques
Kathleen M. Patterson

The decade of the thirties saw the beginning of parallel movements in rehabilitative care. One was counseling and psychotherapy, developed on a traditional base of professional care; the other was a "people's movement" of self-help. For more than thirty-five years, these two helping systems have existed side by side. They have expanded, matured, and grown beyond the expectations of their adherents; yet they have ignored or denied each other, rarely communicated, and have gone about their business as if the other did not exist. Occasionally rumblings were heard, and more often than not they were critical of the other's practices. A few individuals from each system showed interest in the practices of the other, but interactions were rare and superficial. Primarily, each seemed convinced of its "rightness of approach" and chose not to examine its relationship or be examined.

The questions remain : What do the two approaches have in common? Is it possible to share or move between the professional and the self-help model? Or is the self-help process a unique modality of care not now widely known, acknowledged, or accepted by the professions, but a functional part of a total rehabilitative system?

Recently, the professional world has shown more interest in the self-help world as it has become progressively more difficult to ignore its growth in numbers, size, and benefits. The reports of satisfaction by self-help group members and the pragmatic results they have achieved for themselves have been impressive, if not disturbing, to some professionals. These reports seem to be in contrast to the general aura of self-doubt and dissatisfaction permeating the professionals' helping fields. Hard evidence that the professional service system works effectively for

From *Rehabilitation Counseling Bulletin, 18* (1974), 48–58, Copyright © 1974 by American Personnel and Guidance Association. Reprinted with permission from the publisher and authors.

those seeking help is sparse. Too many persons with problems are either not cared for or cared for in an unsatisfactory manner.

Group Types and Purposes

There are two basic types of self-help groups : (a) individuals with a certain condition or problem who have suffered a personal-social deprivation, such as Alcoholics Anonymous (AA) and Recovery, Inc., and (b) groups of families or friends of persons who have a condition or problem, such as Alanon, Alateen, and Parents of Retarded Children. Groups are also referred to as mutual aid groups. The labels, self-help and mutual aid, state concretely the purpose and method of these groups. Help for each member around specific problem areas is the group goal. Although groups of the first type are usually occupied with their personal problem solving and programs, the group members often fulfill an information-giving function to the interested public. Groups of the second type more often engage in advocacy, social action, and program development.

There seems to be a fine line of demarcation between a families/friends self-help group and a voluntary agency, with no clear-cut criteria of distinction. As the group grows in size it tends to develop structure and add services, usually given by professionals. This, of course, changes the original self-help and mutual aid function. The volunteers who join the group help the programs and support a common cause, though they may not share the problem. Examples are hundreds of college students and persons from all walks of life who volunteer their services as companions, foster grandparents, big brothers and sisters, and in other aspects of planning, program development, public information, and fund raising in large and small private agencies. The self-help and mutual aid may not be as clear-cut, at least not explicitly, although Riessman's helper principle (1965) of receiving therapeutic help in the process of helping others may apply.

Katz (1970) described five phases of development by which some self-help groups evolve a more complex organization : origin by disadvantaged persons and relatives, informal organization spread through friends and acquaintances, emergence of leaders, formal organization through rules and by-laws, and use of professional methods and staff. Zola (1972) described the development occurring in another order from voluntary lay associations of American pioneer days to mutual aid societies with membership based on social characteristics of race, religion, and country of origin. The original mutual aid was of a tangible, material type, like money lending, Zola reported. The tangible aid members gave to each other was followed by "aid of a more social psychological nature" (p. 180).

Growth and Development of Self-Help Model

Self-help groups have undergone an impressive growth, although there is no up-to-date total directory or census. Mowrer (1964) reported that Maurice Jackson developed a directory in 1961–62 entitled *Their Brother's Keepers* and listed 265 different types of self-help groups. A recent survey of self-help organizations for the physically handicapped reported over 1,200 groups nationwide (Massachusetts Council of Organizations of the Handicapped, Inc., 1973). In their most recent directory, Alcoholics Anonymous (1973) reported 600,000 members throughout the world, with 405,858 United States members in 14,037 groups. This is a phenomenal story of growth and development, which began with two members in 1935. The Oxford group movement of that day is credited with providing some background for the AA method, though its tenets were considered too rigid by the AA founders (*Alcoholics Anonymous* 1955; *Alcoholics Anonymous Comes of Age* 1957). AA has been used as a model for the development of other self-help groups, such as Synanon, Gamblers Anonymous, Neurotics Anonymous, Weight Watchers, and Overeaters Anonymous. Recovery, Inc., reported in their 1973 directory that they have 950 groups in 46 states and 5 Canadian provinces and 1 group each in Puerto Rico and Israel.

Self-help groups have spread not only across the nation but throughout the world. It is safe to say that more groups exist in the United States and Canada than in other parts of the world. They have spread, at least in contemporary times, from the United States to other countries in the manner of AA and Recovery, Inc. Katz (1964, 1965) reported two quite different self-help programs in England and Poland. The Psychiatric Rehabilitation Association in England has a program of social clubs or groups where numerous self-help functions are carried out for both former and present patients. Although these are done with official support and in official health centers, professionals are in the background, with the patients or clients actually planning, organizing, and directing the programs from counseling to planning job interviews and training. The programs are not limited to professional activities but may include cultural and social functions.

The Polish Union of Invalid Cooperatives exists so that disabled persons and their families may prepare themselves for work through both treatment and training. The cooperatives, not state-owned or managed, are set up on a self-help model. The disabled persons belong to the cooperatives, share in planning, and participate in the rehabilitation programs. Apartments, workshops, and business enterprises, along with counseling, training, and placement, are integral parts of the cooperative program. Participation in the planning and policymaking seems to provide high incentive and motivation toward self-help.

There is no end to the possible number and type of self-help groups. Their potential may be as variable as unsolved human problems or the special needs not met by existing social arrangements. Some behavioral scientists believe that the small group is in fact a new dimension in social organizations, counteracting the isolation of our time and the rigidity of an institution. Rogers (1973) described the emergence of a new kind of person, who uses the small informal group as an alternative to the structured bureaucratic institution. The traditions and structure of AA, for example, permit few organizational structures within or influences from outside. For example, chairpersons rotate monthly, and the work of the group is assumed by members for short periods of time. The group supports itself only by members' small contributions; no contributions from outside are permitted, therefore eliminating a potential source of control.

The Integrity Group movement described by Mowrer (1972) and the Self-Directed Therapeutic Group reported by Berzon and Solomon (1966) are related developments by professionals in counseling and psychotherapy who have used several aspects of the self-help mutual aid model. Frankel and Sloat (1971) described the total process of development of a self-help group for persons with physical, emotional, and social disabilities who wanted group involvement, but existing groups were not available to them. Colbert (1969) reported a program of planned mutual help at the Veterans Administration Hospital at Brentwood, Los Angeles, where the opportunity of giving as well as receiving help was incorporated into the rehabilitation program. This is an example of the use by professionals of a concept long known and practiced by self-help organizations.

Effectiveness of the Self-Help Process

The nature of the self-help process has been commented on by a number of authors (Grosz 1972, 1973; Hurvitz 1970; Jaques 1972, 1974; Katz 1965, 1967, 1970; Mowrer 1972; Riessman 1965; Wechsler 1960; Wright 1971; Yalom 1970). In most cases authors, usually professionals, have read the sparse literature, attended meetings of self-help groups, collected self-reports of members, and, from an outsider's viewpoint, attempted to be objective, empirical observers. Two survey research projects were reported by Grosz and Wechsler. From the perspective of self-help group participant members, some reports have appeared in their own publications, such as the Recovery Reporter, the AA Grapevine, and Paraplegic News. In addition, an AA survey of its own membership was reported (Bailey and Leach 1965).

Positive aspects to members of self-help groups include the following knowledge, therapeutic, and skill dimensions: (a) gaining facts and knowledge of the condition; (b) social learning of coping mechanisms from those who are successfully living with the condition; (c) motivation and support by communicating with others who have shared a similar life experience; (d) the modeling effect of successful problem-solving behaviors which provides reinforcement for new members and for long-term members; (c) self-evaluation of progress resulting from feedback and sharing with members at various stages of problem, knowledge, and levels of coping behavior; (f) identification with the group, providing a tangible sense of belonging, of an individual and social nature, and minimizing isolation and alienation; and (g) in the mutuality of the altruistic concern for others, finding self-help.

The self-help mutual-aid group cannot be ignored as a system for maintaining rehabilitation gain and preventing deterioration of function over time. Modeling effect is provided by members who are coping with stigma problems and functioning adequately in life roles. Positive impact on social attitudes may be an additional gain from the coping behaviors demonstrated. Too frequently negative succumbing aspects of disadvantaged disability are emphasized in the media, particularly for fund-raising purposes (Wright 1969). Observing persons with handicapping problems functioning in the community and living "like other people" cannot help but enhance the quality of life for the able and disabled alike. AA group members report that persons are coming to their groups at earlier ages, which seems to demonstrate a more hopeful and accepting view of the problems presented. And, of course, the value of seeking help early cannot be overemphasized in rehabilitation.

A case study of Recovery, Inc., reported by Wechsler (1960) included the results of two surveys, one of the characteristics and opinions of members and the other of selected psychiatrists, members of the American Psychiatric Association in Detroit and Chicago. The results reported certain potential problem areas which concerned the psychiatrists sampled. These areas included the lack of medical or professional supervision, no system for the screening of members or of training leaders, and certain professional reservations about the Recovery method. The respondents did agree that the group aspect satisfied "the needs of some ex-patients for various forms of group support" (p. 309). The basic criticism resulted from a professional view of services giving little recognition to the validity of the self-help mutual aid group model as part of the total service system.

Recovery was founded in 1937 by Abraham A. Low, a psychiatrist (Recovery, Inc. 1973b). Until his death in 1954, Low underwent years of attack and rejection by his collegues. His biography (Rau, 1971) documented his struggles to establish the self-help method. A recent survey by Grosz (1972, 1973) reflected a change in attitude on the part of the psychiatric profession to the Recovery approach. Grosz related this in part to the general climate of acceptance of the important role of paraprofessionals in mental health. For the last three years, Recovery panels have been a regular event at the annual meeting of the American Psychiatric Association.

Operational Assumptions

The basic operational assumptions of the self-help group approach are as follows:

1. Individuals come together because they have a specific personal problem or condition which they share (e.g., alcoholism, weight-loss, paraplegia).
2. The status of peer relationships is maintained for all members within the group.
3. Peers, sharing the condition or problem, come together with the expectation of helping themselves and each other; that is, both the self-help and mutual aid aspects are central to the group process.
4. Behavior change is expected by and for each member. Learning a new way of life, presumably more satisfying, is undertaken at the individual's own pace.
5. Peers identify with the specific program developed by the group, become committed to its basic beliefs, tenets, and procedures, and actively support the program through practicing its principles in daily life.
6. Although the basic form of interaction is a regularly scheduled group meeting, peers are readily accessible and available to each other as needed outside of group meetings. This interaction is of a one-to-one type relationship, so both group and individual modes of contact are used.
7. The group process consists of actively relating, "owning," and revealing problems, receiving and giving feedback to each other, sharing hope, experiences, encouragement, and criticism in relation to the day-to-day goals of individual behavior change.
8. Members are held responsible for themselves and their behavior. This involves being honest about themselves, both within and outside the context of the group interaction.
9. Group leadership develops and changes from within the group on the basis of giving and receiving help in keeping with the program's purposes and principles.
10. Status comes from helping and being helped effectively, which in turn provides the validity for the program. Status achieved outside the group is of little, if any, value after joining the group; in fact, if it is used manipulatively, it can work against a member's status within the group.

These assumptions have been experientially derived and remain untested, but they are supported pragmatically by the demonstrated help group members receive. Why and how the self-help methods work for so many individuals are common and challenging questions to the professional. Basic themes of many self-help stories shared in the groups are of past experiences and relationships with professionals which were not satisfactory or helpful with their problems. Part of the cathartic value of self-help groups is in sharing past frustrations with other members who have experienced them, knowing there is hope and help within "their program." The self-help experience was described in the words of one member as "a weight of despair being lifted from my life" and "at last I can experience some joy in living" (personal communication, April 1972). It is a common observation and sometimes a surprise to new members and visitors that self-help group meetings are happy occasions with much humor and laughter shared.

The Professional Model:
A Look Within

The feeling held by many self-help group members is that their professional experience or contact has not been helpful and, in some instances, even harmful. That these perceptions are not unrealistic has been verified by the experience of many persons, both professional and nonprofessional, who have attested to the ineffectiveness and fragmentation of much service delivery, By and large professionals still ignore, if not downgrade, the self-help model, although there is evidence that a change in attitude is occurring (Wright 1973). Self-help and professional groups alike seem to be increasingly more open, trustful, and appreciative of each others' unique experience and knowledge.

Tyler (1973) referred to a shift on the part of persons needing help away from the professional therapist to others who understand because they have had the same problems. "Alcoholics Anonymous was perhaps the first herald of this change in the manner in which psychological difficulties were to be dealt with" (p. 1022).

The Lasker Award was given to AA in 1951 by the American Public Health Association. The citation stated : "Historians may one day recognize Alcoholics Anonymous to have been a great venture in social pioneering which forged a new instrument for social action; a new therapy based on the kinship of common suffering; one having a vast potential for the myriad other ills of mankind" (*Alcoholics Anonymous* 1955, p. 573). The role of the helping professional changed from that of a therapist in the medical model to a consultant who suggests rather than prescribes. An equally dramatic change is emerging in the role of the person needing help, from a passive recipient of a service to a consumer who can not only make choices among alternatives, but who also assumes responsibility as the manager of a personal rehabilitative plan. Some problems of professional service delivery may be inherent in the rigid impersonal nature of the bureaucracy and organizations within which agencies exist. Some organizational shifts are apparent in rehabilitation service delivery systems generally, and others are underway (Morris 1973).

Programs of client advocacy have developed over the last decade. The provisions within the Rehabilitation Act of 1973 for consumer participation in program planning and evaluation, a specific client-counselor program planning review process, and program review by a third party make these concerns explicit. They attempt to assure that the clients are truly comanagers of the rehabilitation process. Whether or not the reforms contemplated will be more than paper plans, honestly reflecting humanness and personal concern for individuals with problems in concrete ways, is yet to be tested in practice.

A number of groups have developed statements of need or codes outlining their basic human rights as individuals. Geist and others (1973) called for agencies to develop codes of ethical practices, pointing out the necessity for agency ethic accountability to consumers if individual professional codes of ethical standards are to have real meaning in practice. Clearly, consumer input has already had considerable effect on the service providers, both institutions and professionals' practices, but this is only a small beginning. The professional enterprise itself is in need of careful reexamination. Change in organizations, institutions, and service delivery systems will not modify negative or unhelpful professional attitudes and practices, and it is here that the self-help group experience can be most useful. Its essence of helpfulness seems to pinpoint the areas where professional blind spots and insensitivity exist.

History shows that a self-help group appeared where professionals did not or could not help. The self-help movement is a reflection of professional pressure points due, in part, to a lack of knowledge but also due to rigidity in professional behavior and beliefs. Yet at each junction of a new self-help group development, a few professionals out of step with their colleagues and the times, in thinking and practice, turned the tide to a new approach. For example, the founders of AA, a stockbroker and a physician, both hopeless alcoholics, credit the work of three professionals for the ideas and inspiration that brought AA into existence (*Alcoholics Anonymous Come of Age* 1957, p. 262): W. D. Silkworth, "benign little doctor who loved drunks," William James' great wisdom in his *Varieties of Religious Experience*, and Carl Jung's statement that "science had no answer for the alcoholic." Abraham Low's persistence against professional attacks, referred to earlier, showed the way to a major self-help movement. Charles Dederich, founder of

Synanon, is another example of a person whose beliefs, practices, and courageous struggles were in tune with the needs of persons fighting addiction.

The Relationship of the Professional to the Self-Help Model

During the last three years both authors have had occasion to relate to the two systems of self-care and professional care in new and highly personal ways. The first author moved from a primary professional stance to the study and experience of the self-help approach, and the second author from self-help group experience of long standing to graduate training in rehabilitation counseling. A unique opportunity to share and learn from each helping modality resulted. Although the experiences of self-help and the professional process are unique, it is possible to share and move between these systems, but only under certain conditions. For example, a professional cannot be a self-help group member or leader unless the conditions of common problem, peer relationship, and mutual aid exist. Any other arrangement would be a violation of the self-help model. Professionals who do not or choose not to meet these conditions can relate only in the capacity of visitor-observer. On invitation a professional can act as a consultant or speaker. The professional therapeutic skills as such cannot be used inside the self-help group. That, of course, would also be a violation of self-help precepts.

It may be that both parties to the helping contract can learn what to expect and what to ask of each other and how they relate to the total rehabilitation task. For example, self-help groups might be able to ask professionals to help study aspects of the process self-help groups do so well. The variables of effectiveness within the helping system could be more precisely defined and isolated to study the patterns of this process. Some members drop out of groups while others stay. How many are in each category, and what characteristics differentiate them? What are the characteristics of those who return again and again?

Professionals could learn to ask self-help group members for specific and regular feedback on their help-getting experiences. Members' reactions and suggestions, as consumers of these services, could be effective in improving and humanizing the total service delivery functions. A plan for evaluation of each individual service interaction might be initiated just as courses and professors' performance are evaluated by students. Better Business Bureaus exist to protect consumers and monitor practices. Certainly as much vigilance should be given to human-helping services. Plans might be developed for confronting the social and community barriers that plague both groups, such as public understanding of problems of disability, deprivation, and job and other types of discrimination.

Raising these issues and other questions could lead to an openness in communication which does not now exist between helpers and those on the receiving end of service delivery. The feedback from this interaction might significantly modify therapeutic practices, rehabilitation outcomes, and professional attitudes, resulting in help being given and received more effectively to the contractual standards set by both parties. A more humanized service delivery system could result. Clearly, both models, the self-help and the professional, are necessary parts of a total rehabilitation service system.

REFERENCES

Alcoholics Anonymous. *Alcoholics Anonymous: The story of how many thousands of men and women have recovered from alcoholism.* New York : Alcoholics Anonymous World Services, 1955.

Alcoholics Anonymous. *Alcoholics Anonymous comes of age.* New York : Alcoholics Anonymous Publishing, 1957.

Alcoholics Anonymous. *Alcoholics Anonymous world directory.* New York : Alcoholics Anonymous World Services, spring 1973.

Bailey, M. B. and Leach, B. *Alcoholics Anonymous: Pathway to recovery.* New York : National Council on Alcoholism, July 1965.

Berzon, B. and Solomon, L. N. The self-directed therapeutic group : Three studies. *Journal of Counseling Psychology,* 1966, *13*(4).

Colbert, J. N. Philosophia habilitatus : Toward a policy of human rehabilitation in the post-institutional phase of disability. *Journal of Rehabilitation,* 1969, *35*(5), 18–20.

Frankel, A. and Sloat, W. E. The odyssey of a self-help group. *Psychological Aspects of Disability,* 1971, *18*(1), 41–42.

Geist, G. O., Curin, S., Prestridge, R., and Schelb, G. Ethics and the counselor-agency relationship. *Rehabilitation Counseling Bulletin,* 1973, *17*(1), 15–21.

Grosz, H. J. *Recovery, Inc., Survey: A preliminary report.* Chicago : Recovery, Inc., May 1972.

Grosz, H. J. *Recovery, Inc., Survey: Second report.* Chicago : Recovery, Inc., May 1973.

Hurvitz, N. Peer self-help psychotherapy groups and their implications for psychotherapy. *Psychotherapy: Theory, Research and Practice,* 1970, *7*(1), 41–49.

Jaques, M. E. Rehabilitation counseling and support personnel. *Rehabilitation Counseling Bulletin,* 1972, *15*(3), 160–171.

Jaques, M. E. and Perry, J. W. Education in the health and helping professions : Philosophic context, multidisciplinary team models and cultural components. In J. Hamburg (Ed.), *Review of Allied Health Education,* Vol. 1. Lexington, Ky. : University Press of Kentucky, 1974.

Katz, A. Poland's self-help rehabilitation program. *Rehabilitation Record,* 1964, *5*(3), 30–32.

Katz, A. Application of self-help concepts in current social welfare. *Social Work,* 1965, *10*(3), 68–74.

Katz, A. Self-help in rehabilitation : Some theoretical aspects. *Rehabilitation Literature,* 1967, *28*(1), 10–11, 30.

Katz, A. Self-help organizations and volunteer participation in social welfare. *Social Work,* 1970, *15*(1), 51–60.

Massachusetts Council of Organizations of the Handicapped, Inc. *A directory of organizations of the handicapped in the United States.* Hyde Park, Mass. : Author, 1973.

Morris, R. Welfare reform 1973 : The social service dimension. *Science,* August 10, 1973, *181*(4099), 515–522.

Mowrer, O. H. *The new group therapy.* Princeton, N.J. : Van Nostrand, 1964.

Mowrer, O. H. Integrity groups : Basic principles and objectives. *Counseling Psychologist,* 1972, *3*(2), 7–33.

Rau, N. and Rau, M. R. *My dear ones.* Englewood Cliffs, N.J. : Prentice-Hall, 1971.

Recovery, Inc. *Recovery Inc., National directory.* Chicago, Ill. : Author (60603), January 1973. (a)

Recovery, Inc. *Recovery Inc., What it is and how it developed.* Chicago, Ill. : Author, 1973. (b)

Riessman, F. The "helper" therapy principle. *Social Work,* 1965, *10*(2), 27–32.

Rogers, C. R. *The emerging person: A new revolution.* La Jolla, Calif. : Center for Studies of the Person, 1973.

Tyler, L. E. Design for a hopeful psychology. *American Psychologist,* 1973, *28*(12), 1021–1029.

Wechsler, H. The self-help organization in the mental health field : Recovery, Inc., A case study. *Journal of Nervous and Mental Disorders,* 1960, *130*(4), 297–314.

Wright, B. A. Activism versus passivism in coping with disability. In Ireland National Rehabilitation Board (Ed.), *Proceedings of the Eleventh World Congress of Rehabilitation International, Community Responsibility for Rehabilitation.* Dublin, Ireland : National Rehabilitation Board, 1969.

Wright, B. A. Changes in attitudes toward people with handicaps. *Rehabilitation Literature,* 1973, *34*(12), 354–357, 368.

Wright, M. E. Self-help groups in the rehabilitation enterprise. *Psychological Aspects of Disability,* 1971, *18*(1), 43–45.

Yalom, I. *The theory and practice of group psychotherapy.* New York : Basic Books, 1970.

Zola, I. K. The problems and prospects of mutual aid groups. *Rehabilitation Psychology,* 1972, *19*(4), 180–183.

23

The Contribution of the Physically and Mentally Handicapped to Development

Jean Vanier

Those who live close to wounded people become rather accustomed to hearing talks about how so-called "normal" people should help their unfortunate brothers and sisters. We rarely ask what handicapped people can bring to others. The very thought rarely comes to mind; it seems so remote and farfetched.

And yet I feel deeply that handicapped people have an important part to play in the development of the world, in helping it to find its equilibrium. They can insure that development is not just a development of mind and matter, but a development of the total human person, who is certainly intelligence and creativity, activity and productivity, but who is also a heart, capable of love, a seeker of peace, hope, light, and trust, striving to assume the reality of suffering and of death.

I have had the grace and joy to live with mentally handicapped adults over the last ten years. With friends, we have been able to create some forty-five small homes for men and women who were either roaming the streets, locked up in asylums, or just living idly—though frequently in a state of aggression or depression—with families who did not know how to cope with them. These homes of l'Arche are in France, Canada, the United States, England, Scotland, Belgium, and Denmark, as well as in Calcutta and Bangalore in India; our first home in West Africa is just beginning in the Ivory Coast. Each of these homes welcomes and finds work for eight to ten handicapped men and women and for their helpers or assistants. They try to be communities of reconciliation where

Published in *"Development and Participation—Operational Implications for Social Welfare"* Proceedings of the *XVIIth International Conference on Social Welfare, Nairobi* Kenya, 290–297. (Published 1975 for the International Council on Social Welfare by Columbia University Press, New York & London).

everyone can grow in activity, creativity, love, and hope. Some of the handicapped people leave us and find total autonomy; others, who are more severely handicapped, will stay with us always.

It is this experience of daily living, working, and sharing with my handicapped brothers and sisters that has made me so sensitive to the question of their contribution to the development of our world. A man or woman can only find peace of heart and grow in motivation and creativity if he or she finds a meaning to life. If they are there only to be helped and can bring nothing to others, then they are condemned to a life of simply receiving, of being the last, the most inferior. This will necessarily bring them to depression and a lack of confidence in themselves. This in turn will push them into anguish and make them aggressive towards themselves and others. For them to find real meaning in life, they must find people who sense their utility, their capacity for growth and their place in the community and in the world.

The tragedy of humanity is not primarily the lack of development of peoples, or even poverty. It is the oppression, the despisal, and the rejection of those who are weak and in want. It is the horrible and disastrous inequality of wealth and opportunity and lack of sharing. The tragedy of man is his hardness of heart, which makes individuals and nations endowed with the riches of this world despise and consider as inferior those who are poor and handicapped. They not only refuse to help them; they tend also to reject and exploit them.

The tragedy of mankind is the collective national or religious prejudices and pride which close nations and peoples upon themselves, making them think and act as if they were the elected ones and the others enemies to be rejected and hurt, whose development and expansion should be checked. Our world today, with its terrible divisions and hatred, with its continual sounds of war, with its vast budgets being poured into armaments instead of into works for love and justice, is the result of these prejudices and fears.

The tragedy of our world today is that man is still afraid of man. Far from seeing other individuals and peoples as collaborators in the mystery of universal human growth, we see them as enemies of our own growth and development.

It is of course terribly important that misery and starvation be erased from our earth. It is of course terribly important that everyone has access to social and medical benefits. But it is even more important that the hearts of all men open up to universal love and to the understanding of others, to gentle service to mankind and especially to its weaker members. For if we do not work together to create a world of fraternity and of peace, we will sink in wars, economic crises, and national disasters.

There is a continual struggle in all our countries between traditional religious and moral values, lived through family ties, and economic and industrial development. Highly industrialized countries offer a certain financial prosperity, but so frequently this prosperity has been achieved at the cost of the values of community. Competition and the desire for wealth, individual leisure, and liberty have tended to crush compassion and understanding. So it is that we find old people lingering in homes for the aged, handicapped people in large institutions, and a mass of marginal and suffering people unable to work because of alcoholism, drugs, and social ills. We find thousands of children abandoned and given over to social agencies, a frightening rise in delinquency, and prisons which offer only punishment instead of reeducation and so cause the high rise in recidivism. We find mental disease rampant, because in our search for efficiency we have lost our acceptance of "the other" and prefer to label people "mad" than to understand them. We condemn more and more people to live like strangers, in terrible loneliness, in our large urban conglomerations. The growing population of our cities, our disastrous housing and inhuman working conditions bring a real disequilibrium of the human heart in its quest for love, peace, and truth.

In the small villages of Africa and India, or in rural areas of North America and Europe, there are still sturdy people living simply off the land and artisans bound closely to the matter with which they work. There is deep love and commitment among families. There is a spirit of gentleness and openness, sharing and welcome for the stranger, which has often been lost in the big cities. Certainly this is a generalization, for there are also tribal warfares and social injustices and individual anguishes. But we must not forget the values of fraternity and community held by simple people, which are so often crushed with the coming of economic development. We can see the gradual breakdown of these values as the desire for material possessions is stimulated, as the attractions of big-city leisure activities become stronger, and the older generation and its ways are rejected.

Of course, it is essential that people should develop and find the benefits of greater wealth and security. But it is even more essential that this development take place in a human context that safeguards and strengthens the forces of sharing, participation, and responsibility. Where economic development coincides with the breakdown of cultural and ethnic ties, where villages are destroyed, where children are displaced and men obliged to leave their homes for far-off lands, the situation is extremely serious : it can gradually cause the destruction of what makes a human person a person.

In each of us there is a mixture of weakness and strength. Each of us is born in weakness, unable to fend for ourselves, to find nourishment, to clothe ourselves, or to walk. The growth to autonomy is long and slow, and demands many years of loving education. The period of strength and capacity, during adolescence and manhood, the period during which we are able to act efficaciously and to defend ourselves, to struggle against the forces of nature and environment, is in fact short. After it, we all enter a period of weakness, when our bodies become tired and sick, when we are hurt by the trials and sufferings inherent in human life. And all of us are then called to the last and final poverty of death.

The child in his weakness has all the potential of activity which must grow in him. The strongest of men is inherently weak, because he has a mortal body, and also because he is called to love and is vulnerable to the sufferings of love and of infidelity in friendship; he is weak because he is capable of depression and sadness, drowning in the vicissitudes of life.

The society that encourages only the strong and the intelligent tends to forget that man is essentially weak. We are all potentially handicapped, and we are all created to suffer and to die. So often the search for riches, or hyperactivity in work, is a flight from these essential realities which we must all face one day. What is the meaning of our life, and of suffering, and of death? Are we called simply to be active and to gather wealth, or does man find peace of heart, interior liberty, and happiness in the growth of love? Is it not in service to others, sharing and mutual understanding—which is not mere sentimentality—that we find this inner peace and human fulfillment?

If people do not refind this energy of love and acceptance of their own intrinsic poverty, if they do not discover that joy comes more in giving than in taking, we are heading for more conflict. If we do not grow in the desire to give our lives rather than to exploit and take the lives of others, then we are all doomed to destruction.

In all societies there are vast numbers of weaker brothers and sisters : those who are aged or depressed, those who have been struck by sickness while young and cannot take on a working life. Are these people just misfits who must be gradually eliminated? Are they just people we must try to reeducate so that they become active members of society? Or have they a special place and role in the development of our society? This is the question we must ask ourselves.

My experience of living with the wounded, the weak, is that they have very precious values which must be conserved for the full development of society. Their experience of rejection, their experience of suffering which is a taste of death, has brought them closer to certain realities that others who have not suffered flee and pretend do not exist.

Handicapped people have all the rights of other men : the right to life, to medical and social help, and to work. They are able, when this is recognized, to develop in so many ways. With the right educational and work techniques, many can find their place in the world of work and become totally integrated in that world. I have seen men who at the age of six were judged incapable of any growth, working in a factory at the age of twenty and living quite autonomously. Others who were condemned to asylums, to beggary, or to total inactivity are now finding fulfillment as artisans and enjoying life in the community. With care, loving attention, and the right kind of technical help, many can find their place in society.

Handicapped people, and particularly those who are less "able," are frequently endowed with qualities of heart that serve to remind so-called "normal" people that their own hearts are closed. Their simplicity frequently serves to reveal our own duplicity, untruthfulness, and hypocrisy. Their acceptance of their own situation and their humility frequently reveal our pride and our refusal to accept others as they are.

I had occasion once to appear on television with Helen and some others. Helen has cerebral palsy. She cannot talk, she cannot walk, she cannot eat by herself. She is condemned to a wheelchair for the rest of her life. Her only means of communication is through a typewriter, on which she laboriously expresses her thoughts with two fingers. But Helen has the most beautiful smile. She gives herself through her smile. At one moment in the program, someone asked her if she was happy. She broke out into a big smile and typed : "I wouldn't change my life for anything in the world." Her smile got even bigger, and as the program closed, the camera picked up the last word she was writing : "Alleluia !"

Helen, who has nothing except her joy and her love, revealed to me and to so many who possess the goods of this earth that fulfillment does not come from material riches but from some inner strength and liberty. Through her acceptance of herself and her condition, she showed how poor we are, in all our petty quarrels, pride, and desires.

At a week's meeting with some two hundred people, there was a handicapped man called Glen. He could not use his legs, and he lay on the floor. During the last day, there was a period when each person could express what he felt about the week's activity. Glen propped himself up and just said : "I have only one thing to tell you : I love you all so much." His simple words broke down the barriers of convention and of fear in many of us. He wasn't afraid to talk of love.

So often "normal" people have interior barriers that prevent them from relating with others in a simple way. All of us have deep needs to love and to be loved. All of us are in the conflict of our fear of death and of our own poverty. We so quickly pretend we are more clever, more intelligent, and more powerful than we actually are. So often we flee reality by throwing ourselves into activity, culture, and the struggle for power and prestige. We lose contact with our deep inner selves. Handicapped people do not always have these barriers. In their poverty, they are more simple and loving, and thus they reveal to us the poverty of our riches.

The weaker members of society are total human persons, children of God. They are not misfits or objects of charity. Their weaknesses and special needs demand deep attention, real concern, and continuing support. If we listen to their call and to their needs, they will flourish and grow. If we do not, they will sink into depression, sadness, inward revolt, and a form of spiritual suicide. And we who carry responsibilities will have closed our beings to love and to a strength which comes from God and which is hidden in the smallest and the weakest.

Those who take time to listen to them, who have the inner peace and patience to respond to their silent call, will hear crying in them the great cry of all humanity for love and for peace. A great Dutch psychiatrist has written of the schizophrenic that he is not insane, not made of wood, but is "the loudspeaker from whom the sufferings of our time ring perhaps most clearly" (Foudraine, 1974). The same can be said for all weak and handicapped people who cannot fend for themselves.

If we listen to them, then we, the so-called "normal" people, will be healed of our unconscious egoisms, our hardness of heart, our search for power and for dissipating leisure. We will discover that love, communion, presence, community, and deep interior liberty and peace are realities to be found and lived. We will discover that these can become the inspiration for all men. We will realize more fully that men are not machines or objects to be used, exploited, tyrannized, and manipulated by law and by organizations, but that each one is beautiful and precious, that each one in his uniqueness is like a flower which should find its place in the garden of humanity for the fulfillment and beauty of all mankind.

If each one of us who holds a responsible place in society pays attention to the heartbeats of the smallest, the weakest, and the companionless, then gradually we will make of our countries not lands of competition, which favor the strong and powerful, but lands of justice, peace, and fraternity where all men unite and cooperate for the good of every man.

Then nations will no longer rival each other in their search for power, prestige, and wealth, but will work together. They will turn from fear and from group prejudices and from the creation of large and horribly expensive armies. They will use their intelligence, strength, wealth, and natural resources for the growth of all men throughout the world, and especially for the smallest, the weakest, and the companionless. Mankind will then, through the heart of the poor and those crucified in their flesh, refind the road to unity and universal love, where all can be themselves without fear, growing together in love and in the peace of God, our beloved Father.

REFERENCE

Foundraine, J. *Not made of wood.* London : Quartet Books, 1974.

24

Participant Observation as a Patient in a Rehabilitation Hospital

David J. French
Robert E. McDowell
Robert Allen Keith

The study reported here is part of a program of formulations and research on the nature of the rehabilitation hospital. Previous work has focused on the rehabilitation model currently extant with some suggestions for changes in the model (Keith, 1968, 1969, 1971). In order to understand better the characteristics of such a system, we have devised a number of observational methods for the analysis of social interaction. Unfortunately these methods impose a selective framework and allow the examination of no more than segments of hospital life. To gain some wider insights into the world of the patient, the senior author (D.J.F.) was admitted as a patient for a period of five days.

The use of disguised observation has been reported for a number of different settings. Those of mental hospitals are probably most relevant here, since we know of none which have been concerned with the hospital specializing in physical rehabilitation. It is obvious that some of the information gained depends upon the nature of the institution. The patient society of the small private psychiatric hospital reported by Caudill, et al. (1952) is not that of the 6,000 patient metropolitan state hospital in which the observers of Goldman, Bohr, and Steinberg (1970) became immersed. Nevertheless, some common themes emerge.

The patient-observer is invariably struck by the boredom inherent in institutional routine, where small events become magnified. Deane (1961), who was admitted to a ward where both patients and staff knew him, noted the contrast in the roles of patients and staff. The life of the

Reprinted from *Rehabilitation Psychology*, *19* (1972), 89–95, Copyright © by the American Psychological Association. Reprinted by permission of the publisher and authors.

patient was one of supervised and entirely predictable routine with large blocks of idle time. A review of these accounts makes Goffman's statement more understandable : "To describe the patient's situation faithfully is necessarily to present a partisan view (1961, p. x)."

A second theme, usually noted but not emphasized, is that of emotional strain on the observer. For the disguised observer there is the problem of maintaining the patient role, of playing a part for an extended period of time. The fear of "blowing one's cover" or of betrayal is very real and may produce feelings tinged with paranoia. The hypervigilance involved is emotionally draining. Another common fear is that somehow when the time comes for discharge, the observer might not be released. This fear was particularly marked in the large hospital setting of Goldman, Bohr, and Steinberg (1970). Even though Deane was openly admitted as a nonpatient and was in a familiar setting, he was shaken by the experience, breaking into tears upon his release. For mental hospital patients, the contrast between the life of narrow freedom of choice and the outside world is undoubtedly painfully sharp.

There were several purposes in the present study of a rehabilitation hospital. First, we wanted to have a subjective evaluation of the admissions procedure : what the new patient went through, how much orientation he received, and how ponderous the procedures were. Second, we were interested in how a new patient settled into the routine of the hospital : what adjustments he had to make, and how he began to relate to other patients and to staff in the various departments. Last, we wanted some idea of those attitudes and impressions that patients had about the hospital which might not be given readily to the staff.

SETTING AND ARRANGEMENTS

The setting was a 55-bed hospital specializing in physical rehabilitation. It is a nonprofit, nontax-supported institution with a full range of medical and paramedical professionals represented on the staff. The atmosphere is relaxed in comparison to the acute hospital. Hospital personnel dress in conventional street clothes instead of white uniforms. The physical plant is modern and of pleasant appearance.

The patient-observer (D.J.F.), a young adult, was admitted with the knowledge of only a few hospital administrators. The attending physician, a physical medicine specialist and assistant medical director, assigned a diagnosis of bilateral aseptic necrosis of the femoral heads. This disease would not be manifestly handicapping but would require nonweight-bearing and a wheelchair existence.

During the five-day stay the observer took notes when the opportunity arose. The second author (R.E.M.) made observations during the admission procedure, visited several times, and conducted an interview just prior to discharge which was videotaped. Two days after discharge the third author (R.A.K.) interviewed the observer again to gain his postdischarge reactions.

EXPERIENCES

Transition

The observer was acquainted with the hospital by having visited earlier and by having participated in discussions regarding various operations of the hospital. Prior to entering the hospital, the observer prepared himself by rehearsing the role he was to play as a patient. He had to keep in mind that he was supposed to have hip pain, that he was to be wheelchair-bound, and that he faced an uncertain future regarding normal ambulation.

The patient-observer presented himself on a Friday morning, having applied beforehand for admission. He was transferred from car to wheelchair and given instructions about whom to see. No directions were given about wheelchair manipulation; apparently he appeared to be a young man who could manage. In turn he visited the admissions office, counseling, and social service. It was necessary for him to repeat some basic information several times to different people. A room and bed were assigned, and he was shown where they were located. A nurse explained the general routine of the hospital, although specifics about his own program were not given until Monday, three days later. During this first day he spent much time drinking coffee in the patient dining room with some vague apprehensions that he should be someplace specific. At this point the observer felt at loose ends and a little lonely, since he knew no one. His expressions of anxiety were met by warm support from nurses, although he still felt like an outsider.

The weekend period was one of increasing boredom. Some patients went home for the weekend; many who remained seemed to have little interest in socializing. The observer roamed the halls looking for someone to talk to. When he explored the treatment wing of the hospital and found the rooms locked, he was told that this section was closed to patients on weekends. Even the few recreation facilities available to patients did not appear to be used much. The patients' library was rarely inhabited; the pool table in a lounge area was used most often by staff and visitors. Most patients chose to remain in their rooms. The observer finally telephoned some friends to come visit him.

On Saturday night he wheeled into the patient dining room to find tablecloths and flowers on the tables. His assumption that Saturday night was a special occasion for patients ended quickly when he discovered that the festive setting was for the women's auxiliary, which was having a benefit dinner.

Unforeseen Complications

Increasingly, as the weekend wore on, the observer grew to know and to become close to his four roommates, youths from 17 to 20 years, who had spinal cord injuries or brain damage. The fear of discovery also mounted. He looked for signs, particularly from staff, that they knew he was not a patient. With emotional ties developing, the observer began to have considerable apprehension and guilt about building such close relationships on the basis of simulation. When he left the hospital, the patients would find out about his deception. The feelings he had developed, he felt, represented genuine concern and friendship, but the patients would not see this.

By Sunday evening the pressures on the observer became so great that he broke down and disclosed the simulation to several individuals. First with a visitor, then with two patients, and finally with a nurse, he revealed the nature of the admission. His revelations were accompanied by an outburst of crying and emotional release. Later he observed that he would have been unable to continue without this disclosure to someone in the hospital. The reactions of the two patients were initially quite different. The first, a roommate, was that it was "cool," and if he could have held a pen, he would have liked to do it himself. The second patient, a teenage girl, became angry, retorting, "Who do you think you are, trying to imitate a cripple? You will never know what it feels like." On second thoughts, however, she relented and expressed sympathy for the project.

As far as could be determined, none of the individuals who became aware of the simulation revealed it to anyone else while the observer remained a patient. During the remaining two days in the hospital he was able to continue his role.

For the most part, the observer found the hospital staff to be helpful and, to his eyes, competent and professional. The night crew he found more relaxed and friendly than the day group. The latter maintained a more businesslike air in order to carry out the bulk of planning and treatment. A single incident marred what were otherwise good relations between the observer and hospital personnel. He entered the hospital with a mustache and long hair, an appearance no longer unusual. It created problems with one aide, however. One evening he sat in his room, joking with his roommates. Their banter was about their physical incapacities, e.g., he bet one quadriplegic patient a quarter that he could not get up for breakfast. There was a good deal of hilarity among the patients, but an aide in the room rather abruptly told the observer to shut up. When he tried to find out the reason for her animosity, she would not reply. One patient complained that he was laughing so hard the sleeping pill he had taken would not work. When the observer told the patient to relax and let it take effect, the aide whirled around and said, "You would know about drugs, wouldn't you? You belong down the hall with the rest of the hippies" (a reference to another room of long-haired patients).

While the observer had been the target of some stereotyping prejudice, he had also violated the aide's notion of hospital mores. Making fun of physical disability is permissible for patients (only rarely for staff), but in the aide's eyes he had violated the limits even for patient behavior.

Into the Program

On Monday the observer was seen for a physical examination (by the attending physician who assigned the original diagnosis) and for evaluation by the various departments. Here he was able to weather the scrutiny of staff in occupational therapy, physical therapy, and nursing. Following this series of assessments, he was seen in the new patient conference. This conference, attended by the medical director, assistant medical director, a medical secretary, and various therapists who evaluated the patient, usually comprised about ten or twelve people. When the observer wheeled himself into the room where all these people were sitting in a half circle, his first reaction compared the meeting to a press conference. The purpose of the gathering was to put together all of the information available about the patient and to devise a treatment plan. The patient is present ostensibly to share in this information and to add comments or to ask questions. In this instance, the observer found the proceedings to be intimidating. The number of staff involved and their proficiency at using medical terms made him ill at ease; the opportunity to add his opinion did not seem a real one since he did not feel free to talk in front of so many people. A treatment schedule was drawn up which was appropriate for his diagnosis, and he wheeled out of the meeting.

Leavetaking

Since a main purpose of the admission was to experience the transition from outside to hospital, the patient-observer did not actually begin a treatment regimen. His discharge was arranged for Tuesday, the day after the new patient conference. During the morning he was noted, by the second author (R.E.M.), to have a high level of anxiety. Questioning revealed that he was afraid that for some reason he might not be released as planned. When it was pointed out that he could simply walk out of the hospital, he voiced an additional fear, that he might not be able to walk as he had before. In the office of the admitting physician, he inquired about how he might go about leaving the hospital. The physician suggested that he could simply gather up his things in his room and walk out. The observer was appalled at the possibility of departing in this manner. The entire hospital would now see that he had been faking, particularly the patients whom he had befriended. A compromise was agreed upon, in which he would use a cane. When he returned to his room, his roommates had a difficult time understanding the reasons for his early discharge. The observer muttered something about not being as bad off as first thought and fled. Several patients followed him out to the front door of the hospital, still asking questions.

When he got into his car and drove away, he found that he had to exert great concentration on his driving. During the hospitalization he had spent five days in a wheelchair and had actually begun to experience some pains in his legs. Now he was not certain that they would function the way they should. When he reached home, he was exhausted by the five-day experience. The next day he stayed home to recover.

DISCUSSION

A few hours prior to discharge, a debriefing interview was conducted which was recorded on videotape. The observer's experiences as a patient were still vivid, detailed, and often emotional. Subsequently, the videotape was shown at a meeting of all department heads; the three authors were also present. The reception to the simulation, by now known throughout the hospital, was guarded. Most department heads thought the experiment to be of interest and of value in giving a patient's view. A few expressed reservations about the possible subjective bias of the observer and the potential detriment to patients. About a week later an anonymous note appeared on the desk of the third author, director of research for the hospital, in which was typed a quotation from *Psychology Today* on deception in the social sciences.

In planning for this study, we had paid considerable attention to the possible ramifications of the relationship of the patient-observer to the hospital staff. Partly this reflected some anxiety about the possibility of discovery. We did not spend much time on what might ensue between the observer and patients. In fact, the observer-patient aspect proved to be the more crucial. Even though our goal was to gain some insights into the patient's point of view, our anticipations were more staff-oriented than patient-oriented. We had not escaped the bias present in most hospital professionals.

Certainly the amount of stress encountered by the observer in simulating a patient for five days was greater than we had expected. The participant observer in a mental hospital may have an easier time imitating the role of the mental patient. In the rehabilitation setting an observer-patient is under close scrutiny regarding his physical functioning. A major focus by the professional staff is on changes which indicate whether the patient is profiting from the program. Simulation under such circumstances is not easy.

Entrance into the hospital, while not tedious or unduly time-consuming showed that the transition from outsider to patient produced some strains. The free time at the beginning was a source of uneasiness. Various staff members helped the observer learn the hospital routine, but no one person furnished continuity. The hospital now employs a former patient, a quadriplegic in a wheelchair, as a liaison for incoming patients. He accompanies them through the intake procedure, orients them to the hospital, and is able to impart more "inside" information than the usual staff member might feel free to do.

A central issue in this study concerns the role of deception in gaining information, its impact on patients and hospital staff, and the nature of the information obtained. The pressures felt by the observer-patient and the resultant disclosures of the simulation indicate how intensely he was affected by the situation. An interview with one of the patients to whom the disclosure was made, one of the closer friends made by the observer, did not reveal any particular aftereffects. He had no negative feelings toward the observer or the study; his appraisal of the other patients in the room was that they were not affected one way or another. Staff reactions, even with the anonymous note, did not result in any alterations of working relations with the research unit. The information derived from participant observation is partially subjective, since it comes from the experience of one individual. Nevertheless, it affords an opportunity to sample the effects of immersion in the social system of a hospital much better than the piecemeal picture gained from several discrete objective observations.

The rehabilitation hospital needs considerably more study if we are to understand the nature of its influence on the patient. The length of stay is longer than in the acute care hospital. In addition, the patient is expected to learn new ways of doing things, learning which requires active participation. In such a setting, the potential impact on the behavior of the patient may have long-term effects.

REFERENCES

Caudill, W., Redlich, F. C., Gilmore, Helen R., and Brody, E. B. Social structure and interaction processes on a psychiatric ward. *American Journal of Orthopsychiatry*, 1952, 22, 314–334.

Deane, W. N. The reactions of a nonpatient to a stay on a mental hospital ward. *Psychiatry*, 1961, 24, 61–68.

Goffman, E. *Asylums*. Garden City, N.Y. : Doubleday, 1961.

Goldman, A. R., Bohr, R. H., and Steinberg, T. A. On posing as mental patients : Reminiscences and recommendations. *Professional Psychology*, 1970, 1, 427–434.

Keith, R. A. The need for a new model in rehabilitation. *Journal of Chronic Diseases*, 1968, 21, 281–286.

Keith, R. A. Physical rehabilitation : Is it ready for the revolution? *Rehabilitation Literature*, 1969, 78, 170–173.

Keith, R. A. The comprehensive rehabilitation center as rehabilitation model. *Inquiry*, 1971, 8, 22–29.

Part VIII

Helping Persons with Disabilities

The primary goal of rehabilitation workers is to help persons with disabilities to overcome their deficits and to capitalize on their assets. Although help can be provided through a variety of professional roles— such as those of rehabilitation counselors, nurses, physical therapists, occupational therapists, speech pathologists, physicians, and the like— the common denominator in the helping process is the ability to listen and respond effectively in order to provide support or show under-standing to clients. An understanding of different therapeutic approaches will also be of assistance in the fulfilling of team roles and in the adoption of more helpful techniques.

The question as to what can be therapeutic is discussed in the first article by Whitehouse. In addition to presenting many different modes of therapy, the author presents a lucid discussion of the reasons for a multiplicity of therapies.

In their article written especially for this book, Lasky, Dell Orto, and Marinelli present Structured Experiential Therapy as applied in Rehabilitation (SET–R) as a group method designed to promote intra- and interpersonal growth for physically disabled and nondisabled persons. SET–R emphasizes a strong goal orientation and the application of structured learning experiences as a learning and therapeutic tool. Selected examples of structured experiences are included in Appendix D. Their article includes a survey of significant publications related to group counseling with physically disabled persons.

The rehabilitation setting can be used to promote or retard reinte-gration of persons with disabilities into society. Kutner discusses the impact of the total institution on the resocialization of the adult with disabilities and suggests milieu therapy to provide the patient with an arsenal of social skills. He presents a model of milieu therapy, which can be applied in a rehabilitation setting.

Kerr also looks at the impact of the environment on rehabilitation but from the perspective of helpful and harmful staff expectations. Her discussion assists the rehabilitation worker in answering the question, "Do I help or do I hinder?"

In looking more directly at the interaction between disabled and nondisabled persons, Anthony suggests that in many cases the nondisabled person is not being honest, in a misguided attempt to ease the suffering of the person with a disability. The counselor should therefore not only respond with empathy, warmth, and genuineness toward the client, the author suggests, but he must attempt to improve the client's recognition and understanding of inconsistent feelings and behavior through facilitative confrontation.

Wright presents significant aspects related to removing barriers to the emotional adjustment of persons who have handicaps. These include guidelines for the development of positive self-attitudes on the part of disabled persons, as well as necessary environmental modifications that promote ability rather than disability.

The understanding of the self-concept and of the fallacies that persons with disabilities have about themselves is crucial to the therapeutic method suggested by Kir-Stimon. The importance of joint encounter and commitment in order to facilitate the understanding and modification of distorted perceptions of self is seen as a necessary function of the therapist.

25

The Concept of Therapy:
A Review of Some Essentials

Frederick A. Whitehouse

A review of the major therapies as well as the benefits of occasional means or events to which are attributed favorable responses raises the question as to what can be therapeutic. Furthermore, in all this array (please see List of Categorical Measures), are there some generic principles or at least common elements?

It would seem that almost anything can be therapeutic to some extent, for some people, with certain needs, at a particular moment in time, with a compatible therapist, and with the conviction on the part of the patient that he wishes to be helped and trusts the procedure.

A substantial number of the therapeutic items are only adjunctive at best, and, in some cases, many therapists would not seriously consider usage, while to others the item may be an important emphasis. What is esoteric or irrational to one therapist is another's religion or philosophy. Some of the therapies are almost identical, with innovators giving their own private twists; some are merely elements common to a number of other therapies. Surely, many of the therapies with a physical intent, if successfully applied, would have favorable psychological benefits, and the psychological therapies would in some cases bring about or promote physical improvement.

Some of the "therapies" are pervasive, such as what Beecher[1] has called the "powerful placebo," which can have beneficial, neutral, or harmful effects, and some are as mundane as the glass of beer initiating group therapy, which can be sensory pleasing, physiologically conducive, and socially symbolic.

From *Rehabilitation Literature*, 8 (1967), 238–247. Copyright © 1967 by the National Easter Seal Society for Crippled Children and Adults. Reprinted by permission of the Editor.

An Arbitrary Categorical Listing of Some Therapeutic Measures

Psychological

Acceptance therapy
Active therapy
Activity therapy
Adlerian individual psychotherapy
Anaclitic therapy
Analytic psychotherapy
Assertion-structured therapy
Attitude therapy
Authoritarian psychotherapy
Automated psychotherapy
Autosuggestion therapy
Bedside manner
Behavior therapy
Casework
Catharsis
Character analysis
Client-centered psychotherapy
Coaching-counseling therapy
Cognitive therapy
Combined therapy
Conditioned reflex therapy
Conditioning therapy
Conjoint family therapy
Coordinated therapy
Containment therapy
Cotherapy
Corrective thought process therapy
Couple therapy
Curative therapy
Daseinsanalysis
Dianetics therapy
Deconditioning therapy
Desensitization therapy
Determination therapy
Dilution therapy
Direct analysis psychotherapy
Direct therapy
Discussion-oriented group therapy
Doctor-patient relationship
Double reversal group therapy
Dynamic psychotherapy
Eclectic psychotherapy
Ego-analysis psychotherapy
Eugenic counseling
Evaluative therapy
Existential analysis therapy
Existential counseling
Existential psychoanalysis

Existential psychotherapy
Experiencing therapy
Experiential therapy
Explanatory therapy
Expressive therapy
Family therapy
Flexible psychotherapy
Focal therapy
Free association
Genetic counseling
General practitioner psychotherapy
General semantic therapy
Gestalt therapy
Goal-directed psychotherapy
Group-centered psychotherapy
Group hypnosis
Group therapy
Health counseling
Human relations counseling
Hypnoanalysis psychotherapy
Hypnodelic psychotherapy
Hypnosuggestive therapy
Hypnotherapy
Indirect psychotherapy
Insight therapy
Inspirational group therapy
Interpersonal psychoanalysis
Kindness and attention
Learning theory therapy
Lecture-oriented group therapy
Limit-setting
Logotherapy
Marital counseling
Marriage therapy
Medical counseling
Mental first-aid
Mental health counseling
Mental liquidation therapy
Minor psychotherapy
Moral suasion
"Mourning" therapy
Multiple therapy
Nondirective psychotherapy
Nonverbal group psychotherapy
Nonverbal psychotherapy
Nonverbal suggestive therapy
Objective psychotherapy
Objectivist psychotherapy
Orgone therapy
Paradigmatic psychotherapy

Partnership therapy
Pastoral counseling
Personal counseling
Persuasion
Placebo (mental affect)
Placement counseling
Probation service
Psychedelic therapy
Psychoanalysis
Psychoanalytically oriented psycho-
     therapy
Psychological analysis
Psychotherapy
Rational-emotive psychotherapy
Reality therapy
Reassurance
Reconstructive therapy
Release therapy
Round-table psychotherapy
Sector therapy
Self-therapy
Short psychotherapy
Short-term insight psychotherapy
Spiritual medicine
Strong discipline
Suggestion
Supportive therapy
Suppressive-supportive psychotherapy
Symptomatic psychotherapy
Systematic desensitization therapy
Therapist (self as therapeutic)
Untreatment
Ventilation
Verbal psychotherapy
Vocational counseling
Will therapy

Psychophysical

Alcohol
Antidepressant therapy
Autogenic training
Aversion therapy
Beer therapy
Body reorientation
Causal therapy
Chiropractic
Conditioned reflex therapy
Copulation
Cosmetic surgery
Electronarcosis
Electroshock
Electric sleep
Electrotherapy

Excitation
Hydropsychotherapy
Hypnopsychotherapy
Infantilization
Insulin therapy
Manual arts
Metrazol therapy
Music
Narcosis
Narcosynthetic
Niacin therapy
Nonverbal suggestion
Nonverbal support
Nursing
Occupational therapy
Overstimulation
Pathogenetic
Pavlovian therapy
Physical culture
Physiopharmacotherapy
Placebo
Psychobiologic
Psychomotor catharsis
Psychopharmacologic
Psychosurgery
Rehabilitation therapy
Somatopsychotherapeutic
Speech therapy
Stress
Tranquilizer therapy

Personal-Expressive

Autohypnosis
Autopsychodrama
Baking
Bibliotherapy
Camping
Cosmetic therapy
Creative arts
Dramatic confrontation
Dramatics
Dreams
Enhanced status
Fencing
Fingerpainting
Food preparation
Graphotherapy
Hobbies
Horticultural therapy
Humor
Intellectual diversion
Nondirective play therapy
Service to others

Love
Philanthropy
Play
Poetry therapy
Psychomotor catharsis
Puppetry
Recreational therapy
Reminiscing
Responsibility
Sports
Summer camp
Therapeutic diary

Social

Ceremonials (investiture,
    graduation, etc.)
Companionship
Dancing
Dog (as cotherapist)
Interpersonal relations
Group exercise
Resocialization
Role-playing
Social clubs
Social stimulation
Social therapy
Social participation
Social (ward discussion)
Sociodrama

Social-Spiritual

Alateen (teenagers with alcoholic
    parents)
Alcoholics Anonymous
Cursillo
Fatties Anonymous
Gam-Anon (relatives of gamblers)
Gamblers Anonymous
Mended Hearts, Inc.
Neurotics Anonymous
Parents without Partners
Reach to Recovery (breast removal)
Recovery, Inc.
Synanon
Theotherapy
T.O.P.S. (take off pounds sensibly)
United Ostomy (ileostomy & colos-
    tomy)

Incidental

Diagnostic interview
Electrocardiogram
Psychometrics

Pseudosurgery

Spiritual

Blessing
Christian Science
Confessional
Ethical Culture
Faith healing
Humanism
Jewish science
Medical moralization
Meditation
Prayer
Religion
Religious orders
Silent therapy
Talisman
Spiritualism
Witch doctor
Yoga
Zen Buddhism

Situational

Administrative therapy
Conjoint family and milieu therapy
Day treatment center
Environmental manipulation
Environmental modification
Environmental therapy
Foster home
Group living
Halfway house
Hospitalization
Institutionalization
Isolation
Maintenance therapy
Member employee
Milieu rehabilitation
Milieu therapy
Neglect (as therapeutic)
Patient councils
Personal adjustment training
Prevocational exploration
Psychodrama
Remotivation
Substitute family
Teamwork
Therapeutic community
Therapeutic milieu
Training
Transitional employment
Vacation
Vocational therapy
Work therapy

Educational

Computer psychotherapy
Consultant psychotherapy
Creative dramatics
Educational and re-educational
Experiential
Habit training
Information
Listener-tapes
Mirror image
Movies
Operant conditioning
Photo-self-image
Punishment and reward
Reciprocal inhibition
Remedial
Taped television (of patient and
    therapist for patient review)
Therapeutic study
Tutoring
Vicarious therapy pretraining

Client Involvement

Pseudotherapist
Subtherapist
Unled patient group

Professional Aide

Filial therapy
Family therapy
Friendship
Lay therapy

Physical

Corrective therapy
Diathermy therapy
Exercise
Food
Hydrotherapy
Hyperthermia
Hypothermia

Light therapy
Massage
Oxygen therapy
Physical education
Physical therapy
Relaxation therapy
Sleep
Surgery
Ultrasound

Motivational

Incentive therapy
Money
Rewards

General Medical

Chemical (vitamin, hormones, etc.)
Chiropody
Chiropractic
Coronary vasodilator therapy
Dentistry
Drug
Fever therapy
Homeopathy
Mediate therapy
Medical practice (general)
Medical specialties (19 major, many
    minor)
Naturopathy
Opsonic therapy
Osteopathy
Protein therapy
Radionic
Relief of pain
Sedation
Serotherapy

Pseudotherapy

Magnitizers
Metallotherapy
Orgone box
Tranquilizing chair

The multiplicity of "therapies" may be accounted for by:

1. No One Medicine Cures All

Physical diseases have different causes and may manifest themselves
differently, depending upon the host, and no one pill or method is suitable for all. There are, then, many ways of practicing medical assistance
and coincidentally many ways of giving psychological aid, depending

upon the nature and complexity of cause, individual differences, and the total ecological contribution. Consequently, a single-system approach may not be relevant psychologically.

2. Patient Variance

The great variety of patients and their individual problems and personalities provoke therapists to devise better methods to meet this variance : A conforming of method for particular problem groups, with still greater alteration of technic to suit individuals within this group. Thorne[2] says, "It immediately becomes apparent that a wide variety of methods are indicated for a wide variety of different conditions," and Watson[3] says, "In the opinion of many clinicians, the needs of patients cannot be met with only one technique of treatment. The gamut of human suffering associated with psychological factors is wide. . . ."

Wrenn[4] believes that the skillful therapist knows when to vary the procedure along the directive-nondirective continuum. Finally, Symonds[5] said,

> Under quite different approaches a client will use the therapeutic situations as his own need dictates . . . he will institute his own process of psychotherapy irrespective of the attitude the therapist takes toward him or the words that the therapist utters.

3. Reflection of the State of Knowledge

Watson[3] says, for example, that it is the opinion of some psychotherapists ". . . that the development of schools of psychotherapy (like the development of schools of psychology) is a sign not of considerable knowledge but rather deficiency of knowledge." This is perhaps a rather kind way of excusing sins. We are, we say, very creative, but we unfortunately must rely upon insufficient facts. At least it shows our persistence in probing to seek a better system.

4. Cultural Enterprise

We live in a competitive country in which individual enterprise is admired and respected. Often one does not need to prove a method is better, just that it is new and different. Doing it differently is seen as seeking the truth. This individualism often is a good thing. Yet, frequently it results in cultism and sometimes in exploitation because of economic motivation or just self-enhancement and tends to permit charlatanism. While the price we pay for such freedom of enterprise in human therapeutic affairs is high, it appears to be generally worthwhile.

Evidently, systems and practices vary throughout the world, commensurate with the national culture. Most European countries, according to Bellak,[6] place greater emphasis upon such factors as biology, constitution, heredity, and other organic entities such as the endocrine and metabolic. And, for example, the Russians are generally more physiologically and manipulatively oriented. I suspect that psychotherapeutic practice in Los Angeles may be different from that in Vermont.

5. The Personality of the Therapist

As mentioned in 2 above, it is most often assumed that the therapy is in response to the patient's individuality. Yet, when one reads the literature, one gets the impression that this is not so much the case as therapy is shaped by the personality of the therapist. It is he who devises, in accordance with his own interests, perceptions of the issues, and his own desires and needs.

This variety of systems, with each claiming greater authenticity in terms of productive outcome and perhaps firmer scientific base, may be missing the point. Which therapy is essentially better may be less important than which therapy coincides closer with the individual therapist's needs and personal skills. In fact, each proponent may be correct about his therapy. It is understandably difficult also for a person to appreciate that another therapeutic method that he has not used could be a better therapeutic procedure for him.

It is confusing to find in the literature that a psychotherapist frequently bases his claims upon a very select group of patients : Who these patients were or what were the clear criteria for their acceptance is not stated. Furthermore, what actually was done under what specific circumstantial conditions is often not given. Consequently, comparisons of methods and technics become difficult. I would assume that the patients were basically selected to suit the therapist's own personality; maybe, then, the method or technic is somewhat irrelevant. Frank says, for example :

> It is now clear that psychotherapists of different schools may elicit from their patients verbal productions confirming the theoretical conceptions of that school and that patients sometimes accommodate their memories and dreams to the expectations of the therapist to the point of outright confabulation.[7]

An earlier report by Fiedler speaks in a similar vein :

> The therapeutic relationship created by experts of one school resembles more closely that created by experts of other schools than it resembles relationships created by nonexperts within the same school.[8]

THE THERAPIST

The therapist himself then is an issue of great importance. Alexander said, ". . . The influence of the individuality of the therapist is a crucial, although yet almost completely unexplored factor."[9] Maybe we have been focusing too much upon one side of the two-person model of therapy, and we should not be as much concerned with the various methods and technics of therapy, nor with the variety of patients, but with who the therapist is, what he believes, what his personality is, how much commitment he has, what his image of himself is as a therapist, and what are *his* problems.

In partial support of this, Hill said,

> A therapist is what he does. . . . The choice of what to do, what patients to treat, what goals to set, what techniques to use, or the choice from moment to moment whether to say something or not, or to do something or not; the choice of strategy for the long pull or the tactic of the moment is a choice which is made by the therapist as a predetermined expression of what he *is*, both as a person and as a therapist.[10]

Years ago I had a very insightful experience. It happened when I was puzzling over the various current systems of therapy. Which one was better and why? Did one become this kind of therapist or that? At this point of indecision, I attended a lecture on psychodrama by Moreno (J. L. Moreno, the originator of psychodrama). Actually, it was more a *performance* than a lecture. The dramatic, dynamic quality of his presentation persuaded me that the approach to therapy that he made was particularly suited to his personality, but I knew it would do me no good to go sit at the feet of the master and learn his system. I realized that my personality did not fit that mold. "To thine own self be true," I saw, was what produced vitality, confidence, and genuine expression in one's interpersonal relations. Why, then, do we sell systems, as if one should choose them on the basis of which one claims to be the most scientific, when the right tool in the wrong hands would lead to less effectiveness?

The choice must be compatibility of system and technics with the personality. But this is not static, we change through life, and perhaps so do the patients we accept. We may consciously or unconsciously keep altering our therapies to keep in concert, and we need to be constantly open to what available variations there are or what might be created by us to fit our present maximum expressive effectiveness.

Confidence in one's self and positive convictions about one's method are strongly persuasive factors that tend to generate positive responses. Patient belief in the power of the therapist and his ministrations makes miracles in the sense that Janet[11] has put it :

> From time to time, it has been the fashion to laugh at miracles and to deny that they occur. This is absurd, for we are surrounded by miracles; our existence is a perpetual miracle, every science has begun by a study of miracles. . . . I refer to phenomena which cannot be accurately predicted, and above all to those which cannot be made to occur unfailingly by causing a prior determinant to take place.

Voodoo death,[12] for example, does occur, and faith healers can benefit those who may be persuaded.

The enthusiast may be influencing his patient more by his personality than by his method. The method becomes only the vehicle for this transmission. It may even be that what makes a therapist an expert is his increase in self-expressive ability through the alteration of the chosen system.

For example, there was a surgical operation that not long ago enjoyed some success. It was an operation purporting to increase the blood supply to the heart, useful when a patient had serious angina pectoris. The chest was opened and blood vessels manipulated. A number of highly qualified surgeons reported improvement in their patients, ranging from persons whose pain became less frequent and less severe to those who became able to go back to work. A skeptic then did this study : On one half of a group of patients the real operation was performed, while on the other half merely an incision was made in the chest, resulting in a small scar. Interestingly enough, *greater* improvement was made by those with the pseudo operation : some lost their pain and some, previously incapacitated, went back to work.[13]

The second story is of a patient with long-term chronic asthma whose physician obtained some samples of a new drug that presumably would be helpful. He proceeded to give the patient the new drug and the asthma was dramatically relieved. After a trial period the physician, without the patient's knowledge, substituted a placebo. The patient was beset with his former asthmatic condition. Again the physician secretly substituted the drug, with excellent relief. Placebo again was given with remission and the drug again with symptomatic improvement. The physician, now impressed with the efficacy of the drug, requested another supply. He was informed that the pharmaceutical company, having some question about the new drug, had in his case given him a placebo from the beginning. As long as the physician believed in the value of the pill, it worked, but when he did not, it failed, for somehow the patient got the message.[14]

Rosenthal,[15] a psychologist, found that an experimenter could bias his results by his own undisclosed opinions; i.e., subjects tended to agree with the secret belief of the researcher even though the material was presented objectively.

On the other hand, it is probable that doubts and misgivings about one's ability to help the patient probably cannot be hidden and therefore decrease chances of helping the patient.

This involvement, this interaction with the patient and its nature and degree, may be the most fundamental key to patient advance. Fiedler said :

> The most important dimension (of those measured) which differentiates experts from nonexperts is related to the therapist's ability to understand, to communicate with, and to maintain rapport with the patient.[8]

The therapeutic relationship appears to be an exchange of self-revelation. Unless the therapist is open and unafraid to be himself, the patient may soon sense the apartness, the implied promised giving but the actual withholding. The giving must be of oneself—a oneself that is genuinely concerned with the patient's welfare, indeed with a compassion for the human condition. If the therapist hides, so will the patient. Frank[7] believes that any close contact with the patient over a period of time results in the internalizing of the values and attitudes of the therapist. Strupp[16] also speaks of the warm, empathetic relationship that influences the patient to see the therapist as a model of a maturity to be achieved. Wolberg[17] supports this when he says :

> No matter how passive the therapist may believe himself . . . and no matter how objective . . . there is an inevitable incorporation within the patient of a new ego patterned after the character of the therapist.

There is a favorite example of mine on the less obvious but essential ingredient. A study of the home life of a group of selected children appeared in the *Journal of Educational Sociology*.[18] The investigators found all the horrible things to which we as psychologists would be sensitive. Some of the families had a very domineering father who ran the family with an iron hand; some had the mother in strong control with a weak passive father. Some children were physically whipped, some were seldom censured; some had too much spending money and went to the movies frequently on school nights, staying up late. Some children were never permitted such excess, went to bed early, and had no spending money. There were other aspects about which we might be uncomfortable. This was a study of the home life of *well-adjusted* children. Apparently none of these surface factors carried much weight. The only thread that the investigators could offer was that, regardless of parental management, the children felt a sense of love and acceptance in the home.

Rollo May[19] speaks even somewhat mystically about the patient-therapist relationship when he speaks of a "feeling resonance," analogous to the tendency of one untouched musical instrument to vibrate to the sound of another. Jung, in 1910, in speaking of children said :

> It is not the good and pious precepts, nor is it any other inculcation of pedagogic truths that have a moulding influence upon the character of the developing child, but what most influences him is the peculiarly affective state which is totally unknown to his parents and educators.[20]

This rather unique interaction also has its dangers. Frank, for example, says : "The possibility that the patient may be responding to the therapist's cues and telling him what he wants to hear must always be kept in mind, especially since it can occur without either being aware of it."[7] I am inclined to put this stronger. The pleasing of the therapist, in which the therapist becomes trapped by his apparent successes, can be as Balint and Balint[21] say "mutual seduction." The therapist's acceptance provokes a desire to repay; the therapist, in turn, reinforces this by his attitude. I have observed this particularly in young patients, who soon learn to bring an appreciative smile to the face of the therapist when they regurgitate in their own words what they have consciously or unconsciously received from the therapist. These young people, although they eventually learn to speak a good game, proceed to play the old one because they really have not experienced the change in the real world. I am referring particularly to what may be called the "habilitee."[22]

It is probably impossible for the therapist to avoid some errors of this nature especially because of his personal stake in the process. Perhaps with the greater use of televised sessions, concentrating not only upon the patient but upon the face and posture of the therapist, the therapist may review what may have been taking place.[23] This will not provide any neat solution, for there are still other cues that physical presence brings that cannot be assessed. The recent report in *Science* is thought-provoking. The alteration of the alpha brain wave in one identical twin appeared to change the other twin's alpha wave in another room.[24]

THE THERAPIST'S NEEDS

In this two-person, unrehearsed, improvised drama, we talk usually of the patient's needs but seldom of the needs of the therapist. Generally we select the medium of self-expression suited to our gratification.

The physical therapist would certainly not have chosen physical therapy unless he wished to touch people and was comfortable doing so. With the psychotherapist, one might suspect that it is some combination of a desire for feeling exchange and being intellectually intrigued with the problem to be solved. Possibly the system selected may be a clue to the ascendency of one factor or the other.

The therapist must achieve sufficient satisfaction from the interpersonal exchange, or his dissatisfaction may defeat the patient. What satisfies the therapist certainly is improved patients, but I wonder what more specifically may be the other returns, for I suspect this is not enough. To enter oneself in the process probably results in some personal therapeutic release.

One may hypothesize what some of these factors may be :

The pleasure of being able to give love, have it received and reciprocated.

The release it is to reveal oneself, to examine oneself, not to deny, not to exclude, to be open.

A feeling of power and control that another human being depends upon us.

A security, a relative safeness from the ills and troubles of the patient; it reminds us we are relatively free of such pain. Someone else is climbing the mountain and facing the danger while we observe.

Intellectual intrigue with the puzzle to be worked through.

An enhancement of one's own life by the vicarious experience of many other circumstances.

A feeling of worth and responsibility because one becomes involved in the success or failure of a human being.

A messianic feeling of being the possible savior of a human life and having the power to relieve pain and suffering.

Confirmation of one's competence by the patient's gratitude.

A wise investment of one's efforts; our precious time was not wasted when the patient shows gains.

A feeling of alliance, of commonality with the human condition.

A practice with the disrupting elements of life that strengthens oneself and develops skill in personal solutions.

An enjoyment of the competition for insightful discoveries and their certification when the patient achieves accordingly.

As the patient gains, a feeling of the appropriateness of our chosen field.

Who needs therapy? The therapist does! If his experience is not therapeutic for him, it can be disruptive and even painful. Consequently, when we select the kinds of patient we think we can help, we are also attempting to choose those who can satisfy us. The therapeutic method must suit the therapist, and the therapist must suit the patient. The patient, it would seem, may be helped to some degree by any kind of therapy but not by any kind of therapist, for relating to the therapist is fundamental.

So we are all "patients" needing therapy and needing to give it in some way. We sit on the other side from our patients, and our needs are somewhat different. We cannot help but use the patient to meet our needs within certain rather unclear limitations. There may be no evil in this, because our gain is transmitted to the patient, and his gains reciprocate ours. Interpersonal exchange of any sort by word, by silence, by touch, by manipulation is an exchange of giving and basically self-supporting to each participant.

So when we have "failing patients," we are failing. This again raises the question of the importance of the most appropriate therapeutic method for ourselves.

Shapiro, a physician, apparently would support this, for he says, "Some treatments, then, although ostensibly directed at the patient, may actually function as a treatment for the doctor."[25] And he speaks of this as ". . . mediating psychological change in the patient."

VARIETY OF THERAPISTS

It is important to exercise our bodies for good physical health apart from mental benefit. This physical release provokes a sensuous enjoyment and in addition is a reaching out and touching of our environment in many forms. We define and confirm our assessment of the real world. It also verifies our physical self-identity. We compulsively touch the painted object to see whether the "wet paint" sign is still correct, and we test our skills, our endurance, in sports and recreation. The tired accomplishment of body use is pleasant and relaxing.

We also need the opportunity for verbal release, to keep our inner world in concordance with the external world. The person who talks aloud to himself in solitary confinement and the sensory deprivation experiments show the need for release and for return input. We vary in the means we take and the extent of need for expurgation of feelings as well as certification of beliefs. We choose the therapeutic means and people who satisfy us. A person is picked who can give us an appropriate response to our disclosure or will at least be a good listener. A woman may say some things or discuss some topics with her hairdresser and other things with her best friend or her doctor. The release is geared to the presumed nature, competence, and interest of the listener.

Paredes[26] reports that, as a teaching device for medical students, "We invited an articulate hairdresser to talk about the type of psychological assistance he gave to his customers." Each listener has a particular use, each is accepting, and each is uncritical and supporting about certain revelations. The bartender and clergyman are, then, useful within the particular circumscribed areas. Some of us require a large array of listener roles; with others, a close friend or one's wife may be sufficient, while lesser issues are acted out or "talked out" mentally.

Presumably, if society at large were more therapeutically skilled, we might have a mentally healthier population. Maslow[27] says : "Psychotherapy is not at its base a unique relationship, for some of the fundamental qualities are found in all 'good' human relationships." Later he says : "Certainly, we need not be afraid as professionals of putting into the hands of amateurs these important therapeutic tools : love for other human beings and respect for other human beings."

However, the relationship in psychotherapy is different even if it is not entirely unique, for, as Brill[28] remarks :

> Whitehorn has pointed out what the therapist says to the patient has often been said previously by relatives and friends without effect. It is the relationship that exists, in reality or in fantasy, between the patient and the therapist which lends force and meaning to the therapist's comments or interpretations.

THERAPIST, SYSTEM, METHOD

There is a Germanic epigram : "It is easier to become a father than to be one." The issue of compatibility of therapist, therapeutic system, and methods is, I believe, a serious one. Qualifying for therapeutic practice is, of course, one thing, but operative suitability is another. As in the selection of patients, the selection by a training establishment of candidates may be important if its emphasis is upon a particular school of therapy.

The general practitioner of medicine can set a complicated fracture, but an orthopedic surgeon would more likely do a superior job. A general practitioner can treat rheumatic fever, an internist might be better, a cardiologist still better, and a pediatric cardiologist presumably best. And, the pediatric cardiologist would ordinarily never see an obstetrical patient. The obvious parallel principle is the selection of a system or systems of therapy operation at a certain level, and the selective use of technics compatible with the effectiveness of the therapist.

Vocationally, we select a profession compatible to ourselves. Should not this vocational principle continue to operate and determine what kind of therapist, what kind of system, what variation is best, and what varieties of technics are best suited for individual effectiveness? Matarazzo has called psychotherapy a "highly idiosyncratic art."[20]

PARALLEL WITH RELIGION

We both profit by a system and lose by it. Man is a maker of systems; he forms them and they become comfortable like habits. Systems make one secure. One has a reference point and the aid of fellow adherents; one can blame the system for failure rather than one's judgment. Did I not follow the dicta of the system? I accept it as imperfect, and therefore any error is not my fault.

Religious systems or systems of psychotherapy become binds to freedom, but many of us like to be bound and we enjoy the support it gives to those who pay allegiance. We claim it to be the true faith, or the most scientific, as our justification.

Psychology has inherited from its forebears in religion, in medicine, and in philosophy practices that bear the ancestral body, but onto which we put the psychological face and spirit. Our modern expression of the witch doctor-priest has retained some of the good and evil, some of the rational-irrational aspects. Many of our mechanisms are parallels and derivations of religious practices. Yet, William James[30] said: "It does not follow because our ancestors made so many errors of fact and mixed them with their religion that we should therefore leave off being religious at all."

Whether we are formally religious or not, our practice is religious. It gives help, concern, and love; it respects the individual. We have a priesthood, an authority, an anointed role certified by the high institutional procedures of graduate schools.

In religion, the postulant is baptized and inducted into the faith, and his sins are relieved by his commitment to a doctrine through the intercession of a priest close to God. He worships on the appointed day and at the appointed hour, impressed by the power and charms of the ritual. He is relieved and made whole by his allegiance to holy principles. But he still needs to cope with the devil. He confesses his sins, does penance, and is forgiven. He prays and is fortified from the devil's control, with much turmoil, soul-searching, and emotion, but he, having passed through this ordeal, feels cleansed, stronger, and grateful to achieve a new holy status. He has a model of Christ as accepting, loving, forgiving, and rewarding, giving a security and a shield against evil circumstance.

If one religion does not save him, he goes to another and another until some compatibility is found. One person may respond to the charisma of formal ceremony, sacraments, and pomp and another to a simple, intellectual down-to-earth approach. It may be related to the kinds of "sins" he has and what he believes will expiate them.

Has religion learned the process that we have either stumbled upon or unconsciously based our practice? Is our practice not a "religion" in a disguised form? Should we study religion more closely to learn what it has found through long evolvement, so that we may emulate it for our patients?

A system of psychotherapy often becomes the "religion" of the therapist. How comfortable it is to be a true believer, a member identified with a faith, a missionary with a gospel. Patients are gradually indoctrinated with the dogma and rules of conduct. We expect their faith, their belief, their soul-baring, and we bless them for it, and they benefit from the rebirth. If our patients are not "converted," we are yet reluctant to lose them to another faith. We have offered them love and concern to no avail. But it does not shake our faith, for we have found the truth. We may resist the scepticism of science and the proofs demanded and battle fiercely for our mystical sacramentals.

We speak of the need to make our patients free—free, I suppose, to love themselves, i.e., to accept themselves as an important basis for growth. Schiller said: "There is no freedom but love." Might therapeutic training be essentially a learning of how to give love and how to get our patients to accept it?

Maslow said:

> Human beings have always gone for advice and help to others whom they respected and loved. There is no reason why this historical phenomenon should not be formalized, verbalized, and encouraged to the point of universality by psychologists as well as religionists.[27]

One might say religion has done this, encouraged this, even though it has often been distorted.

Wittkower says in a similar vein: "The aim . . . in becoming a doctor is a savior fantasy regarding primarily the family and, ultimately, suffering mankind in general."[31]

CONCLUSION

Professionals may often use their methods and tools as if there were no other benefits available, other circumstances to be considered, or other professions having offerings of value. Have you met the psychologist who says, "All I need is a Rorschach," as if singleness of tool, as if multiple deductions from one tool, were the apex of clinical performance?

The fact is that our therapeutic methods have limitations, that we are naive in many areas of the total therapeutic spectrum, and that we seldom understand the world of our patients unless we restrict ourselves to therapy with persons of professional status. Not many of us frequent the corner bar, eat hot dogs in the bleachers, dance the watusi, and are familiar with the mainstream of some patients' lives.

There are many other therapies that can be conducive, supportive, ameliorative, or curative for the patient other than psychotherapeutic measures. If we are open-minded and sophisticated in the use of other measures, our therapy, so augmented, may be more effective, longer lasting, and more successful.

Are we and the patient aware of what kinds of environment, what activities, what circumstances in his everyday life may be therapeutic for him? Does he return to the very mode of life that stressed him to the point of maladaptation? Is he sufficiently sensitive to the situations that will make it more difficult for him to maintain his equilibrium? He is, we may be inclined to overlook, a human being with a body requiring exercise and use in a real physical sense. We castigate medicine for ignoring the psyche. Do we not in turn forget the soma?

Consequently, besides relationships with people, the patient needs appropriate exercise, diet, rest, recreation, and spiritual and creative expression. His mind does not operate in a vacuum nor his body in pickled brine. Nemiah said, "It is a truism, often stated but more often forgotten in practice, that the human discords in a patient's daily life are played on the organs of his body."[32] Untolerated physiological stress affects the mind and its ability to function normally. Ill health and pain leave their imprint upon mental equipment. A failing heart may cause a failing brain and, therefore, a failing mind. Psychotic reactions take place with inadequate blood supply.[33] An unhappy job may lead to mental and physical illness. Regardless of the selective process, we select more than mere "emotional" problems.

Science aims to discover unity in a diversity of related events. We organize principles to arrive at a single law that explains all. We do not appear ready to do this for therapy or for psychotherapy. Perhaps pressure in this direction may even be a mistake, since creative developments are still taking place. Furthermore, such efforts with guilt feelings about the insufficiently scientific base of our method may even be irrelevant, if we are trying to emulate a physical science rationale. Colby said, "Psychotherapy is not a science, is not even an applied science and by its nature can never become either of these."[34] Medicine does not have the dream that some magic pill will be found to cure all illnesses. True, there is the hope that what ages the human cell will be found, and thereby the clue to all aging diseases may then be specified. However, diseases have been conquered or alleviated by specific treatment supported by the improvement of ecological community measures that are preventive and that tend to maintain good health by strengthening resistance.

Perhaps our road is much the same : To determine the best specific therapies for certain patients as well as to devote ourselves to the broader problem of improving community mental health. Maslow[27] speaks of "public psychotherapy" and says, "These fundamentals of what we may call lay psychotherapy can be taught from childhood on to any human being at all. . . . One clear task is to teach these facts, to broadcast them far and wide, to be certain that every teacher, every parent, and ideally every human being be given the chance to understand them and to apply them."

Crew[35] speaks of "the disease-evoking qualities of our society and its institutions" and Halliday[36] of a "sick society." We know that many patients are the innocent victims of the institutions and philosophies of their milieu. I have spoken of our ideal goal as "a community of therapists in a therapeutic community."[37] Margaret Mead and others surely illuminate our present cultural strictures into which we either fit reasonably well or become alienated.

Perhaps we are in a position analogous to the new African nation whose educated legislators meet seriously in a modern building, while around the corner tom-toms beat in the jungle. One is still part of the other, related to the other, and must live with some alliance to the other. The therapist has evolved from the witch doctor, is still influenced by him, may even use some of his wiles with a modern stamp, and may continue to learn from his magic. Furthermore, the witch doctor-faith healer is still a competitor, and many people benefit from such services. Some of these people would, in fact, not benefit from ours, because they would not accept us, nor we them. In our case, it may be a formal rejection, because we feel we cannot reach them, or an unconscious one in that, while we apparently accept them as a case, the result is failure.

Our particular magic cannot be universally applied, and we ethically owe those we cannot help a recourse to the more nonscientific therapies that may assuage their troubles.

Anatole France[38] said, "It is true that the scientific reasons for preferring one piece of evidence to another are sometimes very strong, but they are never strong enough to outweigh our passions, our prejudices, our interests."

REFERENCES

1. Beecher, Henry K. The Powerful Placebo. *J. Am. Med. Assn.* Dec. 24, 1955. 159 :17 :1602–1606.
2. Thorne, Frederick C. Further Critique of Nondirective Methods of

Psychotherapy. *J. Clin. Psychol.* July, 1948. 4 :3 :256–263.

3. Watson, Robert I. *The Clinical Method in Psychology. (Science Editions)* New York : John Wiley & Sons, 1963.

4. Wrenn, C. Gilbert. Client-Centered Counseling. *Educ. Psychol. Measurement.* 1946. 6 :439–444.

5. Symonds, Percival M. *Dynamics of Psychotherapy; The Psychology of Personality Change: Vol. 1, Principles.* New York : Grune & Stratton, 1956.

6. Bellak, Leopold. *Contemporary European Psychiatry.* New York : Grove Press, 1961.

7. Frank, Jerome D. The Dynamics of the Psychotherapeutic Relationship; Determinants and Effects of the Therapist's Influence. *Psychiatry.* Feb., 1959. 22 :1 :17–39.

8. Fiedler, Fred E. A Comparison of Therapeutic Relationships in Psychoanalytic, Nondirective and Adlerian Therapy. *J. Consult. Psychol.* Dec., 1950. 14 :6 :436–445.

9. Alexander, Franz. Current Problems in Dynamic Psychotherapy in Its Relationship to Psychoanalysis. *Am. J. Psychiat.* Oct., 1959. 116 :4 :322–325.

10. Hill, Lewis B. On Being Rather Than Doing in Psychotherapy. *Internatl. J. Group Psychotherapy.* Apr., 1958. 8 :2 :115–122.

11. Janet, Pierre. *Psychological Healing: A Historical and Clinical Study.* (2 vols.) New York : Macmillan Co., 1925. Vol. 1, p. 21.

12. Cannon, Walter B. "Voodoo" Death. *Am. Anthropologist.* 1942. 44 :169.

13. Cobb, Leonard A., and others. An Evaluation of Internal-Mammary-Artery Ligation by a Double-Blind Technic. *New Eng. J. Med.* May 28, 1959. 260 :22 :1115–1118.

14. Boshes, Benjamin. The Status of Tranquilizing Drugs—1959. *Annals Internal Med.* Jan., 1960. 52 :1 :182–194.

15. Rosenthal, R. On the Social Psychology of the Psychological Experiment; The Experimenter's Hypothesis as an Unintended Determinant of Experimental Results. *Am. Scientist.* 1963. 51 :268–283.

16. Strupp, Hans H. The Psychotherapist's Contribution to the Treatment Process. *Behavioral Science.* Jan., 1958. 3 :1 :34–67.

17. Wolberg, Lewis R. Comment, p. 565–573, on : Ginsburg, Sol Weiner, and Herma, John L. Values and Their Relationship to Psychiatric Principles and Practices. *Am. J. Psychother.* July, 1953. 7 :3 :546–565.

18. Stout, Irving W. and Langdon, Grace. A Study of the Home Life of Well-Adjusted Children. *J. Educational Sociol.* Apr., 1950. 23 :442.

19. May, Rollo. The World the Patient Constructs. (Lecture at New School, New York City)

20. Jung, C. G. The Association Method. (Translated by A. A. Brill) *Am. J. Psychol.* 1910. 21 :219–269.

21. Balint, Michael and Balint, Enid. *Psychotherapeutic Techniques in Medicine.* London : Tavistock Publications, 1961. 236 p.
22. Whitehouse, Frederick A. Habilitation—Concept and Process. *J. Rehab.* Mar.–Apr., 1953. 19 :2 :3–7.
23. Kagan, Norman, Krathwohl, David R., and Miller, Ralph. Stimulated Recall in Therapy Using Video Tape; A Case Study. *J. Counsel. Psychol.* Fall, 1963. 10 :3 :237–243.
24. Duane, T. D. and Behrendt, T. Extrasensory Electroencephalographic Induction Between Identical Twins. *Science.* Oct. 15, 1965. 150 :367.
25. Shapiro, Arthur K. Etiological Factors in Placebo Effect. *J. Am. Med. Assn.* Mar. 7, 1964. 187 :10 :712–714.
26. Paredes, Alfonso. The Behavioral Science Correlation Clinic as a Teaching Device. *J. Med. Educ.* Jan., 1964. 39 :1 :58–64.
27. Maslow, A. H. *Motivation and Personality.* New York : Harper & Bros., 1954.
28. Brill, Norman Q. The Psychotherapeutic Process, p. 1–25, in : Brill Norman Q., *ed. Psychiatry in Medicine.* Berkeley, Calif. : Univ. of California Pr., 1962. 195 p.
29. Matarazzo, Joseph D. Psychotherapeutic Processes. *Annual Rev. of Psychol.* 1965. 16 :181–224. (Published by Annual Reviews, Inc., Palo Alto, Calif.)
30. James, William. *The Varieties of Religious Experience; A Study in Human Nature.* New York : New American Library, 1958.
31. Wittkower, Eric D. The Psychiatric Role of the General Practitioner, p. 136–160, in : Brill, Norman Q., *ed. Psychiatry in Medicine.* Berkeley, Calif. : Univ. of California Pr., 1962. 195 p.
32. Nemiah, John C. Emotions in Clinical Medicine. *Postgrad. Med.* May, 1965. 37 :5 :523–528.
33. Whitehouse, Frederick A. Cardiovascular Disease and Mental Health. *Rehab. Lit.* May, 1963. 24 :5 :130–139, 148.
34. Colby, Kenneth Mark. Psychotherapeutic Processes. *Annual Rev. of Psychol.* 1964. 15 :347–370. (Published by Annual Reviews, Inc., Palo Alto, Calif.)
35. Crew, F. A. E. The Changing Philosophy of Health. *Health Educ. J.* May, 1955. 12 :2 :117.
36. Halliday, James L. *Psychosocial Medicine; A Study of the Sick Society.* New York : W. W. Norton, 1948.
37. Whitehouse, Frederick A. Basic Concepts in Comprehensive Rehabilitation. *J. Rehab.* May–June, 1959. 25 :3 :4–6, 18.
38. France, Anatole. In : Preface to *Penguin Island.* New York : Modern Library.

26

Structured Experiential Therapy: A Group Approach to Rehabilitation

Robert G. Lasky
Arthur E. Dell Orto
Robert P. Marinelli

Although there is a wealth of information available concerning the theory and practice of group methods used to promote personal and inter-personal growth (e.g., Cartwright and Zander, 1968; Ohlsen, 1970; Shaffer and Galinsky, 1974; Yalom, 1975), little attention has been focused on the use of group procedures specifically designed to meet the needs of physically disabled individuals. Even less attention has been given to reducing intrapersonal and interpersonal stress and stigma often experienced between physically disabled and nondisabled persons. Most frequently, existing group counseling and therapy procedures have been adapted to physically disabled persons (Cook, et al., 1974; Goldman, 1971; Heller, 1970; McClellan, 1972). The specific populations served have included hemodialysis patients (Hollon, 1974; Wilson, et al., 1974), cystic fibrosis patients (Farkas and Shwachman, 1973), deaf persons (Landau, 1968; Robinson, 1965; Sarlin and Altshuler, 1968; Stinson, 1972; Sussman, 1975), blind persons (Manaster and Kucharis, 1972; Shlensky, 1972), stroke patients (Dafflitti and Weitz, 1974; Oradei and Waite, 1974), hemiplegics (Bouchard, 1972), arthritic patients (Henkle, 1975), hemophiliacs (Caldwell and Leveque, 1974), and terminally ill patients (Franzino, et al., 1976). Occasionally group practices have been used with physically disabled persons to assist in vocational counseling (Brondzel, 1963; Rosenberg, 1956; Wilson, 1962). Groups have also been used to assist parents and their disabled children in coping with family difficulties (Heisler, 1974; Hicks and Wieder, 1973).

Unfortunately, group approaches do not generally use behavioral principles to effect individual change. Group procedures have been criticized as dealing with vague and/or questionable goals (Walker and

Peiffer, 1957) and not directly focusing on observable interpersonal difficulties giving rise to maladaptive functioning (Lazarus, 1968; Ullman and Krasner, 1965). Thus, physically disabled and nondisabled persons often spend time in groups that are not goal-directed and focus on questionable internalized problems, often without objective referents. Furthermore, most group approaches use talking as the primary vehicle to promote change, without stressing the importance of corroborative explicit behavioral changes that are measurable and observable. Action rather than talk is necessary for persons to combat problems that hinder personal and interpersonal development.

Issues

While typical approaches used may be facilitative, they are not designed to reduce the interpersonal and intrapersonal stress often experienced between physically disabled and nondisabled persons. These reactions may be of such intensity that disabled and nondisabled persons respond, when interacting, with uncertainty, withdrawal, helplessness, denial, anger, and similar emotions (Shontz, 1975; Wright, 1960). Such responses may be rationalized by thoughts and feelings to reduce uncomfortable anxiety (e.g., "Nobody could like me now that I'm disabled," or, "They think they deserve a free ride from society"). These and similar reactions lead to prejudicial attitudes and a lack of understanding between disabled and nondisabled individuals, which further reinforces mutual exclusionary practices.

Additionally, in an examination of stigma, which Goffman (1963) describes as an attribute that is deeply discrediting, English (1971) found that stigma exists in the lives of most physically disabled persons and generally represents the most salient and frustrating problem to overcome in rehabilitation. But who has the problem, or where does the problem lie? If the nondisabled are aware of the fact that disability is a significant part of a person's existence, and that personal and interpersonal self-worth goes beyond an individual's disability, would that awareness eliminate stigmatizing responses toward the disabled? We think not, and research evidence supports the contention that information is not enough (Anthony, 1969; 1972; Rusalem, 1967). Adverse beliefs, values, and attitudes about the nondisabled are also experienced by the disabled, since the disabled are also people with human frailties and prejudices. Thus, it appears that both disabled and nondisabled persons have interpersonal difficulties, to a greater or lesser degree.

Considering that physically disabled persons have been stigmatized by nondisabled persons and vice versa, and that dysfunctional interpersonal stress frequently is experienced between both groups and leads to maladaptive reactions, it is a challenge to the rehabilitation professions to devise and implement proactive personal and interpersonal growth. Structured Experiential Therapy in Rehabilitation (SET–R) has been developed as a response to this challenge.

Description of SET–R

Structured Experiential Therapy in Rehabilitation is a form of group therapy in which physically disabled and nondisabled individuals meet together to share growth experiences and to develop skills necessary to function more effectively in everyday living. In SET–R, group members are viewed as worthwhile individuals who are attempting to develop their resources to cope more effectively with problems of life and living.

The original rationale for using and developing the group process in a SET–R format was to introduce the dimensions of goal orientation, accountability, mutuality, and skill generalization into group therapy. The impetus for this position was the concern that when the group process is applied in rehabilitation, there is an overreliance on traditional approaches—such as psychoanalytic, encounter, sensitivity—whose impact may be short-lived due to their often random application and lack of a skill-building perspective. While many of the conventional group techniques used are retained in SET–R (e.g., processing of group dynamics, giving and receiving information), the structure and focus of the SET–R group includes several significant variations :

1. *Group composition.* The SET–R group is composed of a heterogeneous group of physically disabled and nondisabled clients. Ideally, there is an equal number of disabled and nondisabled participants in the group. The size of the group is usually eight to ten members including two coleaders. The heterogeneity of the group exposes participants to the process of incidental learning and role-modeling. Explorations of problems which may exist between disabled and nondisabled people are facilitated by heterogeneous group membership.

2. *Group leadership.* Rather than promote a lack of structure and leader noninvolvement, as often stressed in therapy groups (Bach, 1958; Yalom, 1975), SET–R stresses the importance of the leaders' use of their specialized skills, techniques, and experiences and functioning as role models and as facilitators. A major role of the leader is to develop the group systematically and actively so that cohesiveness and mutual concern are quickly attained.

3. *Structured experiential learning.* A key concept in SET–R is the use of structured experiential learning to identify, explore,

evaluate, and act upon specific problem areas of disabled and non-disabled group members. This differs from broad applications of structured learning approaches, such as those discussed by Kurtz (1975), Marks and Davis (1975), and Pfeiffer and Jones (1973). Examples of several structured learning experiences used in SET–R are included in Appendix D. The strengths and limitations of structured experiential learning have been thoroughly discussed elsewhere (Argyris, 1967; Bach, 1954; Kurtz, 1975; Lieberman, et. al., 1973; Rogers, 1970).

4. *Written contract.*   A written contract is given to potential SET–R members prior to their inclusion in the group process. This contract, a modification of a contract developed by Egan (1972), contains information on the goals and general expectations of the SET–R experience. Such a contract has been shown to facilitate the group process by maximizing participants' expectations, establishing basic procedural rules, and minimizing the nonfacilitative levels of anxiety often experienced in unstructured groups. Furthermore, the emphasis of individual and group goals and mutuality of group members is highlighted as soon as possible and not simply left to happen by chance.

5. *Goal orientation.*   SET–R stresses the importance of group participants' working on self-selected goal attainment both within the group experience and externally to it. The early phases of the group sessions are used to help each individual to identify, explore, and evaluate his or her goals. Later phases focus on participants' being accountable by taking responsibility for their goals and actually attaining these through personal effort and group support. An important part of each group session is devoted to feedback from participants on the progress that has been realized between sessions. The importance of personalized goals in a therapeutic group context has been discussed from various theoretical and practical considerations (Carkhuff, 1969; Dell Orto, 1975; Lazarus, 1968; Westmen, 1974).

6. *Mutuality.*   Another emphasis in the SET–R group is upon mutual help. Members are encouraged to become increasingly aware of their obligation to help one another. The use of the explicit contract described above and early group structuring helps to assure that this obligation is agreed upon and demonstrated.

Goals of SET–R

SET–R emphasizes a process that teaches generalizable skills to group members in order to increase their personal and interpersonal effectiveness and to reduce stress and prejudices frequently shared between disabled and nondisabled individuals. The goals of SET–R are specifically stated below :

GOALS OF SET–R

1. To reduce stress and stigma shared between disabled and non-disabled persons and promote more facilitative understanding and actions between people, regardless of disability or nondisability.
2. To develop individual potential by exploring the unknown or by activating the unused resources of group members.
3. To teach life-coping skills by stimulating life experiences through the use of structured experiences.
4. To support progress, using differential reinforcement by group members and facilitators.
5. To provide goal-oriented resources by establishing contact with persons, places, things, and events that can be of benefit to the group and to its members.
6. To evaluate past functioning and improve present functioning of individual group members by requiring peer group accountability and providing peer group perspective on the gains and efforts of the group members.
7. To avoid future problem areas by preparing individuals to cope with potentially difficult situations, using structured experiences both in and outside the group.
8. To expose group members to role models and incidental learning by relating to those persons who have made gains and who can share their skills.
9. To teach group members to identify, implement, and evaluate personal goals.
10. To promote active mutual concern between group members.

The Process of SET–R

SET–R groups develop through three phases, each with distinctive stages. Phase I focuses on the early development of the group and includes (a) the Initiation, (b) the Goal Identification Process, (c) the Goal Exploration and Evaluation Process, and (d) Didactic Intervention. The purpose of Phase I is to acquaint group members with their individual

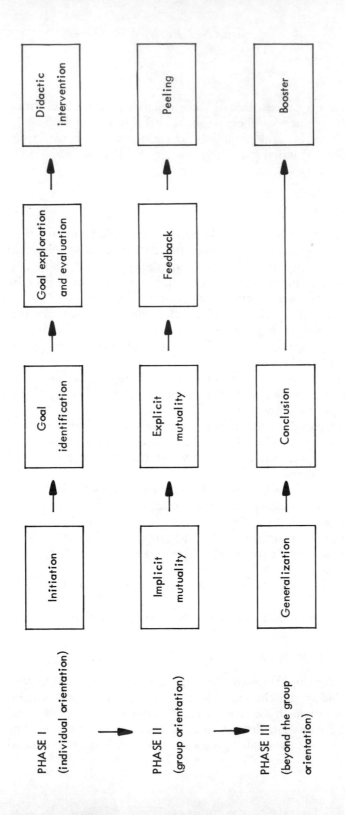

Figure 1. The phases and stages of SET–R.

responsibilities in the group and to have each member identify meaningful personal goals, clarify these goals using descriptive behavioral language, learn how to evaluate individual progress for personal goals, and begin to demonstrate explicit concern for other group members. The focus in Phase I is upon the development of individual responsibility in the group process.

Phase II emphasizes group cohesiveness, implicit and explicit intergroup member responsibility in helping each other attain personalized goals, and in-depth exploration focusing on deeper levels of awareness. Feedback to assess goal attainment successes and limitations is stressed during this phase and may highlight occasional return to Phase I to reconsider individual goal performances. The focus in Phase II is upon developing a group orientation through individual group members' assuming the responsibility to help others.

Phase III is composed of three stages: Generalization, Summary, and Booster. These stages stress the extension of skills beyond the group experience. The phases and stages of SET–R are outlined in Figure 1.

Each of the SET–R stages has a particular focus. These stages and descriptions of their major emphasis are shown in Table 1.

Table 1.   The Phases and Stages in SET–R (Descriptive Summary)

PHASE I: Individual Orientation

Stage 1:   Initiation

Focus	*Description*
"What is the purpose of the SET–R group?"	Prospective members are individually interviewed to determine their potential gains from the group experience and the potential contributions each might have to offer the group. Specific screening criteria include (1) interest and motivation to attain identifiable descriptive goals, (2) an equal number, as far as possible, of nondisabled and physically disabled group participants —six to eight group members are suggested in addition to two coleaders—and (3) having prospective members read the SET–R contract to determine personal thoughts and feelings about the SET–R experience. The SET–R group leaders also assess the prospective member's willingness to discuss personal problems within the group and the person's commitment to change. The group leader can also answer any questions regarding expectations or doubts the prospective member may have concerning participation. The group begins by reviewing member's perceptions of the SET–R experience as described by the written contract.

Stage 2: Goal Identification Process

Focus

"Who has identified their goals and who has not?"

Description

The Goal Identification Process begins with the second group session and may last for several sessions, although this is usually not the case. Each member is expected to make a commitment to the process by presenting goals he or she wishes to attain in the group. These goals are recorded in their SET–R group log, which provides a valuable record, as each member is required to record events occurring both within and outside the group as they relate to group goals. Personal accountability is established as well, since the written goal(s) approximate a personalized committment. If some group members do not have written goals, their reasons for this are explored by the group.

Stage 3: Goal Exploration and Evaluation Process

Focus

"How meaningful are your goals?"

Description

The content and potential implementation of individually presented goals are examined by the group, with an emphasis on reaching agreement that personalized goals are worthwhile. Structured experiences, such as "the Payoff–Goal Evaluation Feedback" (Appendix D), are used to increase responsible feedback and accountability of group members. Close scrutiny of the goal and the program for attaining it provides an opportunity for the group to make suggestions for improvement.

Stage 4: Didactic Intervention

Focus

"How will I know if I am attaining my goals?"

Description

After the group has helped individual members to accurately describe identifiable behavioral goals, the group leaders challenge the group to determine how to evaluate progress. This challenge stresses personal and interpersonal accountability and behavioral change and may lead to changes in individual goals. The group leader then teaches members how to record base rates and goal gains. For example, a physically disabled member, whose stated goal is "to become less self-conscious around the nondisabled," may be taught how to keep a record of his/her level of anxiety within and outside the group using the SET–R group log.

PHASE II: Group Orientation

Stage 1: Implicit Mutuality

Focus

"How can the group help you attain your goals?"

Description

Group members are challenged to take interpersonal responsibility by exploring and evaluating ways in which they may be able to help others to attain their goals. It is not uncommon for goals to be originally stated in global, diffuse terms (e.g. "I want to grow from this group experience") that are not easily adaptable to specific group implementation. The group may help the individual accurately describe goals that are attainable with group assistance. This process begins the transition from personal concerns to extending and reaching out to assist others in the group. Group members may wish to help each other to attain their goals but find that the only way they might help is by offering advice. Since this form of helping is generally not very effective, the group leaders usually intervene with appropriate structured experience or other techniques to assist members to help each other.

Stage 2: Explicit Mutuality

Focus

"Who really gives a damn!"

Description

It is common in most group experiences for group members not to go beyond the "implicit mutuality" stage. An important component of the SET–R process, which is described in the written contract, is genuine concern explicitly demonstrated between group members. Such concern is given verbally and nonverbally. In other words, group members are strongly encouraged to extend themselves to help others in the group attain their goals by giving individual attention beyond the group. For example, a disabled male group member who is having difficulty developing a relationship with a woman may find group members volunteering to assist him by going on a date with him, instructing him in initiating a relationship with a girl, and so on. If there is any question about the intentions of explicit mutuality (e.g. Joan is going out on a date with Sam not because she really cares but because of group pressure), such concerns are processed in the group directly or through a structured experiential learning format. Events reflecting explicit mutuality, including descriptions of personalized learning from the experience, are discussed in the group and recorded in the group log. Again, the concern is that members assist each other, not by talking, but by doing!

Stage 3: Feedback

Focus

"Who is making progress towards their goals?"

Description

Intermittently, a SET–R group begins with a feedback session opened by the leader with a question focusing on progress in goal attainment. Group members have the opportunity to share individual goal-oriented attainments as well as to determine significant contributions by group members (i.e. explicit mutuality) to help each other. Feedback sessions that are intermittently spaced help to keep the group accountable for personal and interpersonal goal attainments. Further, group leaders and members receive feedback on who in the group may be having difficulty with goals or related problems. Such feedback sessions also help group members to reassess their goals and to make changes if necessary.

Stage 4: Peeling

Focus

"Are there important issues about myself which I can now trust the group to help me with?"

Description

As the group develops, greater interpersonal trust is experienced. This leads to increased risk-taking behavior and improves group members' ability to cope with confrontation. Group leaders and/or participants may wish to help others in the group to probe areas of concern that they are unable or unwilling to express. For example, a group member may be using his/her disability in a defensive way to avoid experiencing stress in the group. A perceptive group member might facilitatively confront this person to help him/her become aware of such potentially self-defeating behaviors. Also, the group member who experiences such stress might choose to share this feeling with the group.

PHASE III: Beyond the Group Experience

Stage 1: Generalization

Focus

"How will this goal related experience help me in other areas of my life?"

Description

Group members are again challenged to go beyond the specific goal-related experience and extend upon their goals. Group members may participate in structured learning experiences or the group focus may stress explicit group member involvement beyond the group.

Thus, the SET–R experience must be integrated into the person's value system to generalize the specific skills learned in the SET–R group.

Stage 2: Summary

Focus	Description
"What have I learned? —What am I taking away?"	The members of the group discuss their SET–R experience using an open-ended and structured group discussion format. The latter may be used to focus on significant strengths and limitations of the SET–R experience and on personal sharing of the SET–R log. An important emphasis at this point is the solidarity of the group and generalizing group growth experiences outside the group.

Stage 3: Booster

Focus	Description
"How have I grown since I left the group?"	In order to establish whether group members have generalized significant learnings from the SET–R experience to other areas of their life, a booster session is held one to three months after the last group sessions. This booster is used to focus on current life functioning and to explore any way in which the group might be helpful to individual members who may be experiencing difficulties. Group members may choose to have additional booster sessions if it is agreed by the group that such experiences would be helpful for members' further growth.

SUMMARY AND IMPLICATIONS

Although the group has been used extensively as a significant therapeutic tool, its application to the problems of physically disabled persons has been minimal. When group approaches have been applied, their use has generally been traditional (e.g., encounter, sensitivity, psychoanalytic). SET–R has been uniquely developed to help physically disabled and nondisabled individuals experience each other in a systematic group context, to help overcome interpersonal stress and stigma frequently experienced when disabled and nondisabled persons come together. The group process focuses on personalized goals and group commitment for participants to help each other attain chosen goals. Rather than let the group process evolve in a nondirected manner, the group is directed by the leader(s), using a structured experiential format, to foster quickly the development of a cohesive unit with a group goal of interpersonal concern and explicit investment of time and energy. Group experiences are then generalized to direct life experiences to help members transfer their group learnings to other meaningful segments of their lives.

While this article discusses the use of SET–R with a heterogeneous population, it is readily applicable to homogeneous groups of physically disabled or nondisabled persons. Such an application is possible considering that the SET model (Table 1) is not specifically bound to physically disabled or rehabilitation populations. However, it should be realized that not using a heterogeneous group results in a reduction of focus on the immediate issues of interpersonal stress and stigma.

Although the SET–R model has been used with physically disabled persons (Dell Orto et al., 1976) and variations of it with drug-abusing persons (Dell Orto, 1975), it can be applied to a variety of settings and populations. Its strong goal orientation and emphasis on mutuality provide a powerful tool for the practitioner interested in using a group format maximizing interpersonal growth and the development of skills.

REFERENCES

Anthony, W. A. The effect of contact on an individual's attitude toward disabled persons. *Rehabilitation Counseling Bulletin*, 1969, *12*, 168–171.

Anthony, W. A. Societal rehabilitation : Changing society's attitudes toward the physically and mentally disabled. *Rehabilitation Psychology*, 1972, *19*, 117–126.

Argyris, C. On the future of laboratory education. *Journal of Applied Behavioral Science*, 1967, *3*, 153–183.

Bach, G. R. *Intensive Group Psychotherapy*. New York : Ronald Press, 1954.

Bouchard, V. Hemiplegic exercise and discussion group. *The American Journal of Occupational Therapy*, 1972, *26*, 330–331.

Brondzel, R. Role playing as a training device in preparing multiple-handicapped youth for employment. *Group Psychotherapy*, 1963, *16*, 16–21.

Caldwell, H. and Leveque, K. Group psychotherapy in the management of hemophilia. *Psychological Reports*, 1974, *35*, 339–342.

Carkhuff, R. *Helping and Human Relations—Volume 1*. New York : Holt, Rinehart and Winston, 1969.

Cartwright, D. and Zander, A. *Group dynamics: Research and theory*. New York : Harper & Row, 1968.

Cook, D., Sleater, S., and Kunce, J. Encounter groups and rehabilitation. *The Journal of Applied Rehabilitation Counseling*, 1974, *4*, 157–163.

Dafflitti, J. and Weitz, G. W. Rehabilitation of the stroke patient through patient–family groups. *International Journal of Group Psychotherapy*, 1974, *24*, 323–332.

Dell Orto, A. E. Goal group therapy : A structured group experience applied to drug treatment and rehabilitation. *Journal of Psychedelic Drugs*, 1975, *7*, 363–371.

Dell Orto, A. E. Marinelli, R. P., and Lasky, R. G. *The Application of Structured Experiential Therapy (SET–R) to a Physically Disabled and Nondisabled Group.* Boston : Instructional Resource Center, Sargent College of Allied Health Professions, 1976. (Videotape Package).

Egan, G. Contracts in encounter group. In Pfeiffer and Jones (eds.). *The 1972 annual handbook for group facilitators.* La Jolla, Calif. : University Associates, 1972.

English, R. W. Correlates of stigma towards physically disabled persons. *Rehabilitation Research and Practice Review*, 1971, *2*, 1–18.

English, R. W. Correlates of stigma towards physically disabled persons. *Rehabilitation Research and Practice Review*, 1971, *2*, 19–28.

Farkas, A. and Shwachman, H. Psychological adaptation to chronic illness : A group discussion with cystic fibrosis patients. *American Journal of Orthopsychiatry*, 1973, *43*, 259–260.

Franzino, M., Green, J., and Meiman, G. Group discussion among the terminally ill. *International Journal of Group Psychotherapy*, 1976, *26*, 43–48.

Goffman, E. *Stigma.* Englewood Cliffs, N.J. : Prentice-Hall, 1963.

Goldman, H. Rehabilitation meets the encounter group. *Journal of Rehabilitation*, 1971, *37*, 42.

Heisler, V. Dynamic group psychotherapy with parents of cerebral palsied children. *Rehabilitation Literature*, 1974, *35*, 329–330.

Heller, V. Handicapped patients talk together. *American Journal of Nursing*, 1970, *70*, 332–335.

Henkle, C. Social group work as a treatment modality for hospitalized people with rheumatoid arthritis. *Rehabilitation Literature*, 1975, *36*, 334–341.

Hicks, J. and Wieder, D. The effects of integration group counseling on clients and parents in a vocational rehabilitation agency. *Rehabilitation Literature*, 1973, *34*, 358–368.

Hollon, T. Modified group therapy in the treatment of patients on chronic hemodialysis. *American Journal of Psychotherapy*, 1974, *26*, 501–510.

Kurtz, R. Structured experiences in groups. In J. Pfeiffer and J. Jones (eds.). *The 1975 Annual Handbook for Group Facilitators.* La Jolla, Calif. : University Associates, 1975.

Landau, M. Group psychotherapy with deaf retardates. *International Journal of Group Psychotherapy*, 1968, *18*, 345–351.

Lazarus, A. Behavior therapy in groups. In G. Gazda (ed.). *Basic*

Approaches to Group Psychotherapy and Group Counseling. Springfield, Ill. : Charles C. Thomas, 1968.

Lieberman, M. A., Yalom, I. D., and Miles, M. B. *Encounter Groups: First facts.* New York, Basic Books, 1973.

McClellan, M. S. Crisis groups in special care areas. *Nursing Clinics of North America,* 1972, *7,* 363–371.

Manaster, A. and Kucharis, S. Experiential methods in a group counseling program with blind children. *The New Outlook,* 1972, *66,* 15–19.

Manley, S. A definitive approach to groups. *Journal of Rehabilitation,* 1973, *39,* 38.

Marks, S. E. and Davis, W. L. The experiential learning model and its application to large groups. In J. Pfeiffer and J. Jones (eds.). *The 1975 Annual Handbook for Group Facilitators.* La Jolla, Calif. : University Associates, 1975.

Middleman, R. and Goldberg, G. The concept of structure in experiential learning. In Pfeiffer and Jones (eds.). *The 1972 Annual Handbook for Group Facilitators.* La Jolla, Calif. : University Associates, 1972.

Niewochner, G. The use of group methods in vocational rehabilitation : A review of the literature. *Rehabilitation Research and Practice Review,* 1971, *2,* 49–58.

Ohlsen, M. *Group Counseling.* New York : Holt, Rinehart and Winston, 1970.

Oradei, D. and Waite, N. Group psychotherapy with stroke patients during the immediate recovery phase. *American Journal of Orthopsychiatry,* 1974, *44,* 386–395.

Pfeiffer, J. W. and Jones, J. E. Design considerations in laboratory education. In J. Jones and J. W. Pfeiffer (eds.). *The 1973 Annual Handbook for Group Facilitators.* La Jolla, Calif. : University Associates, 1973.

Robinson, L. Group psychotherapy using manual communication. *Mental Hospital,* 1965, *16,* 24–26.

Rogers, C. R. *Carl Rogers on encounter groups.* New York : Harper and Row, 1970.

Rosenberg, B. Group vocational counseling in a rehabilitation center. *Journal of Rehabilitation,* 1956, *12,* 4–6.

Rusalem, H. Engineering changes in public attitudes toward a severely disabled group. *Journal of Rehabilitation,* 1967, *33,* 26–27.

Sarlin, M. and Altshuler, K. Group psychotherapy with deaf adolescents in a school setting. *International Journal of Group Psychotherapy,* 1968, *18,* 337–344.

Shaffer, J. and Galinsky, M. D. *Models of group therapy and sensitivity training.* Englewood Cliffs, N.J. : Prentice-Hall, 1974.

Shlensky, R. Issues raised in group process with blind pre-college students. *Adolescence,* 1972, *7,* 427–434.

Shontz, F. *The psychological aspects of physical illness and disability.* New York : Macmillan, 1975.

Stinson, M. Group communication for the deaf. *Volta Review,* 1972, *74,* 52–54.

Sussman, A. Group therapy with severely handicapped. *Journal of Rehabilitation,* 1975, *8,* 122–126.

Ullman, L. P. and Krasner, L. *Case studies in behavioral modification.* New York : Holt, Rinehart & Winston, 1965.

Walker, D. E. and Peiffer, H. C. The goals of counseling. *Journal of Counseling Psychology,* 1957, *3,* 204–209.

Westmen, W. A solid front : goal oriented counseling. *Journal of Rehabilitation,* 1974, *40,* 15–17.

Wilson, C., Muzekari, L., Schneps, S., and Wilson, D. Time-limited group counseling for chronic home hemodialysis patients. *Journal of Counseling Psychology,* 1974, *21,* 376–379.

Wilson, E. L. Group therapy experiences with eight physically disabled homebound students in a prevocational project. *Exceptional Children,* 1962, *29,* 164–169.

Wright, B. *Physical disability—A psychological approach.* New York : Harper & Row, 1960.

Yalom, I. *The theory and practice of group psychotherapy.* New York : Basic Books, 1975.

27

Milieu Therapy

Bernard Kutner

The disabled adult must thread his way through the immediate problems of survival and then must regain essential physical skills before attempting to reach the larger goal of resuming a role in life. These are formidable tasks. Not only are there overwhelming personal problems to be managed, but since roles depend upon the needs of society as well as the individual, there may be external blockades to readjustment. For instance, after treatment and retraining, the disabled individual may be denied employment (for which he is now once more suited) because of social rejection, ignorance, or prejudice on the part of prospective employers. Acquiring new roles, readapting old ones, and developing the social skills necessary to enter and manage them are tasks for which milieu therapy may offer one major solution. While exposure of a disabled person to a program of milieu therapy may never cause an employer to feel comfortable with a partially paralyzed person, an epileptic, or an amputee in his presence, the afflicted person, on the other hand, may be better prepared to deal with the prospective employer.

Role Disorders

Disability, among other things, impairs or otherwise seriously modifies previously existing roles to varying degrees : from minor change (i.e. full to part-time student or worker) to complete obliteration (i.e. bedbound patient, retired, recluse). These role damages may be directly attributable to an illness or injury resulting in disability (i.e. brain tumor, spinal cord injury, hemiplegia, etc.) or may be the consequences of changes to the

From *Journal of Rehabilitation*, March/April, 1968 (Vol. 34, No. 2) 14–17 Copyright © 1968 by the National Rehabilitation Association. Reprinted by permission of the author and Editor.

person and to his life circumstances occasioned by lengthy hospitalization, aging, and extended treatment programs. Hence, following a personal health catastrophe, the individual may stabilize finally in the role of invalid, or he may be semiretired or become a permanent resident of an institution.

In the diagnostic work-up and medical treatment plan of the recently disabled patient, it is rather rare to include a listing of the "role disorders" accompanying the illness or injury.[1] One almost never hears of social disarticulations, severed relationships, or fractured associations, but these may, in fact, be concomitants of the physical insult. They require not the cursory attention typically accorded them but specific and purposeful therapy. In a typical treatment milieu, the patient is "motivated" to become more active, he and his family are consulted about the problems of returning home, and he may also be counseled about possible employment. These approaches to the psychological and social aspects of rehabilitation usually involve individual conferences with social workers, vocational counselors, and psychologists. Occasionally, group therapy is employed as a central or secondary technique. Milieu therapy is relatively a newcomer to this field.

Definition

Since the meaning of milieu therapy has taken on such a variety of nuances,[2,3] we should like to make explicit our understanding of it. It is a theory of treatment and a body of associated methods in which the environmental or residential setting is utilized as a training ground for patients to exercise social and interpersonal skills and to test their ability to deal with both simple and complex problems commonly experienced in open society. The treatment program attempts to engage the patient in various social encounters with other patients, staff members, and administrative personnel. These encounters may be group or individual in nature and expose the patient to increasingly challenging problems, to provoke him into personal involvement with the issues at hand and to encourage him to struggle actively toward specified objectives. These experiences provide tests of judgment, of social competence, of problem solving ability, and of social responsibility. They are calculated to deal with a wide range of conditions aimed at significant, positive accomplishments. The therapy involved in this process consists both of the mobilization of the patient's efforts to become involved in the work of the milieu program and of engagement in the specific projects themselves. Hence, to help in presenting a list of grievances to an institution's administrators, a patient must first be up and about, dressed and fed, and prepared to act as a spokesman or committee member, etc. The management of the grievance procedure, its prior preparation, the follow-up of meetings, and so forth, constitute aspects of the work of patients in a milieu program.

To understand how milieu therapy may play a role in the overall therapeutic process, it might be helpful to conceive of the hospitalized, physically disabled patient in psychosocial terms. Looked at solely from a behavioral viewpoint, the patient may appear to the outside observer as a bed-ridden, indolent, dependent, incompetent, socially isolated individual living among strangers, eating unaccustomed food, sleeping and rising and retiring by a schedule not of his own choosing, often dressed in bedclothes, and submitting voluntrily to acts that may involve indecent exposure, inflicted pain, and even dangerous weapons. If his medical condition were of a comparatively minor nature, time-limited and rapidly healing, the individual would not ordinarily establish and retain new habits learned as a patient. When, however, the disabling condition involves a lengthy period of institutional care, the medical problem is serious, and residual malfunctions are involved, there is a greater likelihood that some patients will develop and continue hospital habits of living into their posthospital life. It is for those patients who will tend to adopt the role of chronic invalid—who will become socially isolated, indolent, unnecessarily unemployed or retired, and less than competent to deal with the everyday problems of living—that milieu therapy is most clearly intended.

One of the most deceptive aspects of hospital rehabilitation is the condition of the patient at the time of discharge. For the most part, professional staffs may be satisfied that the patient has attained maximum hospital benefits, i.e., that further treatment would yield little or no medical gain. But, following a strenuous effort to get him to the discharge plateau, there is strong likelihood that the patient may have "peaked out" prior to discharge. It is not surprising to find patients backsliding within a few months following discharge without benefit of supporting staff and hospital. Milieu therapy is also designed to help deter or avoid this common regressive change.

Weapons of Life

To accomplish its major therapeutic objective—helping to retain the benefits of rehabilitative care—milieu therapy must attempt to provide the patient with an arsenal of social skills to overcome frustration with enlightened self-interest and high morale. These "weapons of life" are necessary ingredients to prevent a tendency to capitulate easily in the face of rebuff or rejection, to avoid new and potentially risky social experiences, to become overdependent, and to reduce the utilization of skills learned in the hospital.

To restore the integrity of a set of adult roles following a massive physical insult which leaves serious or severe functional handicaps, specific role retaining methods are indicated. There are such concrete role difficulties as finding and holding employment, assuming normal household responsibilities, and resuming old friendships. Severe disability can, in fact, profoundly modify the individual's life to such an extent that a modified or an entirely new set of roles may emerge. A number of studies have been reported pointing to changes in self-image, negative attitudes toward disability, hypersensitivity, and social self-segregation following a personal disaster.[4,5,6] The traditional approach to this complex of problems has been to concentrate most therapeutic efforts on the restoration of physical functioning, in the anticipation that personal and social readjustments will flow more readily once physical integrity is restored. When difficulties of adjustment occur, social, psychological, and psychiatric services are invoked to help smooth over the rough periods. Milieu therapy, on the other hand, attacks the problem of adjustment to new roles by inducing the patient to adopt and test them as part of the treatment process.

Milieu therapy can be conducted either in the form of a therapeutic community, that is, in the social system within the institution, in which the patient participates as part of a democratically structured social order; or he may take part in a specially designed program within a conventional rehabilitation structure (sheltered workshop, halfway house, day hospital, clinic, or rehabilitation center). Fundamentally, the patient is given the opportunity to engage in activity that is functionally useful and to adopt a variety of testable social roles. These could include some of the following : patient government member and/or officer, committee member and/or officer, work associate, volunteer, nonprofessional assistant, housekeeper-homemaker, as well as such conventional roles as friend, neighbor, colleague, acquaintance, or roommate. The key factor in the role retaining process is the exercise of the role with some degree of professional supervision. The patient's performance is monitored by staff members, and his activities and progress are discussed both within group meetings as well as within patient-staff conferences. To create the opportunities for the conduct of such roles within a hospital, clinic, or other rehabilitation setting, it goes without saying that the organization itself must be geared to permit their free exercise. We cannot here go into the development of a milieu therapy program which others have well described.[2,3] However, some observations about such a program are in order.

Facilitating Environment

The attainment of new roles through the process of milieu therapy requires from several weeks to several months, depending upon the patient and the organizational structure. Patients with little or no experience in group activities, such as work in a voluntary organization or service on a committee, will require a considerable period of time to warm up and learn what is expected of them. Some patients require a period of time to allow themselves to be drawn into the core of a milieu therapy group. They may participate in only a peripheral manner. Some patients are so threatened by group meetings that they take part in the program only in carrying out group decisions rather than in their formulation. Still other patients need experience in overcoming the embarrassment of speaking in a group. A further difficulty is encountered in dealing man-to-man, on an equal-status basis, with staff members who may come from different social, educational, or cultural backgrounds. It may be necessary to hold instructional classes in public speaking to desensitize the individual by slow stages.

As to the contribution of the environment in the facilitation of developing new roles, one major factor is the provision of a wide latitude of permissiveness. The rehabilitation setting may have either the characteristics of the "total institution" or some degree of relaxation of typical institutional controls. The optimal setting for a milieu therapy program is one in which the senior management and staff members are fully cognizant of the need for achieving increasingly greater patient involvement in the group life of the organization. This may eventually lead to a role for patients in management itself. A rigidly structured hierarchy will make this type of involvement quite impossible. Our experience has pointed to the need for a professional interloper who assists patients to achieve status, gain intended goals, and experience the feeling of success, mediating between patient and administration.[7,8] Group social workers have filled this role, and they have helped promote a considerable measure of patient movement. Whether this would have been possible without the willing cooperation of unit directors and clinical chiefs is highly doubtful. The role of the group social worker in rehabilitation medicine is of prime importance, since the patient sees this person as a guide and model in his effort to affect his environment in some noticeable fashion. A repeated sense of achievement, despite the handicap, is a vital element in the social rehabilitation of the disabled person.

Overtraining

The conduct of a milieu therapy program probably has little chance of significant and lasting effect unless it is carried on with determination. In this respect, an important concept in such a program is that of *overtraining*, since both physical and social regression often occur following the completion of a source of conventional therapy.[9] The training of social skills in milieu therapy should lead to an *exaggeration* of role involvement within the institutional framework. Toward this end, the patient should be induced into activities that are *above and beyond* those he would normally enter in community and family life. It is hardly likely, for example, that a worker will soon find himself in face-to-face relationships with supervisory and managerial personnel after he leaves the program. Yet, such confrontations can aid him in meeting and dealing with bureaucracies with the degree of firmness and tolerance necessary to secure needed services.

Since he is almost certain to find himself in situations which require verbal skill, negotiating ability, and monumental patience, the milieu therapy program can increase his threshhold of frustration tolerance, reduce his sense of resignation, and reinforce an enlightened self-interest. While there is certainly no intention to match the individual's experiences in therapy with those he will most likely face in open society, the former contain myriad situations and conditions that would permit the individual to meet and joust with obstacles, barriers, impediments, and frustrations. Success and failure can be examined under the eyes of experienced professional observers, and the individual may thus gain from each such exposure.

There are some clinicians in the psychological, social work, and medical fields who believe that the listless and apathetic patients so frequently seen in rehabilitation settings, especially those with some degree of brain damage, cannot be expected to participate to any high level in environmental therapy. Listlessness, apathy, indifference, and resignation may all be characteristics of individuals who have suffered overwhelming personal reversals. Their social presentation and psychological distance may superficially lead one to the conclusion that little may be expected of them. One may conceive of these psychosocial reactions, however, as concomitants of the illness-disability syndrome, not necessarily intrinsic to the individual, but caused by a multiplicity of interacting personality and environmental factors. A second view of this problem is that the vigorous exercise of new role activities may be self-stimulating and have a cumulative effect. The adoption of one new role may lead to a second and to others in turn, setting off a return flow of other vital social and psychological functions.

The implication of the approach suggested here is that if milieu therapy is offered as part of a treatment plan, that it be a *mandatory* aspect of therapy. If the institution is tooled up to set such a program in operation, patients should be given no opportunity to back away. In the search for a new plateau on which life may be comfortably led, the patient may, with all due tender loving care, sink into abject dependency and chronic invalidism. Moreover, even the seemingly optimistic and enthusiastic patient may, upon repeated rebuffs in the posthospital world, throw in the sponge and regress into a narrow, circumscribed, custodial existence. It is for this reason that milieu therapy should be thought of as an attempt to provide the means for overcompensation on the part of the patient for the noxious circumstances of life that he almost certainly will meet.

Challenge to Administration

The therapeutic milieu in a rehabilitation unit will call for extremes of forbearance and fortitude on the part of both administration and staff. The activation of patients may touch off demands for the satisfaction of material wants and reforms of administrative practices. Patients may seek to shake off the conventional, administratively sound controls that ordinarily keep a large organization in efficient running condition. When they are encouraged to think out and then act upon decisions affecting their lives as patients, almost invariably the impact involves administrative change. The intrusion of patients into the area of administration is often looked upon as an invension of territorial rights that are the exclusive domain of the caretakers. To encourage patients in such endeavors would, on the surface, be only asking for trouble.

The poverty programs which require the representation of the poor on the boards of local organizations managing and dispensing federal funds have faced this same issue. Yet, it is absolutely essential that such participation be part of the program. While many patients will never again be involved in the inner operations of an institution nor sit with professionals and administrators in joint problem-solving meetings, such opportunities are offered in the process of milieu therapy so that significant and relevant involvement in meaningful issues is experienced. Here, the patient can take part, without cognizance of his handicap, in the planning and exercise of useful practices appropriate to institutional programs. The involvement of this patently less competent group in hospital affairs may lead to a degree of inefficiency, and even occasionally to a breakdown, in normal practices. In this case, however, the end would appear to justify the means, since the objective is to help the patient to test the *outside limits* of his capacity to deal effectively with his social environment. The patient as well as the hospital must bend strenuous efforts to maintain a high level of patient interest in the program. The failure of milieu therapy to produce significant effects may be attributed, at least to some extent, to the natural desire of hospital officials to "keep the lid on" and to prevent a patient take-over of what is conceived to be hospital responsibility.

Consider the situation of the patient who has been through such a test of endurance and strength as just described and now must face by himself the exigencies of life. Would he not be better prepared, in fact, to meet and deal with the obviously severe tests to which he will be subjected? The sobering experiences of coping with life problems in the hospital, in our view, will be at least comparable, if not in excess, of those likely to be encountered in the community. A tender, cautious hospital program of milieu therapy will provide little challenge. A tough, unrelenting program, on the other hand, should raise the individual's morale, strengthen his determination, and provide him with an additional measure of resourcefulness and those characteristics of socialization necessary to meet head-on the obligations of normal life. The inclusion of a vigorous program of milieu therapy could be a significant addition to the more conventional therapies available in rehabilitation services.

REFERENCES

1. Weissman, R. and Kutner, B. "Role disorders in extended hospitalization." *Hospital Administration,* vol. 12, no. 1 (Winter 1967).
2. Cumming, J. and Cumming, E. *Ego and Milieu.* New York : Atherton Press, 1962.
3. Stanton, A. and Schwartz, M. *The Mental Hospital.* New York : Basic Books, 1954.
4. Dembo, T., Leviton, G., and Wright, B. "Adjustment to misfortune : a problem of social psychological rehabilitation." *Artif. Limbs;* vol. 3, 1956.
5. Yuker, H. and Block, J. R. *A Scale to Measure Attitudes Toward Disabled Persons.* Human Resources Study No. 5, 1960. Human Resources Foundation, Division of Abilities, Inc., Albertson, New York.
6. Cogswell, B. "Self-socialization : readjustment of paraplegics to home and community." Paper presented at the National Rehabilitation Association national conference, Cleveland, Ohio, Oct. 3, 1967.
7. Lipton, H. and Malter, S. "The social worker as systems mediator on a paraplegic ward." Presented at the 94th annual forum, National Conference on Social Welfare, May, 1967.
8. Weinger, H. J. "The hospital, the ward, and the patient as clients : use of the group method." *Social Work,* vol. 4, no. 4, Oct. 1959.
9. Abramson, A. "The human community in the rehabilitation process." The Seventeenth John Stanley Coulter Memorial Lecture, presented at the annual meeting, American Congress of Rehabilitation Medicine, Miami Beach, Aug. 29, 1967.

28

Staff Expectations for Disabled Persons: Helpful or Harmful

Nancy Kerr

Becoming disabled and finding oneself in a wheelchair alters a person's life situation not only with respect to what he can or cannot do physically —which is often the major focus of rehabilitation personnel—but also with respect to social interactions with others. Of particular importance are the places, activities, and relationships that the disabled person is restricted or barred from entering.

The newly disabled person *knows*, phenomenologically, that he is the same person that he was before the injury to his body occurred. Yet, he is so frequently and persistently placed in inferior status positions by his professional "helpers" that, in time, he is coerced into wondering if he has become a different kind of person. The whole illness and disability experience places him in such new psychological situations where his customary behavior may stimulate responses so radically different from what he is accustomed to that he may often consciously or unconsciously question who he is, what roles are appropriate for him, and what he can expect to be able to do.

The earliest and possibly the critical answers to such identity and role questions come from the hospital or rehabilitation center's personnel in the everyday situations during treatment. In this paper, six pairs of situations drawn from personal experience suggest the implicit questions asked by patients and the subtle, often nonverbal, answers given by hospital and rehabilitation center staff members.

The first situation in each pair illustrates an answer that may lead a paraplegic patient to learn that the problem of adjustment to disability involves more than learning to get around on wheels: It makes explicit

From *Rehabilitation Counseling Bulletin, 14* (1970), 85–94. Copyright © 1970 by American Personnel and Guidance Association. Reprinted with permission of the publisher and author.

the probability that he may have to adjust to being a second-class citizen faced not only with physical obstacles but also with social devaluation. It teaches him that as society views him, he is no longer a responsible, employable adult but psychologically and sociologically a child. The answer given in the second situation in each pair of examples shows how a similar situation was handled in a way that told the patient that he was still a respectable and responsible human being.

I

Patient : Who am I ?

Staff I : *You are a second-class citizen.*

The submissive and devaluating aspects of the *role* of patient are so frequently accepted by both patient and staff that some curious phenomena become apparent only when a person in a wheelchair enters a medical institution as a professional. On countless occasions, I have been wheeling along in treatment settings in various parts of the country, attending to my business as a teacher, researcher, or clinical psychologist, when an attendant or nurse would hustle alongside and challengingly or sarcastically say, "Hey, where do you think you're going?" or sometimes "You're not supposed to be out here—go to your room." On one occasion, solely on the basis of my occupancy of a wheelchair, a nurse tried physically to put me to bed! More than once my wheelchair has been hijacked by an attendant who, without comment, wheeled me to the dining room of his institution.

Although I have no objection to consuming a free meal, in general, following one of the "You can't come in here" comments or "You must go there" actions, I tactfully explain my business. Invariably the response is, "Oh, I'm sorry, I thought you were a patient!" There is immediate recognition by the staff member that his behavior toward me was inappropriate. But there does not seem to be the slightest trace of awareness that the same ordering, grabbing, and shoving would be inappropriate even if I were a patient.

One is reminded of the unwritten rules of the army : "If it moves, salute it; if it's on the ground, pick it up; if it's a lineup, join it." The unwritten rule of perhaps too many rehabilitation personnel often seems to be "If *it's* in a wheelchair, *it* must be a patient—push *it* somewhere else."

Staff II : *You are a human being.*

In good rehabilitation centers, alternative kinds of behavior can be found among institutional personnel. I remember one attendant in particular who was named as "outstandingly helpful" by every person

I interviewed in a study on the meaning of help. Each day when the rest of the staff rushed out of the physical therapy room for a coffee break while leaving me stranded on a floor mat to rest, this gentleman would return to bring me a cup of hot coffee and a portion of whatever goodies were in the dining room. In general, when he had taken a person somewhere, he never failed to wait a moment to ask if there was anything else he could do. He always approached patients from the front where he could be seen (rather than suddenly grabbing their wheelchair from behind); and he asked, for example, if one was ready to go to dinner. He was the person who would stand by and give moral support when a frightened patient was supposed to be transferring into bed independently. (Few people realize that the space between a wheelchair and a bed can look as deep and forbidding as the Grand Canyon!) He was one of those rare people who had the sensitivity to handle hundreds of situations, big and little, in ways that were truly helpful from the patients' standpoint.

There was another attendant in the same institution who was liked by patients almost as well because he practiced the kinds of behavior just described, although his actions appeared to be somewhat less skillful and natural. When I asked him where he had learned to be so considerate, he replied that he had had a course for psychiatric attendants at Michael Reese Hospital in Chicago. When he came to a rehabilitation center, he was surprised to learn that disabled persons like to be treated as *people* just as psychotics do. His approach, however, was pragmatic rather than empathic. He had learned that if he told a patient he was going to be five minutes late; if he asked whether the patient was ready to go; if he chatted about the weather or the topics of the day; then, he found, the patients didn't gripe so much about matters over which he had no control and his job was much easier.

Apparently some people are naturally therapeutic in their relationships with patients, others can be educated to behave nicely and therapeutically even if it doesn't come naturally.

II

Patient :   How hard is it going to be to get around in a wheelchair? Can I really be independent?

Staff I :   *It is going to be very difficult indeed.*

I have a special problem with elevators. If I try to enter one of the elevators for "regular people," usually I am told that I must go to the patient's elevators somewhere in the rear since regular elevators are for regular people and not for wheelchairs or wheelchair people. (Comments, in this situation, about "the patient as nigger" are not appreciated.)

After finding the patient elevator, two potential problems remain : (a) If some observant soul discovers that I am not wearing pajamas or a hospital robe, I may not be allowed in *that* elevator either; (b) Some hospitals have a rule that all patients in transit must be accompanied at all times by an attendant.

Staff II : *You are a responsible person who is quite capable of getting around on your own.*

On the brighter side, some treatment centers have a system that allows mobile patients to go almost anywhere in or out of the institution if they leave a note at the nurses' station specifying where they can be found if needed and when they will return. In institutions using this system, usually, the patients are responsible also for getting thermselves to appointments and therapies on time.

III

Patient : Can a disabled person really go out and earn a living?

Staff I : *Probably not.*

One of the finest and most prestigious rehabilitation centers in the country has excellent ramps and bathroom facilities in all patient areas. The room used for professional meetings, however, can be reached only by a long stairway : There is no elevator. While the patients back on the wards are being told that they can enter or reenter the world of work, apparently no one ever expected that someone in a wheelchair might attend a professional meeting on rehabilitation. If rehabilitation centers contain impassable architectural barriers, how realistic is it to except that other settings will be accessible?

Staff II : *Sure. See for yourself.*

Another well-known rehabilitation center (a well-deserved pat on the back to William Spencer, M.D., and his staff at the Texas Institute for Rehabilitation and Research) employs disabled persons for responsible positions in the organization without discrimination. At one time the bookkeeper, head receptionist, head nurse, building manager, a physician, and many others did their jobs efficiently from wheelchairs. Some of them had extensive arm involvement as well as paraplegia, and some used breathing aids. However, there were no cosmetic criteria. All that was asked was that the person should do his job well. Equally important, there was no physical space in the entire center that was inaccessible by wheelchair. Of course, not every person with a disability can or should work in a rehabilitation center. But the high visibility of *some* workers with serious physical disabilities holding responsible positions and functioning well in them had striking effects on both patients and staff. No amount of reassuring verbalization alone could have yielded the same result. The whole story that employment was possible for the disabled was believed in that setting. And no one dared make impertinent remarks to a person occupying a wheelchair—he might turn out to be one's boss!

IV

Patient :   Do I have any control over my own fate, or am I just a body being run through the repair shop?

Staff I :   *Just put yourself in our hands. We know what's best for you.*

Frank Shontz reported on interesting research at APA a year or two ago in which he demonstrated that at the staff meeting where the patient supposedly participated in his own rehabilitation planning, the "team" did almost all the talking. The few remarks made by the patient were generally confined to "Yes, sir."

When patients inquire about why some therapeutic procedure is being employed, it is not uncommon for them to be told : "It's good for you," or "Doctor's orders."

It is quite possible that patients would be more cooperative and work harder in physical therapy, for example, if they had a very clear idea of what the exercises were intended to accomplish, if they knew *why* the pain should be endured, and if their agreement was solicited in advance. Does any wheelchair-loving paraplegic ever forget the battle over whether or not he was entitled to refuse to learn brace-walking?

Perhaps the most common way of telling the patient that he is a machine in the shop for repair is the habit some staffers have of communicating with the attendant pushing the wheelchair instead of with the patient himself. The patient thus finds himself sandwiched between two white coats with one asking the other, "Now, where does she go?"

Staff II :   *You are an active member of your rehabilitation team.*

I had a physical therapist who, while working within the framework of the medical prescription, let me make every decision possible concerning therapy. To be sure, the initial options were small, like which exercises we'd work on first, or which chair I'd learn to transfer into next. Later I was encouraged to make more crucial decisions such as whether it was more important to me—with my plans and obligations—to be a resident patient or a day patient.

V

Patient : Because I am dependent and must ask for help, am I an inferior or bad person?

Staff I : *You sure are!*

I can think of no single experience more humiliating than having an attendant complain about what a nuisance it is to have to turn you over in bed or give you a glass of water. And yet, the pecking order of most hospitals is such that the only safe way for an attendant to gripe about being overworked is to unleash his hostility on the patient.

Staff II : *We're here to help.*

There are true professionals in every occupation, i.e., people who do their jobs well and graciously even when they don't feel like it. The image they present is that they are pleased to be of service.

For three months following the onset of polio, I had been in intense pain that was relieved temporarily only by being repositioned. I had done battle with a nurse throughout each night about how often I could be turned over. Upon arriving at another hospital, I asked the attendant the first night what the schedule was for turning patients. She seemed surprised and said "There's no schedule. Whenever you feel uncomfortable, just press this button, and I'll be in. That's what I'm here for."

I said, "But ma'am—I'm *always* uncomfortable!"

"That's okay. We'll move you every five minutes if necessary." She fixed me up with the nine pillows I needed in those days. The next morning, when I awoke from my first night's sleep in three months, I discovered that the other 20 patients for whom she cared had had similar experiences.

VI

Patient : Sometimes I worry that being disabled is the same as being a child.

Staff I : *Right!*

Probably no one has ever survived extensive rehabilitation without undergoing one or more of the parties put on by some well-intentioned community group. On such occasions, appropriate patient behavior consists of smiling while someone places a party hat on your head, saying "thank-you" for the lollypop or other goody that traditionally is handed out, and applauding with some enthusiasm when the little darlings from Kook City's School of Elocution, Singing, and Dancing sing "Kookaberra." The consequences of declining to attend such an affair may range from mild reprimands for being uncooperative to a referral to the psychiatrist on suspicion of "situational depression."

Staff II : *You are an adult who happens to be in a wheelchair.*

Probably one good rule of thumb for any recreational therapist might be to ask whether a proposed party is something she herself would like to attend or if she would throw such a party for her own adult friends. In some degree, a seriously ill person may tend to become more egocentric in thought and childish in behavior, but these are transient responses to stress that should be extinguished.

There are many aspects of a patient's medical regimen in which it might be unrealistic to allow him complete freedom of choice. Other regions of the rehabilitation center, such as the recreational activities, for example, are not so circumscribed. The staff has the option of strengthening childish behavior by placing patients in childish situations, or they can use recreational activities, from the very beginning, to create situations that encourage mature freedom of choice, relearning or maintenance of "taking responsibility," and strengthening of the process of decision making.

DISCUSSION

Common questions asked by patients, consciously or unconsciously, have been outlined together with some positive and negative answers they receive from the behavior of the treatment staff in everyday situations. There are many more such questions often unverbalized or unperceived but which, nevertheless, may have marked effects on the rehabilitation process. Unfortunately, there is little objective evidence.

Although there have been a number of excellent descriptive reports of the mental hospital milieu by psychologists and sociologists who have entered such institutions posing as patients, there appear to be no similar participant studies of the social-psychological environment of hospitals or rehabilitation centers. Such studies are needed. Both formal research studies to provide "hard data" and informal participation to increase the understanding of staff would be valuable. The latter could be accomplished easily by any person working with the disabled simply by borrowing a wheelchair and moving into a center for a day, a week, or a month.

The following are obvious possibilities for needed research :

1. What is the nature of staff-patient interactions? In the light of our ignorance, descriptive and counting studies are of first importance, but ultimately such work must lead to the specification of the con-

ditions under which such interactions can become more positive and growth-inducing.

2. What is the social structure of the general hospital or the rehabilitation center? What are the realistic barriers that impede or frustrate patients' psychological progress? Considerable and instructive work along this line has been done for the mental hospital and the mentally ill. Similar studies of the physically ill and the disabled are desirable.

3. On a more limited basis, what can be done within one small aspect of an institution's structure to describe and modify the roles that patients play? In particular, attention might be paid to the restrictions on personal freedom, freedom to choose and select, and the reduced responsibility for one's own fate that seem inevitably to come with living in an institution. What can be done to increase the decision-making powers of the patient? Equally important are studies of patients who have accepted the patient role too well. Under what conditions can staff facilitate their relearning of the mature and responsible adult role?

4. The chronic problem patient who is perceived as too demanding and too dependent is an example of a specific research problem that can be studied independently of institutional structure. Often we jump to the conclusion that such a person has unmet dependence needs stemming from childhood experiences. That may be so. Systematic observation of the social-psychological situation, however, may suggest equally tenable explanations. For example, the patient may fear injury if he attempts new tasks or fear being left alone unaided in situations with which he cannot cope if he ever starts doing things for himself. Sometimes these fears actually may be reasonable; sometimes not. Under such beliefs, however, it is reasonable for the person to play it safe and to insist that someone else take responsibility.

Similarly, a patient may fear the loss of social contact. If the only way a patient obtains attention and social contact is to ask for something, it is predictable that patients will do a lot of asking.

Finally, the level of hostility between patients and staff may be an important variable. If patients and attendants are fighting, the demand "you are going to do this for me—or else" is one way for a patient to sustain his self-esteem, even if it is an unhealthy and less desirable way than some others.

It may be reasonable to start looking for unmet dependence needs only if it is certain that (a) the patient has reason to know that he will succeed in a task that is requested of him; (b) he is not afraid; (c) he is assured of social contact and appropriate attention even if he does take care of himself; and (d) he is not "mad" at anyone. No doubt there are some patients who demand that others do for them what they are well able to do for themselves. Even here, however, the problem is not how to classify them but how to create a therapeutic environment that will help resolve infantile problems.

In summary, the expectations of staff are helpful if they help the patient to gain or regain maturity and self-esteem. They hinder if they impede the patient's progress. *Help,* as Tamara Dembo has said, is whatever the person perceives as help. Such a definition is good to remember because it constantly leads us back to the patient with the simple question : "What can I do to help?" Lee Meyerson has described the ideal helper as being like the blockers on a football team who run interference, clear the paths, create the opportunities, and make it as easy as possible for the patient to take the ball and run with it. That, perhaps, is our major task as rehabilitation workers. It is the patient's ball game and by our appropriate or inappropriate expectations and behavior, we can help or we can hinder.

29

The Physically Disabled Client
and Facilitative Confrontation

William A. Anthony

A physically disabled individual encounters many adjustment problems
that are either precipitated by or complicated by the presence of a
physical handicap. Characteristically, an individual who has not made a
healthy psychological adjustment to his physical disability exhibits gross
inconsistencies and incongruities in his life. Often he has not honestly
confronted himself with the effects of his handicap in many important
areas of functioning, e.g., vocational planning, interpersonal relating, or
sex. The presence of a physical disability has exposed him to destructive
life experiences, which encourage him to develop incongruous feelings
concerning the effects of his disability on who he is and who he wants to
be, and between what he thinks and how he acts on these thoughts.

These incongruous feelings about himself and his disability have
readily apparent behavioral consequences. At a superficial level of awareness, a physically disabled person may deny any negative feelings due to
his disability, but his behavior and deeper feelings may indicate otherwise. Such behavior may be exemplified by—a young woman with a
slight hand deformity who will not participate in any activity which
necessitates the use of her involved hand—a woman with nerve deafness
whose feelings of self-disgust preclude her using the word *deaf*—a
cerebral palsied young man who vehemently states that he will under
no circumstances date a girl who has a physical disability—a college
student with a severe and irreparable speech defect who feels he must
become a preacher—a leg amputee who will never swim for fear of
someone seeing his stump.

The physically disabled person's incongruous feelings usually develop as a result of the contradictory feedback which he receives about himself from significant others, brief acquaintances, and society at large. Their inconsistent responses to the physically disabled individual prevent him from honestly facing his feelings about his intellect, physical capabilities, personality, and/or vocational future. Society's relegation of the physically disabled individual to minority group status often arouses in him unrealistic feelings of ineffectiveness and unworthiness. He is encouraged to act *as if* he were physically normal, yet he is constantly reminded of his disability by architectural barriers, sympathetic charity appeals, and special legislation and agencies for "the disabled." Also, because of his physical dependence on others, he may have to submit to the destructive questions and demands of individuals with whom he might otherwise never interact. His integrated feelings about who he is and what he can become are continuously challenged by his environment.

Male-female relationships are notorious examples of the type of experiences which foment incongruous feelings in the physically disabled person. For example : Out of distorted feelings of pity a girl may pay a great deal of attention to a physically handicapped boy. Responding to her attentiveness as a physically normal boy would, he may ask her out for a date, only to learn by her rebuff that her attentiveness to him has a significantly different meaning than her attentiveness toward a physically normal boy.

Similarly, research evidence has shown that when compared to physically normal children, physically handicapped adolescents are less effective in evaluating interpersonal relationships.[1] Such findings are certainly not surprising. Many important individuals in the physically disabled person's environment interact with him inconsistently—sometimes they respond to the individual himself, and at other times they respond only to his handicap. He is treated as if he were both competent and incompetent, beautiful and ugly, worthy and worthless. Too often the physically disabled individual incorporates as his own feelings the inappropriate and incompatible feelings which others have toward him. In so doing he precludes his own emotional integration.

Why a Dishonest Environment?

Goffman[2] has stated that when physically disabled and normal individuals interact conversationally ". . . these moments will be ones when the causes and effects of stigma must be directly confronted by both sides." Yet on many occasions this is exactly what does *not* happen. Too often the basic effects of the disabled person's handicap on the relationship are glossed over; perceived discrepancies in the physically disabled person's behavior are not articulated, and the interaction between the physically disabled and normal person sinks into mutual dishonesty.

A possible reason for this dishonesty may be attributed to the fact that the physically disabled person's problem is so frightfully real. Every physically normal individual is potentially a physically disabled individual. Unlike most people, the physically disabled person usually cannot hide his problem; it follows him, and the realness of his handicap and its consequences confront each physically normal individual who comes in close contact with him. The physically normal individual, to avoid facing his feelings aroused by the person with a disability, often sugarcoats the reality of the handicap, or perhaps ignores entirely its reality. This lack of honest interaction by the physically normal is often rationalized under the guise of easing the physically disabled individual's suffering. In actuality it may be prolonging the physically disabled person's pain by encouraging him to develop and maintain discrepancies between his real self and his ideal self, and between his thoughts and his behavior.

Treatment

The treatment of psychological problems has been most simply conceptualized as offering the client the inverse of his life experiences.[3] Typically, the counselor who treats the physically disabled client with psychological problems has been instructed to be empathic, warm, and genuine.[4] But the presence of these facilitative conditions is often not sufficient, because the presenting problem may be a result of more than just a previous absence of facilitative conditions. The physically disabled client's psychological difficulties may also be a product of his incongruous feelings which have been aroused by the inconsistent and dishonest responses of others to him, as well as the contradictory roles which society has required him to fill. The counselor, therefore, must be more than empathic, warm, and genuine. He must also be able to recognize and understand these inconsistent life experiences, so that he might confront his client with their incompatible emotional and behavioral consequences. The counselor's confrontation must be accomplished in such a way that the client directly experiences these discrepant feelings and is motivated to resolve them. Facilitative confrontation should play an important role in the treatment of the physically disabled client because the lack of confrontation probably contributed to his present psychological difficulties. Unfortunately, too little is known about the best methods of confronting a physically disabled individual.

Need for Research

Carkhuff and Berenson[5] have reported that counselors who function at high levels of facilitative conditions (counselors rated at level 3 or above on a 5-point rating scale) confront significantly more often and in a different manner than low-level counselors. Their research has suggested that high-level counselors differ from low-level counselors in that the high confront their clients more often with the client's assets than with his limitations, and that the high-level counselors' confrontations tend to increase rather than decrease their clients' level of self-exploration.

Although the manner in which rehabilitation counselors confront their physically disabled clients has as yet not been researched, the present author has measured the faculty and students' level of facilitative conditions in one established rehabilitation counselor training program.[6] In this program, the fourth-semester rehabilitation students were functioning at a significantly higher level of facilitative conditions than first-semester students, with the faculty falling in between the two groups of students and not significantly different from either. However, the fourth-semester students' level of functioning was approximately level 2, and although this is at a level commensurate with the graduates of other helping professions, it is less than a minimally facilitative level (defined as level 3 by the research scales).

By implication from the research studies indicating a positive relationship between the level of facilitative conditions and frequency of confrontation, it may be hypothesized that the students' and faculty's ability to confront a physically disabled client may also be limited. It may be that rehabilitation counselor training programs should place more emphasis not only on the acquisition of facilitative conditions,[7] but also on learning effective methods of confrontation. To accomplish this, more research is needed to determine the most facilitative ways of confronting the physically disabled client with psychological problems.

REFERENCES

1. Cruickshank, W. M. 1952. A study of the relation of physical disability to social adjustment. *American Journal of Occupational Therapy* 6 : 100–109.
2. Goffman, E. 1963. *Stigma*. Englewood Cliffs, N.J. : Prentice-Hall.
3. Carkhuff, R. R. 1967. Toward a comprehensive model of facilitative interpersonal processes. *Journal of Counseling Psychology* 14 : 67–72.
4. Moses, H. A. 1966. A rationale for providing counseling for handicapped students. *Journal of Rehabilitation* 32(6) : 14–15.
5. Carkhuff, R. R. and Berenson, B. G. 1967. *Beyond Counseling and Therapy*. New York : Holt, Rinehart & Winston.
6. Anthony, W. A. 1968. The effects of rehabilitation counselor training on attitudes toward the disabled and on the ability to communicate and discriminate the levels of facilitative conditions. Unpublished doctoral dissertation. State University of New York at Buffalo.

7. Patterson, C. H. 1967. The selection of counselors. Paper presented at the Conference on Research Problems in Counseling, Washington University, St. Louis, Missouri.

30

Issues in Overcoming Emotional Barriers to Adjustment in the Handicapped

Beatrice A. Wright

Four separate aspects of the question of removing barriers to emotional adjustment will be touched on in this paper. The first directly deals with the nature of adjustive attitudes on the part of the person with a disability. The second focuses on a basic difference between rehabilitation of persons with physical disabilities on the one hand, and of culturally and economically handicapped groups on the other, a difference involving special value considerations. The third refers to needed environmental accommodations. The fourth has special reference to the efforts of health and other agencies on behalf of handicapped persons.

Several guidelines to the development of healthy attitudes toward disablement have been differentiated (Dembo, Leviton, and Wright, 1956; Wright, 1960):

1. The first has been called *enlarging the scope of values.* This refers to the necessity, on the part of the person who has a disability, to extend his horizons beyond the disability and self. It implies that there are other values besides physique that are sufficiently attractive to excite the person's interest. It suggests for example that the person become interested in the sports and art world; in entertainment and recreation; in work, study, and play; in sharing with people and enjoying them; in community, national, and international events. Enlarging the scope of values implies that there are different ways to engage widened interests. Where one path is closed because of a disability, other paths adapted to the needs and abilities of the person can be found.

From *Rehabilitation Counseling Bulletin, 11* (1967), 53–59. Copyright © 1974 by American Personnel and Guidance Association. Reprinted with permission from the publisher and author.

2. The second guideline has been called *subordinating physique*. This means that other values should assume greater potency in the person's life than physique. It means that the person has to enhance such values as that of doing what one can, of understanding, of helping, of helping others, and so on, and not allow the importance of physique to override these values.

3. The third guideline is known as *containing disability effects*. It stresses the importance of preventing the spread of the limitations of a disability into nondisability-connected areas. This is particularly important in the case of a visible disability, where the tendency to perceive physical disability as involving mental and emotional disablement as well is so strong. Containment implies that more involved disablement need not be the case, that such spread often reflects unwarranted myths and stereotypes.

4. The last guideline is *upholding asset evaluation*. Within the framework of asset evaluation, not only is emphasis given to what the person can do, but the evaluation takes place in terms of the requirements of the situation rather than in terms of an inappropriate "normal" standard. Attention to what the person cannot do may also be appropriate to situational requirements, but the limitations do not thereby come to represent the essence of the person. Where comparative evaluation is evoked, on the other hand, the person is rank-ordered as "better" or "worse" than someone else, a judgment often leading to wider status connotations. The point to be stressed is that for most, although not all, situations in life, the appropriate principle is that of asset evaluation, a principle that will allow the person to make use of his abilities without being discredited by shame and inferiority resulting from unwarranted comparisons.

These four guidelines should support the development of maturity. In the event of disability (medical or socioeconomic), they should enable a person to view his disability as nondevaluating and to view himself as a person with a disability rather than as a disabled person. But, of course, they do not take place in a vacuum. Specification of important areas in which the words and deeds of society can promote or undermine them will shortly be considered.

In attempting to apply principles of rehabilitation to rehabilitation of the economically deprived (or culturally disadvantaged), a basic difference in the evaluation of disability on the one hand and poverty on the other has to be made clear. We speak of "acceptance of a disability," of "living with a disability," because a disability may be unremediable and because it is, ultimately, the lot of everyone who lives long enough. But we do not speak of "acceptance of poverty" or "living with poverty," because (or at least, when) the unremediability or inevitability of this condition is rejected. One needs to overcome poverty, not live with it.

When overcoming and eradicating a condition is the goal, symbols of that condition almost automatically are stigmatized. And yet, the question of the importance of viewing certain of those symbols as non-devaluating, or even as enabling and ennobling, is raised, just as in the case of disability. For example, in accepting blindness, one needs to view a white cane as a symbol, not of dependency, but of facilitating loco-motion, this being an intrinsically positive evaluation. We know that such positive evaluation must overcome the power of what has been called *spread*, a phenomenon in which association to a negatively evaluated trait tends to be regarded negatively. Thus it is that symbols of poverty also tend indiscriminately to be devaluated.

Consider the speech habits of a deprived people. The rich and complex language of the uneducated, or of the person in the ghetto, or of the poor, etc., could be positively appreciated, were it not inextricably a symbol of the poverty and discrimination that are so rejected. So it is that, in the attempt to overcome poverty, not only are environmental accommodations instituted in the form of head start and job training programs, but language training is also given to *replace* old speech habits. An alternative approach is the notion that the language of the favored group can be taught *without discrediting* the tongue of the ghetto or of the poor, much as one learns a foreign language without devaluating one's mother tongue. Respecting the language of the disadvantaged group helps the person extricating himself from his condition to preserve his own self-respect, for by rejecting the condition he is *not* thereby rejecting everything connected with it, including himself. The example of speech, of course, is used as representative of values at issue in rehabil-itation; i.e., what values to support and what values to reject are just as important in the rehabilitation of the culturally and economically handi-capped as in rehabilitation of the disabled.

Since the development of adjustive attitudes can be fostered by what the world permits the person to do, the need for environmental accommodations must be stressed. The following discussion, drawn from the field of rehabilitation of the physically disabled, may, with some modification, provide some valuable guidelines for programs designed to alleviate poverty.

That the architectural design of public buildings and their facilities should take into account the physical requirements of a wide variety of people is an especially clear example of the continuing need for environ-mental accommodations. Yet only a gesture in this direction is evident around us as one examines means of getting in and out of buildings, telephone booths, toilet facilities, etc.

Another vital application of the principle of environmental accom-modation involves the world of work. The need for reexamining job specifications to make certain that the basis for prescribing physical attributes is legitimate, rather than founded on myth and prejudice, remains imperative. Almost half a century ago, Henry Ford stated that "we are too ready to assume, without investigation, that the full possession of faculties is a condition requisite to the best performance of all jobs" (Ford and Crowther, 1926). We are still unnecessarily limiting job opportunities by such preconceived notions, in spite of the fact that research has shown that the physical capacities required for employees, as indicated in authoritative employment manuals such as those of the United States Civil Service and the United States Employment Service, are too often unnecessarily high in terms of what it actually takes to perform the job adequately, or in terms of what could be effected through simple and inexpensive modification of industrial equipment or work conditions, or both. A not unimportant by-product in some instances has been the benefit of such modifications to all workers.

The question as to who should pay for the cost of needed modifications is a practical one that could best be left to the economist. Income tax deduction for additional overhead on the part of business, as well as contributions from unions, business associations, and private agencies, are suggestive. Designing such accommodations into blueprints prior to construction is, of course, to be recommended, but remodeling as a consequence of wise hindsight should not be bypassed because of financial barriers. What can be afforded, be it by a family, an organization, a business, or a community, is as much—if not more—a function of values as of absolute costs.

When the principle of environmental accommodation is taken seriously, a wide variety of human activities come within its purview. One could add the need to review such public transportation facilities as taxicabs and buses to enable persons with special handicaps to use them. One could include recreation as an area where special arrangements, and sometimes even minor ones, could facilitate participation by persons with disabilities. Effecting appropriate environmental accommodations not only allows fuller participation in society's offerings, it also fosters a general attitude conducive to removing emotional barriers to adjustment of persons with disabilities. It implies recognition and acceptance by that society of the individual's needs, rather than rejection, fear, or indifference.

The notion that formal job qualifications may have little or no relation to actual job requirements is especially germane to problems of economically and culturally handicapped groups. One needs to question whether the required level of education or test score is in fact significantly related to job performance, and to discard such standards where the evidence is lacking. Where there is some justification for these standards, other ways of meeting them need to be considered, as for example, on-the-job training. This type of adaptation is similar, in principle, to the kinds of modification in equipment and work conditions proposed in the case of physical disability.

Equal in importance to environmental accommodations in the removal of barriers to emotional adjustment are attitudes of the nondisabled. Because agencies that work on behalf of persons with disabilities are concerned with public education and because, paradoxically, wrong messages from the point of view of psychological adjustment to disability are so often conveyed in their efforts, an attempt is made here to clarify a source of misconception.

It is proposed that the problems that define the situation of a person with a disability can be either viewed primarily in terms of their negative or tragic aspects, or primarily in terms of constructive possibilities through which the person can gain satisfactions. For brevity, we can say that educational materials may highlight the succumbing aspects of the situation on the one hand, or the *coping* aspects on the other.

Unfortunately, there are many instances in communication media for the public, where the emphasis is on the tragic lives of those with disabilities. This emphasis is based presumably upon the assumption that people will be stimulated by the emotions aroused, either to adopt precautionary health measures to avoid such a calamity, or to contribute time, money, and effort on behalf of the disabled group. Experimental evidence clearly challenges the first assumption. In one study, for example, a strong fear appeal, where the horrors of neglect were emphasized to get people to brush their teeth and visit their dentist, proved to be less effective in producing conformity to recommended protective actions than a minimal appeal that presented relatively matter-of-fact information concerning the functions of teeth and their care, and that rarely referred to the unpleasant consequences of improper dental hygiene (Janis and Feshbach, 1953). With respect to the second assumption, namely, that by emphasizing catastrophic effects people will be stimulated to give, there is no experimental evidence in support or refutation, as far as I know, although there undoubtedly is a large body of accumulated experience. Aside from the issue of monetary return, we can legitimately question the effects of such an emphasis on the attitudes and feelings of the person with the disability, his family, and the broader society.

Three specific examples of the kind of message being questioned will point up the issue. The first is aimed at arousing the public to become inoculated against polio. A cartoon, selected for a Pulitzer award, portrays a small boy on crutches watching wistfully from the sidelines, while other children are vigorously playing football. This cartoon may arouse maudlin sentimentality, pity, and perhaps guilt, but what is being questioned is whether it contributes to the development of adjustive attitudes and constructive action. Portraying the succumbing aspects reinforces the myth that a person with a disability does, in fact, as an overriding characteristic of his life, stand on the sidelines, submerged in the suffering of frustration and rejection. Is this really the fate of a child with polio? Are we lying when we tell parents that the child with crippled legs can participate in sports, can play with nonhandicapped children, can have happy times, even though he will know the suffering of frustration and rejection?

The second example is also aimed at motivating the public to adopt prophylactic measures, in this case against blindness. It depicts a blind man, with tin cup and white cane, shuffling along a city sidewalk. A sign on his back says, "My days are darker than your nights." Beneath the picture appears the caption, "Just be thankful you can have your eyes examined every year or so." What is accomplished by such a communication? We have already referred to evidence that strong fear arousal may serve as a counterforce to constructive action. But what is almost certainly accomplished is reinforcing the view that blindness means the ultimate in despair. The white cane, instead of being regarded as a symbol of trying to cope effectively with the problems presented by blindness, is coupled with the tin cup as a sign of inevitable dependency on the charity of others. Would the agency fostering this public education appeal also submit it to the visually handicapped and their families? The judgment that doing so would ill serve such an audience, it is suggested, provides an excellent criterion for discarding any public communication, for the query sensitizes one to those cognitive and emotional aspects that undermine the adjustment process.

The third example is directly aimed at fund raising on behalf of persons with epilepsy. One leaflet depicts two dejected children, heads bowed and alone. They are introduced by the caption, "Another Tragic Victim of Rejection" and referred to as "*the rejected*." The accompanying text reiterates this aspect of the lot of the epileptic by adding : "There are thousands of boys and girls in this country who are rejected every day . . . rejected by playmates . . . rejected by neighbors . . . rejected by schools. They look forward only to a future of continued rejection."

Might it not be psychologically more sound to present matter-of-fact information about the neurological disorder as such and to leave the affective overtones for constructive efforts on the part of both the person with epilepsy and those who help him? The child could be depicted in the classroom learning with others, on the field playing with others, for these are realities, too, and the call could be for contributions for medical care and other rehabilitation services that would spread these realities still further. Could not people be aroused to contribute their resources by pointing out the need for special education and vocational rehabilitation, the need for research to ameliorate and prevent the condition, etc.? Such an approach casts the very real and difficult problems imposed by epilepsy within a positive framework rather than one that reinforces the maladaptive equation between disability and tragedy. But, one can ask, will emphasis on the coping aspects of disability problems yield as much monetary response in fund-raising campaigns as emphasis on the succumbing aspects? Until systematic research is forthcoming, we do not know, but we can say that educating the public toward maladaptive attitudes toward disability is in any case too big a price.

Despite the basic differences between disability and poverty, both are often presented in fearful and stigmatizing terms. Some appeals for support of "anti-poverty" programs rely primarily on fear, e.g., depicting the horrors of juvenile crime as a consequence of nonsupport of programs, Other appeals present in maudlin and sentimental terms the dire consequences of poverty. It is suggested that these approaches do not serve the needs of the poor any better than they do the needs of the disabled. Instead, the strengthening power of viewing the problems of poverty constructively, in terms of steps to overcome them, is advocated. The danger of the succumbing approach, in which fear and pity are highlighted, is that it stimulates rejection of the poor, rather than rejection of poverty.

The foregoing has sketched out some issues and principles involved in assessing efforts on behalf of handicapped groups, whether the handicap resides in physical, cultural, or economic factors. They deserve a hard look, for the difficult job of rehabilitation ought not be made more difficult by the neglect of important environmental accommodations or by the communication of wrong messages in the very process of promoting rehabilitation programs.

REFERENCES

Dembo, T., Leviton, G. L., and Wright, B. A. Adjustment to misfortune —a problem of social psychological rehabilitation. *Artificial Limbs,* 1956, 3(2), 4–62.

Ford, H. (in collaboration with S. Crowther). *My Life and Work.* New York: Doubleday, 1926.

Janis, I. L. and Feshbach, S. The effects of fear-arousing communications. *Journal of Abnormal and Social Psychology,* 1953, 48, 78–92.

Wright, B. A. *Physical Disability—A Psychological Approach.* New York: Harper & Row, 1960.

31

Counseling with the Severely Handicapped: Encounter and Commitment

William Kir-Stimon

For the past several years I have been working with severe physical handicaps such as multiple sclerosis, the various central nervous system disorders, crippling arthritis, multiple amputations, cerebrovascular accidents (that is, "stroke" cases), and quadriplegia and paraplegia (spinal cord injuries resulting in relatively complete paralysis from the neck down or from mid thorax). These can run the gamut from the totally and permanently disabling to the moderately crippling in effect. One might distinguish between the more obvious handicap (loss of limb) and the hidden conditions (cardiac disability, diabetes), between those of sudden onset (disabling fracture of an ankle) and those that have run a course through the years (cerebral palsy or post polio). For our purposes, however, any such severely damaging condition that affects basic self-concept can be considered illustrative.

There is, among these people, a deep sense of being forlorn, alienated from the rest of the world. The individual is hemmed in physically, usually more than he has ever been in his entire life, a hemming in from which he knows he cannot be extricated. His situation is irrevocable. And for the most part, he can no longer express himself in any significant physical movement; he can vent energy through talk, mentation, or feeling, or at best throw a light ash tray at his therapist—provided even this does not set him off balance physically.

In my experience it is not the specific nature of the disease entity itself that is important, but the way in which it has changed or affected the patient's relationship to himself and his world. Nor is the past itself significant except insofar as it helps us and him to understand what he

From *Psychotherapy: Theory, Research and Practice*, 7 (1970), 70–74. Copyright © 1970 by Division of Psychotherapy, American Psychological Association. Reprinted by permission of the editor and author.

is like now, how he has changed, and where he stands in this point in the process of reintegrating his personality. I am impressed in our attempts to rehabilitate or physically upgrade these patients by the transitional elements in the process itself, the importance of assessing periodically where the patient is at any one moment.

Our job in counseling is to help the patient become what he already is and must be, in the real sense of being, to help him see himself in his situation and move on from his fear of the nothingness he sees himself in or approaching. For the disabled the question is clearly not one of being one's self but of being one's self in a world of animate existence among others who are functioning, developing, being. For these handicapped people find themselves literally in their own eyes as nobodies—doing nothing, being nothing.

I asked a fifty-year-old arthritic who after treatment is able to walk, use his hands, drive a car, even handle a selective job: "How old do you feel?" and he answers truthfully, for him, "I feel 90"—because he is not what he thinks he was before. Therefore, he is nothing, does nothing, is not even betwixt and between.

A quadriplegic boy of twenty-three, who can barely lift a finger and flip a switch on an electric-powered wheelchair, insists on the career of football coach he had once envisioned for himself. He waits return of physical functions that will almost certainly never come back.

A famous musician has a stroke and can no longer play his instrument; he sees his life as over and wants to end it even more quickly, because he sees himself as already dead in any case.

A diabetic girl, who has lost one leg and is about to lose her eyesight, cannot accept living as a blind person, denies there is any visual impairment, and holds on to her past as if it were actually present; she does not perceive the present at all, and is even unconcerned over the two small children she has left home.

Disablement especially is a time for reassessment, for personal rediscovery. When the individual is able to recognize again his own self-worth in the scheme of things and realizes also the worth of the scheme of things in himself, he is in effect no longer disabled.

I would theorize that in this process the disabled person fears "being found out" and recognized as wanting. He seeks absolution from the debt of living for himself by using some of the typical psychological devices we knew so well—denial, withdrawal, projection, etc. In many ways he exhibits a sense of owing something, not of being due something; he is guilty over his own difference, the stigma of being disabled.

The openly aggressive, even the hostile, patient frequently offers a better rehabilitation risk clinically than those disabled who are passive or lack a sense of self-respect or of personal adequacy. To be demanding in a realistic social sense (rather than neurotically so) means to possess a sense of one's rights as a human being. The more "selfish," the more self-centered, are to a degree more self-respecting and have a feeling of personal integrity, of deserving something better, and are often willing to work for it. In the other hand, there are those who all their lives have been awaiting their eventual disability or the fulfillment of their own death; these persons work in many ways toward their own destruction. In fact, attempting to "move" such a person posttrauma to a preexisting equilibrium, unless accomplished quite early in the rehabilitation process, can result in extreme negativism or, if pushed enough, into a severe regression.

We who continue to work with the maimed—maimed in body and in mind—have a responsibility not to triply maim—by crippling the spirit. Counseling is seldom a "safe," stabilized relationship. Between client and counselor, patient and therapist, there stirs from moment to moment a whole world of changing meaning.

An integral factor here may well be the paradoxical need for an admission of self-ness, of differentness, on the part of the "therapist" and a loosening of the boundary between counselor and counselee. Such personal commitment may well make for awareness, and awareness itself—as Keats implied—changes reality. ". . . He who saddens/ At thought of idleness cannot be idle,/ And he's awake who thinks himself asleep."

We, patient and counselor, are each in a triple role—play actor, playwright, and audience at the same time. We act "as though" we were something or somebody, we become "as if" we were an entity—a job, a thing. We play a role written by and for ourselves. I am reminded at this point of Eugene O'Neill's *Strange Interlude* in which the characters on stage stand silent and immobile as the sole existence centers about the speaker in his soliloquy. The severely disabled in the process of reintegration are in a sense similarly physically immobile and emotionally so, powerless, with a feeling of being moved rather than moving.

The emotional rehabilitation process can be thought of in terms of a paradigm, something like this, where the patient says to himself:

Who am I?
I am different than I was.
I don't like me.
Nobody likes me.
I am not worthwhile.
Perhaps I was never worthwhile.
Who was I?
I have no real identity anymore.
I have changed. Nothing is the same as before.
My friends, my family, the world about me has changed.
I am lost.

From here hopefully he might go on as follows:

> I am the same as I was before.
> I have not really changed and the world is the same.
> If it's a mess of a world now, the world was actually the same before. Only I didn't see it.
> I was a fool, an immature child.
> It's all pretty absurd and in a sense amusing.
> Let me confront reality as it is, was, and will be.
> Let me confront myself as I was, am, will be.
> It's all right that I am what I am.
> It doesn't really matter who I am—I may never know anyway.
> Life keeps changing and so do I.
> What matters is where am I now? what am I doing? how can I live? where do I go from here?

In all of this we ask of ourselves and the patient the following: (1) How much loss of function has he actually sustained? Can he look at the world directly face-to-face, even for brief periods? (For example, on tilt table or electric bed?) Is he completely wheelchair-bound, or can he do limited ambulation in the parallel bars? Can he use fingers, hands, wrists? Does he have bowel, bladder, sexual control and feeling? Is he completely bed-fast or on a cart—looking at the world (the ceiling) from a flaccid horizontal position? That is, how much closer to nonbeing, how much closer to death does he see himself? (2) How much magical control has he assumed over his own body? What degree of defensiveness and emotional "invulnerability"? Where is he in the process of assuming himself-in-the-world? (3) Where is he now in relation to his own sense of time in his own life cycle? At what point did he begin to exist individually? Is he ready to experience himself at all? Or is he content with the become, stultified by his present?

We can only take off on the patient's lead. The decisions of any particular moment are his to make, unless it is literally a matter of immediate life and death. There are parallels here, I am sure, for the so-called "normal." Let me recount here a number of fallacies in our working through some of these basic problems with the patient, fallacies on both our part and that of the patient himself.

For the patient:

1. That his life is over. That the moment passed is *the* important one. The fact is, it is probably still to begin. This may not be a matter of reinstitution or reinvestment emotionally, but, if he is not to regress, of a new birth, so to speak. He must learn to exist—perhaps even to breathe differently (through a metal tube, e.g., in the trachea).

2. That he is overly concerned with himself. He is probably not actually concerned enough, is feeling guilty and likely to be distrustful of himself-in-the-eyes-of-others. This is inherent in his distortion of subject-object relations, brought on, or heightened by, his "being different," by his being looked at or upon.

3. That he will be absolved of responsibility because he is ill or an invalid. In this sense he is overwhelmed and immobilized by what he conceives as his situation and responds with "la belle indifférence" that frequently mocks the reactions of a psychopath or sociopath.

4. That he wants to be "normal." For the disabled person with a disturbance in the realm of identity or self-concept, the desire for normalcy is tantamount to the wish for self-dissolution, for losing oneself literally in being another. In this respect, as disabled as he is, he must work through his responsibility for narrowing his own life potentials at this point, for saying in effect "I don't want to be me, I want to be nobody."

5. That he must be either nobody or somebody worthwhile. In this either/or situation in which the severely disabled frequently finds himself, he fails to realize that he is important simply because he exists, despite societal standards of productivity—creation, invention, even procreation. For the severely handicapped person who is labeled totally and permanently disabled and considered unable to earn his own livelihood, this becomes a distinction between being and not being. Personal unproductivity in our society is literally "un-becoming." Whereas, as a matter of fact, personal creativity need not involve a product or an object but might relate more to the very craft of living. This is where such seemingly divergent philosophies as Zen Buddhism, Existentialism, and even Judaism would seem to merge.

For the counselor-therapist some of the fallacies and their implications are these:

1. That one must get the patient well. As a matter of fact, one can only act as guide, mentor, midwife, and, as in any educational endeavor, can only expose another to learning, perhaps attempt to protect him against major hazards. To do otherwise would be to assume the patient's role, to attempt to recreate the other in one's own image, both dangerous and presumptuous. My role as counselor might be conceived as helping the patient to *want* to get well, to help him "get off the fence" so to speak, with an emphasis on doing, acting, and reacting to experience, living spontaneously rather than Hamlet-fashion. We are talking here about his investment in life, his relationship to pain, to waking and sleeping, his available energy for any movement within the rehabilitation process.

2. That the patient be treated as a "sick" person. While in some cases

this may be so where the patient's own life or that of others is at stake, for the most part the individual must be given an opportunity to feel responsible not only for himself but given an opportunity to become aware of his responsibility for others as well. Only in this way can he come to grips with his anxiety and sense of alienation. (This in turn arises in large part from the problem of dual identity : subject-object, doer-thinker, self-other. This is the same insoluble problem in the dualism faced by contemporary physical and biological sciences in their concern over the matter-energy, mind-body problem.)

3. That the patient be made to accept his *future* realistically and his physical limitations. What is important is that he *accept his present more fully*, that he learn to exist without either a *carpe diem* escapist running from or a destructive lashing out. The therapist too, must accept his patient's decision, as long as the latter retains his own self-respect without paralyzing anxiety. He need not find the magic exit for his patient's dilemma. There is no magic in these cases, and the dilemma is part and parcel of his quest—and the counselor's. By attempting to do what he considers good he may be unwittingly creating the reverse.

4. That the therapist act primarily as a scientist, working from cause to effect, according to the maxims of his own particular theory. It is more important—certainly in dealing with the disabled, who are far from complete persons—that the patient learn to know him as a fallible, sometimes incomplete human being—neither as an idol nor in a highly personal intimate sense, since both detract from the naturalness of their relationship. If the patient is to avoid being amorphous, the counselor perhaps should also refrain from being amorphous. This does not change his alter ego status but makes of the therapeutic situation a reciprocal rather than a unilateral affair. He must go beyond the fiction of technology and supposed fact as ultimate truth, beyond tests and test results. Only in the moments where intellect and feeling are beyond symbol can life be experienced per se. This can be "thinking with the belly" or "feeling with the mind," as it has been aptly put.

5. That he is at any time dealing with ultimates, with blacks and whites. In working with the severely handicapped, where the medical picture often appears so clearly delineated, we are forever dealing with the greys. Every situation is a field of forces and has a permeable border. The counselor must beware of narrowing not only his own outlook but that of his patient in the process. Treatment is always a "brink" situation, a risk situation. He and the patient may at times reach a point where the distinction between self and world, knower and known, feeler and felt, grow more and more

indistinct. It must be remembered that the world of reality for the severely disabled is in any case a rather nebulous one.

6. That illusion and dream are harmful. One must have the courage to dream, to believe in one's dream, to go beyond what the conformist world would consider reality, to find in a sense one's own reality. This I see as important for both counselor and patient. For the severely disabled, fitting one's particular illusion into the needs of the workaday socioeconomic world is frequently an impossibility. This is where the sheltered shop, the half-way house, and similar devices have real meaning. They lend a flavoring of reality to a restricted kind of existence. However, let us not confuse dream and illusion with hallucination. The man with a bilateral hip disarticulation as the result of an accident who is now walking with crutches and artificial legs and who works and drives his own car and supports his own family is a reality. So too is the quadriplegic who is getting his degree in law or the severely handicapped post-polio working as a typist-receptionist in a living-in situation. So, too, unfortunately, is the paraplegic who committed suicide because his particular illusion had little basis in the world outside himself.

Because of the seriousness of the situations in which the disabled find themselves, the counselor's task becomes at the same time both more vague and more definite. Where patient limitations are so clear-cut and the emotional involvement so total, communication between therapist and counselee must be on a one-to-one level, and not as able-bodied to disabled, or doctor to patient. The encounter is one in an existential sense between one human being and another, with commitment on both sides. We risk failure when we hold off and relate as I-to-It rather than I-to-Thou. The patient fears being untapped and facing the pain he may have fought all his life to avoid. What do we fear in our relationship with him? How free the patient becomes to release and handle his suffering will depend in great part on how free we feel to work with him. Let each one of us be as circumspect as he needs be, in the light of his own limitations.

> "In each hour the human race begins . . .
> To keep the pain awake, to waken the desire . . .
> (that is) the first task of the genuine educator of our time."

APPENDIX A

Significant Books Related to the Psychological and Social Impact of Physical Disability

The following books are significant contributions to the understanding of the psychological and social impact of physical disability. The organization of this listing is based on date of publication, with newer books listed first.

The Psychological Aspects of Physical Illness and Disability by Franklin C. Shontz, published by Macmillan Publishing Company, New York, in 1975.

This book touches upon a variety of psychological problems related to sickness and disability.—When is a person sick? How do people adapt to illness and disability and the accompanying stress? What role do the treatment facilities play in the psychological adjustment of their patients and clients?—The emphasis throughout the book is upon the treatment of the patient as a personal entity worthy of individual attention and respect.

Medical and Psychological Aspects of Disability edited by A. Beatrix Cobb, published by Charles C. Thomas, Springfield, Illinois, in 1973.

The purpose of this book is to transmit pertinent medical and psychosocial concepts surrounding common disabilities, with which the rehabilitation counselor must work. It is a collection of 16 originally written chapters by psychologists, physicians, and educators who brought together medical, psychological, educational, and rehabilitation factors related to individual disabling conditions.

Rehabilitation Practices with the Physically Disabled, edited by James Garrett and Edna Levine, published by Columbia University Press, New York, in 1973.

This book is divided into three sections : The Rehabilitation Scene,

The Disabilities, and The International Scene. Thirteen of sixteen originally written articles focus upon individual disabling conditions and their implications for medical and rehabilitation practice. Two articles introduce the reader to rehabilitation as it is practiced in the United States and to consumer issues. One article is devoted to international rehabilitation. This book is an excellent source of practical information about specific disabling conditions.

The Social Psychology and Sociology of Disability and Rehabilitation by Constantina Safilios-Rothschild, published by Random House, New York, in 1970.

A provocative, thorough description of the organizational and behavioral manifestations of physical disability and the challenges that they pose to sociological and psychological inquiry. This book represents a complete survey of the theoretical and empirical implications that disability and rehabilitation pose to sociology and social psychology.

Loss and Grief: Psychological Management in Medical Practice, edited by Bernard Schoenberg and Associates, published by the Columbia University Press, New York, in 1970.

This book defines concepts and practices for professionals who handle matters related to loss and grief. It deals with the psychological aspects of loss as a result of physical illness and disability as well as a result of death. It consists of 26 originally written chapters broken down into five sections: Psychological Concepts Central to Loss and Grief; Loss and Grief in Childhood; Reaction to the Management of Partial Loss; the Dying Patient; and Humanistic and Biologic Concepts Regarding Loss and Grief.

Physical Disability and Human Behavior by James McDaniel, published by Pergamon Press, New York, in 1969.

Pertinent theory and research as they apply to psychology and physical disability are presented in this book. It provides compact, comprehensive summaries of theoretical positions, in a manner that is understandable to practitioners and college students.

Physical Disability—A Psychological Approach, by Beatrice Wright, published by Harper & Row, New York, in 1960.

Relating physical disability to psychology, this book provides the reader with conceptual understanding and practical information regarding the impact of disability. The wealth of concrete examples and nontechnical language make this book of value to a wide range of readers, both professional and nonprofessional.

A Man's Stature by Henry Viscardi, published by the John Day Company, New York, in 1952.

Probably the best of the books discussing personal accounts of disability, *A Man's Stature* presents Henry Viscardi who, although born with underdeveloped legs, overcame his disability and succeeded in helping people with a disability and opening society's eyes to others who have suffered disability. "Must" reading for those who plan to work with disabled people.

Journal of Social Issues, All of Volume 4, published in 1948.

Although not a book, this entire issue, devoted to the theoretical, cultural, and practical problems that physically disabled persons have in society, is of such relevance that it must be considered a significant contribution to the field of physical disability. Solutions to employment and other social problems discussed in that issue are finally being realized.

APPENDIX B

Significant Journals Related to the Psychological and Social Impact of Physical Disability

The Journal of Applied Rehabilitation Counseling is a quarterly journal published by the National Rehabilitation Counseling Association, 1522 K Street, N. W., Washington, D.C. 20005.

This journal is concerned with issues of importance to the practicing rehabilitation worker, particularly the rehabilitation counselor. The focus is upon implications for practice with a de-emphasis of technical and research issues.

Journal of Chronic Diseases is published monthly by Pergamon Press, Maxwell House, Fairview Park, Elmsford, New York 10523.

This journal is concerned with various phases of chronic illness for all age groups, including long-term medical and nursing care, impact of chronically ill on the community, and rehabilitation needs.

The Journal of Physical Medicine and Rehabilitation is a monthly professional journal published by the American Congress of Rehabilitation Medicine and the American Academy of Physical Medicine and Rehabilitation, 30 N. Michigan Avenue, Chicago, Illinois 60602.

This journal focuses upon the field of physical medicine and rehabilitation. Articles include medical, psychological, and social issues as they relate to physical medicine and rehabilitation.

Journal of Rehabilitation is a semi-monthly professional magazine published by the National Rehabilitation Association, 1522 K Street, N.W., Washington, D.C. 20005.

The journal is concerned with the rehabilitation field in general. Articles cover a broad expanse of interests and are usually nontechnical and nonresearch in nature.

Psychosomatics is a quarterly international journal published by the Academy of Psychosomatic Medicine, 922 Springfield Avenue, Irvington, New Jersey 07111.

This journal explores the role of emotional factors in the daily practice of comprehensive medicine.

Psychosomatic Medicine is a semi-monthly journal published by the American Psychosomatic Society, 265 Nassau Road, Roosevelt, New York 11575.

This journal is concerned with fostering knowledge concerning psychosomatic problems.

The Rehabilitation Counseling Bulletin is a quarterly journal published by the American Rehabilitation Counseling Association, 1607 New Hampshire Avenue, N.W., Washington, D.C. 20009.

This journal focuses upon articles illuminating theory and practice and exploring innovations in the field of rehabilitation counseling. It contains a substantial proportion of articles related to psychological issues in disability.

Rehabilitation Literature is a monthly journal published by the National Easter Seal Society of Crippled Children and Adults, 2023 W. Ogden Avenue, Chicago, Illinois 60612.

This journal is intended for use by professional personnel in all disciplines concerned with rehabilitation of the handicapped. The Article of the Month provides an in-depth analysis of a selected rehabilitation issue, while reviews of books and articles allow readers to remain current regarding rehabilitation.

Rehabilitation Psychology is published by the Rehabilitation Psychology Division of the American Psychological Association, 1200 Seventeenth Street, N.W., Washington, D.C. 20036.

It publishes original investigations, theoretical papers, and evaluating reviews relating to the psychological aspects of illness, disability, retardation, and deprivation.

APPENDIX C

Organizations Serving the Physically Handicapped

Alexander Graham Bell
Association for the Deaf
3417 Volta Place, N.W.
Washington D.C. 20007
(202)337–5220

Organization and purpose

The Alexander Graham Bell Association for the Deaf is an international organization, founded in 1890, whose goal is to foster supportive environments and programs directed to the preparation of the hearing-impaired child and adult to participate independently in the life of his family, community, and country. The Association provides information services for parents, educators, libraries, hospitals, and clinics, physicians, nurses, students, and others interested in the hearing-impaired. It also maintains a specialized library of hearing and speech containing over 20,000 volumes and extensive clipping and pamphlet files.

American Cancer Society, Inc.
219 East 42nd Street
New York, NY 10017
(212)867–3700

Based on Committee for the Handicapped, *Directory of Organizations Interested in the Handicapped,* Washington, D.C.: 1975.

Organization and purpose

Founded in 1913, the American Cancer Society's major purpose is to organize and wage a continuing campaign against cancer and its crippling effects, through medical research, professional and public education, and service and rehabilitation programs. The Society conducts programs of public and professional education, along with service and rehabilitation programs at the national and local levels.

American Congress of Rehabilitation Medicine
30 N. Michigan Avenue
Chicago, IL 60602
(312)236–9512

Organization and purpose

The American Congress of Rehabilitation Medicine exists for the purpose of providing a scientific forum for communication among the many disciplines concerned with rehabilitation medicine. It has a membership of more than 2,000 practicing professionals, educators, and scientists who are working actively for the advancement of rehabilitation medicine. The organization focuses its programs and meetings on research findings, and new practice, knowledge, and techniques of interest to all professionals in the rehabilitation field.

American Foundation for the Blind, Inc.
15 West 16th Street
New York, NY 10011
(212)924–0420

Organization and purpose

The American Foundation for the Blind, Inc. (AFB) is a private, national organization whose objective is to help those handicapped by blindness to achieve the fullest possible development and utilization of their capacities and integration into the social, cultural, and economic life of the community. The Foundation serves as a clearing-house on all pertinent information about blindness and services to those who are blind.

American Occupational Therapy Association
6000 Executive Blvd.
Rockville, Maryland 20852
(301)770–2200

Organization and purpose

The American Occupational Therapy Association is the professional organization for occupational therapists and occupational therapy assistants.

American Physical Therapy Association
1156 15th Street, N.W.
Washington, D.C. 20005
(202)466-2070

Organization and purpose

The American Physical Therapy Association, founded in 1921, is a membership organization whose purpose is to meet the physical therapy needs of the people through the development and improvement of physical therapy education, practice, and research and to meet the needs of its members through identification, coordinated action, communication, and fellowship.

American Public Health Association
1015 18th Street
Washington, D.C. 20036
(202)467-5000

Organization and purpose

The American Public Health Association (APHA) was founded in 1872 and has 30,000 members. The Association is a professional organization of physicians, nurses, educators, engineers, environmentalists, new professionals, social workers, podiatrists, pharmacists, dentists, industrial hygienists, and other community health specialists.

American Rehabilitation Counseling Association
1607 N.H. Avenue, N.W.
Washington, D.C. 20009
(202)483-4633

Organization and purpose

ARCA, a division of the American Personnel and Guidance Association, is a national professional Association dedicated to the advancement of the theory and practice of rehabilitation counseling.

American Speech and Hearing Association
9030 Old Ceo'town Road
Washington, D.C. 20014
(301)530-3400

Organization and purpose

The purposes of the American Speech and Hearing Association are to encourage basic scientific study of the processes of individual human communication with special reference to speech, hearing, and language; promote investigation of disorders of human communication and foster improvement of clinical procedures with such disorders; stimulate exchange of information among persons and organizations so engaged; and to disseminate such information.

Bureau of Education for the
Handicapped, U.S. Office of Education
400 Maryland Avenue, S.W.
Washington, D.C. 20202
(202)245–9661

Organization and purpose

The Bureau of Education for the Handicapped was established in 1967 for the purpose of coordinating and administering all Office of Education programs for the handicapped.

Council of Organizations
Serving the Deaf
P.O. Box 894
Columbia, MD 21044

Organization and purpose

The Council of Organizations Serving the Deaf (COSD) is a central clearing-house and contact point for information and combined action by member organizations. Since 1967, the Council has worked to eliminate social and economic barriers that handicap deaf persons.

Council of State Administrators of
Vocational Rehabilitation
1522 K Street, N.W.
Suite 836
Washington, D.C. 20005
(202)659–9383

Organization and purpose

The Council of State Administrators of Vocational Rehabilitation is composed of the chief administrators of the public vocational rehabilitation agencies for physically and mentally handicapped persons in the states, the District of Columbia, and the four territories. These agencies constitute the state partners in the State-Federal program of vocational rehabilitation services provided under the Rehabilitation Act of 1973. The organization provides a forum to enable administrators of state vocational rehabilitation agencies to study and discuss matters relating to vocational rehabilitation and its administration.

Disabled American Veterans
3725 Alexandria Pike
Cold Spring, KY 41076
(606)441–7300

Organization and purpose

The DAV's paramount objective is to promote the welfare of the service-connected disabled veteran and his dependents, and to provide a service program to assist such service-connected disabled veterans and their dependents in their claims before the Veterans Administration and other government agencies.

Epilepsy Foundation of America
1828 L Street, N.W.
Washington, D.C. 20036
(202)293–2930

Organization and purpose

Founded in 1967 after a series of mergers, the Epilepsy Foundation of America is the national voluntary health agency leading the fight against epilepsy in the United States.

Federation of the Handicapped, Inc.
211 West 14th Street
New York, NY 10011
(212)242–9050

Organization and purpose

The Federation of the Handicapped, founded in 1935, is a private, nonprofit organization whose purpose is the vocational rehabilitation of the disabled.

Goodwill Industries of America
9200 Wisconsin Avenue
Washington, D.C. 20014
(301)530–6500

Organization and purpose

Founded in 1902, Goodwill Industries of America and its member local Goodwill Industries provide vocational rehabilitation services, training, employment, and opportunities for personal growth as an interim step in the rehabilitation process for the handicapped, disabled, and disadvantaged.

International Association of Rehabilitation Facilities, Inc.
5530 Wisconsin Avenue, No. 955
Washington, D.C. 20015
*(301)654–5882

Organization and purpose

In 1969, the Association of Rehabilitation Centers and the National Association of Sheltered Workshops and Homebound Programs merged to form the International Association of Rehabilitation Facilities, Inc. with the purpose of assisting in development and improvement of services of member facilities in providing services to the handicapped.

Muscular Dystrophy Associations of
America, Inc.
810 Seventh Avenue
New York, NY 10019
(212)586–0808

Organization and purpose

Muscular Dystrophy Associations of America, Inc., a nonsectarian voluntary health organization, was founded and incorporated in 1950 to foster research seeking cures or effective treatments for muscular dystrophy and related neuromuscular diseases.

National Association of the Deaf
814 Thayer Avenue
Silver Spring, Maryland 20910
(301)587–1788

Organization and purpose

The National Association of the Deaf is a private organization founded in 1880 for the purpose of promoting social, educational, and economic wellbeing of the deaf citizens of the United States.

The National Association for Mental Health, Inc.
1800 North Kent Street
Arlington, Virginia 22090
(703)528–6405

Organization and purpose

The National Association for Mental Health is a private organization with 1000 local affiliate chapters whose aim is to improve attitudes toward mental illness and the mentally ill; to improve services for the mentally ill; and to work for the prevention of mental illness and to promote mental health.

National Association of the
Physically Handicapped, Inc.
5473 Grandville Avenue
Detroit, Michigan 48228
(313)271–0160

Organization and purpose

The Association of the Physically Handicapped, Inc., seeks to promote the economic, physical, and social welfare of all physically handicapped persons.

National Association for Retarded Citizens
2709 Avenue E East
POB 6109
Arlington, Texas 76011
(817)261–4961

Organization and purpose

The National Association for Retarded Citizens is a membership organization whose purpose is to further the advancement of all ameliorative and preventive study, research, and therapy in the field of mental retardation, to develop a better understanding of the problems of mental retardation by the public, to further the training and education of personnel for work in the field, and in general to promote the general welfare of the mentally retarded of all ages.

National Congress of Organizations of the
Physically Handicapped, Inc.
7611 Oakland Avenue
Minneapolis, Minnesota 55423
(612)861–2162

Organization and purpose

The National Congress of Organizations of the Physically Handicapped, Inc. is a national coalition of the physically handicapped and their organizations. The organization serves as an advisory, coordinating, and representative body in promoting employment opportunities, legislation, equal rights, social activity, and rehabilitation.

National Easter Seal Society for
Crippled Children and Adults
2023 West Ogden Avenue
Chicago, IL 60612
(312)243–8400

Organization and purpose

The National Society conducts a three-point program in service, education, and research at the national, state, and local levels; programs serve all types of physically handicapped children and adults.

National Federation of the Blind
Suite 212
1346 Connecticut Avenue, N.W.
Washington, D.C. 20036
(202)785-2974

Organization and purpose

The purpose of the National Federation of the Blind (NFB) is the complete integration of blind people into society as equal members. This objective involves the removal of legal, economic, and social discrimination and the education of the public to new concepts concerning blindness.

National Multiple Sclerosis Society
257 Park Avenue South
New York, NY 10010
(212)674-4100

Organization and purpose

The National Multiple Sclerosis Society was founded in 1946. Its major objectives are to support research, to conduct lay and professional education programs concerning the disease, to administer patient services, and to carry out worldwide programs of information and idea exchange regarding multiple sclerosis.

National Paraplegia Foundation
333 N. Michigan Avenue
Chicago, IL 60601
(312)346-4779

Organization and purpose

The National Paraplegia Foundation was founded in 1948 with the objectives of : (1) improved and expanded rehabilitation and treatment of those sufferings spinal cord injuries; (2) expanded research on a cure for paraplegia and quadraplegia; (3) removal of architectural barriers to the handicapped; (4) increased employment opportunities for the handicapped; (5) accessible housing and transportation.

National Rehabilitation Association
1522 K Street, N.W.
Washington, D.C. 20005
(202)659-2430

Organization and purpose

The National Rehabilitation Association is an organization of professional and lay persons dedicated to the rehabilitation of all physically and mentally handicapped persons.

National Rehabilitation Counseling Association
1522 K Street, N.W.
Washington, D.C. 20005
(202)296–6080

Organization and purpose

The National Rehabilitation Counseling Association is a private organization founded in 1958 with the objectives of (1) developing of professional standards for rehabilitation counseling, (2) promoting professional training for rehabilitation counseling, (3) supporting rehabilitation counseling as it contributes to the interdisciplinary approach to the solution of problems in rehabilitation, and (4) fostering research to advance knowledge and skill in rehabilitation counseling.

Office of Handicapped Individuals
Department of Health, Education, and Welfare
330 Independence Avenue, S.W.
Washington, D.C. 20201
(202)245–6644

Organization and purpose

In 1974, through the authorization of the Rehabilitation Act of 1973, the Secretary of Health, Education, and Welfare announced the formation of this office. Its primary focus is the review, coordination, reformation, and planning related to policies, programs, procedures, and activities within all Federal agencies relevant to the physically and mentally handicapped. The intended result is the maximum effectiveness, sensitivity, and continuity in the provision of services for handicapped individuals by all programs.

Paralyzed Veterans of America
7315 Wisconsin Avenue
Suite 301–W
Washington, D.C. 20014
(301)652–3464

Organization and purpose

The principal thrust of efforts by the Veterans is toward improved programs of medicine and rehabilitation not only for veterans, but for all the spinal cord afflicted.

Partners of the Americas
Rehabilitation-Special Education Program
2001 S Street, N.W.
Washington, D.C. 20009
(202)332–7332

Organization and purpose

The Partners of the Americas is currently the largest people-to-people program between the United States and Latin America, and is commited to fostering a closer relationship and understanding between our peoples.

PREP, the rehabilitation and special education program has been one of the largest areas of activity since 1966. The purpose of PREP is to increase opportunities and improve programs for persons with handicaps in the Americas.

The President's Committee on
Employment of the Handicapped
Washington, D.C. 20210
(202)961–3401

Organization and purpose

The President's Committee on Employment of the Handicapped was established by the President of the United States in 1947. Since then, every President has given his personal and active support to full employment opportunities for the physically and mentally handicapped.

The objective of the Committee is to help the handicapped help themselves.

Rehabilitation International USA
17 East 45th Street
New York, NY 10017
(212)682–3277

Organization and purpose

Rehabilitation International USA (RIUSA) was founded in 1971 to offer international services to the U.S. rehabilitation community, as well as draw upon the expertise of the U.S. rehabilitation community for the benefit of the handicapped worldwide. It is also the U.S. affiliate of the

Rehabilitation International, a network of national agencies in more than 60 countries dedicated to helping all the disabled.

Rehabilitation Services Administration
Social and Rehabilitation Service
330 C Street, S.W.
Washington, D.C. 20201
(202)245–6726

Organization and purpose

The Social and Rehabilitation Service administers programs of the United States Department of Health, Education and Welfare that deal with the handicapped, dependent families and children. Of the several agencies and offices of the Service, the Rehabilitation Service Administration is principally concerned with the rehabilitation of the handicapped.

United Cerebral Palsy
Associations, Inc.
66 East 34th Street
New York, NY 10016
(212)889–6655

Organization and purpose

United Cerebral Palsy Associations is a national voluntary health organization dedicated to a continuing overall attack on cerebral palsy. Its primary function is to seek solutions to the multiple problems of cerebral palsy, with affiliates providing direct services to the cerebral palsied in states and communities.

The Veterans Administration
810 Vermont Avenue, N.W.
Washington, D.C. 20420
(202)389–2044

Organization and purpose

The Veterans Administration established in 1930 administers a broad range of programs providing medical care, rehabilitation, education and training, income support, and other benefits for eligible disabled veterans and their dependents.

APPENDIX D

Structured Group Experiences in Rehabilitation

The structured experiences included in this appendix are used in conjunction with the treatment approach discussed in Structured Experiential Therapy: A Group Approach to Rehabilitation (Chapter 26). In addition, they can be used as experiences which have the following goals :

1. Broaden the reader's perspective of disability.
2. Sensitize the readers to their own attitudes and reactions to disability and disabled persons.
3. Personalize the reading of the book.

Designed to supplement the chapter presentations, the structured experiences are envisioned as steppingstones to both class discussion and outside experiences.

Experience I
Picasso or Michaelangelo?:
Increasing Self-Awareness through Projected Disability

Developed by
Arthur E. Dell Orto, Robert G. Lasky, and Robert P. Marinelli

Physical disability is seldom of concern for nondisabled individuals. However, not being aware of the potential for illness or severe disability may adversely keep the nondisabled out of touch with important aspects of himself or herself which have a direct impact on current functioning. For example, a person may become extremely worried about various trivial aspects of life, and this worry drains away a significant degree of emotional energy needed to function more effectively. An existential awareness of the fragility of life and the strong possibility of experiencing physical disability can help the nondisabled person to become aware of disowned aspects of self and better focus on more meaningful aspects of living. Likewise, physically disabled persons may feel that their disability is final and do not entertain the possibility that further injury is possible. Increased self-awareness of present happenings is necessary to maximize here-and-now growth processes rather than worry about the past or focus on future occurrences. "What has passed has passed; the future is yet to be; all that exists is *now*."

Goals

1. To sensitize participants to the potential impact of physical disability on their lives.
2. To facilitate self-disclosure and feedback.
3. To explore aspects of oneself through a medium other than talking.
4. To increase personal awareness of the importance of maximizing the potential of present, or "here-and-now" functioning.
5. To assist participants in exploring aspects of themselves that they might not be presently aware of or underutilizing.
6. To facilitate interaction between disabled and nondisabled persons.

Group Size

Small groups of six to ten participants.

Time Required

Approximately one and one-half hours.

Materials

1. Blank pieces of $8\frac{1}{2}$ x 11 inch paper.
2. Pencils for all participants.

Physical Setting

Participants are seated in small groups in a circle.

Process

1. The facilitator forms small groups of six to ten participants, describes the goals of the experience, and gives each person two blank pieces of paper and a pencil.
2. Participants are asked, "Draw a picture of yourself and include your whole body."
3. After five to ten minutes the facilitator announces, "Stop! You have just acquired a severe physical disability through an accident. Take your second sheet of paper and draw yourself as a person having a severe physical disability." (10 minutes)
4. The facilitator then asks participants to hold up their first drawing (present self) so that group members can see each drawing. Group members are asked to observe any characteristics of the drawing that may infer something about the person. Participants are then asked to share their observations with group members. (10 minutes)
5. The facilitator asks participants to hold up their second drawing and to draw inferences. Participants then share their inferences with the group. (10 minutes)
6. Participants are asked to hold up drawings and to look for further clues concerning characteristics of each participant. (10 minutes)
7. The facilitator asks participants to pause and reflect momentarily on this experience and to write down individually two major learnings that were experienced.
8. Group members are asked to share their learnings with the group and discuss the process in terms of the stated goals.

Variations

1. The facilitator could distribute a brief questionnaire with incomplete sentence stems and ask participants to complete the questionnaire in relation to the first, and then the second, drawing.
2. Participants might focus on the impact of their disabled selves in relation to adjustments they would have to make, how the disability would affect significant others, etc.
3. Participants might be challenged to volunteer their services for one week to assist people having the disability they chose.
4. The facilitator could specify the disability (e.g., spinal cord injury, brain damage, blindness).

Experience II
Half a Sentence

Developed by
Arthur E. Dell Orto, Robert P. Marinelli, and Robert G. Lasky

Introduction

People respond to different things in a variety of ways. One interesting stimulus to elicit a response is the sentence completion. This exercise attempts to gather individual responses to stimuli that focus upon physical disability.

Setting

Group setting in a relaxed manner.

Material

Paper and pencil.

Process

The teacher or leader reads the stimulus sentence. The group writes down their responses. After the exercise, the responses are compared and discussion begins.

HALF A SENTENCE

1. Being deformed
2. My wheelchair
3. I see my brace
4. Yesterday at the hospital
5. Being paralyzed
6. Losing one's sight
7. Deafness will
8. Not being able to run

9. Hospitals can
10. Doctors have
11. Pain will
12. A wheelchair in a car
13. My blind wife
14. As a child with polio
15. My friend, who lost both legs, will

Variations
The group can modify or expand this list.

Discussion
This section of the exercise should focus on the variation in the response and the explanation for them.

Experience III
The Unexpected

Developed by
Robert P. Marinelli, Arthur E. Dell Orto, and Robert G. Lasky

Introduction

The onset of a disability touches many areas of a person's life. It effects the manner in which individuals respond to themselves (intrapersonal) and the manner in which others respond to them (interpersonal).

Goals

To sensitize the participant to the lifestyle changes that may occur as a result of disability.

Process

Imagine that your physical functioning is beginning to change. You have been noting problems with your physical coordination, particularly as you have been stumbling a lot lately. As a result of a medical consultation, you are informed you have muscular dystrophy. In a small group, discuss the impact of this information upon you and those with whom you come into contact. In your discussion, respond to the following questions :

1. How would you respond? Consider your thoughts, feelings, and behaviors in your response.
2. Would your family and friends be accepting of you and your illness? Which one, if any, would reject you, and why?
3. Discuss the impact of this information on your future. Consider vocational aspiration and marital plans.

Variations

1. Rather than focusing upon the present, the participants are asked to consider the impact of disability upon themselves as a child or adolescent. Consider important factors as they relate to developmental issues in your response.
2. The focus can be upon disability occurring to a family worker or close friend.

Experience IV
Payoff — Goal Evaluation Feedback

Developed by
Robert G. Lasky, Robert P. Marinelli, and Arthur E. Dell Orto

Introduction

People very often have difficulty giving and receiving feedback from one another. Verbal feedback is often given in vague, nonexplicit messages that may be misunderstood by the recipient and lead to further communication difficulties. The person who responds with the statement, "I really like everybody in this group," is very often avoiding specific, direct, and individualized confrontations that might more accurately reflect feelings about group members. Thus, by giving general feedback, one avoids risk-taking and the opportunity to share personal growth experiences. One way to overcome this potential difficulty is to use a medium other than verbal communication, which is explicit and direct, where persons giving feedback must take responsibility for their feedback. This feedback is particularly important when evaluating a person's goals. The following structured learning experience was designed to help group members in this regard.

Goals

1. To take responsibility for individualized feedback in a group situation.
2. To share positive and negative aspects of giving and receiving direct interpersonal feedback.
3. To experience increased risk-taking behavior by giving specific feedback symbolically.

Group Considerations

Participants should have had at least two sessions together to experience one another in order to be able to share meaningful and direct interpersonal feedback.

Group Size

Small groups of six to eight participants.

Time Required

Approximately two hours.

Materials

Envelopes for all participants, each containing a penny, a nickle, a dime, a quarter, and a half-dollar. If the group is larger than six members, two or more of these coins may be used as necessary.

Physical Setting

Participants are seated in a circle or semicircle.

Process

1. The group leader discussed the importance of giving and receiving feedback, focusing on the above goals and their ramifications.
2. The group leader distributes one envelope, containing one each of the above coins, to each group participant.
3. Group members are instructed that each envelope contains the coins described. They are also given the following guidelines:
   a. Each participant is to give feedback to other group members by giving the coin which most accurately describes the member's

perceptions. For example, a group member may evaluate the worth of other members' goals, giving the highest amount (half-dollar) to the member who has the most meaningful goal, the lowest amount to the person who has the least meaningful goal, etc.

    b.   Participants must give away all their coins.

    c.   Participants are requested to use notebooks to write down the names of group members, followed by the amount of feedback they plan to give each group member.

    d.   Participants are asked to write down the total amount they expect to receive from the group.

4.   The group leader announces a group member, then passes a cup around the group for each member, who then deposits the chosen coin.

5.   Group members tally their feedback, focusing on the amount and type of coins received. They are asked to pause and reflect on this feedback.

6.   The group leader asks questions such as, "Who believes they expected the most money?" "Who thinks they received the most?" ". . . the least?" etc.

7.   Each of the above and similar exploratory statements may be discussed in the group focusing on participants' self-perceptions, perception of the general and particular feedback, etc.

8.   The group shares significant learnings experienced by this exercise.

Variations

1.   The amount of coins may vary so that a member may give self-feedback.

2.   Group participants may be asked to give feedback at a subsequent session by bringing objects other than coins which accurately convey their impressions.

NAME INDEX

SUBJECT INDEX